Corrective and Distributive Justice

Corrective and Distributive Justice

From Aristotle to Modern Times

IZHAK ENGLARD

OXFORD
UNIVERSITY PRESS

OXFORD
UNIVERSITY PRESS

Oxford University Press, Inc., publishes works that further Oxford University's objective of excellence in research, scholarship, and education.

Oxford New York
Auckland Cape Town Dar es Salaam Hong Kong Karachi Kuala Lumpur Madrid Melbourne Mexico City Nairobi New Delhi Shanghai Taipei Toronto

With offices in
Argentina Austria Brazil Chile Czech Republic France Greece Guatemala Hungary Italy Japan Poland Portugal Singapore South Korea Switzerland Thailand Turkey Ukraine Vietnam

Published by Oxford University Press, Inc.
198 Madison Avenue, New York, New York 10016

Library of Congress Cataloging-in-Publication Data

Englard, Izhak.
Corrective and distributive justice : from Aristotle to modern times / Izhak Englard.
p. cm.
Includes bibliographical references and index.
ISBN 978-0-19-538007-1 ((hardback) : alk. paper) 1. Justice (Philosophy) 2. Aristotle. 3. Aristotle. Nicomachean ethics. 4. Ethics. I. Title.
B105.J87E54 2009
172'.209—dc22
ISBN 978-0-19-538007-1 2008037368

Note to Readers
This publication is designed to provide accurate and authoritative information in regard to the subject matter covered. It is based upon sources believed to be accurate and reliable and is intended to be current as of the time it was written. It is sold with the understanding that the publisher is not engaged in rendering legal, accounting, or other professional services. If legal advice or other expert assistance is required, the services of a competent professional person should be sought. Also, to confirm that the information has not been affected or changed by recent developments, traditional legal research techniques should be used, including checking primary sources where appropriate.

(Based on the Declaration of Principles jointly adopted by a Committee of the American Bar Association and a Committee of Publishers and Associations.)

To my wife, Jocheved, at the occasion of our golden wedding

Contents

Preface

THIS STUDY IS QUITE AN AMBITIOUS PROJECT: To retrace the long and complex history of the Aristotelian conceptual distinction between distributive and corrective justice from antiquity to the present day. True, for many centuries Aristotle's works on ethics have laid rather dormant, but their revival in medieval times constituted a major event in the Latin Christian world. Thus, Aristotle's *Nicomachean Ethics* became an important source in scholasticism. No wonder that Aristotle's analysis of the notion of justice as one of the cardinal virtues attracted the attention of the scholastics and provoked protracted discussions and controversies. A vast literature was the result, a literature which is of no easy access to the contemporary scholar. Not only many works have remained in manuscripts, dispersed in libraries all over the Christian world, but also many of the printed works are rare books guarded in a great number of libraries. A taste of the richness of that literature one can get from the recent important work of David A. Lines, *Aristotle's Ethics in the Italian Renaissance (ca. 1300–1650): The Universities and the Problem of Moral Education* (Leiden 2002), where the list of Latin works on the *Nicomachean Ethics* in Italy alone comprises more than 170 items. If we add other countries, like Spain, France, Belgium and Germany, the numbers would go into many more hundreds. I, therefore, had to limit the scope of the studied literature. The result was a concentration on the printed books that were accessible to me. This criterion inevitably caused a certain amount of arbitrariness. However, I am convinced I have succeeded in giving a genuine and rather complete picture of the scholastic literature. This sentiment is based upon the fact that the discussions of some of the late scholastics refer in great detail to the whole relevant literature. By studying them, it is highly probable that very little has been overlooked, and most likely nothing of importance. The same appears to be true for the rich post-scholastic literature.

The work on this project extended over many years and I owe thanks to a great number of persons and institutions. First, I would like to thank the

Max-Planck-Institute for European Legal History in Frankfurt am Main, Germany, where on the initiative of its director, Professor Michael Stolleis, I twice got a fellowship for doing research at the Institute's library. Special thanks go to Father Dr. Udo Lang, librarian of the excellent and rich library of the Benedictine Monastery of Einsiedeln in Switzerland, where I spent many days studying the rare books. I am grateful to Professor Reinhard Zimmermann, Director of the Max-Planck-Institute for Comparative and International Private Law in Hamburg, for giving access to his private collection of Roman-Dutch law books. Thanks equally to the librarians of the Columbia University Law School in New York, where I taught a seminar in the fall semester of 2007. The list of the other libraries, whose hospitality I enjoyed, is rather long; among them: École Biblique of the Dominican St. Stephen's Priory at Jerusalem; Jewish National and University Library, Jerusalem; Zentralbibliothek Zürich, Switzerland; Rechtswissenschaftliches Institut der Universität Zürich; Universität Greifswald, Germany; Herzog-August Bibliothek, Wolfenbüttel, Germany; Universität Trier, Germany; Stadtbibliothek Trier; Priesterseminar Trier; Bayerische Staatsbibliothek, München, Germany; Philosophisch-Theologische Hochschule Sankt Georgen, Frankfurt am Main, Germany; Union Theological Seminary, New York; Beinecke Library at Yale University, New Haven, Connecticut. To all of them my sincere thanks.

An important and vital source of the research has been the more recently established digitized libraries of ancient books and modern articles accessible through the Internet. I used in particular the following sources: *Early English Books Online, The Digital Library of Classic Protestant Texts, The Digital Library of the Catholic Reformation, Jstor, and Verteilte Digitale Inkunabel-bibliothek.*

Introduction

ARISTOTLE IN THE FIFTH BOOK of his *Nicomachean Ethics* analyzes the notion of justice as a virtue. Justice as complete virtue is called by him legal or universal justice; justice as partial virtue is called particular justice. Inside the notion of particular justice, Aristotle makes the seminal distinction between distributive justice and corrective justice. The idea is that there are basically two different situations that require two different kinds of justice. In a very general and simplistic way, one could say that the difference is between a situation where justice is oriented towards creating a new state of affairs (distributive justice), and one where its purpose is to restore a certain equilibrium (corrective justice). Aristotle defines some characteristic features that make the difference between the two kinds of particular justice: distributive justice follows a geometric proportion according to the respective merits of the recipients; the transactional equality under corrective justice is according to an arithmetical proportion. As a result, the latter treats the litigants as equal, whatever their prior virtues and merits may have been. On the contrary, under distributive justice, the prior merits of the parties are at the basis of their original rights.

In this book we retrace the history of this distinction between corrective and distributive justice: its interpretation and use from antiquity to the present day. Our endeavor is what in German is called "*Begriffsgeschichte*", the history of concepts. It assumes that the meaning of terms is imbedded in cultures. In our context, we will map throughout the ages the fundamental controversies about the understanding and significance of the distinction, and, most importantly, the different and changing purposes of its use.

Two important restrictions on the scope of our scholarly enterprise: First, we take the text of Aristotle as transmitted to the later ages. Hence, we are not concerned with the complex, manifold and controversial textual and philological questions of Aristotle's work. Neither do we deal with the philosophical sources of the author nor, more specifically, with the relationship to Plato's work. These topics have been treated extensively by experts of classic literature and philosophy. Second, we retrace the history of the use of the conceptual distinction in its formal dimensions without going into the substance of the respective notions of justice. Thus, e.g. the concept of merit is central to distributive justice, but in Aristotle's own understanding its substance varies with the different forms of the political regime. The same phenomenon exists in relation to corrective justice: the restoration of a disrupted equilibrium is conditioned upon the unjustness of the disruption. However, the basis of that unjustness must be found in a substantive value system that transcends the formal concept of corrective justice. We will describe the modern attempts to integrate form and substance, but we will reserve judgment on the validity of the substance of justice as such.

As a matter of fact, the amazing modern revival of the Aristotelian distinction—especially in the U.S. tort scholarship—is at the origin of our idea to inquire into its history. Starting in the 1970s, the classic distinction "conquered" the minds of American legal scholars and literally hundreds of papers, a symposium, and many chapters in books, were dedicated to the topic. The vigor of this trend is not yet abating. We thought that a look into the work and the minds of earlier generations might deepen our understanding of the modern concerns. Moreover, we might even learn something about the very nature of the distinction and its inherent problems. The results of the historical enquiry went far beyond our expectations. It turned out that Aristotle's conceptual idea has occupied the most brilliant philosophical, legal, and theological minds for generations.

In the light of the enormous amount of relevant literature—and as stated in the Preface—we limited ourselves to the printed books, but the problem arose of how to proceed in presenting the vast historical material. The option is between a topical and a chronological arrangement. We found the first possibility impractical because of its complexity. Moreover, in many instances the author's basic viewpoint directly influences his conclusions in relation to a variety of topics. We chose, therefore, the chronological order that has the great advantage of placing the views of the individual authors into a given historical period. A certain disadvantage of this way lies in the inevitable repetitiousness of topical issues. However, it is outweighed by the integral description of the individual scholar's outlook. In some instances, we deviated slightly from the strict chronological sequence in order to describe related views in proximity.

We didn't apply any prior selection among the very great number of authors dealing with the Aristotelian notions of justice, but presented in the book all of those whose work we could find in the libraries. As mentioned in the Preface, we didn't succeed in finding all the books—some of which are mentioned by past authors—but we believe that at least all the important ones are treated in our work.

The manifold views are presented in a neutral, objective way. The result of our scholarly endeavor is, therefore, somewhat encyclopedical. We intended to bring before the reader the immense richness of past literature, that to a great part is practically inaccessible, and leave it to him to evaluate the content and, if appropriate, to draw conclusions in relation to contemporary discussions. The reader will find plenty of criticism in the writings of the authors. However, some central themes of scholasticism are hardly relevant anymore for most of the modern readers, such as the problem of whether Divinity is subject to corrective or distributive justice. We limited our own few critical comments to some views of contemporary authors in tort law.

The book is divided into seven chapters. Five of them are chronologically linked: The Starting Point: Aristotle's Classification of Justice; High Scholastics; Late Scholastics; Post-Scholastic Writers; and The Modern Use of Aristotle's Forms of Justice. Two chapters deal with specific issues: A Special Theological Problem: Divine Justice; and Jewish Commentators. These two chapters are equally internally arranged according to a chronological order. The five chapters indicate a hiatus of more than one thousand years between Aristotle's *Ethics* and medieval commentators. None of the ancient commentaries has been preserved.

In the appendix we deal with the iconography of the two kinds of justice as depicted by the famous fourteenth-century fresco cycle of Ambrogio Lorenzetti in the Palazzo Pubblico of Siena, Italy. We believe that our research may help to resolve one of the problems that arose from Lorenzetti's inclusion of punishment in the representation of distributive justice. The appendix deals also with miniatures in two fourteenth-century illustrated manuscripts of Oresme's translation into French of Aristotle's *Nicomachean Ethics* that was presented to the French King Charles V.

May we add a personal note: The discourse with all these outstanding scholars of past times was for us a wonderful intellectual experience. It taught us modesty toward our own mental capacities.

ONE

The Starting Point

Aristotle's Classification of Justice

ARISTOTLE'S FAMOUS ANALYSIS of the notion of justice in the Fifth Book of his *Nicomachean Ethics* remains unsurpassed.[1] It has exercised an enormous influence throughout the ages and remains relevant to this very day.[2] Aristotle's starting point is the concept of virtue: justice can be a complete virtue or a partial one. Justice as complete virtue is called by him the legal or universal justice; justice as partial virtue is called particular justice.[3] The distinction between these two virtue-related notions of justice can be better illustrated by referring to their opposites: manifold vices, such as lasciviousness, cowardice, and anger; hence, universal justice is reached by overcoming these different vices. Particular justice, on the other hand, means the

---

1. A general remark: I am not concerned with the complex, manifold, and controversial textual and philological questions of that book. Thus, according to some authors, the Fifth Book of that work originated in Aristotle's other work on ethics, the *Eudemian Ethics*. Some think it is the other way around. On the controversy, *see* R.A. Gauthier and J.I. Jolif, *L'éthique à Nicomaque* (2è éd., repr. Leuven 2002) t. I, 1, at 70–74.

2. H. Coing, *Grundzüge der Rechtsphilosophie* (3. Aufl., Berlin 1976) 17–18: "Wie die gesamte Philosophie des Aristoteles, so hat auch seine Theorie der Gerechtigkeit eine ungeheure Wirkung entfaltet. Diese beginnt schon im Altertum; aber der Höhepunkt liegt im Mittelalter. Vom 13. bis zum 17. Jahrhundert beherrscht der Aristotelismus die Universitäten Europas, und darin kommt seiner Ethik keine untergeordnete Rolle zu. Auf Aristoteles bauen die philosophischen Systeme der Hoch- und Spätscholastik auf, und damit auch der Thomismus, der für das katholische Denken im 19. Jahrhundert so entscheidende Bedeutung gewonnen hat." On the lasting importance of Aristotle's analysis and the problem of its understanding, *cf.* the comment of G. Del Vecchio, *Giustizia e diritto* (2a ed., Roma 1934) 4: "In verità, nella grande opera aristotelica le considerazioni sulla giustizia sono molteplici, e siffattamente intrecciate, attraverso numerose distinzioni (le quali dovevano offrire buon giuoco a quelle ancor più numerose degli Scolastici), che nessuna dottrina sullo stesso argomento può, ancora ai giorni nostri, prescindere dagli elementi meditati già dallo Stagirita. Il che è tanto più notevole, in quanto l'esatta ricostruzione del pensiero aristotelico presenta ancora, per questa parte, difficoltà gravissime, contro le quali molti pur dei migliori interpreti consumarono invani i loro sforzi." For a critical attitude on these constructive efforts, *see* D. Bostock, *Aristotle's Ethics* (Oxford 2000) 54, note 1.

3. EN 1130a9, 1130a14–16, 1130a32–34, 1130b6–8.

overcoming of a particular vice, namely that of desiring more than what belongs to oneself (*pleonexia*).[4] The outcome of that vice is inequality; hence, particular justice is the justice of equality (*iustitia aequalitatis*).[5] It has been suggested that the Aristotelian basic distinction between universal (legal) justice and particular justice may have its origin in the ancient dual divinities of Themis and Dike, one representing the divine-royal commandments, the other the law immanent in humanity.[6] On the other hand, it is noteworthy that Aristotle in defining the "legal" justice does not elaborate on the specific content of that general law and its relationship to ethics. He seems to emphasize the mental attitude and the habit of abiding by the law of the state as the basis of all virtue, without examining the inherent value of the specific legal system. The latter may, indeed, be only incompletely just and, therefore, of merely hypothetical (relative) value.[7]

Inside the notion of particular justice, Aristotle makes the seminal distinction between distributive justice and corrective justice, which is the topic of this essay. The terms "distributive" and "corrective" have come down to us through the medieval Latin translations of Aristotle's *Nicomachean Ethics*, especially through the influential commentary on that book by the great scholastic philosopher and theologian Thomas Aquinas (1225–1274).

4. EN 1129a32 (πλεονέκτης=pleonektes); *see* G. Bien, "Gerechtigkeit bei Aristoteles," *Die Nikomachische Ethik* (O. Höffe, ed., Berlin 1995) 145–147. For a critique of the notion of "greed" in connection with particular justice, *see* J.O. Urmson, "Aristotle's Doctrine of the Mean," *Essays on Aristotle's Ethics* (A.O. Rorty, ed., Berkeley 1980) 157, at 164–166, 170; *see also* B. Williams, "Justice as a Virtue," *ibid.*, at 189–199.

5. This has been contested by some modern writers, *see*, e.g., J.R. Lucas, *On Justice–ΠΕΡΙ ΔΙΚΑΙΟΥ* (Oxford 1980) 171–184.

6. R.Hirzel, *Themis, Dike, und Verwandtes—Ein Beitrag zur Geschichte der Rechtsidee bei den Griechen* (Leipzig 1907) 164–165; *cf.* the comments of Gauthier and Jolif, *op. cit.*, II, 1, at 325–326; *see* especially on the various interpretations of the two mythical figures G. Del Vecchio, *Justice—An Historical and Philosophical Essay* (A.H. Campbell, ed., Edinburgh 1952) 6–8, notes 4–14, at 15–17; on the etymology of δίκη *see also ibid.*, 170.

7. K. Hildenbrand, *Geschichte und System der Rechts—und Staatsphilosophie: Das klassische Altertum* (Leipzig 1860) 282–284. Compare the author's interesting comment on the possibilty of viewing justice as a means between injustice, conceived as the vice of arbitrary disregard of the law (ἀδικία), and injustice conceived as the vice of excessive adherence and insistence on the letter of the law (ἀκριβοδίκαιος). Aristotle himself did not choose to adopt this idea (*ibid.*, 284–286); *cf.* generally, D. Bostock, *Aristotle's Ethics* (Oxford 2000) 56–57. Concerning the latter work, we cannot refrain from mentioning the author's peculiar supercilious style in commenting on Aristotle's classic work. For a defense of Aristotle's notion that justice is the medium between doing injustice and suffering injustice, *see* the Jesuit scholar Tarquinius Gallutius (Tarquinio Galluzzi) (1574–1649), *In Aristotelis quinque priores Moralium libros ad Nicomachum, Nova interpretatio, explanatio, quaestiones* (Paris 1632) Lib.5, Cap.5, Quaest. 3, 952–953.

Aristotle himself used for distributive justice the Greek term "dianemetic."[8] The concept of corrective justice is more complex. Aristotle uses the terms of "diorthotic"[9] and "epanorthotic."[10] In Latin, this kind of justice has received a great number of translations, among them: *iustitia regulativa, directiva, correctiva, correctrix, commutativa, commutatrix, rectificativa, emendativa,* and *iustum in corrigendo.*[11] Hugo Grotius (1583–1645) called it *iustitia expletrix,* whereas for the other (distributive) form of justice he used the term *attributrix.*[12] The corresponding notion in other European languages reflects generally these traditional translations, but one finds also some modern ideas like "interactive justice."[13]

For the better understanding of later manifold uses and interpretations of the Aristotelian distinction concerning the forms of justice, it is vital to give first a short description of Aristotle's ideas on this topic as expressed in his *Nicomachean Ethics.*

Let us quote the basic relevant passages concerning the said distinction:

> Particular justice on the other hand, and that which is just in the sense corresponding to it, is divided into two kinds. One kind is exercised in the distribution of honour, wealth, and the other divisible assets of the community, which may be allotted among its members in equal or unequal shares. The other kind is that which supplies a corrective principle in private transactions. This Corrective Justice again has two sub-divisions,

8. διανεμητικὸν, EN 1131b27; 1132b24; 1134a3. In Latin, the most usual translation is "*iustitia distributiva*"; more rare: "*iustitia divisiva,*" or "*distributrix.*" *See also infra* note 12.

9. EN 1131a1, 1131b25 (διορθωτικὸν).

10. EN 1132a18 (ἐπανορθωτικὸν).

11. One of the most influential medieval Latin translations of Aristotle's *Nicomachean Ethics* was that of Robertus Grosseteste Lincolniensis (1168–1253); *see Aristoteles Latinus,* XXVI 1–3, Ethica Nicomachea (Bruxelles, Leiden 1972–4). This translation uses for corrective justice the term "*iustitia directiva.*" A revised edition of that translation—according to some scholars edited by William of Moerbeke—was used by Thomas Aquinas in his famous commentary on EN written about 1271–1272. *See Aristoteles Latinus,* XXVI 1–3, fasc. Primus (1974) CCXXXIX–CCXLV. *See also* additional translations: Joannes Magirus (d. 1596), *Aristotelis Ethica Nicomachea Commentationes* (R. Walker, ed., Oxford 1842) 239, mentioned the notion of "justitia oeconomica"; J.H. von Kirchmann, *Erläuterungen zur Nikomachischen Ethik des Aristoteles* (Leipzig 1876) 92, used the Latin term "*justitia constitutiva.*" On the term "*iustitia emendativa*" or "*iustitia emendatrix,*" *see* Gregorius Christianus Gebaverus (Gebauer) et Burchardus-Christianus Behr, *De Iustitia et Iure* (Göttingen 1738) 16. For a critical discussion of the notion's various translations, *see* Paul Lapie, *De Justitia Apud Aristotelem* (Paris 1902) 17–18, note 1. The author prefers "corrective justice."

12. *De iure belli ac pacis,* Lib. 1, Cap. 1, § VIII. Joannes Magirus (d. 1596), *Aristotelis Ethica Nicomachea Commentationes* (R. Walker, ed., Oxford 1842) 239, mentioned the notion of "*justitia politica.*"

13. R. Wright, "The Principles of Justice," 75 (2000) *Notre Dame L. Rev.* 1859, 1883.

> corresponding to the two classes of private transactions, those which are voluntary and those which are involuntary. Examples of voluntary transactions are selling, buying, lending at interest, pledging, lending without interest, depositing, letting for hire; these transactions being termed voluntary because they are voluntarily entered upon. Of involuntary transactions some are furtive, for instance, theft, adultery, poisoning, procuring, enticement of slaves, assassination, false witness; others are violent, for instance, assault, imprisonment, murder, robbery with violence, maiming, abusive language, contumelious treatment.[14]

Describing in more detail the idea and form of distributive justice, he says:

> It follows therefore that justice involves at least four terms, namely, two persons for whom it is just and two shares which are just. And there will be the same equality between the shares as between the persons, since the ratio between the shares will be equal to the ratio between the persons; for if the persons are not equal, they will not have equal shares; it is when equals possess or are allotted unequal shares, or persons not equal equal shares, that quarrels and complaints arise. This is also clear from the principle of "assignment by desert." All are agreed that justice in distribution must be based on desert of some sort, although they do not mean the same sort of desert; democrats make the criterion free birth; those of oligarchical sympathies wealth or in other cases birth; upholders of aristocracy make it virtue.[15]
>
> Thus the just involves four terms at least, and the ratio between the first pair of terms is the same as that between the second pair. For the two lines representing the persons and shares are similarly divided; then, as the first term is to the second, so is the third to the fourth; and hence, by alternation, as the first is to the third, so is the second to the fourth; and therefore also, as the first is to second, so is the sum of the first and third to the sum of the second and fourth. Now this is the combination effected by a distribution of shares, and the combination is a just one, if persons and shares are added together in this way. The principle of Distributive Justice, therefore, is the conjunction of the first term of a

---

14. EN 1130b30–1131a9; Aristotle, *The Nicomachean Ethics: with an English translation by H. Rackham* (London and Cambridge, Mass. 1962) 267. (Among the many English translations of Aristotle's *Nicomachean Ethics* we prefer to use this translation published in the series of The Loeb classical library, hereafter quoted: Loeb-Rackham).

15. 1131a18–29 (Loeb-Rackham, 269).

proportion with the third and of the second with the fourth; and the just in this sense is a mean between two extremes that are disproportionate, since the proportionate is a mean, and the just is the proportionate. This kind of proportion is termed by mathematicians geometrical proportion; for a geometrical proportion is one in which the sum of the first and third terms will bear the same ratio to the sum of the second and fourth as one term of either pair bears to the other term. Distributive justice is not a continuous proportion, for its second and third terms, a recipient and a share, do not constitute a single term.[16]

The notion of corrective justice appears to be more complex:

The remaining kind is Corrective Justice (διορθωτικόν), which operates in private transactions, both voluntary and involuntary. This justice is of a different sort from the preceding. For justice in distributing common property always conforms with the proportion we have described since when a distribution is made from the common stock, it will follow the same ratio as that between the amounts which the several persons have contributed to the common stock; and the injustice opposed to justice of this kind is a violation of this proportion. But the just in private transactions, although it is equal in a sense (and the unjust the unequal), is not the equal according to geometrical but according to arithmetical proportion. For it makes no difference whether a good man has defrauded a bad man or a bad one a good one, nor whether it is a good or a bad man that has committed adultery; the law looks only at the nature[17] of the damage, treating the parties as equal, and merely asking whether one has done and the other suffered injustice, whether one inflicted and the other has sustained damage. Hence the unjust being here the unequal, the judge endeavours to equalize it: inasmuch as when one man has received and the other has inflicted a blow, or one has killed and the other been killed, the line representing the suffering and doing of the deed is divided into unequal parts, but the judge endeavours to make them equal by the penalty or

16. 1131b3–16 (Loeb-Rackham, 271–273). For a modern explanation of Aristotle's mathematical formula, P. Lapie, *De Justitia Apud Aristotelem* (Paris 1902) 19–23.

17. In the original text the term used is διαφορά, which caused some difficulties of translation. *See* the comment of E.J. Weinrib, "Aristotle's Forms of Justice," *Justice, Law, and Method in Plato and Aristotle* (S. Panagiotou, ed., Edmonton 1987) 133, 135, note 9; reprinted in 2 (1989) *Ratio Juris* 211, 212, note 2.

> loss he imposes, taking away the gain. For the term "gain" is used in a general way to apply to such cases, even though it is not strictly appropriate to some of them, for example to a person who strikes another, nor is "loss" appropriate to the victim in this case; but at all events the results are called "loss" and "gain" respectively when the amount of the damage sustained comes to be estimated. Thus, while the equal is a mean between more and less, gain and loss are at once both more and less in contrary ways, more good and less evil being gain and more evil and less good loss; and as the equal, which we pronounce to be just, is, as we said, a mean between them, it follows that Justice in Rectification (ἐπανορθωτικὸν) will be the mean between loss and gain.[18]

We shall pause here for a moment in order to point out, and comment upon, some of the central issues of the Aristotelian text.

The distinction between the two forms of justice seems to be an original idea of Aristotle. There might be a certain affinity with Plato's observation on two kinds of justice in the distribution of goods between the members of the *polis*, one distribution by lot and the other on the basis of geometric equality.[19] However, whereas in Plato's view, the former kind is one of inferior justice, in Aristotle's conception both forms of justice, distributive as well as corrective justice, are equally implementing the idea of strict equality. In other words, distributive and corrective justice are equally appropriate to achieve justice, though each in a different way as required by the different basic situation.[20]

In Aristotle's conception, distributive justice is based, as mentioned in the quotation above, on desert, merit (ἀξία, *axia*). The author explicitly mentions a variety of criteria, each according to the different political system: freedom (democracy), wealth or nobility (oligarchy), and virtue (aristocracy). It is noteworthy that Aristotle identifies here democracy with the merit of freedom, whereas in his *Politics*,[21] he founds democracy on the absolute equality of all citizens, and hence a distributive justice based on numerical equality. In any event, it clearly follows that Aristotle's concept of distributive justice is a purely formal one, since the "merit" at its basis differs according the political system.[22]

---

18. 1131b25–1132a19 (Loeb-Rackham, 273–275).
19. Laws VI 757 b–e; V 737 c, 744 c; *cf.* Gorgias, 508a.
20. Gauthier and Jolif, *op. cit., supra* note 1, II, 1, p. 349.
21. Pol. VI 2 1317b 3–10.
22. *Cf.* the commentary on the *Nicomachean Ethics* by the Benedictine Cardinal Josephus Saenz de Aguirre (1630–1699), *Philosophia Moralis Ab Aristotele Tradita Decem Libris*

The concept of corrective justice appears to be much more complex. Aristotle distinguishes between two transactional relationships, one voluntary and the other involuntary.[23] In both, the form of corrective justice is applicable. It has been noted that the term "corrective" is better suited to involuntary transactions than to voluntary ones.[24] In fact, some scholastics used for the general description of the two forms of (corrective) justice the Latin term of *iustitia directiva.*[25] However, the most common Latin term throughout the ages was *iustitia commutativa.*

Aristotle describes a number of important distinctive features of corrective justice as compared to distributive justice: First, the different nature of equality. In relation to distributive justice the equality is a "geometric" proportion between four terms, being based on a criterion of respective

---

Ethicorum ad Nicomachum: A Joanne Argyropilo Byzantino latine reddita; Nunc perpetuo Commentario literali & Scholastico, plenissime illustrata, Pars Prima (Rome 1698), Lib. Quintus, Cap. III, 208. The author refers to Aristotle's own preference in his *Politics.* For a popular historical analysis of the various political systems on the background of the criterion of distributive justice, *see* Count Don Emanuele Tesauro (1581–1677/78), *La Filosofia Morale Derivata Dall'Alto Fondo Del Grande Aristotele Stagirita* (Torino 1671) 365–370. Among the more modern authors emphasizing the formal character of distributive justice, *see* M. Salomon, Der Begriff der Gerechtigkeit bei Aristoteles (Leiden 1937) 29; H. Kelsen, "Aristotle's Doctrine of Justice," *What is Justice? Justice, Law, and Politics in the Mirror of Science* (Berkeley 1957) 110, 127–128; E.J. Weinrib, "Corrective Justice and Formalism: The Care One Owes One's Neighbors," 77 (1992) *Iowa L. Rev.* 403, 411–413; F.D. Miller, Jr., *Nature, Justice, and Rights in Aristotle's Politics* (Oxford 1995) 71, 124–126; Gabriel Danzig, "The Political Character of Aristotelian Reciprocity," 95 *Classical Philology* (2000) 399, 400. It has been observed that Aristotle's intention by relying on "merit" for the distribution of political rights did not relate to political achievements but to political capacities, U. Wolf, *Aristotele's "Nikomachische Ethik"* (Darmstadt 2002) 106–107. *See also infra* 184–185, 193.

23. EN 1131b26 (ἑκουσίοις; ἀκουσίοις). *Cf.* P. Moraux, *À la recherche de l'Aristote perdu—Le Dialogue "Sur la Justice"* (Louvain 1957) 118–119, note 27.

24. *See* the discussion on the relationship between commutative and corrective justice, G. Del Vecchio, *Justice—An Historical and Philosophical Essay* (A. H. Campbell, ed., Edinburgh 1952) §6, note 9, 61–62.

25. Aristoteles Latinus: EN 1131a1 (diorthotikon=[iustitia] directiva); and *see* in particular EN 1132a18 (epanorthotikon=directivum [iustum]), 1132b21 (antipeponthos=contrapassum). *See* generally on the controversy concerning these translations, Gauthier and Jolif, op. cit., II, 1, pp. 358–359. In these authors' view the Greek terms diorthotikon and epanorthotikon are of identical meaning; *see also ibid.*, at 363–364; *see also* G. Del Vecchio, *Justice—An Historical and Philosophical Essay* (A. H. Campbell, ed., Edinburgh 1952) 59–60, note 8. Some modern authors use the scholastic notion of "directive justice" as the generic (superordinate) term for the subdivision of "commutative justice," limited to voluntary transactions, and "corrective justice," designed for involuntary ones; *see* J. Saint-Arnaud, "Les définitions aristotéliciennes de la justice: leurs rapports à la notion d'égalité," 11 (1984) *Philosophiques* 157, 164. However, the authoress thinks that Aristotle was mistaken in viewing corrective justice as applying an arithmetic proportion, since the punishment is proportional to the wrong; *ibid.*, 169.

merit. Thus, the ratio of the merits between two persons should be proportional to the ratio of the distributed goods among them. The equality in the framework of corrective justice is an "arithmetic proportion" between supposedly two terms. Corrective justice's aim is to restore the original positions of both the person who suffered the loss and the person who gained the profit at the other's expense. Aristotle describes the "correctively just" as the arithmetic mean between the part of the earner and the part of the loser.[26]

A second distinctive feature of corrective justice is that the law considers only the extent of the damage caused; it, therefore, treats the litigant parties as equal, whatever their prior virtues and merits may have been.[27] This approach contrasts with that of distributive justice, where the prior respective merits of the parties are at the basis of their original rights.

Let us return to an additional, important passage of Aristotle, discussing the relationship between justice and retribution, called by him *antipeponthos* (ἀντιπεπονθὸς). The scholastics have translated the latter term literally into the Latin *contrapassum*[28]; modern scholars prefer to use the term of reciprocity.[29] Aristotle states:

> The view is also held by some that simple Reciprocity is Justice. This was the doctrine of the Pythagoreans, who defined the just simply as "suffering reciprocally with another." Reciprocity however does not

26. Gauthier and Jolif, *op. cit.*, II, 1, p. 368.

27. EN 1132a2–5.

28. But *see* Dominicus de Soto, *De iustitia et iure Libri decem*, Lib. 3, Quaest. 5, Art. 4, (Lyon 1559), 176, who prefers the Latin term: *repassio. See also* Tarquinius Gallutius (Tarquinio Galluzzi) (1574–1649), *In Aristotelis quinque priores Moralium libros ad Nicomachum, Nova interpretatio, explanatio, quaestiones* (Paris 1632), Lib.5, Cap.2, 894, who translates: "*reciproca perpessio*"; *see also ibid.*, 928, Cap. 5: "*reciproca et mutua perpessio*." The same author suggests also the Latin expression: "*retaliatum*," *ibid.*, 942. *See also* Joannes Magirus (d. 1596), *Aristotelis Ethica Nicomachea Commentationes* (R. Walker, ed., Oxford 1842) 247, who translates "*reciproca aut mutua passio*." Some translated the notion straightway with *"lex talionis": Aristotelis ad Nicomachum Filium de Moribus, quae Ethica nominantur, Libri decem, Ioachimo Perionio Benedictino Cormoeriaceno interprete* (Paris 1547) 43; finally, one finds also the notion of "*repatientia*," such as in the Latin translation of Michael of Ephesus' commentary by Johannes Bernardus Felicianus: *Commentaria in Aristotelem Graeca Versiones latinae temporis resuscitarum litterarum*, Band 11, 1 (Charles Lohr ed., Stuttgart 2006) 106b. As D.D. Raphael, *Concepts of Justice* (Oxford 2001) 50, notes, the literal translation in English is "suffering in return"; *cf.* A. Trendelenburg, *Historische Beiträge zur Philosophie*, Vol. III (Berlin 1867) 404, who translates into German: "das Gegenempfangen."

29. David George Ritchie, "Aristotle's Subdivisions of Particular Justice," 8 *The Classical Review* (1894) 185–192, suggested the notion of "catallactic justice," coined by Richard Whately (1787–1863). Some modern authors translate: "requital" or "reciprocation."

> coincide either with Distributive or with Corrective Justice . . . For in many cases Reciprocity is at variance with Justice: for example, if an officer strikes a man, it is wrong for the man to strike him back: and if a man strikes an officer, it is not enough for the officer to strike him, but he ought to be punished as well. Again, it makes a great difference whether an act was voluntary or involuntary [done with or without the consent of the other party]. But in the interchange of services Justice in the form of Reciprocity is the bond that maintains association: reciprocity, that is, on the basis of proportion, not on the basis of equality.[30]

As we shall see later, this passage created considerable difficulties of interpretation. Thus, the example of the officer who hits another man or is hit by him seemed to contradict Aristotle's own assumptions about the nature of commutative justice. Indeed, one of the major problems concerned the exact relationship of retribution (punishment) to the other two forms of justice. Not surprisingly, a number of conflicting solutions have been advanced throughout the ages: (1) retribution makes part of distributive justice; (2) it is part of corrective justice; (3) it is a third form of justice; (4) it is a distinct idea

---

30. N 1132b21–1133b33. (Loeb-Rackham, 279–281). On the question whether Aristotle's description of the Pythagorean conception corresponded to reality, *see* G. Del Vecchio, *Justice—An Historical and Philosophical Essay* (A.H. Campbell, ed., Edinburgh 1952) 42–50; the author notes (at 45): "And therefore, if it is true—and there seems to be no doubt—that Hippodamus belonged to the Pythagorean school, the objection advanced by Aristotle against that school, that it did not succeed in deriving from its concept of equiparation or 'requital' a criterion appropriate to the two types of justice, is manifestly without foundation" (footnote omitted). *See also* Ritchie, *op. cit.*, 190: "There is, in any case, little reason to believe that the Pythagoreans intended their conception of justice as *τὸ ἀντιπεπονθὸς* to mean merely 'tit for tat.'" It is noteworthy that some scholastic scholars remarked that the Pythagoreans were not so stupid as to assume that hitting a king entails an equal punishment as hitting a plebeian. *See, e.g.*, Michael Salon, *Controversiae de iustitia et iure atque de contractibus* (Venezia 1608) Tom. 1, Quaest. 61, Art. 3, Concl. 2, at 105: "Observandum est hic, iudicio multorum Pitagoreos non aliter iudicasse, quam hic docemus cum Th.se Arist. falso illorum sententiam interpretari: non erant enim tam stupidi, ut non intelligerent, maius crimen esse afficere regem vulnere quam plebeium, et ita esse dispari poena plectendos, unde quamvis absolutè suam sententiam protulerint." *Compare also* Gregorius de Valentia (ca. 1550–1603), *Commentarii Theologici, Tomus Tertius, Secundae Secundae Divi Thomae* (Ingolstadt 1595), Disp. 5, Quaest. 5, 1163: "Ubi tamen Philosophus non ait (ut Sotus lib. 3. de Iustit. q.5.art. 4 & alij quidam putarunt) eam Pythagoreorum sententiam fuisse quoque sententiam Rhadamanti; sed ait, Pythagoreos quidem dixisse, Rhadamentum secundum eam juris normam iudicandum putavisse."

that can be applied to the basic two forms of particular justice. The controversy has not been resolved until this very day.[31]

A final comment on the formal character of the Aristotelian distinctions of distributive and commutative justice[32]: Hans Kelsen claimed, in a critical analysis of Aristotle's notions of justice, that their formal essence constitutes an ideological basis for justifying the existing, substantive legal order.[33] Against this critique it has been argued that Aristotle's philosophical approach was fundamentally one of practical hermeneutics, based upon a common sense view of human society. It had no aspiration whatsoever to rationally define universal ethical rules in the Kantian spirit.[34]

---

31. On this controversy, *see* Gauthier and Jolif, *op.cit.*, II, 1, pp. 369–372. *See* in addition Gabriel Danzig, "The Political Character of Aristotelian Reciprocity," 95 (2000) *Classical Philology* 399, 402, 404 and *passim*. The latter author considers reciprocity to be the second part of Aristotle's corrective justice, namely that dealing with voluntary transactions. A similar view has been maintained already by Karl Hildenbrand, *Geschichte und System der Rechts—und Staatsphilosophie: Das klassische Altertum* (Leipzig 1860) 291, 298. *See also* H. Nef, *Gleichheit und Gerechtigkeit* (Zürich 1941) 89–91. See especially on the whole topic: G. Del Vecchio, *Justice—An Historical and Philosophical Essay* (A.H. Campbell, ed., Edinburgh 1952) 52–53, and notes 10–12, pp. 65–67. For a recent claim that retribution constitutes a third form of justice, *see* Ronen Perry, "The Role of Retributive Justice in the Common Law of Torts," 73 (2006) *Tenessee L. Rev.* 177, 183–186. Some scholars view punishment as part of universal (legal) justice; *infra* at notes 142, 203, 322, 718.

32. *See* in this context the remark of C.A. Emge, *Geschichte der Rechtsphilosophie* (Berlin 1931) 35: "Das Aristotelische Prinzip der Gerechtigkeit ist also in Wirklichkeit ebenso formal wie sein Prinzip des Ethischen: das 'Mittlere' die μεσότης."

33. H. Kelsen, "Aristotle's Doctrine of Justice," in *What Is Justice? Justice, Law, and Politics in the Mirror of Science* (Berkeley 1957) 110, 128: "Aristotle's definition of distributive justice is but a mathematical formulation of the well-known principle *suum cuique*, to each his own, or to each his due. But this tautology has the important function of legitimizing the positive law which, as a matter of fact, fulfills the task, which legal philosophy is not capable of fulfilling—to determine what is everybody's due." In relation to corrective justice, *see ibid.*, 131; *see also* at 125, note 52.

34. W. Kersting, "Kelsen und Aristoteles," *Griechische Philosophie im Spiegel Hans Kelsens* (R. Walter, W. Jabloner, K. Zeleny, eds., Wien 2006) 15–30, esp. at 28–30.

TWO

High Scholastics

THE RELATIVELY FEW EARLY GREEK COMMENTATORS on Aristotle's *Ethics*, whose writings were preserved,[35] did not add much to the distinction between the two forms of justice. Unfortunately, the commentary of Aspasius (ca. 100–150) on the relevant Book Five of the *Nicomachean Ethics* has not been preserved[36]; the same is true for Eustratius (ca. 1050–1120).[37] The other authors, whose writings came down to later generations, basically relied on the original text of Aristotle.[38] Of some influence in relation to Aristotle's distinction of justice, is the commentary of Michael of Ephesus (eleventh to twelfth centuries).[39]

---

35. H.P.F. Mercken, "The Greek Commentators on Aristotle's *Ethics*," *Aristotle Transformed: the ancient commentators and their influence* (R. Sorabji, ed., London 1990) 407–443. The author speaks (at 407) of the "shortage of commentary on Aristotle's *Ethics* from the heyday of commentary writing, which stretches from Alexander in the third century AD to Simplicius in the sixth." The composite Greek commentary comprises texts from five authors, spread over eleven centuries: Aspasius and two anonymous scholiasts from the second century AD; Michael of Ephesus, professor at Constantinople, and Eustratius, Metropolitan Bishop of Nicaea, both eleventh to twelfth century. Mercken, *ibid.*, 408; *see also* J. Barnes, "An Introduction to Aspasius," *Aspasius: The Earliest Extant Commentary on Aristotle's Ethics* (A. Alberti and R.W.Sharples, eds., Berlin 1999) 13–16.

36. Mercken, *ibid.*, 409.

37. Mercken, *ibid.*, 410–419.

38. The relevant remaining commentaries on Book 5 are that of the scholia and that of Michael of Ephesus. *Cf.* Mercken, *ibid.*, 428–436.

39. Mercken, *ibid.*; D.A. Lines, *Aristotle's Ethics in the Italian Renaissance (ca. 1300–1650): The Universities and the Problem of Moral Education* (Leiden 2002) 39–40. For the Latin translation of that author by Johannes Bernardus Felicianus: *Aristotelis Stagiritae Moralia Nicomachia cum Eustratii, Aspasii, Michaelis Ephesii* (Paris 1543); Reprint: *Commentaria in Aristotelem Graeca Versiones latinae temporis resuscitarum litterarum*, Band 11, 1 (Charles Lohr ed., Stuttgart 2006). On the Aristotelian notions of justice, *see ibid.*, 99b–110a. The commentary of Michael of Ephesus shows a predilection for the explanation of the different (mathematical) proportions.

After the important rediscovery of Aristotle's writings by Arab philosophers in the early medieval era,[40] these authors, equally, repeated the former's view about the two forms of justice without much further analysis.[41] A good example is the important Arab philosopher Averroes (Ibn Rushd) (1126–1198), who wrote the *Middle Commentary on Aristotle's Nicomachean Ethics*.[42] In relation to our topic, this author basically restated the thoughts of Aristotle. One short comment of his is nevertheless noteworthy. It concerns the above-mentioned example of the officer who hits a citizen or is hit by him. Averroes notes the apparent contradiction in Aristotle's work about the nature of equality in retribution, namely the taking into account of a person's prior status. His answer is that the difference in the solution is a result of the different measure of damage.[43]

The situation changed dramatically in the Christian West in the twelfth and thirteenth centuries in the wake of the Latin translations of Aristotle's *Ethics* as well as those of some Arabic commentaries.[44] The reception of Aristotle's works constituted, indeed, a major event in Western thought creating the central intellectual movement of scholasticism. It put into focus the vexing problem of the relationship between theology and philosophy. Among the manifold issues dealt with by the scholastics, we find also

---

40. *The Arabic Version of the Nicomachean Ethics* (A.A. Akasov and A. Fidora, eds., Leiden 2005), Introduction by D.M. Douglas, 1–109.

41. *Cf.* generally on the place of Aristotle's *Ethics* in the Arab world, L.V. Berman, "Le Commentaire moyen d'Ibn Rushd sur l'Ethique à Nicomaque dans la littérature hébraïque du moyen âge," 13 (1977) *Archives Juives* 19, 20–21.

42. A Latin translation of Averroes; commentary was made by Hermannus Alemannus (Teutonicus) in 1240: *Averroes: Commentarius medius in Aristotelis Ethicam; Aristotelis Opera cum Averrois commentariis*, Tertium Volumen, *Aristotelis Stagiritae Libri Moralem totam Philosophiam complectens, cum Averrois Cordubensis In Moralia Nicomachia Expositione Et in Platonis Libros de Republica Paraphrasi* (Venezia 1562; reprinted Frankfurt 1862). *See also* L.V. Berman, *Averroes' Middle Commentary on Aristotle's Nicomachean Ethics in the Hebrew Version of Samuel Ben Judah* (Jerusalem 1999) (in Hebrew).

43. *Aristotelis Opera cum Averrois commentariis, op. cit.*, fol.71b,M; L.V. Berman, *Averroes Middle Commentary, op. cit.*, 185, §16. Averroes considers the hitting officer to be more punishable, since his malice (*malitia*) is more intense. The Hebrew text is in this respect somewhat ambiguous; *cf.* Berman's comment *ad locum*. *See* the critical remark on Ibn Rushd by the Jewish commentator Josef Ibn Shem Tov (1400–1460), *infra* 113–114.

44. J. Brams, "Der Einfluss der Aristoteles-Uebersetzung auf den Rezeptionsprozess," *Albertus Magnus und die Anfänge der Aristoteles—Rezeption im lateinischen Mittelalter* (Honnefelder et al. eds., Münster 2005) 37–39; G. Endress, *Der arabische Aristoteles und sein Leser: Physik und Theologie im Weltbild Alberts des Grossen* (Münster 2004); D.A. Lines, *Aristotle's Ethics in the Italian Renaissance (ca. 1300–1650): The Universities and the Problem of Moral Education* (Leiden 2002) 45–48.

the notion of justice. The scholastics went into the moral and theological foundations of justice on the background of the classical definitions, among them the more formal Aristotelian concepts.[45] The relationship between the universal (or legal) justice and the particular justice became also an important topic for scholastic and post-scholastic scholars.[46] However, given the limited framework of this work, we will concentrate on the specific use of the Aristotelian distinction between distributive and commutative justice.

This brings us to an incidental remark concerning the place of Roman law in our specific context. In Justinian's *Digesta* there is a famous definition of justice in the name of Ulpian: "*Constans e perpetua voluntas ius suum cuique tribuens*."[47] There exists an age-old, fundamental controversy among scholars as to what extent Roman jurisprudence and law in general, and this definition in particular, were influenced and inspired by Aristotle's writings and by Greek philosophy.[48] Be that as it may, the fact remains that this traditional Roman law definition did not use the Aristotelian bipartite division of particular justice. Hence, Roman law as such did not contribute anything to the understanding of the distinction between distributive and corrective justice. As we will see in the later developments, the reaction of Roman law jurists to the Aristotelian distinction moved from its positive identification with Ulpian's definition, through indifference to open hostility.

Returning to the early scholastics, foremost mention must be made of the German Dominican scholar Albertus Magnus (1206–1280), who was one of the first authors to write an extensive commentary on Aristotle's *Nicomachean Ethics*.[49] He dealt with the problem of the exact relationship between the two

---

45. *See* on this development J.W. Baldwin, "The Medieval Theories of the Just Price: Romanists, Canonists, and Theologians in the Twelfth and Thirteenth Centuries," 49 (1959) *Transactions of the American Philosophical Society* 1, 58–63.

46. *See, e.g.*, the dissertation dealing with that issue on the background of Roman law: Cajus Henricus Nährman, *Exercitatio Academica De Justitia Universali* (Praes. Samuelus Rachelius, Kiel 1675).

47. Digest. 1.1.10. pr.: "Justice is the constant and perpetual will to render each his due."

48. *See* the discussion on this issue in G. Del Vecchio, *Justice—An Historical and Philosophical Essay* (A.H. Campbell, ed., Edinburgh 1952) 55–56, notes 24–29, at 72–76, and *see* especially the editor's reference to Schulz, *History of Roman Legal Science* (Oxford 1946), in note 26.

49. Albertus Magnus, *Super Ethica Commentum et Quaestiones*, lib. V, in *Opera Omnia edenda curavit Institutum Alberti Magni Coloniense*, B. Geyer Praeside, Tomus XIV, Pars I (W. Kübel, ed., Münster 1968–1972) 306–389. This commentary was written between 1250 and 1252 at Cologne. Albertus Magnus wrote a second commentary, *Ethica*, around 1262, that has received little attention among scholars. *See* J. Müller, "Ethics as a Practical Science in Albert the Great's Commentaries on the *Nicomachean Ethics*," *Albertus*

notions of (particular) justice. In this context he referred to Cicero's general definition of justice that equally mentioned dignity, but as a common element of justice; the author distinguished this more general notion of dignity from the specific use made by Aristotle's analysis.[50] Moreover, Albertus Magnus discussed a number of additional traditional definitions of justice.[51] Another major concern of that author was the relationship between justice and virtue. He specifically referred to the argument that denied justice of constituting a virtue, since the mean of justice related to things, whereas the mean of virtue concerned persons. The author's answer is significant: Nothing prevents the medium of a thing to be also the medium in relation to persons. This is the situation in respect of justice. The mean of our actions is that of our passions. In the case of commutative justice, the mean is not conceived to be different in relation to different persons, except where the damage itself varies, and not because of the person's condition. Thus, where a prince has been hit, the whole community suffers, because he is a public person; this would not be true where a private person had been hit. Correspondingly, when a prince hits somebody, there is less shame than if another person had hit him, because the prince, in view of his jurisdiction, has a kind of justice mixed in, which the other person has not.[52]

Magnus: Zum Gedenken nach 800 Jahren: Neue Zugänge, Aspekte, und Perspektiven (W. Senner, ed., Berlin 2001) 275–285. On the historical importance of Albertus Magnus in philosophy and especially in ethics, *see* L. Honnefelder, "Die philosophiegeschichtliche Bedeutung Alberts des Grossen," *Albertus Magnus und die Anfänge der Aristoteles-Rezeption im lateinischen Mittelalter* (Honnefelder et al. eds., Münster 2005) 249, 270–273. For an earlier discussion by Albertus Magnus of Aristotle's notion of justice, *see* A.T. Canavero, "Alberto Magno: La giustizia dopo lettura del V libro dell'*Etica Nicomachea*," 12 (1986) *Medievo* 111.

50. *Ibid.*, Lectio V, pp. 329–330, Lectio VI, p. 335 v. 69–70: "Iustitia est habitus animi communi utilitate conservata suam cuique tribuens dignitatem." The quotation is of Cicero, *De inventione*, lib. 2, c. 53, n. 160. See the interesting comments in relation to a parallel text in Albertus Magnus's sermons by U. Meier, "Die linke und die rechte Waagschale der Justiz. Die Rezeption der aristotelischen Lehre der Teilgerechtigkeiten bei Albertus Magnus und Ambrogio Lorenzetti," *Gerechtigkeiten im gesellschaftlichen Diskurs des späteren Mittelalters, Festschrift zum 60. Geburtstag von Eberhard Isenmann* (G. Annas and P. Schulte, eds., Berlin 2008) (forthcoming).

51. *Ibid.*, 336–338, Lectio VI.

52. *Ibid.*, Lectio VI, p. 338 v. 60–75: "Ad secundum dicendum, quod nihil prohibet medium virtutis esse medium rei, quando est idem medium rei et quoad nos. Et sic est in iustitia; quod enim sit medium ipsius etiam quoad nos, patet ex hoc quod est in operationibus nostris sicut medium aliarum in passionibus nostris. Nec accipitur diversimode medium secundum diversas personas in directiva iustitia nisi propter maius vel minus damnum et non propter condicionem personae; si enim percutitur princeps, laeditur tota communitas, eo quod ipse est persona publica, quod non contingeret, si esset privata persona

However, in spite of a number of important clarifications, Albertus Magnus basically followed Aristotle's way of expounding the distinction between commutative and distributive justice.[53]

A deeper and more critical analysis of the Aristotelian distinction was undertaken by the most eminent disciple of Albertus Magnus, the Dominican Thomas Aquinas (1225–1274), the dominant figure of scholasticism whose decisive influence lasted for centuries. In his major work, the *Summa Theologiae*, Thomas, in responding to specific questions, expounds more analytically the distinction between the two forms of justice.[54] In relation to distributive justice, the author notes that here common property is distributed to the individual according to the latter's excellence (*principalitas*) in

---

percussa; et ideo de omni principe simile iudicium. Similiter quando princeps percutit aliquem, est minoris deformitatis, quam si percutiat alius, quia habet quoddam iustitiae admixtum propter iurisdictionem, quam habet ipse et alius non habet."

53. *Cf.* the author's short restatement of the Aristotelian distinction in Albertus Magnus, *Opera Omnia*, Tomus Nonus (Jammy, ed., Lyon 1651), *Commentarii in Matthaeum*, Cap. V, p. 72; with slight textual changes in *Opera Omnia, etc. edenda curavit Institutum Alberti Magni Coloniense*, W. Kübel, Praeside, Tomus XXI, Pars I, *Super Matthaeum* (Münster 1987) Cap. V, 6, p. 109: "Sed attendendum, quod Iustitia dicitur duplex; specialis, & generalis. Specialis est, quae est ius suum reddens secundum rationem: aequalis inter plus & minus: damni et lucri in distribuendis, & commutandis; sicut dicit, *Aristoteles in quinto Ethicorum*. Commutans enim cum aliquo in aliquo contractu, & putans se esse deceptum & esse in damno: & ita minus habere quam valeat res, quam emit, vel vendidit, venit ad iudicem; & ille audiens adversarium, aestimat per rationem, aequalitatis valorem rei, & addit ei, qui minus in lucro, & plus habet damni. Similiter autem si aliquid sit distribuendum, iudex stipendia distribuit pro merito & dignitate uniuscuiusque. Haec est ergo iustitia specialis."

54. *Summa Theologiae*, II–II, *Quaestio* 61 art. 1–4. Naturally, the author equally deals with the notion of general, universal justice. In his view, general justice is called legal justice, because the function of law is to regulate the common good, on the basis of which the individual adapts himself to the law that coordinates the acts of all virtues with the common good. *See ibid.*, II–II, Quaestio 58, art. 6. For a discussion of the notion of legal justice with an extensive bibliography, *see* G. Del Vecchio, *Justice—An Historical and Philosophical Essay* (A.H. Campbell, ed., Edinburgh 1952) 33–37, note 15. However, as mentioned above, we are exclusively concerned with the distinctions of particular justice. It has been rightly observed that—contrary to Aristotle's formal approach to justice—Thomas Aquinas introduced a substantive notion of justice based on practical human reason and oriented toward the common good; M. Lutz-Bachmann, "The Discovery of a Normative Theory of Justice in Medieval Philosophy: On the Reception and Further Development of Aristotle's Theory of Justice by St. Thomas Aquinas," 9 (2000) *Medieval Philosophy and Theology* 1–14; on the Thomist notions of common good and legal justice, *see also* N.J. Paulhus, "Uses and Misuses of the Term 'Social Justice' in the Roman Catholic Tradition," 15 (1987) *The Journal of Religious Ethics* 261, 262–268.

the community.[55] The mean according to distributive justice is not determined according to the equality between things, but according to the proportion between things and persons.[56] However, Aquinas observes that distribution of common goods is sometimes made not from goods belonging to the state, but to a single family; in the latter case, the distribution of the common goods can be made by the authority of a private person.[57]

In this context, however, it had been remarked that Aristotle, in discussing retribution (ἀντιπεπονθὸς), apparently contradicted himself. He criticized, on the one hand, the Pythagorean principle of retribution because it did not take into account the social status of the wrongdoer and that of the injured person (ordinary man and officer). On the other hand, in his earlier discussion of corrective justice, Aristotle emphasized that the law looks only at the nature of the damage, treating the parties as equal.

Thomas Aquinas, both in his major work *Summa Theologiae*[58] and in his *Commentary on the Nicomachean Ethics*, referred to this apparent contradiction in Aristotle. In his *Commentary*, Thomas Aquinas, after stating the problem,[59] suggested—probably influenced by his teacher Albertus Magnus[60]—that the

55. *Summa Theologiae*, II–II, Quaestio 61, art. 2: "Et ideo in distributiva iustitia tanto plus alicui de bonis communibus datur quanto illa persona maiorem principalitatem habet in communitate."

56. *Ibid.*

57. *Ibid.*, Quaestio 61, art.1, ad tertium: "Quamvis etiam distributio quandoque fiat bonorum communium non quidem civitati, sed uni familiae: quorum distributio fieri potest auctoritate alicuius privatae personae." John Finnis, *Natural Law and Natural Rights* (Oxford 1980) 186, in his critique of Robert Nozick's opposition to redistributive taxation, makes the following statement: "On Aquinas's view, anyone in charge of an item of 'common stock' will have duties of distributive justice; hence any property-holder can have such duties, since the goods of this earth are to be exploited and used for the good of all." We doubt very much the accuracy of that statement. The fact that a property holder has a duty toward the needy (*Summa Theologia*, II–II, Quaestio 66, art. 2c; Quaestio 32, art. 5 ad 2) does not mean that it makes part of distributive justice in the Thomist-Aristotelian sense. Aquinas speaks explicitly of distribution of common goods on the basis of authority. *Cf.* J. Gordley, "Morality and Contract: The Question of Paternalism," 48 (2007) *Wm and Mary L.Rev.* 1733, 1737, 1739: "While the virtue of distributive justice is typically exercised by those in authority, that of liberality is exercised by private persons who choose to enrich others at their own expense."

58. *Summa Theologiae*, II–II, Quaestio 61, art. 2.

59. *S. Thomae Aquinatis in Decem Libros Ethicorum Aristotelis ad Nicomachum Expositio* (R.M. Spiazzi ed., 1949) Lib. V, Lect. 8, § 969: "Videtur autem hoc esse contra id quod philosophus supra dixerat, quod in iustitia commutativa non attenditur diversa conditio personarum, sed lex attenditur solum ad differentiam nocumenti."

60. *Supra* at note 52.

solution was to be found in the nature of the damage. Corrective justice (called by Thomas as mentioned: *iustitia commutativa*) was directed in cases of injuries toward the compensation of the damage. However, in case of personal injury, this damage might differ according to the social status of the injured person. Hence, equal compensation (retribution) in all cases of this kind would be wrong. Thomas mentioned in this context that hitting a superior officer implied, in addition, damage to the state. However, where there was damage to exterior things, equal compensation would be just, since the damage was independent of the person involved.[61]

---

61. *Ibid.*: "Sed attendendum est quod ibidem Philosophus dixerat quod in commutativa iustitia lex attenditur solum ad differentiam nocumenti. Manifestum est autem quod quando nocumentum attenditur circa subtractionem rei exterioris, puta pecuniae, non variatur quantitas nocumenti secundum diversam conditionem personae, sed quando est nocumentum personale, tunc necesse est quod quantitas nocumenti diversificetur secundum conditionem personae. Manifestum est enim quod maius est nocumentum quando aliquis percutit principem, per quod non solum personam ipsius sed totam republicam laedit, quam si percutit aliquam personam privatam. Et ideo non competit iustitiae in talibus simpliciter contrapassum." [St. Thomas Aquinas, *Commentary on Aristotle's Nicomachean Ethics* (C.I. Litzinger, transl., Notre Dame 1993) Book V, Lect. VIII, 308: "But it should be noted what the Philosopher had said was this: in commutative justice the law considers only the nature of the damage. It is clear that when damage is considered in the taking of an external thing—money for instance—the amount of damages does not vary according to a person's rank. Still when the injury is personal, the extent of the injury necessarily changes according to the rank of the person. Obviously, worse damage is done when someone strikes a ruler, by reason of the fact that the injury is done not only to the person of the ruler but also the whole commonweal. Therefore, reciprocation is not suitable for justice in matters of this kind"] In the same sense *see* the comment on Aristotle's *Nicomachean Ethics* in *Textus ethicorum Aristotelis ad Nichomachum iuxta antiquam translationem cum familiarissimo commentario in eundem et compendiosis questionibus ac dubiis circa litteram emergentibus ad mentem doctissmorum virorum magistrorum Martini magistri Johannis buridani maiore pro parte decicis* (Paris ca. 1496), fol. 65a: "Dicitur quod hoc non provenit ex dignitate principis per se: sed ex maiori vel minori nocumento illato. Qui enim percutit principem non iniuriatur solum principi in persona eius: sed toti communitati cuius vices gerit. Plus enim ledit communitatem qui ledit partem eius nobiliores quam qui viliores." *See also* Tarquinius Gallutius (Tarquinio Galluzzi) (1574–1649), *In Aristotelis quinque priores Moralium libros ad Nicomachum, Nova interpretatio, explanatio, quaestiones* (Paris 1632), Lib.5, cap. 4, p. 920–921 (quoting Buridanus): "Recte quidem Aristotelem dicere repercutiendum et puniendum esse qui Principem percussit, Principem ipsum, qui alium percusserit, non esse percutiendum: non tamen hoc proficisci ex Principis dignitate per se, sed ex minori; vel maiori damno, quod est illatum. Nam qui percutit Principem, non Principi solum iniuriam facit, nec eius personae tantummodo contumeliosus est, sed toti etiam Republicae, cuius obtinet vices ac locum. Damnum adeo, quod in ea commutatione perpenditur, est gravissimum, idque iustitia primum intuetur ac per se; personae vero conditionem respicit ex accidenti, vel consequenti"; *see also ibid.*, cap. 5, pp. 928–930; *see* in this sense also the commentary of the scholar Donatus Acciaiolus (1429–1478), in *Aristotelis Stagiritae Peripateticorum Principis Ethicorum ad Nicomachum libri decem, Ioanne Argyropylo Byzantio interprete, nuper ad Graecum exemplar diligentissime recogniti, & cum Donati Acciaioli Florentini*

In the *Summa Theologiae* the relevant question posed was the following: Apparently the dignity of a person is relevant both in distributive justice and in corrective justice, since in the latter, the punishment is more severe for a person who hits a prince than for one who hits an ordinary person. How can this be explained on the background of Aristotle's distinction between geometric and arithmetic proportion, the latter being the characteristic feature of corrective justice?[62] The answer given is that in relation to acting and suffering, the quantification of the thing [damage] differs, whereas in distributive justice the position of the person as such is taken into account.[63]

---

viri doctissimi Commentariis castigatissimis, denuo in lucem editi (Paris 1541) 87b: "Dicendum ad hanc dubitationem, quod philosophus loquitur ibi de iis quem communiter eveniunt. Praeterea videtur ibi accipere privatas personas, at siquis percusserit virum in magistratu constitutum, non punitur, quia personam illam tamquam privatam percusserit, sed quia videtur percussisse rempublicam, cum ille publicam personam gerat ut apparet exemplo allato."

62. *Ibid.*, Quaestio 61, art. 3.

63. *Ibid.*: "Et ita conditio personae in distributiva iustitia attenditur secundum se: in commutativa autem secundum quod per hoc diversificatur res." In this sense also the commentary of the Dominican scholar Dominicus de Soto (1494–1560), *De iustitia et iure Libri decem*, Lib. 3, Quaest. 5, Art. 2 (Salamanca 1556), at 244, (Lyon 1559), at 174: "Respondetur, qualitatem personae in utraque iustitia perspici: attamen in distributiva per se: ut scilicet per augmentum personae augeatur proportio ad alium: cumulatioris namque meriti est in viro ingenuo comitas & humilitas, quam in homine inferioris sortis: sed tamen in iustitia commutativa dumtaxat attenditur persona quatenus inde augetur quantitas iniuriae, quae ad aequalitatem resarcianda est." For a similar explanation of Aristotle's assumed contradiction: Josephus Saenz de Aguirre (1630–1699), *Philosophia Moralis Ab Aristotele Tradita Decem Libris Ethicorum ad Nicomachum: A Joanne Argyropilo Byzantino latine reddita; Nunc perpetuo Commentario literali & Scholastico, plenissime illustrata*, Pars Prima (Rome 1698), Lib. Quintus, Cap. V, 216, §4: "Respondeo nihil inconsequentiae esse in doctrina Aristotelis. Priori enim illo loco egit de justo correctivo secundum ea, quae communiter accidunt; non autem semper, & absque distinctione ulla. Communiter autem loquendo, justum correctivum exigit, ut arithmetica proportio plene servetur inter injuriam & poenam: quia justum correctivum prout extenditur ad casus frequentes not attendit dignitatem qualitatemque inaequalem personarum, sed solum qualitatem injuriae, & poenam arithmetice ipsi proportionatam. In praesenti autem sermo est de justo ipso correctivo prout attendit utrumque, & habitudinem injuriae ad poenam, & offensi ad offendentem, juxta inaequalem utriusque dignitatem. Insuper & eo loci agebatur de injuria personae privatae ad privatam; hic vero de injuria personae publicae, cuius dignitas in Magistratu resplendet. Pythagorei autem contrapassionem ubique constituebant, & nulla distinctione facta." In this sense also the Jesuit scholar Franciscus Pavonius (1585–1637), *Summa Ethicae sive Introductio in Aristotelis, Et Theologorum Doctrinam moralem* (Mainz 1621) 430: "Interdum tamen per accidens attenditur personae dignitas, nimirum cum ex dignitate personae crescit valor rei, ut accidit in compensandis iniurijs, quae eo sunt maiores, ac proinde maiorem compensationem exigunt, quo persona offensa est dignior." A slightly different explanation is given by Count Don Emanuele Tesauro (1581–1677/78), *La Filosofia Morale Derivata Dall'Alto Fondo Del Grande Aristotele Stagirita* (Torino 1671) 379. In the latter's view one has to

A special article is dedicated to the relationship between retribution (*contrapassum*) and the two forms of justice.[64] The question posed is the following: Why should retribution not be considered the common principle of both forms of justice, since both refer to the merits of persons? Hence, why does Aristotle claim that there is no identity between justice and retribution? The answer given is the following: Retribution in corrective justice has different forms. One has to distinguish the causing of injuries to another person from voluntary transactions. But in both cases, the leading principle is equal retribution according to the circumstances. In case of wrongful acts, the punishment has to take into account the fact that injury has been caused not only to a private person, but also to the state by menacing the latter's protective security.[65] In voluntary transactions, the retribution has to be made by a proportionate measure effectuated through money. In this way, retribution is commutative justice.[66]

However, retribution does have no place in distributive justice. In the latter, equality is not measured according to the proportion between things, or according to the proportion between the suffering and the act, whence it is called "*contrapassum*"; but it is measured according the proportion between things and persons.[67] Thomas adds that where a person receives compensation for his services to the community, it is commutative justice and not distributive justice. In the latter, a person does not receive benefits according to his expenditures, but according to his status in proportion to that of another person.[68]

---

distinguish between measuring the injury and measuring the punishment. In relation to the injury, one applies a geometric proportion by taking into account the specific circumstances and persons; but in relation to the punishment one has to adopt an arithmetic proportion without taking into account the persons: the greater the injury, the greater the punishment; for an equal injury an equal punishment.

64. *Summa Theologiae*, II–II, *Quaestio* 61, art. 4.

65. *Ibid.*: "Ed ideo punitur in hoc quod multiplicius restituat, quia etiam non solum damnificavit personam privatam, sed rempublicam, eius tutelae securitatem infringendo." This idea is repeated by the Dominican Archbishop of Florence, Antoninus Florentinus (1389–1459), *Summa Theologica*, Pars III (Venezia 1480), Titulus V, Cap. II.

66. *Ibid.*: "Et sic contrapassum est commutativum iustum."

67. *Ibid.*:"In distibutiva autem iustitia locum non habet. Quia in distributiva iustitia non attenditur aequalitas secundum proportionem rei ad rem, vel passionis ad actionem, unde dicitur contrapassum: sed secundum proportionalitatem rerum ad personas, ut supra dictum est."

68. *Ibid., ad tertium:* "In distributiva enim iustitia non attenditur aequalitas eius quod quis accipit ad id quod ipse impendit, sed ad id quod alius accipit, secundum modum utriusque

Another objection raised in the *Summa Theologiae* against the Aristotelian distinction related to restitution is the following way:

Restitution is repayment of something taken away. Now something may be taken away from a man not only in commutation but also in distribution, as when, in distributing, one gives a man less than his due. Therefore restitution is not more an act of commutative than of distributive justice.[69]

The answer given to that objection is the following:

Compensation is made by the distributor to the man to whom less was given than his due, by comparison of thing with thing, when the latter receives so much the more according as he received less than his due: and consequently it pertains to commutative justice.[70]

In summary, a number of things have to be noted in relation to Thomas Aquinas's interpretation of the Aristotelian distinction. Retribution (*contrapassum, antipeponthos*) is at the basis of corrective (commutative) justice. However, retribution is not a simple equal measure, as assumed by the Pythagoreans, but a proportionate measure, adapted to the circumstances that determine the specific quantum of damage. It includes punishment for misdeeds, the measure of which takes into account the violation of the public interest in the individual's security. In voluntary transactions, the tool that determines the proportional value of things is money. Here, Thomas Aquinas, in his *Commentary* on Aristotle's *Ethics*, adds: "But this one standard which truly measures all things is demand."[71] This includes all commutable things inasmuch as everything has a reference to human need. Articles are not valued according to the dignity of their nature, otherwise a mouse, an animal endowed with sense, should be of greater value than a pearl, a thing without life. But they are priced according as man stands in need of them for its own use."[72]

---

personae." Thomas Aquinas follows the Aristotelian approach of a mere formal criterion of distributive justice (*supra* at note 22). *See* S. Lippert, *Recht und Gerechtigkeit bei Thomas von Aquin: Eine rationale Rekonstruktion im Kontext der Summa Theologiae* (Marburg 2000) 86–87. The author calls it an empirical approach, as distinguished from a normative one.

69. *Summa Theologiae*, II–II, *Quaestio* 62, Art. 1, Obj. 3; (transl. Fathers of the English Dominican Province, London 1929) 169.

70. *Ibid.*, 170. See the extensive treatment of the relationship between restitution and the two forms of justice according to Aquinas in Manuel Moix Martinez, *ΔIKH—Nuevas perspectivas de la justicia clásica* (Madrid 1968) 518–560.

71. In the original Latin: *indigentia*, need. *See infra*, note 182.

72. St. Thomas Aquinas, *Commentary on Aristotle's Nicomachean Ethics* (C.I. Litzinger, transl., Notre Dame 1993) Book V, Lect. IX, §981, p. 312; *S. Thomae Aquinatis in Decem Libros*

Finally, distributive justice's function is to distribute common goods exclusively according the respective status of citizens.

It is highly possible that the brief mentioning of "contrapasso" by Dante Alighieri (1265–1321) in his *Divine Comedy*[73] evokes the Aristotelian and scholastic concept of retribution in the context of divine justice.[74]

Another important figure of High Scholasticism is the Franciscan scholar Johannes Duns Scotus (ca. 1265–1308), who did not hesitate to contest a number of Thomas Aquinas's theological and philosophical assumptions.[75] In relation to the Aristotelian distinction, it is interesting to note that in one place Duns Scotus affirms that punitive justice has to be distinguished from commutative justice, since it is exercised neither for the sake of the punished nor for that of the punisher, but for the sake of the law and furthermore for that of the public good.[76] However, in another place Duns Scotus affirms, when dealing with divine justice, that commutative justice has to do with punishment and reward, so that rewards are dealt out as if in compensation for merits and punishments for sins.[77] He adds that commutative justice

---

Ethicorum Aristotelis ad Nicomachum Expositio (R.M. Spiazzi ed., 1949) Lib. V, Lect. IX, § 981, p. 270: "... hoc autem unum, quod omnia mensurat secundum rei veritatem est indigentia, quae continent omnia commutabilia, inquantum omnia referuntur ad humanam indigentiam; non enim appretiantur secundum dignitatem naturae ipsorum: alioquin unus mus, quod est animal sensibile, maioris pretii esset quam una margarita, quae est res inanimata: sed rebus pretia imponuntur, secundum quod homines indigent eis ad summum usum." *Cf.* James Gordley, "Equality in Exchange," 69 (1981) *Calif. L. Rev.* 1587, 1604, at note 93.

73. *Inferno* XXVIII, 136–142. Bertran de Born, whose brain-pan had been separated from its source in his trunk, explained this punishment as a retribution for splitting apart in his life father and son: "Così s'osserva in me lo contrapasso."

74. *See* the excellent analysis by Peter Armour, "Dante's *Contrapasso*: Context and Texts," 55 (2000) *Italian Studies* 1–20; *cf. also* M. E. Smith, "Punishment in the Divine Comedy," 25 (1994) Cumb. L. Rev. 533, 540.

75. On the lasting influence of Duns Scotus in general, J. Schmutz, "L'héritage des subtils, cartographie du scotisme de l'âge classique," 57 (2002/1) *Les études philosophiques* 51–81.

76. *Quaestiones in libro IV sententiarum* in *Opera Omnia*, t. 9 (Lyon 1639) Lib. 4, Dist. 14, Quaest. 2, p. 36: "Est ergo iste actus iustitiae punitivae, quae distinguitur contra iustitiam commutativam, &etiam contra amicitiam. Et fortè iste actus est nobilior inter omnes actus iustitiae in communi, excepto actu praemiationis: quia ille est proprius legislatori, & nulli alij conveniens, nisi ex commissione à iudice, quasi vice eius." *Cf.* Gregorius Dev, *Ethica seu ethica generalis ad mentem Ven. J. Scoti D. Subtilis* (Jerusalem 1906) §174, p. 104.

77. *Op. cit., Opera Omnia*, t. 10 (Lyon 1639) Lib. 4, Dist. 46, Quaest. 1, n. 4, p. 240: "Ad propositum, commutativa propriè respicit punitionem, & praemiationem ut scilicet pro meritis quasi commutando, reddantur praemia, & pro peccatis supplicia. Distributiva respicit quasi naturas, & perfectiones superadditas, ut scilicet naturae distribuatur perfectio sibi proportionata."

cannot be in God in an unqualified sense with respect to creature, since there cannot be equality between them in an unqualified sense. But in a way there can be equality according to proportion, as between a master and his slave. For it is fitting for a generous master to reward his slave with a greater good than the slave can actually deserve, and yet his doing so is still in keeping with proportion: just as the slave does what is his to do, the master repays him with what is his to give; and the same is true in punishing him less than he deserves.

Distributive justice, on the other hand, can be in God in an unqualified sense, since in an unqualified sense he can give natures the perfections that are due to or suitable for them in accordance with the levels [of goodness] that make them perfect [after their kind].[78]

Later commentators have made an effort to reconcile the two passages.[79] Among them the Polish Franciscan scholar Marianus Costenus deserves special mention.[80] He argues that only commutative justice is a real and proper kind of particular justice, since both distributive and vindictive justice cannot be counted as veritable kinds of justice. Distributive justice concerns the distribution of common goods according to a geometric proportion.

However, the individual citizens don't have a strict right to these goods. Likewise, the dignity of persons is not an object of justice, but merely of the virtues of deference and respect. Thomas Aquinas teaches that favoritism (*acceptio personarum*) is the opposite of distributive justice; but according to him the rendering of reverence and honor is not a kind of strict justice, but belongs to what he calls "potential" parts of justice. Duns Scotus, when dividing justice into legal, commutative, distributive, and vindictive justice, emphasizes the aspect of the "other-directness" (*ad alterum*) of these virtues. He intends, therefore, to use the term justice in its wide sense—like he does

78. *Ordinatio*, 4, d. 46, q. 1. Translation by Thomas Williams from the Wadding edition; *Quaestiones in libro IV sententiarum*, in *Opera Omnia*, t. 10 (Lyon 1639) Lib. 4, Dist. 46, Quaest. 1, n. 4, pp. 240–241. On Duns Scotus's notion of justice as a moral virtue and its relationship to will, *see* Giovanni Pizzo, "La giustizia nella dottrina della volontà di Giovanni Duns Scotus," 81 (1989) *Rivista di Filosofia neo-scolastica* 3–26. The problem of divine justice will be specifically treated in Chapter 4 of this book.

79. *Cf.* the comment by Antonius Hiquaeus (1586–1641), *Quaestiones in libro IV sententiarum*, in *Opera Omnia*, t. 9 (Lyon 1639) Lib. 4, Dist. 14, Quaest. 2, nn. 33–36, pp. 39–40; *see infra* 55–56.

80. Marianus Costenus, *Aequilibrium Iustitiae Seu Tractatus Speculativus & Moralis De Iure Et Iustitia, De Obiecto, & Subiecto Dominij, De Restitutione, De Contractibus, De Iudice, & Iudicio / Iuxta doctrinam Venerabilis P.F. Ioannis Duns Scoti* (Poznan 1641).

in relation to friendship, obedience, and goodness—and not justice in its strict sense. Hence, distributive justice is not a proper kind of justice.[81]

The same is true for vindictive justice.[82] Vindictive justice may be directed toward the good of the revenging person, then it constitutes an act of charity against oneself; or it may be directed toward the good of another person, then it may be an act of friendship. As a result, vindication may be an act of different virtues. If it concerns the common good, then it enters the category of "legal justice," since its immediate objective is the preservation of the law.

The author then quotes the above-mentioned apparently contrary statement of Duns Scotus, where the latter qualifies punishment as a kind of commutative justice.[83] Costenus relies on Duns Scotus's wording of "*quasi commutando*," affirming that accordingly vindication is not a proper act of commutative justice, but merely by a kind of imitation. In conclusion: Vindictive justice is not a specific kind of particular justice; the only real kind of particular justice is commutative justice, since it is based upon a strict duty-right relationship.[84]

It seems that Duns Scotus's view on punitive justice being part of distributive justice was accepted by a great number of later scholastics and scholars. Thus, in a general commentary on Aristotle's *Nicomachean Ethics* made by scholars of the Coimbrian school, it is assumed, without further discussion, that punitive and remunerative justice fall into the category of distributive justice.[85]

---

81. *Ibid.*, 22–23. However, when dealing with the effects of distributive justice, the author recognizes a duty of restitution for the damage caused to the state by the inadequate distribution of common goods (p. 27): "Quod Principes Reipublicae aliquis ratione officij sui, stricte obligatur communitati ad bona communia iuste distribuenda, quod non iuste distribuat, obligatur ad restitutionem damnorum secutorum, contra rationem boni communis ex iniqua distributione, sicut Oeconomus aliquis, iussu domini, conducens operarios inique, tenetur ad restituenda damna secuta, ex iniqua conductione messorum." It appears, therefore, that he bases the duty of compensation on commutative justice. On the other hand, the ruler is not liable toward the worthier citizen who was not elected to the office. The author mentions specifically that the King of Poland is not liable in restitution (*ibid.*): "Ratio est, quia Rex Poloniae, non ita stricte obligatur Reipublicae, ad haec bona communia distribuenda, in rem boni communis Reipublicae, sicut Dux Venetorum, ut constat ex rotula iuramenti."

82. *Ibid.*, 23–24.

83. *Supra* at note 76.

84. *Ibid.*, 24: "Ergo vindicativa, non est proprie, ac presse iustitia specialis: consequenter sola commutativa est iustitia proprie dicta, quae ex sua essentiali ratione, in illo in quo est, debitum stricte sumptum, & in altero ad quem est, ius stricte sumptum, supponit."

85. *In Libros Ethicorum Aristotelis ad Nicomachum Aliquot Conimbricensis Cursus Disputationes* (4a ed., Cologne 1603), Disp. 9, Q. 1, art. 2, col. 89–90: "Rursum dividitur justitia

Interestingly, a different view on the classification of punitive justice was voiced by Fra Domenico Cavalca (ca. 1270–1342), the Italian Dominican writer of spiritual treatises in the vernacular. In his famous *Lo Specchio della Croce*,[86] he considers vindictive justice to be a third kind of justice besides commutative and distributive justice.[87] He affirms that on the cross Christ demonstrated all three forms of justice.[88]

---

in distributivam & commutativam. Distributiva est, *quae in rectem distribuendo versatur.* Haec autem in duo membra secatur, in remunerativam, & punitivam. *Remunerativa est quae iubet honores, magistratum, munera & beneficia, aliaque id genus pro cuiusque dignitate & meritis, secundum Geometricam proportionem dispensare.* Punitiva *est, quae similiter, ut par est, suppliciis affici iubet.*" In the same sense: Eustachius a Sancto Paulo (Le Feuillant Eustache de Saint Paul) (1573–1640), *Summa Philosophiae Quadripartita*, Secunda Pars, Quae est Ethica (Paris 1611) 161 [edition: Cologne 1629, 105]: "Est autem distributiva iustitia duplex; altera remunerativa, quae honores & magistratus, & alia id genus beneficia pro cuiusque dignitate & meritis distribuit; altera punitiva, quae similiter nocentes, ut par est, suppliciis afficit"; Cornelius Valerius (1512–1578), *Ethicae Seu Moralis Philosphiae Brevis Et Perspicua Descriptio* (Antwerpen 1672) 43. It seems that the classification of punishment under distributive justice was then widely accepted; see the popular book for beginners on the Institutions of Justinian by the Spanish scholar Antonius Perezius (1583–1672) who taught at Leuven: *Institutiones Imperiales Erotematibus distinctae* (Editio novissima, Anwerp 1675) I, I, p.1: "*Distributiva* in praemiis & poenis pro cujusque merito distribuendis aequalitatem servat; seu tribuit pro factis unicuique quod suum est. Cum autem facta sint vel bona vel mala, pro bonis praemia redduntur, pro malis poenae, servata geometrica proportione." *See* equally the very popular law dictionary of the Heidelberg law professor Johann Kahl, alias Calvinus Wetteranus, (1550–1614), *Lexicon Iuridicum Caesarei* (Geneva 1612) 1482, "Iustitia": "Prior [iustitia distributiva] pertinet ad praemia & poenas distribuendas pro ratione & varietate meritorum: altera versatur circa contractus & aequabilium rerum permutationes, paresque compensationes." However, the contrary view can also be found: Jacob Spiegel, *Lexicon iuris civilis* (Basel 1549) 319, "Iusticiae particularis": "Hac [iusticia commutativa] autem utimur, non solum in contractibus, sed etiam in iudicijs, in poenis: non solum ubi damnum & lucrum, sed etiam ubi delictum & poena aestimantur."

86. Domenico Cavalca, *Lo Specchio della Croce: Testo originale e versione in italiano corrente a cura di P. Tito Sante Centi* (Bologna 1992) Capitolo 29, pp. 234–237.

87. *Ibid.*, 234: "La giustizia si divide in tre modi, cioè in giustizia vendicativa, che sta in punire; commutativa, che sta in non ingannare e satisfare i debiti; ed in distributiva, che sta in distribuire a ciascuno bene ed onore, secondo che è degno."

88. *Ibid.*, 234–236. In the author's view, Christ demonstrated vindictive justice by vindicating the sin in himself, showing by this how much he was displeased with sin, to an extent that he wanted to have satisfaction (*vendetta*) and justice done by his own death. Commutative justice was shown by Christ by paying the Devil for the liberation of men a higher price than was owed to him. The death of Christ was a greater thing than the damnation of all men in the world. Distributive justice was done by Christ on the cross when giving everybody according to merit. Thus, the Apostles he left his peace and the persecution of the world; the mother he left the [preferred] disciple; the [repenting] robber the Paradise; the soldiers his clothes; Godfather his soul; Joseph [d'Arimatea] his body. The examples of the author are hardly compatible with the Aristotelian notion of equality. *See* the comment of J. Polzer, "Ambrogio Lorenzetti's 'War and Peace' Murals Revisited: Contributions to

Another influential High Scholastic scholar is the French philosopher and scientist Johannes Buridanus (Jean Buridan) (ca. 1300–ca. 1358) who dared to deny the difference of kind (*species*) between commutative and distributive justice.[89] In his view, the difference resided merely in the matter (*in materia*); moreover, he was of the opinion that distributive justice and commutative justice are two forms of the same virtue.

Finally, it is noteworthy that the Neapolitan Post-Glossator, Lucas de Penna (ca. 1323–ca. 1390), though familiar with Aristotle and Aquinas, used the distinction between the two kinds of justice merely in order to classify their negatives, the acts of injustice that constitute their violations.[90] Thus, among the vices opposed to distributive justice, he enumerates a series of acts that fall under the heading of *acceptio personarum* (favoritism), such as unjust judgment, unjust accusation, false testimony, and unconscientious legal arguments. Another kind of acts that oppose distributive justice are those that run counter to religion, such as superstition, idolatry, invocation of demons, perjury, and sacrilege.[91] Violations of commutative justice are damages caused by means of involuntary transactions, such as homicide, mutilation, theft, and robbery, as well as damages caused by unjust judgments; similar violations can also occur in connection with voluntary transactions, such as damages caused by fraud and usury.

---

the Meaning of the 'Good Government Allegory,'" 23 (2002) *Artibus et Historiae* 63, 81: "In essence, Cavalca's text shows that, in the hands of the less enlightened, or in treatises intended for popular consumption, lofty speculation easily lost its philosophical coherence."

89. *Questiones Joannis Buridani super decem libros ethicorum Aristotelis ad Nicomachum* (Paris 1513) Lib. 5, Quaest. 7, at 98a–99a. He argues that distribution is not limited to public goods, since it can be done by individuals in relation to their specific property; moreover, proportional (geometric) distribution can be applied by merchants. For a favorable modern comment on Buridan's view, *see* G. Del Vecchio, *Justice—An Historical and Philosophical Essay* (A.H. Campbell, ed., Edinburgh 1952) 57, note 2.

90. Lucas de Penna, *Commentaria In Tres Posteriores Libros Codicis Iustiniani* (Lyon 1597), Cod. X, Tit. X, Lex V, nos. 28–34, pp. 49–50. *See* generally W. Ullmann, *The Medieval Idea of Law As Represented By Lucas De Penna* (London 1946). In relation to our topic the author remarks (at 39–40): "The corresponding Aristotelian notions of distributive and commutative justice are employed to show that crimes are simply violations of justice in either of these senses; the right to punish is based on the supposed violation of justice."

91. *Ibid.*, nos. 31–33. The author counts among the violation of religion also the observance of Mosaic law after the truth of the Evangile.

THREE

Late Scholastics

BETWEEN THE FIFTEENTH AND SEVENTEENTH CENTURIES a great number of scholastics wrote commentaries on the influential works of Thomas Aquinas, who remained the dominant figure in Western religious thought. Other important scholastic works were dedicated to moral theology and ethics, as well as to general philosophical problems. The latter bore witness to the lasting overwhelming position of Aristotle's works. Many of these late scholastics expounded the Aristotelian concept of justice and especially the distinctions between commutative and distributive justice.

We shall proceed by describing the different scholastic views in relation to that topic in a basically chronological order. In spite of the manifold and variegated opinions, it is, however, possible to point out some major general tendencies of these important works. This we shall do in a few preliminary remarks.

One major concern of these scholastics was to defend Thomas Aquinas's view on the essential character of the Aristotelian distinction against the mentioned contrary opinion of Buridanus.[92] In relation to the distinction itself, one strong new tendency was to enhance it by means of an additional element: the intensity of the right and the duty. Accordingly, only under commutative justice there was a perfect duty-right relationship; distributive justice created a much weaker claim against the distributor. On the other hand, the emphasis upon the intensity of the relationship implied a weakening of the geometric-arithmetic elements that were so prominent in the

92. *See, e.g.*, the comment on Aristotle's *Nicomachean Ethics* in *Textus ethicorum Aristotelis ad Nichomachum iuxta antiquam translationem cum familiarissimo commentario in eundem et compendiosis questionibus ac dubiis circa litteram emergentibus ad mentem doctissmorum virorum magistrorum Martini magistri Johannis buridani maiore pro parte decicis* (Paris ca. 1496), fol. 63a–b. The ample discussion of the questions and doubts was probably written by Magister Martinus, who might be the theologian Martinus of Biberach (d. 1498). As will be seen in the following pages, many other late scholastic scholars objected to Buridan's view. On Buridan's view, *supra* at note 89.

traditional approach. Moreover, the very dichotomous character of the distinction was considerably weakened: many scholars saw no problem in defining certain legal situations as a combination of the two forms of justice.

Furthermore, many late scholastics followed Thomas Aquinas's specific interpretations of Aristotle's views. Thus, as noted above, many scholars adopted Aquinas's explanation of Aristotle's apparent contradiction between the essence of commutative justice and the example of the hitting of the prince, as given in the discussion of retribution (*contrapassum*).[93]

Let us start with Dominican Archbishop of Florence, Antoninus Florentinus (1389–1459), who, in his *Summa theologica*, followed closely in the steps of Thomas Aquinas by maintaining the distinction between distributive and commutative justice.[94] In his summary work, he often paraphrases the statements of Aquinas. Thus, in discussing distributive justice, he emphasizes the practical insights of Aquinas. He repeats almost literally the opinion of Aquinas, that when electing a person to a public office, the better one should be preferred. However, legally it suffices to elect a good one, even if there might be a better one. In that case, the election cannot be impugned in court, since otherwise every election would entail litigation (*calumnia*). Nevertheless, in respect of the conscience of the electors, the better person should be elected to the office.[95]

---

93. *Supra* 16–18. As mentioned above, Aquinas followed here his teacher Albertus Magnus.

94. Antoninus Florentinus (1389–1459), *Summa Theologica*, Pars III (Venezia 1480), Titulus V, Cap. II, III.

95. *Ibid.*, Cap. III, §2. The author explicitly relies on Thomas Aquinas, *Summa Theologica*, II–II, *Quaestio* 63, art. 2, ad Obj. 3. The topic of electing persons to public or ecclesiatical offices became an important issue in many scholastic treatises. Some required the election of the better candidate, others claimed that it suffices to elect a good one. On the various opinions *see* Bartholomaeus Mastrius de Meldula (1602–1673) *Theologia Moralis Ad mentem DD. Seraphici, & Subtilis concinnata, et in disputationes vigintiocto distributa* (Editio Secunda, Venezia 1681), Disput. VI, Quaestio 1, §4, p. 134. The author sides with those authors who find it sufficient to elect a good candidate, even if there is a better one. However, the situation changes where the candidates were invited with a promise that the best candidate will be elected. In this case, not only the welfare of the state is involved, but equally a duty toward the candidates to elect the best one. The question of the electors' liability was widely discussed on the background of the Aristotelian distinction, *see, e.g.*, the work of the Spanish Bishop Didacus (Diego) Covarruvias y Levya (1512–1577), *Opera Omnia* (Madrid 1610) Pars 2, §7, 489–493; for a more recent statement of the elector's legal liability toward the subjects who suffered damage as a result of the "unjust or inconsiderate election," *see* Thomas Mauritius Richeri (1733–1797), *Universa Civilis et Criminalis Jurisprudentia Juxta Seriem Institutionum ex Naturali et Romano Jure Depromta*, Tomus I (Lodi 1826) §15, 59; *see also* generally on the distribution of offices, Thomas Holzclau S.J.

More original and influential is the work of the Spanish Dominican scholar Francisco de Vitoria (ca. 1483–1546).[96] In relation to the Aristotelian distinction, he concluded that a debt under corrective justice is stricter than one under distributive justice. He stated:

> If Petrus owes me ten ducats, the debt is that he renders me the equal amount. Yet in distributive justice not so much is owed. Given that I am suitable for a certain office, then when the King does not give it to me, he does not cause me as much injustice as if it had been mine . . . Equally, note that it is possible that a debt occurs in distributive justice as well as in commutative justice, nevertheless a greater debt is in commutative justice; hence if here a mistake is made a greater injustice is done.[97]

Another important Spanish Dominican scholar was Domingo de Soto (1494–1560), who elaborated in a lengthy discussion the distinction between the two forms of justice on the background of the works of Aristotle and Thomas Aquinas.[98] He maintained, against Buridanus, that the two forms differed in their essence (*specie*). In his view, commutative justice is based upon a real and proper debt; distributive justice merely a kind of a debt. Moreover, they differ also in relation to their object, their notion of equality and their form. Finally, they consist in two different virtues. Thus, distributive justice takes into account the prior position of the parties. The author gives the following example: the stomach is a common member of the body, but it

---

(1716–1783), *Theologia Dogmatico-Polemico-Scholastica*, Tractatus II, *De Jure Et Justitia*, Pars II, *De Justitia* (Würzburg 1768) 46–59.

96. De Vitoria was the founder of the famous Spanish "School of Salamanca," owing its origin in part to the revival of Thomism which had been established at the University of Paris during the last decades of the fifteenth century; *see* A.R.D. Pagden, "The Diffusion of Aristotle's Moral Philosophy in Spain, ca. 1400–ca. 1600," 31 (1975) *Traditio* 287, 308–309.

97. Francisco de Vitoria, *De justitia*, vol. 1 (V. Beltrán de Heredia, O.P., ed., Madrid 1934) 2.2, Quaest. LXI, Art. 2, 3: "Est notanda differentia inter justitiam commutativam et distributivam, quia commutativa est magis stricta. Si Petrus debet mihi decem ducatos, debitum est ut reddat totidem. Sed tamen in justitia distributiva non est tantum debitum. Dato ego sim idoneus ad unum officium, si rex illud non mihi daret, non mihi faceret tantam injuriam sicut si esset meum . . . Item, nota quod licet debitum cadat in justitia distributiva et commutativa, tamen majus debitum est in commutativa justitia; et ideo si hic erretur, fit major injuria." *See* generally on Vitoria's notion of justice, D. Deckers, *Gerechtigkeit und Recht—Eine historisch-kritische Untersuchung der Gerechtigkeitslehre des Francisco de Vitoria (1483–1546)* (Freiburg 1991).

98. Dominicus de Soto; *De iustitia et iure Libri decem* (Lyon 1559) Lib. 3, Quaest. 5, Art. 1–4, at 171–178.

does not distribute an equal amount of food to the feet as to the eyes, nor the same to the liver as to the spleen; but each according to its nature and dignity.[99] Vindictive justice necessarily makes part of commutative justice, since under it neither goods nor evils are distributed, but punishment is meted out in equivalence of the crime.[100]

Another staunch defender of Thomism was the Spanish Dominican scholar Domingo Báñez (1528–1604), professor of theology at the University of Salamanca.[101] In his commentary on Aquinas's *Summa*, after a rather lengthy discussion of the general notion of justice, he shortly summarizes the conclusions on the two different kinds of particular justice.[102] Thus in distributive justice, the mean is according to the proportion between things and persons: the more dignity a person has in the state, the greater is his part of benefits. In commutative justice, the equality is between things: one owes the other person as much as one has received from him.[103]

The author equally rejects Buridan's view that declared the difference between the two kinds of justice to be merely accidental and not *in specie*. Buridan's view runs counter Aristotle and the schools of both philosophers and theologians.[104] The specific differences between the two kinds of justice are the following: distributive justice functions between state and citizen, the whole versus the part; commutative justice constitutes the order between citizens, i.e., between the individual parts of the community. The foundation of the obligation is different.[105] Moreover, according to the opinion of all, the violation of commutative justice entails a duty of restitution; in relation to distributive justice the opinions of jurists and theologians are divided as to the existence of a duty of restitution.

---

99. *Ibid.*, 174, Art. 2.

100. *Ibid.*, Art.1, 4, at 172, 178.

101. Domingo Báñez, who was referred to as *praeclarissimum iubar* ("the brightest light"), became famous also as one of the spiritual directors and confessors of Saint Teresa of Avila (1515–1582).

102. Dominicus Bañes, *Decisiones De Iure & Iustitia, Tomus Quartus* (Douai 1615) 15–29.

103. *Ibid.*, 46.

104. *Ibid.*

105. *Ibid.*: "In iustitia distributiva repetitur ratio debiti eo quod id, quod est totius, videlicet reipublicae, debetur, aliquo modo parti, scilicet, civi. Debetur autem non tanquam illi applicatum: sed applicandum tanquam proprium. In commutativa vero debetur aliquid civi, tanquam iam proprium & applicatum illi, & tanquam ipsiusmet civis & partis, ergo."

Finally, the opposite vices of the two kinds of justice are different: The opposite of distributive justice is *acceptio personarum* (favoritism); the opposite of commutative justice is injustice without a specific denomination.[106] It is true that sometimes in commutative justice the dignity of a person is taken into account. This occurs in personal injury cases but, contrary to distributive justice, not always and not formally and directly for the purpose of distributing common goods. In situations of distributive justice, the greater the number of worthy people is, the less each of them will obtain from the public goods to be distributed.

Commutative justice is concerned with equality; hence the purpose of taking into account an injured person's dignity is to adequately compensate him for his injury. As a result, the fact that there is a plurality of worthy people in the state does not detract from the amount of compensation to be paid to the individual injured person.[107]

In relation to vindictive justice, the author equally follows closely in the steps of Aquinas. The exercise of vindication by a judge falls under the heading of commutative justice, since the judge is duty-bound not only to care for the common good, but equally for the good of the individual citizen, namely to preserve him from injury. Moreover, the judge receives contributions and income not only from the state but also from the individual citizens in order to ward off injuries from the latter. Should the judge neglect his duty of protecting the citizens from theft and robbery, he will under commutative justice be liable to pay them compensation for the damages.

A dignitary, whose reputation has been blemished by others, has a duty under commutative justice to claim judicial vindication if he cannot recover otherwise his good reputation. He is obliged under commutative justice to exercise his public function, but cannot do it as long as he is in bad repute. Hence, he is under a commutative- justice-duty to claim vindication. He can legally be forced by his subjects to claim judicial revenge and punishment.[108] However, a claim by a private person for judicial vindication is not based upon a legal duty, but merely upon a moral one.[109]

---

106. *Ibid.*, 46–47.

107. *Ibid.*, 47.

108. *Ibid.*

109. *Ibid.*, 47–48. The author, relying on Aquinas's *Summa Theologiae* (II–II, Quaest. 80 and Quaest. 108, art. 2) concludes: "Dicimus enim quod iustitia vindicativa proprie loquendo non est iustitia Cardinalis & perfecta, quae dividitur in hac divisione." The author disagrees with the contrary opinion of De Soto (*supra* at note 100) by arguing (48): "Atque

The above-mentioned argument of de Vitoria[110] was further developed, under the influence of Aquinas's work, by the Flemish Jesuit theologian Leonardus Lessius (1554–1623).[111] In his view, where, e.g., a person or a body has a perfect right to receive a certain amount of money according to a proportion determined by law, by custom, or by a donator's disposition, then by the same act the two forms of justice coincide. Thus, where the person, having that right under strict law, receives less than the proportion due to him, there is a concomitant violation of both commutative and distributive justice.[112] On the other hand, where something is distributed according to a proportion, without the recipient having a right to it under strict law, then distributive justice does not include commutative justice. Hence, the violation of the proportion by the distributor is not a wrong obliging restitution under corrective justice; it is a nevertheless a sin against distributive justice.[113]

The topic of the Aristotelian distinction between commutative and distributive justice was dealt with extensively by another, most influential, Spanish Jesuit scholar, Francisco Suárez (1548–1617), who was a contemporary of Lessius. In his work dealing with questions of justice and law,[114] after stating six traditional distinctions between the two forms of justice,[115] he adduces

---

adeo, qui petit vindictam, licet reddit par ei, qui intulit iniuriam, non tamen reddit per commutationem: quia non ex debito legali."

110. *Supra* 29.

111. Lessius, *De iustitia aliisque virtutibus morum libri quattuor* (Lugd., 1630) Lib. 2, Cap. 1, Dubit. 4, p. 15.

112. *Ibid.*: "Quare minus dando quam opportet, simul violatur Iustitia utraque: distributiva, quia non datur secundum proportionem dignitatis quam habet ad alios: commutativa, quatenus non datur aequale iuri quod ipsi acquisitum est."

113. *Ibid.*: "Unde non fit ipsis iniuria, quae ad restitutionem obliget, etsi aliis conferantur: peccat tamen distributor contra Iustitiam distributivam." In this sense also Iohannes De Lugo (1583–1660), *De Iustitia et Iure* (Lyon 1652) Tom. 1, Disp. 1, Sect. 3, n. 51, p. 15. The latter explains that restitution is problematic from two points of view. If the distributor corrects the faulty distribution by means of his own personal property, then the originally intended distributive proportion is still not achieved, since the common goods remain distributed incorrectly. If he restores the original proportion by taking away the excessive part from the recipient and transferring it to the right person, then he violates commutative justice, since the former recipient had acquired a strict right of property. The original transfer of ownership was not affected by any error in substantia. (*ibid.*, n. 53). These arguments are repeated by Florentio de Coque, *De Jure, Justitia et Annexis Tractatus Quattuor* (Bruxelles 1708) 6; A. Pottier, *De Jure et Justitia* (Liège 1900), Diss. II, n. 22; A.F.M. Sweens, *Institutiones Theologicae de Virtute Cardinali Justitiae* (Haaren 1913) 180–181.

114. F. Suárez, *Questiones de iustitia et iure*, in J. Giers, *Die Gerechtigkeitslehre des jungen Suárez* (Freiburg 1958) 100–109, Disp. 4, Quaest. 3–4.

115. Suárez, *op. cit.*, Disp. 4, Quaest. 3; Giers, *op. cit.*, 101–102.

in a rather nominalistic, critical way, a number of counterarguments.[116] Thus, even in the basic situation of commutative justice, such as the payment of a debt, there can be cases where a distributive principle is applied.

This happens where there is a multitude of creditors and the debtor has insufficient funds: payment is made proportionally.[117] On the other hand, where there is only one candidate for distribution, the situation becomes one of commutative justice. Nevertheless, Suárez maintains the fundamental difference between the two forms of justice by emphasizing less the difference in the objectives of justice (distribution versus restitution) and more the legal character of the claim.[118] Remaining in the scholastic tradition, he considers the claim in distributive justice to be imperfect and therefore weaker than that of commutative justice that is necessarily based upon a strict right.[119]

In a special section, the author deals with classification of revenge (*vindicatio*).[120] In his view, revenge makes part of the traditional forms of justice. If it is applied by a judicial authority, then it constitutes commutative justice, since the judge is duty bound to exercise penal jurisdiction in the framework of his assumed judicial task. The idea of a contractual or administrative judicial duty as an additional basis of commutative justice seems to be an original contribution of Suárez, since the traditional scholastic view referred the commutative dimension of revenge exclusively to the required equivalence between crime and punishment.[121] In Suárez's view, the role of commutative

116. Giers, *op. cit.*, 176.

117. Disp. 4, Quaest. 3: "Quod in propriu actu commutativo accidere posse, patet in restitutione: si quis habeat multos creditores et non possit unicuique tantum reddere quantum debet, tenetur enim dunc servare dictam proportionem." *Cf.* in this sense also Iohannes De Lugo (1583–1660), *De Iustitia et Iure* (Lyon 1652) Tom. 1, Disp. 1, Sect. 3, n. 46 *in fine*, 13: "Similiter quando debitor non potest integre solvere creditoribus, servat quandam speciem iustitiae distributivae; sed revera intenditur aequalitas cum debito absoluto singulorum, licet per accidens non possit obtineri propter debitoris inopiam."

118. In connection with Suárez's view that distribution of award to a single person according to his dignity is basically still an act of distributive justice, *see* the detailed defense by the Jesuit scholar Petrus Hurtadus De Mendoza (1578–1651), *Disputationes de Homine sive de Incarnatione Filii Dei* (Antwerpen 1634) Disp. 12, Sect. 15, §§237–243, pp. 119–120.

119. Giers, *op. cit.*, at 176–181; in this sense also De Mendoza, *ibid.*, §§244–250, 120–121: "Respondeo, ex sola iustitia distributiva numquam oriri obligationem restituendi; quando autem oritur, est a iustitia commutativa"; *see also ibid.*, §§255–256, 122–123.

120. Suárez, *op. cit.*, Disp. 4, Quaest. 4; Giers, *op. cit.*, 107–109.

121. Giers, *op. cit.*, at 181–186. The relevant authors are Thomas Aquinas, *Summa Theologiae*, II–II, *Quaestio* 80, art. 1; Cardinal Thomas de Vio Cajetanus (1469–1534), in his commentaries

justice in the case of private revenge is essentially limited to the prevention of excess.

The elements of the Aristotelian distinction are elaborated in great detail by Suárez in a special work dedicated to the question of divine justice.[122] His starting point is the following definition of commutative justice: The constant and perpetual will to give everybody his own full right, i.e., what is his specific property or what morally is its equivalent.[123]

The definition intentionally omits the arithmetic proportion, that according to the traditional view distinguishes commutative justice from distributive justice, the latter applying a geometric proportion. In Suárez's opinion, the two proportions are not mutually exclusive. Thus, in commutative justice situations, sometimes a geometric proportion is applied, as in the case of a plurality of creditors facing insufficient funds of the debtor.

Moreover, in these cases, the prior debts might be preferred over posterior ones, which again is not a simple arithmetic proportion. Equally, in situations of distributive justice, where there is only one benefit to be granted or one single candidate to the benefit, no geometric proportion is applied, but rather an arithmetic one. The argument that in case of one candidate, there is nevertheless a comparison to all those who don't have equal merits—this argument is not convincing, since in commutative justice situations it could

---

on Aquinas, *Summa Totius Theologiae S. Thomae De Aquino Cum Commentariis Et Opusculis Thomae de Vio Caietani Cardinalis S. Xisti* (Venezia 1588) II–II, Quaest. 80, 108 art. 2; Dominicus Soto, *Libri decem de iustitia et iure* (Lyon 1559) Lib. 3, Quaest. 5, Art. 1–2, 4; the latter author, insisting on the specific difference between the two kinds of justice, rejects Buridanus's view mentioned above (at note 89). However, a similar idea to that of Suárez, was voiced by the Jesuit scholar Ludovicus Molina, *De Justitia et Jure Opera Omnia* (Geneva 1732) Tom. 1, Tract. 1, Disput. 12, n. 12, p. 14. Since this work appeared first in 1593, after the lectures given by Suárez in Rome (1584), it is possible that Molina was influenced by Suárez. The same argument is repeated by a number of authors, among them: Gabriel (di San Vincentio), *De Iustitia et Iure* (Rome 1663) Disp. 1, Quaest. 18, nn. 265–266, p. 91; Florentio de Coque, *De Jure, Justitia et Annexis Tractatus Quattuor* (Bruxelles 1708) 7, arguing that the violation of vindictive justice imposes upon the judge a duty of restitution; A.F.M. Sweens, *Institutiones Theologicae de Virtute Cardinali Justitiae* (Haaren 1913) 182, relying on Gotti (1664–1742) *De jure et justitia*, Quaest. 3, n.17.

122. Franciscus Suarez, *De Justitia Dei, Varia Opuscola Theologica, Operum Tomus Decimus* (Venezia 1741) 285–323.

123. *Ibid.*, 292, Sect. II, §2: "Nam, sicut justitia definitur, quod sit constans & perpetua voluntas, jus suum unicuique tribuens, ita justitia commutativa definiri potest, quod sit constans & perpetua voluntas unicuique tribuens jus suum proprium, id est, tale, ut vel sit proprium dominium rei, vel illi moraliter aequivaleat." The author affirms that this definition, even if differently worded, corresponds in its substance to the traditionally accepted one; *ibid.*, 293, §5.

equally be argued that the creditor is compared to all those who don't have any right, in order to be paid by preference.[124] As a result, the two forms of justice cannot be distinguished according to different proportions.[125]

However, this does not entail the conclusion that Buridan is correct in denying the essence of the Aristotelian distinction. As a matter of fact, the vice of unjust preference (*acceptio personarum*) does not run counter to commutative justice, but it is contrary to distributive justice; this is a sign that the two forms of justice are different. However, in Suárez's opinion the distinction is based upon the nature of the right that constitutes the object of justice. The object of commutative justice is the full right of property or its moral equivalence. On the other hand, where something is due to a citizen from the common goods of the state on the basis of his dignity and in proportion to it, that right of the citizen is not in the nature of property, since the goods were never in his ownership. Hence, the benefits are not owed to him on the basis of a prior right. The duty arising from a prior right is, therefore, much stronger. As a result, its violation gives rise to a duty of restitution, contrary to a right based on mere dignity.[126] Where a number of persons have an equal measure of dignity, none of them has a specific right to the benefit. However, after the benefit has been given to one of them, a right of property is acquired; depriving the person of that property would now be against commutative justice. Hence, the great difference existing between a full property right (*ius in re propria*) and the right to obtain a common good (*ius ad rem communem*).[127]

This difference between the natures of the rights is sufficient to establish the distinction between commutative and distributive justice.[128] The emphasis

---

124. *Ibid.*, 307, Sect. III, §11: "Idem esse potest frequens in distributione honoris, qui nunc quidem inter multos distribuitur, nunc autem uni soli fit. Quod si forte dicant in his actionibus semper includi comparationes ad indignos vel non habentes talem titulum meriti: eadem ratione dicam justitiam commutativam comparare creditorem cum aliis, qui nullum jus habent, ut illi potius, quam aliis solvat."

125. *Ibid.*: "Videtur ergo ex dictis omnibus concludi, non posse has iustitias precise distingui ex habitudine seu ordine ad huiusmodi varias proportiones, seu aequalitates: & consequenter adaequatam rationem iustitiae distributivae non posse consistere in illa aequalitate proportionum constituenda." *See also ibid.*, 322, Sect. VI, §11.

126. *Ibid.*, §§13–14, pp. 307–308.

127. *Ibid.*, 308, §15.

128. *Ibid*, §16: "Ex his ergo concludo; hanc diversitatem iurium sufficere ad distictionem constituendam inter iustitias; & hanc esse propriam & primariam rationem distinguendi commutativam a distributiva." The author rejects the views of Durandus and Paludanus, according to which the duty under distributive justice is necessarily based upon

upon the basis and the nature of the right is relevant in an additional context: the relation to dignity. It is wrong to assume that only distributive justice is concerned with a person's dignity. The violation of a person's dignity or reputation engenders a claim to compensation under commutative justice, since dignity here is based upon an existing proper and strict right. The situation is generally different where the issue is the granting of honor to a person. Thus, a person does not have a duty, as such, to enhance the reputation of another by his acts. In rare cases, however, there might be a duty under commutative justice to honor a person whose specific right to it is based upon a special authority or power.[129]

The ideas of Suárez are basically repeated in the work of another contemporary, Portuguese Jesuit scholar Fernandus Rebellus (1548–1608).[130] This author equally insists, against the opinion of Buridanus, that the two forms of justice are different in species. On the other hand, the violation, by the person charged with distribution, of his duty to distribute, creates a duty of compensation under commutative justice. In his discussion of punitive justice, the author mentions the opinions of Duns Scotus, Thomas Aquinas, Caietanus, and De Soto. He remarks that judicial administration of punitive justice implies a number of different kinds of justice: As far as the judge exercises his official function, he falls under a duty of contractual, commutative justice; as far as he punishes the offender in order to restore the inequality between the latter and the victim, he applies commutative-punitive justice; as far as he is concerned with the public interest (*bonum commune*), he applies legal (universal) justice.

As far as the punishment is intended to serve the proportion between the pain and the fault of the delinquents, it is not unreasonable to assert with Duns Scotus that punishment belongs to distributive justice. A delict creates a duty toward the victim, but equally one toward the community. However, the duty toward the victim is stricter than that toward the community. The victim asks for satisfaction that equals the measure of the offense, hence he demands commutative justice. On its part, the community, by punishing the offender, distributes goods; those, though being evils for the offender, are, as

commutative justice: *ibid.*, Sect. VI, §§13–15, pp. 322–323. On the other hand, it is possible that the two forms of justice are joined in one situation: thus, a state official may be obliged under a contract to exercise distributive justice; *ibid.*

129. *Ibid.*, §20, p. 309.

130. Fernandus Rebellus, *Opus de Obligationibus Iustitiae, Religionis et Caritatis* (Lyon 1608) Lib. 1, Quaest. 3, Sect. 3–4, pp. 20–25.

Aristotle teaches, remedies for the evils.[131] Moreover, as the distribution of goods among citizens is not based upon a strict right against the state, so the contrary duty of the delinquents toward the state to suffer the punishment is of a similar kind.[132]

It is interesting to note that the view concerning the distributive-justice-character of punishment seems to have been commonly accepted by scholars of the Coimbrian School in Portugal. Thus, in a general commentary on Aristotle's *Nicomachean Ethics*, first published by the Jesuit College of Coimbra in the last decade of the sixteenth century, it is stated that distributive justice has to be divided into a remunerative and a punitive part: the latter orders to inflict upon delinquents punishments according to a geometrical proportion.[133]

Another important Spanish Jesuit scholar, Luis de Molina (1535–1600), starts with the traditional distinction between a quantitative (arithmetic) equality in commutative justice and a proportional (geometric) equality in distributive justice.[134] But he notes that sometimes in the framework of commutative justice an image of distributive justice is created. Thus, where partners invested different sums into the enterprise, the profits are divided proportionally according to the rate of investment. However, this is basically a simple arithmetic equality according to commutative justice based upon the contract of partnership.[135] Relying on Aquinas, Molina explains that the state, when entering transactions with individual citizens, is subject to commutative justice. Thus, the state is duty-bound under commutative justice to pay salary to its soldiers, judges, and public officers.[136]

The author then relates to the mentioned argument of Buridanus (ca. 1300–ca. 1358), claiming that there is no difference between the two forms of justice, since the violation of distributive justice creates a debt based

---

131. *See also ibid.*, Lib. 1., q. 4, s. 6, at 36–37, quoting Aristotle: "Poena sunt medicamenta peccantium."

132. *Ibid.*, 24.

133. *In Libros Ethicorum Aristotelis ad Nicomachum Aliquot Conimbricensis Cursus Disputationes* (4a ed., Cologne 1603), Disp. 9, Q. 1, Art. 2, col. 89–90. *See supra* note 85.

134. Ludovicus Molina, *De Justitia et Jure, Editio Novissima* (Mainz 1659) Tom. 1, Tract. 1, Disput. 12, col. 23, §3.

135. *Ibid.*, col. 24, §4. The same argument is further developped by the Jesuit Cardinal Iohannes De Lugo (1583–1660) in his *De Iustitia et Iure* (Lyon 1652) Tom. 1, Disp. 1, Sect. 3, n. 46, p. 13.

136. *Ibid.*, col. 24, §9: "Nec in his iustitia distributiva intervenit."

upon commutative justice.[137] Molina's answer is that the violation of distributive justice creates a new debt, one of restitution that is naturally based upon the idea of arithmetic equality.[138] Moreover, the judge in exercising his judicial function is fulfilling a commutative duty toward his employer, the state. A violation of that duty entails a commutative duty of compensating the ensuing damage.[139]

In relation to vindictive justice, Molina remarks that, as far as the punishment is measured according to the extent of the wrong, it makes part of the arithmetical proportion of commutative justice; but, as far as it merely punishes the offender without compensating the victim, it is not achieving perfect commutative justice.[140]

The Spanish Augustinian scholar Petrus de Aragon (1545–1592), professor of theology at the University of Salamanca, equally rejects, in his commentary on Aquinas, the view of Buridanus.[141] In relation to vindictive justice, he considers it to fall under commutative justice, since there is a simple equality between guilt and punishment. In addition, vindictive justice is ruled also by legal justice (*iustitia legalis*), since punishing delinquents enables the state to be governed in peace and calmness.[142] Distributive justice is generally based upon a geometric proportion according to the varying merits of the recipients.

However, it may happen that, given enough resources, the individual recipient will get a reward that is arithmetically equal to his merit. This will occur on the day of the Last Judgement, where the divine rewards, to be

---

137. *Supra* at note 89.

138. *Ibid.*, col. 25, §11.

139. *Ibid.*, §12.

140. *Ibid.*, §13: " . . . nihilominus deficere a perfecta ratione iustitiae, quatenus poena, quae pro iniuria & delicto sumitur, damnum illarum non resarcit, sed solum patitur reus, quantum iustum est pro delicto pati, cum tamen damnum integrum perseveret." The same argument is repeated by the Jesuit scholar Tarquinius Gallutius (Tarquinio Galluzzi) (1574–1649), *In Aristotelis quinque priores Moralium libros ad Nicomachum, Nova interpretatio, explanatio, quaestiones* (Paris 1632), Lib.5, Cap.2, Quaest. 3, p. 900: "Sed quia poena ipsa, quam ultrix haec Iustitia ad vindicandum scelus imponit, haud compensat, resarcitve damnum illatum, sed solum facit, ut tantumdem patiatur reus, quantum equum est ipsum pro perpetrato crimine perpeti, ex perfecta ratione commutantis iustitiae multum desiderat. Quare, ne sub commutante quidem continetur, nec inter partes peculiaris Iustitiae proprias numeratur, sed inter eas, quas nominant potentiales ex D. Thom. 2,2, quaest. 108."

141. Petrus de Aragon (1545–1592), *In Secundam Secundae Divi Thomae Doctoris Angelici Commentaria.De Iustitia Et Iure* (Lyon 1596) Quaest. LXI, Art. I, 84.

142. *Ibid.*

distributed by divine grace, are inexhaustible.[143] In relation to retaliation (*contrapassum*), the author distinguishes between retaliation in kind—like eye for eye—and a proportionally quantified retribution that can be made by monetary compensation.[144]

The German Lutheran scholar Joannes Magirus (d. 1596) in his extensive commentary on the *Nicomachean Ethics*,[145] specifies that the arithmetic proportion may be applicable even in the framework of distributive justice; namely, where the merits of the persons involved are identical, then under the very principle of geometric proportion, the arithmetic one is applied. The same is true in relation to punishment for equal crimes.[146]

Gregorius de Valentia (ca. 1550–1603) is another important Jesuit scholar who deals with the Aristotelian distinction on the basis of Thomas Aquinas's *Summa*.[147] He claims that the rejection of the notion of strict reciprocity (*contrapassum* or *retaliatio*) in commutative justice is based upon the idea that things are not universally equal, since their value depends upon the concrete circumstances, i.e., upon their evaluation according to the individual market.[148] He equally rejects the above mentioned opinion of Buridanus, according to which there is no specific difference between commutative and distributive justice.[149]

---

143. *Ibid.*, Art. II, 87. The author adds a touching prayer: "Faxit Deus, ut illius beatissimae distributionis ex sua benignitate participes simus."

144. *Ibid.*, Art. IV, 90. The author notes—relying on Aquinas and Aristotle—that for this purpose the money (*numisma*) has been invented. He adds an etymological comment: "Unde numus dicitur a nomos, Greco vocabulo, quod idem significat, quod lex, quasi numus fit lex, regula, & mensura valoris uniuscuisque rei."

145. Joannes Magirus (d. 1596), *Aristotelis Ethica Nicomachea Commentationes* (R. Walker, ed., Oxford 1842) 245. The author, a physician and philosopher, was Professor and Dean of the Faculty of Philosophy at the University of Marburg.

146. *Ibid.*, It appears that this author considers punishment to fall generally under distributive justice; *cf.*, *ibid.*, 228: "Nam justitiae distributivae propria actio est, recte distribuere bona vel mala externa pro conditione, merito, dignitateque personarum: veluti sunt *honores, praemia, labores, officia:* item, *poenae et supplicia*"; but, *see ibid.*, 247, where punishment is conceived as a case of commutative justice.

147. Gregory of Valencia, a native of Spain, served many years as a professor of theology in Ingolstadt, Bavaria.

148. Gregorius de Valentia, *Commentarii Theologici, Tomus Tertius, Secundae Secundae Divi Thomae* (Ingolstadt 1595) Disp. 5, Quaest. 5, 1163–1164.

149. *Ibid.*, at 1164–1168. The author uses mainly the arguments of Thomas Aquinas. He emphasizes that, except in cases of compensating injuries, commutative justice (in transactions) does not take into consideration the dignity of persons, but only the value of things.

Another Spanish Jesuit scholar who discussed at length the various approaches to the Aristotelian distinction was Luisius Turrianus (Luis de Torres) (1562–1655), professor of theology at the Complutense University (Alcalá de Henares).[150] The author starts the discussion on the validity of the distinction with the negative view of Buridanus. He admits the force of the latter's arguments, although the common opinion of scholars accepts the essential nature of the traditional distinction. The author is critical of a number of arguments aimed at justifying the distinction. Thus, he rejects the distinction based upon the stricter nature of commutative justice. In his view, a strict right of restitution is given also in the framework of distributive justice. The act of restitution itself is always an act of commutative justice. He equally rejects the distinction assumedly grounded in the difference between a strict *ius in re* (commutative justice) and a weaker *ius ad rem* (distributive justice).

Finally, some scholars assume that the difference lies in the measure of the mental effort to implement or violate the respective kinds of justice.[151] Thus, distributive justice is much easier to realize, as well as to violate, than commutative justice requirements. The author rejects this attempt of justifying the essential nature of the distinction. In his view, the only rationale lies in the different kinds of equality: commutative justice is based upon an arithmetic equality of things; distributive justice upon a geometric, proportional equality.[152] The author follows basically the approach of Gabrielis Vasquez (1549–1604), who was critical of the views of Francisco Suárez (1548–1617). Thus, where there is only one benefit to distribute, or, especially, where there is one single candidate for the benefit, the situation becomes one of commutative justice, since there is no geometric proportion.[153] On the other hand, in case of a debtor's insolvency toward a plurality of creditors, the proportional, partial payment of debts is an application of both forms of justice.[154] However, where the debtor fully pays the differently sized debts of creditors, it remains a commutative justice situation, since payment is not based upon a comparison between the creditors, but exclusively on the

---

150. Luisius Torrianus, *Disputationum in secundam secundae D. Thomae, De Iustitia*, Tomus alter (Lyon 1621) Disp. V–VII, col. 59–88.

151. *See, e.g.*, in this sense Petrus de Aragon (1545–1592), *In Secundam Secundae Divi Thomae Doctoris Angelici Commentaria.De Iustitia Et Iure* (Lyon 1596) Quaest. LXI, Art. I, 84.

152. *Ibid.*, Disp. VII, Dubium I, col. 83–85.

153. *Ibid.*, Disp. VI, Dubium I, col. 75–77.

154. *Ibid.*, col. 77–78.

respective measure of the individual debt.[155] The duty under distributive justice may also arise from a binding contract.[156] In agreement with Vasquez, and contrary to the view of Suárez, the creditor is obliged, under commutative justice, to accept in payment of his debt what is judged according to the rules of justice as equivalent. There might be, however, a difference between a contractual and delictual debt. Thus, e.g., where a horse has been stolen, the owner has a right to demand its specific restitution—if feasible—and cannot be obliged to accept any equivalent substitute.[157]

The Bishop of Antwerp, Joannes Malderus (1563–1633), in his commentary on Thomas Aquinas, is rather closely following the ideas of the latter.[158] In his view, the allocation of a benefit to a single person of merit still falls under distributive justice.[159] Distributive justice differs in kind (*specie*) from commutative justice, like music and geometry differ from arithmetic, since the latter's object is much simpler.

Moreover, in order to fall under distributive justice, it is not enough that common goods are distributed. Thus, payment out of public money of a strict debt owed by the state, such as for a lease or the payment of soldiers according to merit, is not distributive justice but commutative justice.[160] Relying on Suárez's *Iustitia Dei,* the author objects to the view that any claim of distributive justice necessarily arises out of commutative justice. This would cancel the very distinction between the two forms of justice.[161] Finally, he observes that sometimes in a certain matter, both kinds of justice may occur.[162]

155. *Ibid.*, Disp. VII, Dubium II, col. 85–86.

156. *Ibid.*, col. 86–87.

157. *Ibid.*, Disp. V, Dubium IV, col. 72–73.

158. Ioannes Malderus, *De Virtutibus Theologicis et Iustitia et Religione Commentaria Ad Secundam Secundae D. Thomae* (Antwerpen 1616) 280–281, Dubium IV.

159. *Ibid.*, 280: "Ut iustè appropriet, curare debet, ne huic parti dando habeat plus qui minus dignus est, aut minus habeat qui dignior est. Qua circumspectione quia utitur collator, etiam quando unus solum dignus est beneficio Ecclesiatico, patet etiam tunc eiusdem collationem ex Iustitia distributiva fieri."

160. *Ibid.*: "Quomodo militibus respublica distribuit stipendia pro meritorum diversitate. Neque tamen ibi Iustitia est distributiva, sed commutativa. Si enim servatur proportio Geometrica, servatur tamen propter se solum Arithmetica, quamvis inde consequatur ibi etiam altera."

161. *Ibid.*, 281.

162. *Ibid.* The author gives an example according to which a person receives from the state an amount of money and distributes part of it to the poor: "Is tenebitur ita distribuere ex utraque Iustitia; ex commutativa quidem, quia ad certam & aliquotam partem totius summae singulis illis pauperibus quaesitum est Ius strictum, dominio aequiparabile; ex

The Jesuit scholar Thomas Sanchez of Cordoba (1550–1610) states that if a person prefers his less needy friend in giving charity, it is a sin against charity, but not against distributive justice.[163] Similarly, if a person invites all citizens to a meal, except his enemy, it is a sin (*scandalum*), but again not against justice.[164]

The Flemish theologian Johannes Wiggers (1571–1639), professor at the Catholic University of Louvain (Leuven), bases his conclusions on the writings of Thomas Aquinas.[165] The author's starting point is the validity of the distinction between distributive and commutative justice. The distribution of common goods, of public offices and charges is primarily the function of public officials; commercial transactions are generally made between private persons. Commutative justice concerns the equality between the exchanged things; distributive justice relates to the parity between proportions, taking into account the condition of persons.[166]

However, sometimes the state or the ruler commits itself or himself to a commutative justice duty under a private transaction. Thus, in case of paying salary to soldiers or recompense to workers for services rendered, the measure of the payment is according to the contractual agreement relating to the value of the service and not to the status of the person.[167] In this connection, the author mentions the argument that in these cases of commutative justice, a proportional measure is applied that is not different from that used in distributive justice. Moreover, where the distributor gives to one person less than his status requires, the latter has a right under commutative justice for compensation.

---

distributiva autem, quatenus ipse censetur hic manus reipublicae,ex cuius aerario tali proportione pauperes isti Ius quoddam remotius habebant tantundem percipiendi."

163. Thomas Sanchez, *Consilia Moralia, De Iustitia et Iure*, Tomus primus (Cologne 1653), Lib. II, Cap. 1, Dub. 1, p. 121. The author relies on Salon, 2.2, Quaest. 6, Art.1.

164. *Ibid.*: "Sexto infertur, quod si quis ex proprijs bonis invitaret ad coenam omnes cives, & solum excluderet inimicum, non peccaret peccato acceptionis personarum, sed tantum peccato scandali; quia hoc non est contra iustitiam."

165. Ioannes Wiggers, *Commentaria De Iure Et Iustitia Caeterisque Virtutibus Cardinalibus Cum Adnexis De quibus tractat Divus Thomas in 2.2 a quaest. 47. usque ad quaest. 171* (Louvain 1639) Tract. I, Caput I, Dubium IV, pp.18–20.

166. *Ibid.*, n.12, pp. 18–19: "Nam finis intrinsecus prioris, scilicet commutativae, est constituere equalitatem inter datum & acceptum: posterioris autem, scilicet distributivae, finis est constituere paritatem inter proportionem & proportionem, ut nimirum talis sit proportio inter res quae diversis distribuuntur, qualis est inter conditiones personarum attendi debitas in eiusmodi distributione."

167. *Ibid.*

As a result—thus the additional argument goes—distributive justice does not seem to constitute a different kind of justice.[168] The author then defends the distinction against the two mentioned objections. He argues that it is a mere accidental fact that sometimes in a commutative justice situation a proportion similar or identical to that of distributive justice is used. This proportion is not intended *per se*, but only as a means to determine the equality between things. This is not the case where the state distributes common goods; in this case, the whole basis is the proportion between the quality or status of persons and the quantity of the things to be distributed.

In relation to the second objection, the author admits that the violation of the distributive criterion by the distributor may grant the recipient a (strict) commutative justice right for compensation. This is, e.g., the case where under a will a certain amount of wheat is to be distributed to the poor according to their respective need. In the author's view, this is a situation where simultaneously both a commutative and a distributive justice right are violated.

However, the distributive justice is not accidental, but entirely intended *per se*. Moreover, not in every case the violation of distributive justice engenders an obligation of restitution. Thus, where public offices or benefits are to be distributed among the worthy, a sinful neglect of the guiding criterion does not entail a right of restitution.[169]

The author's final conclusion is interesting: The division of justice into the mentioned two members is rather one of analogy than of species. Of principal significance is commutative justice, since it presupposes a strict and absolute right. The right under distributive justice is weaker. Hence, the definition of justice suits best commutative justice.[170]

The Jesuit scholar Tarquinio Galluzzi (1574–1649), in his lengthy commentary on the first five chapters of Aristotle's *Nicomachean Ethics*, expounds

---

168. *Ibid.*, n. 13, p. 19.

169. *Ibid.*, n. 14–16, pp. 19–20.

170. *Ibid.*, 20, n. 17: "Ex hic potest colligi: Iustitiae divisionem in duo praedicta membra, potius esse analogi in analogata, quam generis in species: & principale significatum esse iustitiam commutativam, cui enim propijssime convenit definitio iustitiae supra assignata: nam haec per se praesupponit Ius absolutum & strictum: non sic iustitia distributiva, ut ex iam dictis patet: sed de hac per se loquendo supponit tantum aliquod quasi conditionatu, & ius remissius . . .Dixi autem, quod distributiva per se non praesupponit ius absolutum & strictum: quia aliquando potest accedere ius tale, sed tunc etiam eatenus ibi locum suum habet commutativa, ut ex ante dictis potest intelligi: quare consequens est, iustitiae rationem principaliter & proprijissime cerni in iustitia commutativa."

the substantive difference between the two forms of justice.[171] He equally observes that commutative justice refers also to the state, when the latter engages into private transactions with citizens.[172]

The author insists upon the formal character of the notion of distributive justice, since the criterion of the oligarchy (wealth)—mentioned by Aristotle—is conceived to be "corrupt and depraved."[173] Moreover, even in the preferred governmental system of aristocracy, the criterion of virtue is not always relevant; thus, the government may decide to distribute common goods to the needy and poor. In this case, should the distributor insist upon the criterion of virtue, he would violate the very rule of distributive justice.[174]

Distributive justice may, in principle, relate also to one single person whose merits bestow upon him the privilege to obtain the benefit. Aristotle, when speaking of at least two persons, refers merely to the more usual case.[175]

Tarquinio Galluzzi endorsed Thomas Aquinas's view that retaliation is specific to commutative justice.[176] He emphasizes that retaliation has no place in the distribution of common goods to the citizens, a distribution that is exclusively based upon their relative merits.[177] The author then proceeds to analyze closely the notion of retaliation and its relationship to commutative justice. In his view, one has to distinguish between two forms of retaliation: one that is in the Pythagorean sense, the exact and arithmetic measure of the gain or the loss, and the other that constitutes their proportional and geometric measure. In other words, inside commutative justice there are two measures, one arithmetic and one geometric. The geometric, proportional measure is the general rule in involuntary commutations, in crimes and delicts. Exact retaliation is generally excluded. Indeed, the punishment for a

---

171. Tarquinius Gallutius (Tarquinio Galluzzi) (1574–1649), *In Aristotelis quinque priores Moralium libros ad Nicomachum, Nova interpretatio, explanatio, quaestiones* (Paris 1632), Lib.5, Cap.2–5, pp. 899–953. Galluzi taught in Rome at the Jesuit institution Collegio Romano; on his commentary, in general, *see* D.A. Lines, *Aristotle's Ethics in the Italian Renaissance (ca. 1300–1650): The Universities and the Problem of Moral Education* (Leiden 2002) 325, 374–376, 533.

172. *Ibid.*, 901.

173. *Ibid.*, 910.

174. *Ibid.*

175. *Ibid.*

176. *Ibid.*, 942–943, Cap. 5.

177. *Ibid.*

delict is meted out in accordance with the specific circumstances, taking into consideration the status of the victim, the state of mind of the perpetrator, and other aggravating or mitigating circumstances. Moreover, a just retaliation would require the compensation of the victim; but exact retaliation punishing the perpetrator does not compensate the victim's damage.[178]

However, even in voluntary transactions, the strict arithmetic proportion does not constitute a just measure of retaliation. Where goods are exchanged, their respective value in money is the result of the people's mutual needs (*indigentia*), which is a matter of geometric proportion. Hence the (arithmetic) price expressed in money is itself primarily based upon a geometric proportion.[179]

As a result, only very few voluntary transactions are based upon the idea of strict arithmetic retaliation, such as loans and guaranties, where an identical object or amount of money has to be restituted to the creditor. Even in donations, the recipient may, by his thanking and praising of the donator, enhance the latter's reputation and standing in the eyes of the public. This constitutes compensation according to a geometrical proportion.[180]

In the author's view, Aristotle's critique of the Pythagorean conception is not directed against the very notion of retaliation, but against its identification with strict arithmetic proportion.[181] The general opinion that in voluntary transactions commutative justice is based upon arithmetic proportion has to be understood in the following sense: The parties among themselves refer to the monetary value of the object which is to be exchanged. Here the proportion is arithmetic. But the (pre)established monetary value of the object itself is based upon a geometric proportion, being the result of people's mutual needs.[182]

---

178. *Ibid.*, 944.

179. *Ibid.*, 945: "Itaque in commutationibus voluntariis arithmetica talio non potest ponere medium absque geometrica proportione, quae per comparationem ad maiorem, vel minorem indigentiam, ex qua pretij constituitur aequalitas, in utraque re commutanda, ipsam parit proportionem arithmeticam, cuius vi res immediate permutantur, non enim commutamus nisi pretio arithmetice constituito. Pretium autem ipsum costitui non potest absque illa comparatione ad humanam indigentiam maiorem aut minorem: quae comparatio per geometricam proportionem fit, quia in aliquo est maior, in alio minor."

180. *Ibid.*, 946.

181. *Ibid.*, 947.

182. *Ibid.*, 947. Today, one would probably speak of demand and supply. See especially the author's extensive discussion on the measure of things' value and on the function of money, *ibid.*, at 947–952. On the contribution of the late scholastics to the economic theory in general, *see* G. Ambrosetti, "Diritto privato ed economia nella seconda scolastica," *La seconda*

We have already mentioned Galluzzi's defense of Aristotle's critical comment in relation to the Pythagorean doctrine of *antipeponthos*, a defense that is identical to that of Thomas Aquinas.[183] However, in this context it is interesting to note that Tarquinio Galluzzi raises against the very idea of a strict *talio* the following argument: A person, who killed another by imprudence, could not be killed the same way, since any punishment would necessarily be an intentional act.[184]

Finally, Galluzzi makes an attempt to explain Aristotle's use of the notion of gain in the context of delictual actions[185]: In his view, the gain here is not what the wrongdoer receives in fact from the victim, but it is rather an estimation of his state of mind: Since he intends to cause the damage to the victim, he is deemed to obtain the victim's loss as his profit. In other words, the wrongdoer considers it worthwhile to cause the loss; but, since the victim is not willing to suffer the loss for that price, the former is deemed to gain the actual amount of the victim's loss.[186]

In the author's view, the same is true in case of distributive justice. Where the distributor violates the established criterion for the distribution, by awarding more or less than the merit of the recipient would require, the former is deemed to make a profit. His act is based either on the friendship

---

scolastica nella formazione del diritto privato moderno (P. Grossi, ed., Milano 1973) 23; J.A. Schumpeter, *History of Economic Analysis* (New York 1954) 87–107. Some modern translators of Aristotle and Aquinas use the term "demand" instead of "need" (χρεία, *chreia; indigentia*), though the two notions are not identical. *See* Lindsay Judson, "Aristotle on Fair Exchange," 15 (1997) *Oxford Studies in Ancient Philosophy* 147–175, at 158–160; J. Gordley, *The Philosophical Origins of Modern Contract Doctrine* (Oxford 1991) 97–98; see especially Gabriel Danzig, "The Political Character of Aristotelian Reciprocity," 95 (2000) *Classical Philology* 399, 412–415.

183. *Supra* note 61.

184. However, this argument was by no means novel. It had been used long before in relation to the *lex talionis* of the Twelve Tables, as recounted by Aulus Gellius, *Noctes Atticae*, XX.1. 14–17; *see* Joannes Magirus (d.1596), *Aristotelis Ethica Nicomachea Commentationes* (R. Walker, ed., Oxford 1842) 249; *see also* the same argument with reference to Gellius, F. Burgersdicius (Franco Burgersdijck) (1590–1635), *Idea Philosophiae Tum Moralis Tum Naturalis Sive Epitome Compendiosa utriusque ex Aristotele excerpta, & methodice disposita* (Editio quarta, Oxford 1637), Cap. XXII, §19, col. 301–302.

185. *Ibid.*, 921–924.

186. *Ibid.*, 922: "Is vero qui laesus est, ne lucro quidem & compendio aureorum mille laedi vellet, ac propterea tantum ille qui laedit lucratus putatur, quanti qui laesus est aestimat laesionem suam. Denique allij qui de laesione iudicant, cuiusmodi iudices sunt, laesionem ipsam aestimant pretio: ideoque decernere videntur, in eius qui laesit lucro tantum esse positum pretium, quanto ipsi damnum illatum, & maleficium aestimarunt."

for the preferred person, or on the hatred for the one discriminated against; in both cases he is deemed to make a profit by satisfying his volition.[187]

The author is aware that where the wrongdoer, who has to pay compensation for the victim's loss, is in addition to it punished by a judge, it goes beyond the symmetry between gain and loss. The author considers the punishment as a different act of commutative justice implemented by the judge.[188]

The important Austrian Jesuit moral theologian Paul Laymann (1574–1635) dedicated to the Aristotelian distinction a relatively very short chapter.[189] However, in a brief comment, the author introduces what seems to be a new aspect of the traditional distinction. He claims that distributive justice is basically not the same kind (*species*) as commutative justice, but merely of an analogical nature. The fundamental difference is that distributive justice is not specifically oriented toward another person and neither does it constitute a strict debt.[190]

In relation to the category of involuntary transactions, namely those arising from delicts, the author remarks that here the gain does not always correspond to the damage. Nevertheless, the idea of equality can be applied in this case like in voluntary exchanges: The measure of the damage caused is tantamount to the measure of compensation.[191]

---

187. *Ibid.*, 923. It seems, therefore, that this author views the violation of the distributive criterion as a matter of distributive justice. *Cf. supra* at note 161.

188. *Ibid.*, 923–924: "Quod si is, qui facit iniuriam, puniatur a iudice, non ideo damnum pati ex iniurosa illa sua, iniustaque dicitur actione (inde quippe lucrum facit saltem secundum aestimationem) sed ex actione Iudicis aequa, illum plectentis, & pari damno ex iustitia commutante afficientis."

189. Paulus Laymann, *Theologiae Moralis Compendium Absolutissimum Et In Quinque Libros Partitum*, Pars Prima (Vienna 1753), Lib. III, Sect. V, Tract. I, Caput IV, pp. 427–428. A slightly different version appears in an earlier printing of the book: *Id., Theologiae Moralis Liber Tertius. De Iustitia Et Iure Et Caeterisque Cardinalibus Virtutibus* (München 1625) 33–34; Laymann's book influenced the work on moral theology attributed recently to the Jesuit Friedrich Spee (1591–1635), *Theologia moralis explicata: Ein Friedrich Spee zugeschriebenes Werk aus der Zeit des Dreissigjährigen Krieges* (H. Weber, ed., Trier 1996) XXVIII. In the latter work, the distinction between distributive and commutative justice is also treated very briefly according to the traditional understanding; *ibid.*, 162 (74r).

190. Laymann, *Theologiae Moralis Compendium Absolutissimum*, *op. cit.* 428, §2: "Haec divisio non est in species univocas, sed analogas; quia distributiva non est propriè ad alterum, nec tam strictè debita." The same idea is mentioned by the contemporary Flemish theologian Johannes Wiggers (1571–1639), *supra* at note 170.

191. *Id., Theologiae Moralis Liber Tertius*, *op. cit.*, 34: "Tametsi vero in hac posteriore specie iustitiae commutativae non semper ita appareat lucrum, sicut apparet damnum: (Nam qui alteri v.g. domum per iniuria exussit, nihil lucri tulit, sed solum damnum intulit) nihil tamen hoc obstat ijs quae dicta sunt: quia nihilominus servari potest aequalitas

Finally, the author states that vindictive justice (*iustitia vindicativa*) is very remote from a real kind of justice, since punishment does not compensate for the injury inflicted upon the victim.[192] Following Thomas Aquinas, the author dedicates a special chapter to the issue of restitution.[193] He affirms that restitution is always an act of commutative justice. Hence, where a wrong has not caused any material damage, the satisfaction of the victim is necessarily of a vindictive nature. However, vindictive justice is a matter of the public authority. The exclusive function of restitution, as an act of commutative justice, is to restore the damage caused. In cases of distributive justice, one has to distinguish between two different situations.

First, where the distribution of public goods is mainly in the interest of the state—like the bestowal of public functions or the grant of ecclesiastical benefits—the passing over the worthy does not confer them a strict right for indemnity. Such a right may arise in favor of the state if it suffered damage from the distribution of public goods to the unworthy. The situation is different where the distribution of goods is mainly in the interest of the recipients. This is the case, e.g., where the military commander distributes the spoils of war to the soldiers according to their respective merits or dignity. The violation of the distributive-justice-criterion entitles the individual, affected soldier to restitution from the commander's own property. However, in the author's view, this claim is based—contrary to the opinion of some scholars—not upon distributive justice but upon commutative justice. The restitution or compensation is determined according to an arithmetic and not a geometric equality.[194]

The mentioned scholastic idea that the validity of the distinction is not based on the difference in proportion but rather upon the nature of the obligation, has been equally adopted by the Spanish Jesuit moral theologian Ferdinandus de Castro Palao (1581–1633).[195] After describing the arguments

---

quasi cuiusdam commutationis; ut quantum acceptum, aut quantum damni illatum fuit, tantundem restituatur, aut resarciatur."

192. *Id., Theologiae Moralis Compendium Absolutissimum, op. cit., ibid.*, §3: "Justitia vindicativa plurimum recedit a verae Justitiae proprietate, eo quod damnum illatum non ad aequalitatem reddat; siquidem poena, quae pro delicto infligitur, proprie non compensat, aut tollit debitum."

193. *Id., Theologiae Moralis Liber Tertius, op. cit.*, Sect. V, Tract. II, 77–122.

194. *Ibid.*, 78.

195. Ferdinandus de Castro Palao, *Operis Moralis de virtutibus & vitiis contrariis, in varios Tractatus, & Disputationes Theologicas distributi, Pars Septima De Iustitia et Iure* (Lyon 1651) Tract. XXXI, Punctum IV, 43–44.

in favor of Buridan's opinion, that denied the correctness of the distinction, the author explains that the decisive criterion is not the arithmetic or geometric proportion, but the nature of the arising obligation. Distributive justice does not give rise to a strict right-duty relationship. It is, therefore a different kind of justice.[196]

Finally, the author discusses the vindictive justice. Here, in his view, one has to distinguish: In relation to the offender who has to suffer the punishment, it is not an act of justice, since he does not demand it and submits to it involuntarily. In relation to the judge, in is an act of commutative justice, since he fulfills a duty toward the state. In relation to the victim, demanding the punishment, the author mentions the view that it does not constitute a complete kind of justice, since the victim does not get by it compensation of his injury. However, the author is of the opinion that punishment remains a proper kind of commutative justice. The punishment, even if it does not repair the physical damage, nevertheless repairs it morally according to the common judicial estimation.[197]

The question of vindictive justice is treated quite extensively by the Jesuit scholar of Spanish extraction, Juan de Dicastillo (1584–1653).[198] The author notes that one has to distinguish between three relevant factors: the delinquent to be punished, the community, and the injured victim. In relation to the delinquent, the punishment is not a proper act of justice, but part of potential justice. It constitutes neither commutative nor distributive justice, since both the delinquent and the punisher have no right to the punishment. This is evident in

196. The author mentions the known cases where in situations of commutative justice a proportional distribution takes place, such as in case of a debtor with insufficient funds facing a plurality of different creditors. A contrary example mentioned is that of allocating a benefit according to merit to a single candidate. The author concludes (*ibid.*, 43): "Quocirca non ex proportione Arithmetica, vel Geometrica hae iustitiae distinguendae sunt, ut convincit ratio superius allata, sed ex iure diverso, quod utraque satisfaciendum respicit: nam iustitia commutativa respicit ius sub stricta obligatione satisfaciendum. Secus vero iustitia distributiva. Ex quo fit hanc divisionem non esse generis in species, sed analogi in sua analogata. Ut notavit Laymann, *dicto* cap. 4. eo quod iustitia distributiva, non sit propria iustitia, cum ius proprie debitum non respiciat."

197. *Ibid.*, 43–44: "Nam esto Physice' damnum factum, & iniuria illata punitione delinquentis non reparetur, reparatur tamen moraliter & secundum communem hominum aestimationem. Ob quam causam pro iniuria corporis, vel famae pecuniam ab inferente solent iudices exigere. Cum vero corporalem punitionem infligunt delicto commensuratam, eo ipso offensus immunis ab iniuria iudicatur."

198. Ioannes De Dicastillo, *De Iustitia Et Iure Ceterisque Virtutibus Cardinalibus Libri Duo* (Antwerpen 1641) Lib. II, Tract. I, Disput. II, Dub. V, 168–169. The author, born in Naples, served as professor of theology in Toledo, Murcia, and Vienna.

relation to the offender who does not want the punishment. With respect to the punishing agency, it is not an act of distributive justice, since no common goods are distributed. It is neither a case of commutative justice, as neither the state nor the judge, acting for the latter, have a commutative justice right toward the delinquent obliging him not to sin. The delinquent violates only legal justice (*iustitia legalis*),[199] and that violation does not give rise to a commutative-justice-right in favor of the state.[200] The injured victim may have a commutative-justice-right for compensation, but this does not relate to the infliction of the punishment.[201] However, in relation to the judge acting *ex officio*, punishment constitutes an act of commutative justice: The judge by virtue of an express or implied contract is duty-bound toward the state and the victim to impose the adequate punishment upon the delinquent. The judge, when neglecting his duty to punish offenders, might be liable for the damage caused to the state and the private citizens.[202] Moreover, the act of vindictive justice, insofar it is directed toward the public welfare, makes part of legal justice, as a duty imposed upon the public authorities.[203] Finally, the author insists that—contrary to the view of Cajetanus—vindictive justice does not constitute a different kind of commutative justice. Where there is an act of commutative justice, as explained above, it constitutes a material part of this kind of justice.[204]

In relation to the distinction between the two kinds of justice, the author—relying on Francisco Suárez—considers their substantial difference to reside in the rigor of the underlying rights: commutative justice concerns a strict right of property, or a right morally equal to property. Distributive justice relates to a less strict right, one based upon the dignity or condition of a person granting him, as a member of the community, a proportional part of the common goods. As a result, only the violation of commutative justice gives rise to a duty of restitution.[205]

---

199. *Supra* at note 3.

200. *Ibid.*, 168, §101: "Ex violatione autem solius Iustitiae legalis non adimitur Republicae aliquid suum, quod illi iam esset aliquo modo appropriatum, ergo satisfactio publica per poenam, non est actus Iustitiae commutativae, ac proinde, nec Iudex, nec Respublica ad eam habet Ius Iustitiae commutativae."

201. *Ibid.*, §102.

202. *Ibid.*, 168–169, §§103–106.

203. *Ibid.*, §107.

204. *Ibid.*, §108.

205. *Ibid.*

The Spanish Jesuit, Cardinal Juan De Lugo (1583–1660), dealing with the mentioned arguments of Buridanus, claims that the person charged by the state to distribute common goods, violates, by not distributing them according to geometrical proportion, both distributive and corrective justice. He violates distributive justice as against the subjects of the state, since their claim is not based upon a strict right; he violates commutative justice as against the state since he, the distributor, is by contract obliged to distribute the goods correctly. This contractual duty confers upon the state a personal, strict right.[206] The author insists upon the distinction between the nonstrict character of a duty by a superior to distribute common goods proportionally and the strict duty of a subordinate to fulfill his (contractual) obligation to follow the superior's instructions.[207]

In relation to the distribution of burdens among citizens, Cardinal De Lugo comes to an interesting conclusion: it is a combination of distributive and commutative justice. On the one hand, the act of imposing burdens and duties on citizens according to their individual possibilities and the necessities of the state makes part of distributive justice. On the other hand, excessive requirements by the state from the individual violate commutative justice, since it signifies taking away from him without justification what belongs to him under strict right.[208]

Finally, in the same line of ideas, a punishment that exceeds the measure of the delict violates commutative justice, since it violates the strict right of the defendant to his life and bodily integrity. Moreover, it violates equally punitive justice that requires a punishment according to merit; hence it constitutes a kind of distributive justice.[209]

The French Cistercian scholar Eustache de Saint Paul (Eustachius a Sancto Paulo) (1573–1640), professor at the Sorbonne in Paris, follows closely the Aristotelian tradition in his relatively short discussion of the notion of

---

206. Iohannes De Lugo, *De Iustitia et Iure* (Lyon 1652), Tom. 1, Disp. 1, Sect. 3, n. 48, p. 14. In this sense in relation to the restitutionary duty of a judge, *see* Florentio de Coque, *De Jure, Justitia et Annexis Tractatus Quattuor* (Bruxelles 1708) 6–7.

207. *Ibid.*, n. 49 (distribution under a will).

208. *Ibid.*, 16, n. 56–57: " . . . et hoc quidem videtur pertinere ad iustitiam commutativam; nam subditus habet ius strictum; ne ab ipso exigatur plus oneris, quam eius conditio potest et debet ferre."

209. *Ibid.*, n. 58. The author remarks that if God, who is not subject to commutative justice, would excessively punish an offender, He would nevertheless violate punitive justice (but *see also ibid.*, n. 60–61).

particular justice.[210] He explains that distributive justice has a double function: The one—*iustitia remunerativa*—distributes honors, public functions and other similar benefits according to dignity and merit; the other—*iustitia punitiva*—inflicts in a similar way punishment upon criminals. Commutative justice comprises voluntary contractual transactions (nominate and innominate ones), as well as involuntary, delictual transactions.

Firmly in the scholastic tradition is equally the ethical treatise of the Italian Jesuit theologian Franciscus Pavonius (1569–1637).[211] Relying exclusively on Aristotle and Aquinas, the author explains that at the basis of arithmetic proportion lies a transaction, voluntary or involuntary. After describing a variety of voluntary contracts, he states that in case of delicts, it is assumed that between the parties a kind of contract has been passed according to which the injurer has to restore the loss and to suffer the punishment.[212] The right arising from voluntary contracts is called *ius commutativum*, that from delicts *emendativum*. The distinction between commutative and distributive justice is based upon formal and material reasons. Formally, they differ in their notion of equality: arithmetic against geometric proportion. However, they agree in their measurement of equality that is made not according to the nature of things, but according to their need and utility. Contrary to distributive justice, commutative justice does not take into account the dignity of parties, but only the value of things. However, in certain circumstances the value of things is influenced by personal dignity, as in case where the injury caused is increased in view of a person's dignity, thus requiring a greater amount of compensation. Materially, the two forms of justice differ in their function: distribution of common public benefits and charges[213] as against exchanges or compensation of private property. Private transactions may be, as mentioned above, voluntary or involuntary.[214] Finally, vindictive justice is

210. Eustachius A Sancto Paulo, *Ethica Sive Summa Moralis disciplinae, in tres partes divisa* (London 1658) Part. III, Tract. III, §11, Quest.V, 123–126.

211. Franciscus Pavonius, *Summa Ethicae: Sive Introductio In Aristotelis, Et Theologorum Doctrinam Moralem* (Oxford 1633), Disp. 3, Quaest. 2, col. 278–335.

212. *Ibid.*, Prop. 3, col. 286: "Est autem maleficium, seu delictum, genus quoddam contractus, tum quia qui iniuriam faciunt, & accipiunt, contrahere quodammodo inter se videntur, tum quin qui damnum infert alteri, quasi contrahit cum lege, ut ablatum restituat, & praeterea poena plectatur."

213. Elsewhere, the author explains that distributive justice can be exercised not only by the ruler, but equally by subjects who, when getting more as their part, restore it to the person entitled to it; *ibid.*, Prop. 10, col. 331.

214. *Ibid.*, Prop. 6, col. 304–305.

part of commutative justice, since it corresponds arithmetically to the damage caused.[215]

The Irish Franciscan scholar Anthony Hickey (Antonius Hiquaeus) (1586–1641), in his commentary on Duns Scotus,[216] discusses at length the Aristotelian distinction. After mentioning the negative opinion of Buridanus,[217] he supports the essential distinction between the two forms of justice on the ground that distributive justice—contrary to commutative justice—does not grant a strict right to the beneficiary of the public good. Moreover, distributive justice takes into account not only the personal merits, but also the dignity of the person. As a result, sometimes a debt based on a strict right of commutative justice must yield to a debt founded in dignity. Thus, where a person endowed with dignity, but devoid of resources, cannot pay a debt of commutative justice without losing dignity, he will not be bound to pay the debt. The preservation of his dignity is more important for the state than the satisfaction owed to an individual.[218]

The author then explains the case of one single benefit or one single candidate as being an accidental occurrence in distributive justice. Generally, it relates to a plurality of persons. But the criterion remains the proportional measure of dignity.[219]

The author then refers to the case of an insolvent debtor facing a plurality of creditors. Here, the solution is a proportional one: first, the earlier debtors are preferred over the later ones in payment; second, the (insufficient) assets of the debtor are distributed among the creditors proportionally according to the measure of the individual debt. The proportional solution in a commutative situation is again accidental. It is not based on the quality of the persons, but on the equality of the object. The preference of prior debtors is

---

215. *Ibid.*, Prop. 8, col. 317.

216. Johannes Duns Scotus, *Quaestiones in libro IV sententiarum*, in *Opera Omnia*, t. 10 (Lyon 1639) Lib. 4, Dist. 46, Quaest. 1, pp. 241–243.

217. Hiquaeus notes that the Franciscan Pater Smising (1580–1626) (*De iustitia Dei*, n. 72), apparently follows Buridanus.

218. Duns Scotus, *cit.*, *Opera Omnia*, t. 10 (Lyon 1639) Lib. 4, Dist. 46, Quaest. 1, pp. 242: "Non attenduntur autem in hac distributione solum merita personalia, sed etiam dignitas personae; & talis aliquando est debitum fundatum in hac dignitate, ut ei cedat debitum stricti iuris, quod est ex iustitia commutativa. Unde communis resolutio illa authorum, si aliquis in dignitate constitutus non possit detractis omnibus superfluis, solvere debitum commutativae conservando dignitatem, eum non teneri tum solvere, quia eius dignitas conservata magis necessaria est Reipublicae, quam satisfactio debita particulari."

219. *Ibid.*

based upon the fact that the delay of payment has caused them greater damage; moreover, they have a prior right in the assets of the debtor. The same is true for the proportional payment of the creditors: the greater the debt, the greater the damage. The proportion maintains, therefore, as far as possible the equality among the creditors.[220]

The Franciscan scholar John Ponce (Johannes Poncius) (1603–1672), of Irish origin, dedicated in his philosophical work a rather extensive discussion to the Aristotelian distinction, declaredly in the spirit of Duns Scotus.[221] His first comment refers to the situation where only one benefit is attributed to one person according to the latter's merit. In his view, contrary to De Lugo's analysis, it remains a pure act of distributive justice, even if no attention is paid to other people. In other words, distributive justice does not require a plurality of persons or a plurality of benefits.[222] Moreover, he explains that distributive justice is still maintained where the (geometric) proportion of the respective merits is observed, even if the sum total of the benefits distributed are less than the merits would (objectively) require.[223]

The second comment concerns the above-mentioned cases where in a commutative justice situation a proportional-geometric solution is applied; namely, the case of an insolvent debtor vis-à-vis a number of different creditors, and that of different investors in a common enterprise.[224] The author follows the views of Suárez and De Lugo[225]—as against those of Vasquez and Turrianus[226]—who consider the cases to fall exclusively under corrective justice.

---

220. *Ibid.*, 242–243, at 243: "Ad casus autem illos in specie respondetur, ideo in primo casu praeferri antiquiores secundum commutativam, quia, caeteris paribus, maius damnum passi ex mora solutionis, & praeterea, quia prius habuerunt ius in debitorem, & eius bona: ut ergo servetur aequalitas quantum fieri potest, & iuris anticipati, & damni incursi, praeferuntur caeteris."

221. Ioannes Poncius, *Philosophiae ad Mentem Scoti Cursus Integer* (Lyon 1659) 352–354.

222. *Ibid.*, 352, §30: "Iustitia distributiva non ita respicit in quolibet actu suo plures, ut res danda debeat inter eos partiri; nec ita etiam ut exercens actum eius semper debeat actu de pluribus cogitare"; *ibid.*, §31: " . . .non tamen inde sequitur quod in quolibet actu respiciantur plures, aut fiat partitio rei collatae; sed sufficit ad rigorem istius nominis, quod iustitia habitualis inclinet ad distribuenda bona inter plures, quando id debet fieri, & quod quemadmodum inclinat ad dandum unum, aut plura beneficia uni merenti, ita inclinaret ad dandum alterum alteri similiter merenti."

223. *Ibid.*, 353, §33.

224. *Ibid.*, 353, §§34–35.

225. However, the author criticizes some specific aspects, here as elsewhere, of De Lugo's analysis.

226. *Cf. supra* 40.

The author equally supports the view that the decisive criterion is the intensity of the legal relationship: commutative justice gives rise to a strict right-duty relationship; as a result, its violation bestows upon the affected party an absolute right to restitution. In the case of distributive justice, the relationship does not give rise to a duty of restitution.[227] Finally, the author refers to vindictive justice. He follows the view that from the point of view of the judges who, under a contract with the state, are committed to the administration of justice, punishing the offenders is a matter of commutative justice. But, if the punishment is meted out without a special contract, according to a person's discretion, then it falls under distributive justice.[228]

Another attempt to defend on similar lines the opinions of Duns Scotus was undertaken by the Italian Franciscan scholar Bartholomeo Mastri da Meldula (1602–1673).[229] The author first repeats the classical criteria of the Aristotelian distinction between distributive and commutative justice: The former compares objects to persons, giving rise to a geometric proportion; the latter compares objects among themselves, giving rise to an arithmetic proportion.[230] However, according to the author, both categories of justice can be divided into a rewarding one (*praemiativa*) and a punitive one (*punitiva, vindicativa, retributiva*).[231] In other words, rewards and punishments can be measured proportionally, as under distributive justice, or equally like by exchange, as under commutative justice. In this way, the author appears to try to resolve the above-mentioned apparent contradiction in the writings of

---

227. *Ibid.*: "Ad quaesitum principale autem existimo obligationem illam oriri ex iustitia commutativa, & hanc consequenter nonnunquam observare proportionem geometricam; quia in casibus praemissis observari debet illa proportio, & quod obligatio provenit ex commutativa patet, quia quod solvitur creditoribus & sociis est ipsorum, & nisi detur illis obligatio restitutionis remanet, quod autem datur ex iustitia distributiva non est illorum quibus datur, nec manet obligatio restituendi. Quod vero ad praxim attinet perinde prorsus est qua iustitia proveniat illa obligatio, sufficit enim cognoscere quod sit illa obligatio & quod non observans illam teneatur ad restitutionem."

228. *Ibid.*, 354, §37.

229. Bartholomaeus Mastrius de Meldula, *Disputationes Theologicae In Tertium Librum Sententiarum Quibus ab adversantibus, tum Veterum, tum Recentiorum iaculis, Scoti Theologia Vindicatur* (Venezia 1675) Disputatio Septima, De Virtutibus Moralibus, Quaest. VIII, De Iustitia, Art. II, 469–471.

230. The same ideas are repeated in another book of the author, Bartholomaeus Mastrius de Meldula, *Theologia Moralis Ad mentem DD. Seraphici, & Subtilis concinnata, et in disputationes vigintiocto distributa* (Editio Secunda, Venezia 1681), Disput. Tertia, De iustitia et iure, §1, p. 69.

231. *Id., Disputationes Theologicae In Tertium Librum Sententiarum, ibid.*, §178, p. 469. *See also ibid.*, Disput. Tertia, Quaest. V, Art. 1, §150, p. 162.

Duns Scotus.[232] The major difference between the two forms of justice lies, according to the author, in the intensity of the underlying right: The object of commutative justice is a perfect right, the violation of which obliges to restitution, whereas the violation of a distributive justice right does not *ex se* oblige to restitution. However, in case of a wrongly executed distribution, a strict right of restitution might be attached to it. Thus, if money is distributed in violation of a predetermined proportional criterion, then the distributor sins against distributive justice, but at the same time also against commutative justice. He will, therefore, be held liable to restitution toward that person who has been injured by him. The same is true when the ruler distributes charges and taxes upon the citizens without distinguishing between rich and poor. He, too, sins not only against distributive justice, but equally against commutative justice, since the poor has a strict right in respect of his property that has been taken away from him. In many other cases, however, where public honors are distributed according to dignity and merits, the ruler or distributor has no duty of restitution toward the person injured.[233]

The author then mentions four difficulties concerning the traditional understanding of the two forms of justice. The first one relates to the denial by Buridanus of the specific nature of the distinction. The author mentions the contrary common view, according to which the distinction is *in specie*: the forms of justice differ in relation to the mode of equality (proportional versus quantitative), and they differ in respect of the duty of restitution.[234] The second difficulty arises from the fact that sometimes in a commutative justice situation a geometric proportion is applied. This happens in case of a plurality of creditors facing an insolvent debtor, as well as in case of an

232. *Supra* 35–36. The author specifically mentions Duns Scotus, Lib. 4, Distinct. 46, Quaest. 1.

233. *Disputationes Theologicae, ibid.* The notion of restitution is discussed in detail in the other mentioned book of the author: Bartholomaeus Mastrius de Meldula, *Theologia Moralis Ad mentem DD. Seraphici, & Subtilis concinnata, et in disputationes vigintiocto distributa* (Editio Secunda, Venezia 1681), Disput. Septima, Quaestio Prima, Articulus Primus, §§3–9, pp. 147–149. The author insists that restitution is exclusively an act of commutative justice: "Recte ergo fieri potest, ut obligatio non inferendi damnum, ad iustitiam distributivam pertineat, & ex ea oritur non vero obligatio illud resarciendi, sed ex commutativa; & ratio est, quia mutatur ratio iuris in utraque obligatione; quamvis enim ex distributione mala obligatio restituendi in distributore oriatur, hoc tamen non est ex mala & iniqua distributione precise, sed quia ea supposita debetur plus alicui, ut servetur geometrica proportio, & iniquus distributor dat minus, ac proinde quod inique abstulit illi, est restituendum ex vi iustitiae commutativae, ut patet ex exemplis adductis in probatione asserti."

234. *Disputationes, cit.*, §179.

association dividing profits unequally among the partners. Moreover, as mentioned above, a violation of distributive justice may create, in favor of an individual person, a duty under commutative justice that is of an arithmetic nature. In view of these difficulties concerning the geometric and arithmetic proportions,[235] the author—after discussing the various opinions—concludes that it is preferable to distinguish between the two forms of justice on the basis of the nature of the right created by them: Commutative justice engenders a perfect right, distributive justice a merely imperfect one.[236]

The third difficulty relates to the question whether commutative justice is composed of one single (formal) kind or of different ones (*species*). The author accepts the view that there are different kinds, in view of the different rights at the basis of commutative justice, giving rise to different kinds of duties.[237] The fourth difficulty concerns the question whether distributive justice requires always a plurality of objects and persons. The author, preferring the opinions of Suárez and Poncius over that of Cardinal De Lugo, namely, that distributive justice can be applied to one single benefit without having regard to a plurality of persons. Yet, the tendency of distributive justice is to allocate a plurality of things to a plurality of persons where that is feasible.[238]

The Jesuit scholar Louis de Mairat (Ludovicus Maeratius) of Troyes (1577–1664)[239] makes an extensive attempt to refute the view—which he relates to Suárez[240]—that based the distinction between the two forms of justice on the existence or absence of a (prior) full property right to a thing, or at least of a full right to its equivalence. In the case of commutative justice, one deals with a preexisting full ownership right to a thing; in the case of

235. *Ibid.*, 470, §182: "Quare cum medium geometricum, quod ponitur distinctivum distributivae, possit convenire commutativae; & medium arithmeticum, quod ponitur distinctivum commutativae, posset convenire distributivae; plane hoc semel concesso non possent amplius ex hoc capite commutativa, & distributiva specie sufficienter distingui."

236. *Ibid.*, §§181–183, p. 470.

237. *Ibid.*, §§184–185, pp. 470–471.

238. *Ibid.*, §186, p. 471: "Itaque eatenus dicitur iustitia distributiva proportionem geometricam servare, quatenus quando res distribuenda est capax partitionis, & distributionis secundum proportionem ad merita, & qualitates aliorum, ita fiat."

239. Ludovicus Maeratius, *Disputationes in Summam Theologicam S. Thomae*, Tomus Secundus, *Tractatus de Iustitia et Iure* (Paris 1633) Disp. XI–XII, pp. 501–512.

240. Franciscus Suarez, *Operum Tomus Decimum, Varia Opuscula Theologica, De Justitia Dei* (Venezia 1741) Sect. III, §14, pp. 307–308; *supra* 33–35.

distributive justice, no such right exists in relation to the person entitled to a benefit from public goods according to his dignity. The author declares that he adopts the contrary view of Gabrielis Vasquez, who represents the traditional, more common opinion among the theologians.[241]

The author then proceeds to deal with each of the arguments that denied the relevance of the proportional criterion. In relation to the case where only one benefit is accorded to the most meritorious person, he maintains that this is still based upon a geometric proportion, even if on an imperfect one.[242] On the other hand, it is true that in a situation of commutative justice—such as in the case of a plurality of creditors—the payment may follow a geometric proportion according to the size of the respective debts. However, this specific proportion is accidental to commutative justice, since at the base of it stays a debt of an arithmetic proportion. This original debt is not founded upon any comparison with other rights. Hence, by its nature it is grounded in an arithmetic equality.[243] The same is true where in a distributive justice situation, based upon a geometric proportion, the accidental result may be an arithmetic proportion.[244]

The author then refers to what he considers to be the weightiest objection, namely, the cases where, by acts of commutative justice, a duty of geometric proportion is established.[245] Three exemplary cases are discussed: 1) According to a will, one hundred gold coins are to be distributed among ten specific poor people, in proportion to the degree of their respective need. The execution of the will is intended to be a matter of geometric equality. 2) Under a partnership contract, the profits are to be distributed proportionally according to the amount of the partners' respective investments. 3) The case of a debtor who has insufficient funds to pay the full amount of his debts to a plurality of creditors. The payment is made proportionally to the respective amounts given to him by the individual creditors. Here again the geometric

---

241. Maeratius, *ibid.*, 501.

242. *Ibid.*, Sect. II, p. 504.

243. *Ibid.*, 505: "Dicitur autem commutativa per se constituere aequalitatem arithmeticam, per accidens geometricam: quia quod ex natura sua spectat, hoc solum est, nempe ius unum, & adaequatio iuris istius: ius, inquam, unum per se seorsim, non per comparationem ad alterius aut plurium iura consideratum, cuius iuris adaequatione constituitur, ut patet, aequalitas arithmetica."

244. *Ibid.*: "Unde facile intelligitur, quam ob causam similiter dicatur distributiva iustitia constituere per se geometricam aequalitatem, & per accidens arithmeticam."

245. *Ibid.*, Sect. III, pp. 505–507.

equality is evident. The objection to the criterion of proportionality in relation to the two forms of justice is based upon the premise that the three mentioned acts constitute commutative justice. The author contests this premise, claiming that all three transactions constitute proper distributive justice, since they are directly based upon a geometric proportion. Contrary to the opinion of Molina, not every duty arising out of a contract is necessarily one of commutative justice. Thus, a prince, who obliges himself under a contract that the booty obtained from the enemies be distributed among the soldiers according to a geometric proportion, is bound under distributive justice. Moreover, there is no need that the objects of distribution are goods of the community; it suffices that they are intended to be distributed according to a geometric proportion. In this context, the notion of common goods means that a plurality of people may have a common right to a full or partial possession.[246]

In the situation of the third mentioned case, where a debtor with insufficient funds has to pay the creditors according to a geometric proportion, a violation by the debtor of the right of an individual creditor constitutes a violation of both commutative and distributive justice. His primary duty to pay the debt is founded in commutative justice; the proportional payment in case of insolvency is based upon distributive justice. Hence—assuming the difference *in specie* of commutative and distributive justice—the nonpayment of a proportional part to an individual creditor sins against both forms of justice.[247] If, on the other hand, the two forms are not essentially different, but constitute one single virtue, then the nonpayment is one single sin committed on the basis of two different precepts.[248]

The author then discusses Buridan's opinion, according to which the two forms of justice are *not* different *in specie*.[249] Rather surprisingly, Maeratius agrees with Buridan, against the opinions of Aquinas and the majority of

---

246. *Ibid.*, 506: "Quod si per bona communia intelligantur ea omnia, ad quem possidenda, vel tota, vel ex parte, multi commune ius habent, sic concedo quidem distributivae iustitiae materiam propriam esse bona hoc sensu communia, sed nego tres praedictos actus circa bona hoc ipso sensu communia non versari, versantur enim, ut perspicuum est."

247. *Ibid.*, 507.

248. *Ibid.*: "Sicut cum unus idemque unius virtutis aut vitij actus est duobus praeceptis, uno naturali, altero positivo, imperatus, aut vetitus, & omittitur, vel committitur, unicum peccatum est, quod ex duplici praecepto tanquam ex duplici capite ortum habet, quorum quodlibet seorsim sufficiebat, ut idem peccatum contraheretur."

249. *Ibid.*, Sect. IV, pp. 507–509.

theologians. In the author's view, the virtue that lies at the base of the two forms of justice is identical. They are merely sub-categories of the same virtue. Like in the framework of commutative justice, there are different situations, which do not justify the creation of additional forms of justice, so the differences between commutative and distributive justice fall under the same species of justice. The two forms do not differ, neither in the substance (intensity) of the right, nor in the substance of equality. Thus, both the rights under commutative justice and those under distributive justice constitute specific property (*dominium*) or its equivalence. The difference in the number of persons—commutative justice concerns the property of one person, distributive justice the property of a plurality of persons—this difference is not of essence.[250]

Equally, the difference between the geometric and arithmetic proportion is not of essence. Thus, the act of giving alms to one single poor according to his need, or to a plurality of poor persons proportionally to their individual need—these acts are based upon one identical virtue: compassion. The same is true for the two forms of justice.[251] Moreover, the criterion of dignity is not exclusively applied in distributive justice; it is relevant also in cases of compensating an injured person. The latter's dignity may increase the compensation. Hence, it is not different in essence from a case of comparison of dignity in relation to a plurality of persons having a right in the distribution of benefits.[252]

Finally, the author agrees with the traditional opinion that punitive justice (*iustitia vindictiva*) does not constitute a different species of justice.[253]

The Italian Jesuit scholar Francesco Amico (1578–1651), professor of theology at Naples, Aquila, and Graz, specifically argues that the distinction between the two forms of justice does not reside in the geometric or arithmetic proportions, but rather in the basis of the obligation.[254] The reason is that

---

250. *Ibid.*, 508: "Vel quia ius commutativae proprium est unum, & unius numero personae, ius vero proprium distributivae est multiplex, & in multis personis existens: at inter unum & multa, quando nulla alia differentia est, quam unitatis & multitudinis, non est differentia essentialis, alioquin inter unum & multa eiusdem infimae speciei individua essentialis differentia intercederet."

251. *Ibid.*, 509: "Sic actus iustitiae, quo ius unius solius adaequatur, & quo proinde aequalitas arithmetica constituitur, & quo proinde aequalitas geometrica constituitur, videntur esse unius specie virtutis actus, imo & esse unius eiusdemque speciei."

252. *Ibid.*

253. *Ibid.*, Disp. XII, pp. 510–513.

254. Franciscus Amicus, *Cursus Theologici Tomus Quintus De Iure et Iustitia* (Antwerpen 1650), Disp. XI, *De iustitia*, 142–143.

in a number of commutative transactions a geometric proportion has been laid down. Thus, a person may dispose of a certain sum in favor of the poor according to their respective need. The legator is bound by commutative justice to distribute the money according to a geometric proportion. Similarly, a person may sell certain merchandise that is priced according to the quality in a geometric proportion.[255] Hence, the distinction lies in the intensity of the right: commutative justice is based upon a perfect right *in re*, distributive justice upon an imperfect right *ad rem*.[256] Vindictive justice exercised by a judge constitutes commutative justice, because the judge is under a contractual duty to administer justice. The judge has no right to exercise mercy, contrary to the prince who may for the public good grant pardon. A judge who deviates from vindictive justice, violates either the right of the victim (by a too lenient punishment) or the right of the offender (by imposing a too heavy punishment). The author admits, that, in principle, a violation of distributive justice by the prince creates a commutative justice right of compensation, not of the individual citizens, but of the community as such.[257]

The Benedictine Abbot of Einsiedeln, Augustinus II, Reding von Biberegg (1625–1692),[258] equally rejects Buridan's opinion and asserts that the distinction is not accidental but *in specie*. He relies on the different intensity of the rights created by the two forms of justice and the difference in the proportions, the one arithmetic and the other geometric. He refers to the famous argument that in the case of an insolvent debtor toward a plurality of creditors, commutative justice applies a geometric proportion; and in the case of one single benefit to distribute, no geometric proportion is applied.

The author argues that in the first case, the debt was created under commutative justice without comparison between the single creditors. The payment uses geometric proportion by accident and in a secondary way, in order to create equality between unequal creditors. It remains, therefore,

255. *Ibid.*, §182.

256. *Ibid.*, §§183–186: "Iustitia commutativa & distributiva distinguuntur formaliter ex diverso iure, in quo fundantur; quia illa funditur in iure perfecto, & in re; haec in in iure imperfecto, & ad rem."

257. *Ibid.*, pp. 144–145.

258. Augustinus II, *Theologia Scholastica In Secundam Secundae Divi Thomae Ad Normam Theologorum Salisburgensium*, Tomus XII, De Jure Et Justitia (Einsiedeln 1687) Quaest. I, Artic. I, Controversia III, 5–6; Augustinus Reding A Biberegg, *Questiones Theologicae de Jure et Justitia in 2.2. D. Thomae Aq. 56 usque ad Quaest. 78* (Einsiedeln 1673) 15–23.

commutative justice.[259] Correspondingly, distributive justice relates essentially to a plurality of persons subject to comparison. It bestows the benefit upon the person of greatest merit or dignity. Hence, it applies always a geometric equality.[260] In relation to vindictive justice, the author reaffirms the opinion of Thomas Aquinas that it is based on commutative justice. However, he limits it to its exercise by a judge, since then the latter's function makes part of a contractual duty.[261]

A detailed analysis of the distinction between commutative and distributive of justice has been undertaken by the Jesuit scholar Christoph Haunold (1610–1689), professor of theology at the Universities of Freiburg/Breisgau and Ingolstadt. He starts with the general proposition that the two kinds of justice, being based upon an obligation, don't create in the receiving party an obligation to respond with an act of gratitude.[262] He then describes four different views on the nature of the distinction between the two kinds of justice: 1) Buridan's opinion that denies its essential character; 2) the very common view that bases it on the difference between an arithmetic and a geometric proportion; 3) the "ingenious" view of Martinus Esparza (1589–1669), according to which there is no difference in the strictness of the rights; distributive justice relates equally to a strict right-duty relationship, the violation of which entitles to restitution. Distributive justice has to be based upon a prior law or contract; otherwise it is a mere act of generosity and munificence. Distributive justice is exclusively concerned with the conferral of public functions which have to be executed for the common good. Hence, the difference between the two kinds of justice relates to the object of the duty: the welfare

259. *Ibid.*: "Est proinde de essentia Iustitiae *commutativae*, ut per se intendat *arithmeticam* aequalitatem cum iure alterius stricto, licet per *accidens* & *secundario* aliquando videatur servare proportionem *geometricam*."

260. *Ibid.*, 5–6: "Deinde justitia *distributiva essentialiter* respicit plures, inter quos fieri debet comparatio, cui, ceu digniori sit potius jus ad bonum aliquod communitatis, v.g. beneficium vacans. Ergo cum ista Iustitia non respiciat singulorum jura absolute spectata, sed cum comparatione ad alios, ita ut in bonorum communium distributione sit eijus potior habenda ratio, qui meritis ac dignitate alios in communitate antecedit, consequenter Iustitia *distributiva* servat semper *geometricam* aequalitatem."

261. *Ibid.*, 6. The idea of a judge's contractual duty seems to have been introduced by Suárez, *supra* at note 121.

262. Christophorus Haunoldus, *Controversiarum De Justitia Et Jure Privatorum Universo Nova Et Theorica Methodo In Decem Tractatus Et Quatuor Tomos Digestarum*, Tomus Primus (Ingolstadt 1671) Tract. II, Caput I, Controversia I, §§7–14, pp. 68–70. The author notes that it is different in relation to Divinity. In God there is no proper distributive justice; divine rewards are based upon grace and kindness, hence a duty of gratitude (*ibid.*, §9).

of the community versus the interests of private persons.[263] 4) The fourth view considers the distinction to be grounded in the different intensity of the respective duties: The duty under distributive justice, concerned with the distribution of public goods, is not strict and its violation does not create a duty of restitution.

The author adopts that last approach.[264] He bases his conclusion on the following arguments: The difference between arithmetic and geometric proportion is not sufficient, since in some situations distributive justice uses an arithmetic proportion and commutative justice a geometric one[265]; where the members of a community have, under a law or a contract, a strict right *ad rem* to the common goods to be distributed, that distribution is an act of commutative justice[266]; the right of restitution is always based upon commutative justice[267]; the distribution of charges and contributions is basically an act of commutative justice with some aspects of distributive justice.[268]

The German theologian Ewaldus Marchius (active around 1660) states in his summary of the notion of justice that it is commonly divided into legal, commutative, distributive, and punitive justice.[269] Distributive justice relates to meritorious citizens, punitive justice to malicious ones. Judges, who receive salaries from the state, are obliged under commutative justice to punish offenders. Distributive and commutative justice may coexist in one act, according to the existence of a strict duty.[270]

---

263. *Ibid.*, Controversia VI, §§90–92, pp. 84–85: "Itaque secundum hanc auctorem differt denique justitia distributiva a commutativa, quod illa respiciat principaliter bonum communitatis in distributione officiorum cum praedicta obligatione, cum econtra Iustitia commutativa principaliter attendat Ius personae privatae, & nullam inducat obligationem solvendo, quod illi debetur."

264. *Ibid.* He notes that this is the view of Suárez, Rebellus, Lessius, Lugo, Joan. Di Castillo.

265. *Ibid.*, §§94–98, pp. 85–86. The author uses the traditional examples of distribution of a single benefit, insolvency in relation to a plurality of creditors, distribution of proportional profits in a commercial enterprise.

266. *Ibid.*, §§99–101, p. 86.

267. *Ibid.*, §101.

268. *Ibid.*, §109, p. 88.

269. Ewaldus Marchius, *Nucleus tractatus Practici De Iure Et Iustitia* (Köln 1658) 5–9.

270. *Ibid.*, 8–9: "Praeterea, in eodem actu, concurrere potest IUSTITIA Commutativa & Distributiva, cum dividitur aliquid stricto iure debitum. Quod si vero fiat distributio rerum, quae hoc stricto iure non debeantur, secundum conditionem personarum, ut fit in distributione beneficiorum; tunc distributiva non includit commutativam."

The Bavarian Franciscan (Recollector) scholar Patricius Sporer (ca. 1620–1683) analyzes the different aspects of punishment.[271] From the point of view of the judge, who exercises his official punitive function, it constitutes commutative justice as in relation to the state and the victim; the punishment itself, being meted out in accordance with the measure of the crime, has a likeness to commutative justice; however, when considered proportionally in relation to other offenders, it is similar to distributive justice. But, since punishment is not a distribution of common goods, nor does it compensate the victim, it belongs neither to distributive nor to commutative justice. It constitutes, therefore, an imperfect kind of justice.

The Bavarian Franciscan moral theologian, Anacletus Reiffenstuel (1642–1703), adds an additional subdivision to both of the two categories of justice: a rewarding one (*praemiativa*) and a punitive (*punitiva*) one. Thus, under distributive justice, honors and other benefits may be awarded according to the proportion of merits, but also punishments may be meted out varying according to the different societal status of the offender. The same is true under commutative justice; on the one hand, rewards can be distributed equally without taking into account the condition, dignity, or status of the recipient; on the other hand, punishments may be imposed in an equal measure according to the offence, again without taking into account the prior condition of the offender.[272] A similar approach was adopted by another seventeenth-century Franciscan scholar, the Silesian Amandus Hermann. This author affirms that both *iustitia praemiativa* and *iustitia vindicativa* can be referred to both commutative and to distributive justice. On the one hand, reward is an exchange for work and punishment an exchange for guilt; on the other hand, both forms of justice determine respectively the reward or the punishment according to the proportion of the merit or the demerit.[273]

The view that a duty under distributive justice is weaker than one under commutative justice has been challenged by various scholars. Thus, the Discalced Carmelite Gabriele da San Vincenzo (1601–1671), in a treatise published in 1663, criticizes the view of Suárez by arguing that this specific

---

271. Patritius Sporer, *Theologia moralis decalogalis et sacramentalis* (Ed. 2a, I. Bierbaum, ed., Paderborn 1903) Tomus 2, p.16.

272. A. Reiffenstuel, *Theologia Moralis* (Venezia 1736) Tract. 7, De Iustitia et Jure, distinct. 2, q. 2, n. 19, pp. 235–236.

273. Amandus Hermann, *Ethica Sacra Scholastica, Speculativo-Pratica, Seu Tractatus & Disputationes Morales De Virtutibus, Ad mentem Joannis Duns Scoti Doctoris Subtilissimi, & profundissimi* (Würzburg 1698) Tract. VI, Disp. I, Quaestio II, p. 363.

distinction between the two forms of justice cannot be found in the writings of Aristotle or Thomas Aquinas.[274] These forms of justice have different forms of equality, but they are not different in the substance of the right. The rights under both forms of justice have the same force.[275] Moreover, the author assumes that even in case of one single office or one single candidate to the benefit, there is still a situation of distributive justice, since potential other candidates remain excluded.[276] He disagrees with Molina's view that any obligation arising out of a contract is exclusively one of commutative justice. Gabriele argues that nothing prevents a person to assume an obligation to distribute goods of his property according to a geometrical proportion of distributive justice. In his view, these cases represent a combination of commutative justice and distributive justice: There is a personal obligation to apply distributive justice.[277]

Petrus Barbay (d. 1664), professor of philosophy in Paris, states in his commentary on the *Nicomachean Ethics*,[278] that a certain situation may at the same time belong both to distributive and commutative justice. Thus, the obligation of the soldier to serve in the military, and the king's obligation to pay the remuneration, fall under commutative justice; but the measure of the salary, according to the specific kind of military service, makes part of distributive justice. The author distinguishes between three kinds of distributive justice: remunerative, vindictive (or punitive), and civil: the first distributes honors and other public goods according to merit and dignity; the second kind constitutes an equality between punishment and offense; the third kind

274. Gabrielis a S. Vincentio, *De Iustitia et Iure* (Rome 1663) Disp. 1, Q. 19, n. 275, at 94: "Nec inveniet Suarez apud Aristotelem, nec apud S. Thomam suam illam distictionem duplicis iuris, unius, quod est proprium dominium rei, aut ei aequivalens; et alterius, quod nec est proprium dominium rei, nec ei aequvalens; et quod illus prius sit objectum iustitiae commutativae, et hoc distributivae."

275. *Ibid.*, 94–95, n. 276–277: "Antecedens ostenditur, nam ius, quod spectat iustitia commutativa est dominium proprium, aut aequivalens; sed etiam dominium quod spectat iustitia distributiva est proprium, aut aequivalens, ergo. Haec minor ostenditur; nam tanti valet ius, quod spectat iustitia distributiva, quanti valet illud, quod spectat commutativa."

276. *Ibid.*, 95, n. 279.

277. *Ibid.*, 95–97, n. 280–283. The author counts among these cases the traditionally discussed ones: 1) legacy for the poor under a will, to be distributed proportionally; 2) proportional investment in a commercial enterprise; 3) multiple creditors of an insolvent debtor.

278. Petrus Barbay, *Commentarius in Aristotelis Moralem* (Editio quinta, Paris 1690) 306–309.

distributes public charges, such as taxes and military service, according to the individual's condition.

However, the author denies the presence of proportion in a number of situations. His assumption is that proportion requires at least four elements: two things and two persons. This condition is absent in punishment, since there the equality is merely between crime and punishment; in remunerative (distributive) justice, it lacks where there is only one indivisible benefit for distribution. Moreover, arithmetic proportion can never be present in commutative justice. Thus, in case of different rates of investment by merchants, the distribution of profits occurs in a geometric proportion; the same is true in sales, where the price of any merchandise is calculated according to a basic unit: if one ell is sold for three moneys, then eight ell sell for twenty-four. Finally, where the price is equal to the specific merchandise, then there is again no proportion, since there are no four elements.[279]

The work of the French Jesuit Jacques Channevelle (1620–1699) on the *Ethics* according to the Aristotelian principles remains in the Thomist scholastic tradition.[280] The safeguard of strict rights is the function of commutative justice, not of distributive justice. Hence, restitution is the exclusive act of commutative justice.[281] The author analyzes, on the basis of Aristotle's work, the price of goods and the function of money. In relation to need (*indigentia*) as the measure of a good's value, the author explains that one has to distinguish between the need of the poor and the need of the rich. The former need is based upon necessity, the latter upon luxury.[282]

In relation to the Aristotelian discussion of retaliation (*antipepontos, repassio, ius talionis*), the author distinguishes between "simple" and "analogical" retaliation.[283] The former has place neither in distributive nor in commutative justice. In distributive justice, attention is paid to the respective status of the persons; in commutative justice, the goods exchanged are not identical, and in case of injury, the retribution cannot be of a perfect identical nature. Thus, where an

279. *Ibid.*, 307–309.

280. Iacobus Channeville, *Ethica Seu Philosophia Moralis juxta principia Aristotelis* (Paris 1666) 1040–1053.

281. *Ibid.*, 1044, 1050.

282. *Ibid.*, 1048: "Duplex quippe indigentia, altera pauperum: altera divitum. Illa necessariis contenta: haec supervacaneas opes ad potentiam, & voluptates operose conquirit. Illa dicitur indigentia necessitatis: haec exuperantiae: utraque causa, & mensura permutationis."

283. *Ibid.*, 1051.

injury is caused by inadvertence, it is impossible to reciprocate inadvertently, since any vindictive act will be done intentionally.[284] On the other hand, analogical, proportional retribution (*talio*) is applicable in both kinds of justice.

The Benedictine scholar Paul Mezger (1637–1702) in his work on the scholastic theology according to Thomas Aquinas follows rather closely the great predecessor.[285] Distributive and commutative justice are different in kind according to the traditional distinctions: private transactions versus distribution of public goods; measure of things against condition of persons; arithmetic equality versus geometric proportion; however, by accident the geometric proportion may be absent, such as in case of one single person of merit, or a plurality of equally meritorious persons[286]; strict right and duty of restitution versus neither of the two.

The Praemonstratensian theologian of Antwerp, Florentius de Cocq (1648–1693), starts his short discussion with quotations from Thomas Aquinas.[287] He emphasizes that commutative justice is often annexed to distributive justice. Thus, the duty of restitution is always based upon commutative justice, since distributive justice, as such, does not grant the recipients a strict right. Distributive justice requires the distribution of common goods according to a geometric proportion. Once the required proportion has been violated, the original intent is no more applicable, since the common goods have already been distributed. The restitution of equality comes now from the private property of the wrongful distributor. The conferral of a public function to an unworthy person obliges the official to compensate the state for the ensuing damage. This obligation is again based upon commutative justice resulting from a contractual duty of the official to prevent damage

---

284. *Ibid.*, 1052: "Nemo enim injuriam ulciscitur imprudens, sed sciens, volensque." This example has obviously been taken from Gellius (*supra* at note 184), an author mentioned on p. 1051.

285. Paulus Mezger, *Theologiae Scholasticae Secundum Viam D. Thomae Aquinatis, Doctoris Angelici*, Tomus III (Augsburg 1719), Tract. XI, Disp. XXIV, Art. II, pp. 250–251.

286. *Ibid.*, 250: "Unde si quando proportio *geometrica* intermittitur a justitia distributiva, est per accidens, & ex defectu materiae, veluti cum non adest nisi unus dignus, cui conferatur beneficium, vel plures sunt aequaliter digni, tunc enim solum defectu materiae cessat aequalitas proportionum, quo tamen non obstante, quia per se loquendo non contingit haec partium raritas aequalitas, distributiva vero per se respicit jus distributivum partium qua talium, ideo justitia distributiva in geometricam aequalitatem adhuc per se inclinat."

287. Florentius De Cocq, *De Jure, Justitia Et Annexis, Tractatus Quatuor, Theologico-Canonice Expositi; Juri communi, & variorum Regnorum particulari, Maxime Tamen Juri Belgico Accomodati* (Bruxelles 1687) 5–7.

from the state.[288] Vindictive justice is, according to Aquinas, based upon commutative justice. Punishing delinquents is a contractual duty of the judge, who will be liable for the damage caused by the breach of that duty.

Firmly in the mainstream of the Thomist scholastic tradition is also the Slovenian Jesuit theologian Simon Karchne (1649–1722), chancellor of the University of Graz. He affirms, following Cardinal De Lugo, that the formal object of distributive justice is not a strict right in the public goods, but a lesser right based upon dignity and merit.[289] Hence, any right for restitution is necessarily based upon a violation of a commutative justice right. Thus, the violation of distributive justice by a neglect of observing the respective merits does not imply a duty of restitution. The situation is different where there is a specific contract, promising some members a distribution according to merit; the contract gives rise to strict right under commutative justice.[290]

In general, commutative justice applies an arithmetic proportion, but in some situations—such as distribution under a will of money to the poor according to their respective need, or the proportionate payment of creditors in case of insolvency—a geometric proportion is used.[291] Vindictive justice constitutes a species of justice only in relation to the state and the judge. The latter, by accepting the office, is duty-bound, under an express or implied contract with the state, to punish proportionally the delinquent. As a result, the judge has no right to remit the punishment, since he is bound by law to care for the common good. However, the power of pardon is given to the ruler, because a declaration of judicial clemency is very conducive to the common good.[292]

The Italian Jesuit scholar Domenico Viva (1648–1726), in his popular *Cursus Theologicus*, starts with the assumption of four different kinds of justice: commutative, distributive, legal, and vindictive.[293] Among these different kinds, only

---

288. *Ibid.*, 7. The author speaks of a virtual contract.

289. Simon Karchne, *Dissertationes Juridico-Theologicae De Jure, & Justitia Ad Praxim Fere Omnium Statuum Directae, Plurimisque Rarioribus Quaestionibus Instructae* (Augsburg 1714), Dissertatio IV, Art. I, §II, pp. 279–280, n. 278.

290. *Ibid.*, §III, p. 281, n. 280.

291. *Ibid.*, §II, p. 280, n. 278.

292. *Ibid.*, p. 281, n. 279. The author adds that a judge, when failing to exercise vindictive justice, is liable under commutative justice to compensate the community or the private person for the resulting damage.

293. Dominicus Viva, *Cursus Theologicus Ad Usum Tyronum elucubratus, & in quotidianis Praelectionibus Suis Auditoribus traditus*, Pars Quinta, *De Justitia, & Jure* (Ignatius Viva, ed., Köln 1716) Disp. III, Quaest. I, Art. II, pp. 121–131.

commutative justice relates to a strict right; hence, the concept of justice is used with respect to the different kinds in an analogous and not in an identical sense.[294] A right of restitution arises only from a violation of commutative justice.

In some situations, the violation of distributive justice implies a contemporaneous violation of a commutative obligation. This is the case where a person is charged by a will to distribute a certain amount of money according to merit. The beneficiaries acquire a strict right to receive their part of money, obliging the failing distributor to restitution. The situation is different in the case of public offices; the worthier don't have a strict right to the office. Hence, the ruler who violates distributive justice is not bound to restitution. The same is true for a person who does not help the very poor, or sells with profit corn or another commodity by help of his monopoly. That person merely sins against charity. Free of responsibility is also the bystander who does not extinguish the fire of a burning house—which he could easily do—as long as he is not a watchman or servant.[295] Vindictive justice is concerned with the welfare of the community and not with private rights of property.[296]

The French scholar of theology at the Sorbonne, Honoré Tournély (1658–1729), equally affirms that distributive justice is not a strict form of justice. However, the person who causes injury by the unjust distribution to the community or to individuals is bound to restitution on the basis of commutative justice.[297] Vindictive justice belongs partly to distributive justice and partly to commutative justice. It pertains to distributive justice, since the offender's suffering in relation to another person is proportional to the injury caused by him. It belongs, according to Aquinas, to commutative justice, since the punishment is equal to the guilt; the latter is greater the more dignified is the injured person. Moreover, the judge is bound by his office to impose the punishment. The violation of the vindictive justice often gives rise to a restitutionary duty on the part of negligent judges, like the duty of a paid gardener who lets the weeds suffocate the good semen.[298]

---

294. *Ibid.*, 126–127. This idea was voiced by Paul Laymann (1574–1635), *supra* 47, at note 190.

295. *Ibid.*, 130–131.

296. *Ibid.*, 126.

297. Honoratus Tournely, *Cursus Theologicus Scholastico-Dogmaticus* (Köln 1734), *Tractatus de Justitia Et Jure*, 533.

298. *Ibid.*, 534. The author terminates the discussion by stating that the division of justice into legal, distributive, and commutative is legitimate.

The German scholar Augustinus Michel (1661–1751), professor of law and theology, starts also from the premise of four kinds of justice: commutative, distributive, legal, and vindictive.[299] Commutative justice is based upon a strict property right; distributive justice upon a lesser right, namely, that of a person's aptitude. The latter does not give rise—in case of violation—to a right of restitution.[300] The major distinction between distributive and commutative justice resides in the different proportions: arithmetic and geometric. The author then proceeds to respond to five traditional objections raised against that difference.

1) The case of the vacancy of one single public office. The author's answer is that in this situation of distributive justice, since the criterion is the dignity of a person and not the quantity of things, the proportion remains a geometric one even in the absence of other persons. 2) The case of proportional distribution of profits to investors in a commercial society. In this situation of commutative justice, the arithmetic proportion is clearly applied, since the profit is measured according to the quantity invested and not according to the dignity of a person. 3) The case of an insolvent debtor facing a plurality of creditors. Here again the quantity of money paid to the single creditors corresponds to that accepted from them; hence an arithmetic proportion is observed.[301] 4) The case of a testator who left some property to the poor, to be distributed according to their quality and need by the executor of the will. Here, one has to distinguish between a twofold obligation imposed upon the executor: one based upon commutative justice, in favor of the whole community of poor, conceived quasi as one person; the other, based upon distributive justice, vis-à-vis the individuals obliging the executor to distribute according to their quality and need. The executor, failing to distribute the property, will be held to restitution under commutative justice; if he deviates

---

299. Augustinus Michel, *Jus Et Justitia Juridico-Theologico Tractata* (Augsburg and Dillingen 1697) §I, p. 3. The author notes that the Legists classify vindictive justice under distributive justice.

300. *Ibid.*, §IV, p. 9. In the same sense, starting from the four kinds of justice, the Jesuit scholar Paulus Opffermann, *Tractatus De Jure Et Justitia Ad Usum Theologiae Candidatorum* (Mainz 1747) 607–611. This author observes, however, that the infliction of an exorbitant punishment constitutes a commutative injustice, since the defendant has a strict right not to be punished unjustly.

301. *Ibid.*, 10–11: "Quis non videt hanc & similes omnes objectiones niti sinistro illo conceptu proportionis geometricae? Quis non videt clarissime, isthoc casu haberi respectum quantitatis singulis ad quantitatem a singulis acceptam, adeoque observari proportionem arithmeticam?"

from the criterions of quality and need, he will sin against the virtue of distributive justice by the vice of *acceptio personarum.* 5) The case, mentioned in Justinian's *Digesta,*[302] where a husband left a will according to which his property shall be distributed the following way: If his wife gives birth to a son, then the latter will receive 2/3 or 8/12 and his wife 1/3 or 4/12; if she gives birth to a daughter, the daughter will get 1/3 or 4/12 and his wife 2/3 or 8/12. Now, the wife gave birth to twins, a son and a daughter. According to the solution under Roman law, the succession should be distributed in the following way: the son will receive 4/7, the wife 2/7, and the daughter 1/7. Hence, a geometric proportion in a commutative justice situation. The author gives the following explanation: In that case, commutative justice pays *per accidens* attention to the geometric proportion as a means to find out the arithmetic proportion, or rather the intention of the testator.

Finally, the author maintains that between father and son, master and servant, husband and wife, a commutative justice relationship may exist based upon a property right. Thus, the son in relation to *peculium Castrense,* the servant in relation to his bodily integrity, the wife in relation to her dowry, paraphernalia, etc.[303]

A similar approach, based upon the scholastic literature, is adopted by the Neapolitan Jesuit scholar Nicola Mazzotta (1669–1737) in his work on moral theology.[304] Among the mentioned four kinds of justice, only commutative justice is based upon a strict right in way that its violation entitles to restitution.[305] The division into the different kinds is, therefore, of an analogical nature.[306] In situations of distributive justice, there may be included a strict right of commutative justice implying a right of restitution. The author then illustrates this phenomenon by a number of concrete cases: Distribution by a military commander of the enemy's booty according to the soldiers' merit; grant of ecclesiastical benefits to the worthiest on the basis of prior competitive exams; distribution of money under a legacy to students according

---

302. Dig. 28.2.13, in the name of Julianus.

303. *Ibid.*, §VI, p. 14–15.

304. Nicola Mazzotta, *Theologia MoralisAd Mentem Praecipue R.P. Claudii La-Croix,* Tomus Secundus (Venezia 1760) Tract. IV, Disput. I, Quaest. II, Cap. I–III, pp. 190–194.

305. The author notes (*ibid.*, 190) that commutative justice is also called "*Justitia vulgaris,*" because it is commonly applied ("*quia passim vulgo exercetur*").

306. *Ibid.*, 190–191. In relation to vindictive justice, the author states: ". . . sed neque haec est justitia stricte accepta, cum nec Judex habeat ius proprietatis ad exigendum poenam, nec delinquens ad dandam."

to a criterion of merit. In all these situations the recipients have a prior strict right—based upon an express or implied agreement—entitling them to restitution in case the distributor violates the criterion of merit.[307] In the absence of a commutative-justice-right, the violation of legal, distributive, or vindictive justice, as such, does not entitle the damaged person to restitution.[308] The imposition of a disproportionate punishment by the judge obliges him to restitution, since it is a violation of a commutative-justice-right of the delinquent (in case of an exaggerated punishment) or that of the state or of the citizens (in case of remission).[309]

The Belgian Dominican scholar Charles-René Billuart (1685–1757), in his commentary on Thomas Aquinas's *Summa*, affirms that, in principle, nothing prevents an act belonging at the same time to both forms of justice.[310] He relates to the argument that in the case where common (public) goods are distributed in recompense for public services, as, e.g., to soldiers who fought bravely, this is a matter of both distributive and commutative justice. However, the author opines that the mentioned case is rather one of commutative justice, since it deals with a recompense for services, a recompense that is measured according to the actual service and not according to the status of a person.[311]

In the view of the seventeenth-century French Dominican scholar, Hyacintus Chalvet, meting out punishment, as well as awarding recompense for merits, is the privilege of the prince or of the magistrate; hence, both acts fall under the heading of distributive justice.[312]

---

307. *Ibid.*, 192.

308. The author illustrates, relying on Lessius, a number of situations where there is no concomitant commutative-justice-right. Thus, there is no liability of a witness who keeps silent, or a of a criminal who evades punishment. The witness has a right to keep silent; the criminal has no strict duty to suffer punishment (*ibid.*, 193).

309. *Ibid.*, 194. Remission of punishment is, however, the privilege of the supreme Judge or the ruler. Hence, liability is imposed soleley on an inferior judge.

310. Carolus Renatus Billuart, *Summa S. Thomae Hodiernis Academiarum Moribus Accommodata Sive Cursus Theologiae, Secunda Secundae, Tractatus de Jure et Justitia* (Venezia 1787) Dissertatio 5, Art. 3, p. 207: "Quamvis enim hae Justitiae distinguantur, saepe tamen contingit eas at eundem actum concurrere; quia nihil vetat eandem rem utriusque Justitiae titulo deberi."

311. *Ibid.*

312. Hyacintus Chalvet, *Sanctus Thomas Aquinas ex Utroque Suggestu sive Theologia Moralis Angelici Doctoris in Conciones Digesta*, Tomus Octavus (Caen 1676) Lib. 2, Cap. 4, p. 131: "Iustitia distributiva ad solum illum spectat, qui toti praeest communitati; videlicet Principi, vel Magistratui . . . Solus autem Princeps supremum habet in omnes subditos

On the other hand, the Italian Dominican Cardinal Vincent-Louis Gotti (1664–1742), basically repeated in his scholastic textbook the Thomist analysis of the subject.[313] In a lengthy discussion of the Aristotelian distinction, he maintained that the right arising out of distributive justice was weaker than that based on commutative justice.[314] In relation to punishment, called by the author *justitia vindicativa*, he declared that, if applied by a judge, it belonged to commutative justice, since the judge is legally bound to administer punitive justice. Moreover, punishment is meted out according to the measure of the offense and aimed also at compensating the victim.[315] The author then adds that the implementation of vindictive justice is imposed not only upon the judge or the prince, but equally upon the offender himself, who by suffering the punishment is rendering the just and the equivalent to the victim, to the state and to the law.[316]

Firmly in the Thomist scholastic tradition stands equally the Bavarian Jesuit scholar Anton Mayr (1673–1749), professor of theology at the Universities of Freiburg and Ingolstadt.[317] In his view, there exists an important difference between commutative justice and distributive justice. The former is based upon a strict right of property, the latter upon a lesser right, since the recipients don't have, before the actual distribution, a right of disposition over the common good. As a consequence, the violation of the distributive-justice-right—though it can be called an injustice in a broad sense—does not entitle the victim to restitution, except if it constitutes at

---

dominium iurisdictiones; ergo & illius dumtaxat erit optime de Republica meritos proemiare, improbos vero poenis mulctare . . . Actus ergo distributionis, qui est communium bonorum, pertinet solum ad praesidentem communibus bonis." The author follows closely Thomas Aquinas in his discussion of the Aristotelian distinction: *ibid.*, Caps. 3–4, pp. 126–131.

313. Vincentius-Ludovicus Gotti, *Theologia Scholastico-Dogmatica Juxta Mentem Divi Thomae Aquinatis Ad Usum Discipulorum*, Tomus Secundus (Venezia 1750) Tractatus 13, De Jure & Justitia, Quaest. 3, Dubium 2, pp. 552 et seq.

314. *Ibid.*, 552: "Jus vero inspectum a justitia distributiva non est jus fundans rigorosum debitum sed solum debitum exigentiae, & condignitatis."

315. *Ibid.*, §4.

316. *Ibid.*, Sect. XXIII: " . . . sed esse [justitia vindicativa] etiam in reo, recompensante malum, quod egit: & per poenam, quam sustinet, reddente vel laeso, vel Reipublicae, vel legi justum, & aequivalens."

317. Antonius Mayr, *Theologia Scholastica Tractatus Omnes In Universitatibus Provinciae Germaniae Superioris Societatis Jesu Tradi Solitos Et Quaestiones In Iis Praescriptas Complexa*, Tomus II (Ingolstadt 1732) Tractatus VIII, Disputatio I, Quaest. II.

the same time a violation of a commutative-justice-right.[318] The latter right may arise out of an express or implied agreement with the state obliging the distributor to divide common goods according to merit.

Moreover, by the very order to distribute public goods, the community may grant the recipient a certain *ius ad rem* which belongs to commutative justice.[319] The author refers to the objections against the validity of the distinction between the two forms of justice that is based upon the difference of proportion. He relies upon the traditional responses to the examples of the debtor's insolvency in regard to a plurality of debtors and the distribution of profits according to the measure of a partner's individual investment. The fact that in these cases a geometric proportion is applied is merely accidental, since basically the arithmetic proportion is adequate. Similarly, where the merits are equal, an arithmetic proportion may accidentally be applied in a distributive justice situation. Moreover, commutative justice may accidentally deal with a plurality of persons, as distributive justice may accidentally concern one single person.[320]

It is true, that in certain commutative justice situation—like in the case of a horse's theft—simple arithmetic equality is not sufficient, since the owner has a right to the restitution of the specific horse.[321] Vindictive justice belongs to commutative justice in two senses: in respect to the judge who, by a contract with the community, is duty-bound to impose a punishment that is proportional to the delict; in respect to the victim who suffered damage by the delict. The delinquent's duty to suffer the punishment might be viewed as part of legal justice.[322]

---

318. *Ibid.*, §§45–47, pp. 11–12. The author defends quite at length Ulpian's definition of justice against a variety of objections.

319. *Ibid.*, §63, p. 15. The author insists that the right of restitution must be based upon commutative justice and be grounded in a right of property; *ibid.*, §64, p. 16.

320. *Ibid.*, §§58–61, pp. 14–15.

321. *Ibid.*, §60: "Dominus non habet tantum ius ad equum qualemcunque, sed ad hunc in individuo, cui formaliter aequalis non est equus alius; quia per hunc non satisfit potestati ligitimae obligandi alios, ne hunc in individuo equum sine voluntate domini auferant."

322. *Ibid.*, §44, p. 11, §62, p. 15. In relation to retribution (*contrapassum*), the author distinguishes between "physical" and "moral" retribution. The former is an identical, reciprocal act, the latter takes into account the specific circumstances of the situation. Only the latter is an act of justice: "Si autem contrapassum sumatur moraliter, hoc est, si laedens, non tantum physice aequale patiatur, e.g., rusticus alapam pro alapa regi inflicta: sed moraliter aequale, id est, juxta aestimationem prudentum aequale, non alapae tantum physicae sumptae, sed sumptae moraliter, una cum dignitate regis, tunc erit contrapassum

Another theologian, who is following closely in the footsteps of Aquinas, is the Italian Dominican Daniello Concina (1687–1756).[323] Vindictive justice is part of commutative justice: punishment, applied by the judge, is measured according to the violated right of the victim.[324] Commutative justice constitutes a reward or a punishment in respect of the acts of citizens; distributive justice, to the contrary, is a distribution of benefits based upon the personal qualities of citizens.[325] The two forms of justice are of a different kind. A right under commutative justice is a strict right; under distributive justice, a mere imperfect one. However, whenever a strict right arises in a distributive-justice-situation, it is based upon commutative justice. Thus, where a person charged with distributing benefits violates his task, he is subject to a claim in commutative justice.[326] The two forms of justices, though being joined together, are essentially of a different kind.[327]

A similar view is expressed by the Belgian theologian Peter Dens (1690–1775), president of the Seminary of Mechlin.[328] It seems, however, that he considers vindictive justice to be included in both commutative and distributive justice.[329] Following the same line of ideas is the eighteenth-century

---

morale, & justitia circa hoc versabitur" (*ibid.*, §80, p. 19). The biblical *lex talionis* is limited to the cases where physical and moral retribution are identical; *ibid.*, §81.

323. D. Concina, *Theologia Christiana Dogmatico-Morale*, Tomus Septimus, *De Iustitia Et Iure* (Roma 1750) Caput IV, pp. 9–14.

324. *Ibid.*, §5, p. 10: "Iustitia denique haec ad alterum est: quia iudex alius est a persona laesa. Igitur officium quo iudex ulciscitur iniurias illatas subditis, est actus iustitiae commutantis, imperatus a iustitia generali, seu legali propter bonum commune."

325. *Ibid.*, §VII: "Iustitia commutativa respicit quid boni, aut mali subditi egerint; contra iustitia distributiva spectat quid boni, quid habilitatis, quid capacitatis candidati subditi habeant ad sustinendam dignitatem, gradum &c." An identical argument one finds in Franciscus Henno (1662–1714), *Theologia Dogmatica Moralis et Scholastica*, Tomus IV, *De Jure et Justitia, De Statu Religioso ac de Incarnatione* (Editio 15, Madrid 1795) Tract. II, Disp. 1, Quaest. 4, p. 6.

326. *Ibid.*, §X, p. 12: "Si dispensator partitionem factam diminueret ex arbitrio, si vel unum argenteum retineret post designationem factam; laederet iustitiam commutantem, & restitutioni esset obnoxius. En aequalitatem arithmeticam quam ponit iustitia commutans."

327. *Ibid.*, §XI, p. 13: "Coniunctio unius speciei cum altera non inferit, sed supponit obiectorum diversitatem. Ergo si duae sunt iustitiae species coniunctae, duae sunt iustitiae species absolute consideratae."

328. Petrus Dens, *Tractatus De Jure Et Justitia, De Contractibus In Genere, Et De Usitatioribus In Specie* (Liège 1786) 8–9.

329. *Ibid.*, 8: "Justitia particularis subdividitur in commutativam & distributivam, sub quibus etiam continetur vindicativa: est autem commutativa sola proprie dicta justitia ante definita."

German Franciscan theologian Moritz Cuer.[330] He adopts the view that both kinds of justice, commutative and distributive, can be subdivided into a rewarding justice (*praemiativa*) and a punitive one (*punitiva*).[331] An interesting comment refers to the compensating function of commutative justice. The author stipulates that in order to be compensable, the injury must be caused "unjustly." An injury is considered unjust only when caused deliberately. Hence, a completely indeliberate injury—apart from a contract—does not entail an obligation of reparation.[332]

The tripartite division of justice is also at the basis of the short discussion by the French Lazarist theologian Pierre Collet (1693–1770).[333] He illustrates, by a number of examples, situations where the violation of distributive justice is accompanied by a concomitant violation of commutative justice entailing a duty of restitution. In relation to vindictive justice, it seems that the author classifies it under the heading of distributive justice.[334]

The Premonstratensian scholar Joseph Prickartz (b. 1696), professor at the University of Cologne, affirms the correctness of the division of justice into three categories: commutative, distributive, and legal.[335] The division is based upon the difference in the respective notions of equality: arithmetic equality between the rights and duties of private or quasi private persons[336]; geometric equality between the right of private persons against the community

---

330. Mauritius Cuer, *Theologia Moralis Cum Connexis Dogmatibus*, Tomus II (L. Kemper, ed., Münster 1792) 411–415.

331. *Ibid.*, §497, p. 413, note *). The source of this idea is probably Bartolomeo Mastri da Meldula (1602–1673), *supra* at note 231.

332. *Ibid.*, §498, p. 413, note **): "Ut laesio juris alterius proprie injusta dici possit, debet esse *deliberate* posita: nam ad prorsus indeliberata dari nequit obligatio. Igitur nec alius jus habere potest, ut illa ponantur, aut omittantur. Ex hoc modo deducitur, quod damnum alteri omnino indeliberate datum, praescindendo a contractu, non inducat obligationem reparandi."

333. Petrus Collet, *Institutiones Theologicae Ad Usum Seminariorum*, Tomus Tertius (Editio Sexta, Paris 1784) *Tractatus de Justitia*, Cap. I, pp. 2–5.

334. The author opens his analysis with the statement that justice is divided into general justice (which is also called public and legal justice) and particular justice which is subdivided into commutative and distributive justice. In his conclusion he defines distributive justice as " . . .quae partibus reddit quod ipsis debitum est, tum in praemiis, tum in poenis." Its neglect by a judge can be accompanied by a duty of restitution, like the neglect of a garden by a salaried gardener (*ibid.*, 4).

335. Josephus Prickartz, *Theologia Moralis Universa*, Tomus IV, *De Jure & Justitia* (Köln 1764) 36–38.

336. The author's intention in relation to "quasi private person" are situations where the community enters into a private transaction.

in relation to common goods to be distributed; equality between the supreme right of the ruler or magistrate—for the preservation of the common welfare—in relation to the property or to the acts of the subjects and the corresponding duties of the latter. The author states that vindictive justice belongs to commutative justice and, therefore, does not constitute a fourth kind of justice.[337]

As a matter of fact, many of the modern works on moral theology reflect the scholastic discussions and controversies. The views differ on the nature of distributive justice and on the essence of the distinction between the different kinds of justice. Some authors continue to claim that only commutative justice is a strict and perfect kind of justice and that the distinction between legal, distributive, and commutative justice is not univocal, but merely analogical.[338] On the other hand, some modern authors claim—especially when dealing with the notion of social justice—that rights under distributive justice are no less stringent than those under commutative justice.[339] These authors conceive social justice to constitute part of distributive justice.[340]

---

337. *Ibid.*, 37–38: "Justitia *Vindicativa*, per quam authoritate publica puniuntur malefactores, non est quarta species, sed pertinent ad justitiam commutativam, non tantum, quia servat aequalitatem arithmeticam inter poenam, & delictum, sed magis, quia ordinatur ad reparationem injuriae per delictum malefactoris illatae, quod est officium justitiae commutativae. Deinde hujusmodi reparationem facit judex ex officio, ergo ex tacito contractu, ergo imperante justitia non alia, quam Commutativa." In a special section, the author, dealing with favoritism as the opposite of distributive justice, describes the cases where a less worthy person may legitimately be preferred over a worthier one (*ibid.*, 59 et sqq.).

338. *See, e.g.*, the French Capuchin theologian Timotheus A Podio-Luperio (Timothée de Puyloubier), *Theologia Moralis Universa*, Tomus Secundus, *De Virtutibus moralibus* (Paris 1903–1904) 200–202.

339. A.-J. Faidherbe, *La justice distributive* (Paris 1934). This author equally claims, relying on the commentary of Cajetanus (IIa–IIae, Q. 63, art. 4), that a judicial judgment is always an act of distributive justice, *ibid.*, at 97–105. However, the explanation given by Cajetanus is that the form of a judgment concerning a transaction (implying the taking and giving of personal property) belongs to distributive justice, since it is based upon the idea of a correct proportion in relation to the debt. (*Summa Totius Theologiae S. Thomae De Aquino Cum Commentariis Et Opusculis Thomae de Vio Caietani Cardinalis S. Xisti* (Venezia 1588), II–II, q. 63, art. 4, at 152a–b). This reason is very remote from the concept of social justice. For a more reserved attitude to the notion of social justice, *see* A. Tanqueray, *Synopsis Theologiae Moralis et Pastoralis, Tomus Tertius de Virtute Justitiae et de Variis Statuum Obligationibus* (ed. 10a, Paris 1936) Sect. 25–26, at 14–15.

340. But *see* C.K. Allen, *Aspects of Justice* (London 1958) 31: "But whatever 'social justice' does mean, it is certainly something very different from 'distributive justice' as Aristotle conceived it, for that was a matter of allocation of goods and privileges among a small body of free citizens, all of whom were what would today be called 'capitalists' (or perhaps 'bourgeois')." *See* especially the critical analysis—on the basis of the Thomist tradition—of

No wonder, that also in relation to punishment (*iustitia vindicativa*), the controversy on its classification continues. Many authors, among them more modern ones, tend to classify it under distributive justice, since the infliction of the penalty is proportional to the offence.[341] On the other hand, some modern Catholic authors of moral theology tend to separate the different aspects of punishment.[342]

A final comment: there can be no doubt that the Thomist tradition exercised and continues to exercise a decisive influence upon modern Catholic moral theology.[343]

---

the relationship between the concept of social justice and the Aristotelian notions of justice: N.J. Paulhus, "Uses and Misuses of the Term 'Social Justice' in the Roman Catholic Tradition," 15 (1987) *The Journal of Religious Ethics* 261; *cf. also* G. Del Vecchio, *Justice—An Historical and Philosophical Essay* (A.H. Campbell, ed., Edinburgh 1952) 37–39, note 15.

341. In this sense: the Jesuit theologian Thomas Grebner, *Philosophia Moralis Sive Ethica Et Jus Naturae Secundum Principia Orthodoxa Ad Usum Auditorum Philosophiae Accomodata* (Editio secunda, Würzburg 1761) 207; A. Vincent, *Theologia dogmatica et moralis ad mentem S. Thomae Aquinatis et S. Alphonsi di Ligorio accurate explanata auctoribus professoribus theologiae seminarii Claromontensis e Societate Sancti Sulpicii* (Ed. 5a, Paris 1889) 3, n. 1. The latter author mentions the view that, in relation to the judge acting ex officio, punishment falls under commutative justice. *See also* the discussion on distributive justice, *ibid.*, at 239–242. The author suggests that a violation of the rules of a competition for office entitles the candidate, who should have been elected, to restitution. For the view that punishment makes part of distributive justice *see also* G. de Varceno, *Compendium Theologiae Moralis ex Opere Morali Scavini, Gury et Charmes* (Ed. 11, Torino 1898) 468: "Unde justitia distributiva duplex est, nempe remunatoria, et vindicativa."

342. According to Timotheus A Podio-Luperio (Timothée de Puyloubier), *Theologia Moralis Universa*, Tomus Secundus, *De Virtutibus moralibus* (Paris 1903–1904) 202, vindictive justice makes part of distributive, legal and commutative justice: "Justitia vindicativa speciem justitiae particularem non efformat, sed ad unam ex tribus jam enumeratis reducitur. Ad distributivam nempe revocari potest, cum sit principis officium reis imponere poenas proportionatas; ad legalem, si princeps in vindicando bonum commune sibi proponat; denique ad commutativam, quatenus judex, virtute contractus cum republica initi, delicta punire tenetur. Unde non raro judex, si sit negligens aut connivens, justitiae commutativae violatae reus erit."

343. *See, e.g.*, the work of the Italian Jesuit scholar Antonius Ballerinus, *Opus Theologicum Morale In Busenbaum Medullam*, Vol. III (Absolvit et edidit Dominicus Palmieri, Prati 1890) 14–25.

FOUR

A Special Theological Problem

Divine Justice

INTERESTINGLY, THE SUBSTANCE of and the relationship between distributive and corrective justice was discussed by theologians in relation to Divinity. This discussion constituted the natural continuation of the fundamental general problem concerning the relationship between Divinity and justice. In other words, the general question was whether mankind had a legitimate claim of justice toward Divinity.

Already Aristotle had stated that it would be ludicrous to assume the existence of a divine virtue and practice of justice.[344] However, in Christianity the problem presented itself quite differently, since the Aristotelian conception of divine activity being restricted to mere contemplation contradicted the biblical tradition. The latter assumed Divinity's active intervention in human affairs and personal fates, both in this world and in the world to come. Hence, quite early the fundamental problems of the exercise of divine justice were discussed, such as the general relationship between divine and human justice, and, in particular, the vexing question of the connection between divine justice and divine mercy.

The church fathers tended to elevate the perfect divine justice highly above the human one, the latter inevitably being imperfect.[345] The problem of divine

344. EN X, 8, 1178b 10–24: "The Gods, as we conceive them, enjoy supreme felicity and happiness. But what sort of actions can we attribute to them? Just actions? But will it not seem ridiculous to think of them as making contracts, restoring deposits and the like? . . . If we go through the list we shall find that all forms of virtuous conduct seem trifling and unworthy of the Gods."

345. *See* Johannes Chrysostomus, *In Psalmum*, V, § 4, in Migne, *Patrologia Graeca*, vol. 55, p. 67; Augustinus, *Epistolae* CXX, Cap. IV. §§ 19–20, in Migne, *Patrologia Latina.*, vol. 33, p. 461–462; *Id.*, *Contra secundam Juliani responsionem*, Lib. III, Cap. 24, in Migne, *op. cit.*, vol. 45, p. 1256sq.; Gregorius Magnus, *Moralium*, Lib. V, Cap. XXXVII, § 67, in Migne, *op. cit.*, vol. 75, p. 716–717. *See also* the work of the Jesuit Cardinal Robertus Bellarminus (1542–1621), *De Controversiis Christianae Fidei, Adversus huius temporis Haereticos*, Tomus Quartus (Venezia 1599), col. 949.e: " . . . qui dicunt, sententiam Davidis esse, non posse hominem iustificari, si comparetur ad Deum, non quod non sit in homine iusto

justice, compassion and grace turned into a major subject of theological discussions.[346] Since we are exclusively concerned with the Aristotelian distinction between corrective and distributive justice, we will limit ourselves to one rather typical discussion by one of the founders of scholasticism, Anselmus, Archbishop of Canterbury (1033–1109). In a touching personal address to God he says:

> For, though it is hard to understand how your compassion is not inconsistent with your justice; yet we must believe that it does not oppose justice at all. Because it flows from goodness, which is no goodness without justice; nay, that it is in true harmony with justice. For, if you are compassionate only because you are supremely good, and supremely good only because you are supremely just, truly you are compassionate even because you are supremely just. Help me just and compassionate God, whose light I seek; help me to understand what I say. Truly, then, you are compassionate even because you are just. Is, then, your compassion born of your justice? And do you spare the wicked, therefore, out of justice? If this is true, my Lord, if this is true, teach me how it is.[347]

---

vera iustitia, si absolutem consideretur, sed quia tanta est puritas, & sublimitas iustitiae Dei, ut omnis hominum, & Angelorum iustitia, cum ea comparata, iniustitia esse videatur"; *see also ibid.*, col. 946.b. *See also* G. Del Vecchio, *Justice—An Historical and Philosophical Essay* (A.H. Campbell, ed., Edinburgh 1952) p. 5, note 2, at 13, p. 24, note 6, at 29–30. The poverty of human justice was also a topic for the Reformers; *see, e.g.*, Huldrych Zwingli, *Von götlicher und menschlicher Gerechtigheit* (Zürich 1523).

346. For a detailed discussion of the different opinions of scholastic scholars, *see* Fernandus Rebellus (1548–1608), *Opus de Obligationibus Iustitiae, Religionis et Caritatis* (Lyon 1608) Lib. 1, Quaest. 4, Sect. 1–6, pp. 25–38. On early sources suggesting a harmonization between the two concepts, *see* R. Kretschmar, *Alger von Lüttichs Traktat >De misericordia et iustitia<: Ein kanonistischer Konkordanzversuch aus der Zeit des Investiturstreits* (Sigmaringen 1985) *passim.*

347. Anselmus, *Proslogion*, Cap. IX, in Migne, *Patrologia Latina*, vol. 158, p. 232: "Nam etsi difficile sit intelligere, quomodo misericordia tua non absit a tua iustitia, necessarium tamen est credere, quia nequequam adversatur iustitiae quod exundat ex bonitate, quae nulla est sine iustitia, immo vere concordat iustitiae. Nempe si misericors es qiua es summe bonus, et summe bonus non es nisi quia es summe iustus: vere idcirco es misericors, quia summe iustus es. Adiuva me, iuste e misericors deus, cuius lucem quaero, adiuva me, ut intelligam quod dico. Vere ergo ideo misericors es, quia iustus. Ergone misericordia tua nascitur ex iustitia tua? Ergone parcis malis ex iustitia? Si sic est, domine' si sic est, doce me quamodo est." It has to be remembered that Anselm's concept of justice preceded the medieval reception of the Aristotelian notion and was, therefore, of a different nature; *cf.* M. Dreyer, "Veritas—Rectitudo—Iustitia, Grundbegriffe ethischer Reflexion bei Anselm von Canterbury," 64 (1) (1997) *Recherches de Théologie et Philosophie médiévales* 67–85. Compare in this context also the assertion by Petrus Abelardus (1079–1142): "Now it can no more be attributed to God's injustice that He does not inflict the penalty which the guilty merit than it can be the case of those who

The basic assumption is therefore that clemency makes part of divine justice.[348] However, the perfect omnipotence of God excludes the dimensions of equality and reciprocity with human beings, dimensions that underlay the concept of human justice.[349]

Many scholastic theologians denied, as did Thomas Aquinas,[350] the existence of commutative justice in relation to Divinity; they tended, however, to

---

deserve reward and are not given it"; *Abailard's Ethics* (J. Ramsay McCallum, transl., Oxford 1935, repr. New York 1976) 71.

348. See in this sense also the Franciscan Alexander Halensis (1185–1245), who follows in the steps of Anselmus of Canterbury: Alexander de Ales Anglus, *Universae Theologiae Summa* (Venezia 1576) Quaestio XXXIX, Membra 1–2, p. 98a–b. The author also deals with the question which divine intention precedes, that of justice or that of clemency? The author distinguishes between different meanings of these notions. *Cf. also* M. Zehetbauer, *Die Polarität von Gerechtigkeit und Barmherzigkeit—Ihre Wurzeln im Alten Testament im Frühjudentum sowie in der Botschaft Jesu: Konsequenzen für die Ethik* (Regensburg 1999) 354–361.

349. *See also* the discussion on the relationship between divine justice and mercy by Thomas Aquinas (1225–1274), *Summa Theologiae*, Ia, *Quaestio* 21, Art. 3–4; Ricardo de Mediavilla (Richard of Middletown) (1249–1308), *Super Quatuor Libros Sententiarum Petri Lombardi* (Brescia 1591) Lib. 4, Disp. 46, Art.1, Quaest.1; Johannes Duns Scotus (1265–1308), *Ordinatio*, 4, Disp. 46, Quaest. 1–4. On the history of the related doctrine of justification, *see* A.E. McGrath, *Justitia Dei—A History of the Christian Doctrine of Justification* (Cambridge 1986). The author, who does not deal specifically with the use of the Aristotelian notions of justice, remarks (vol. 1, at 70): "The theologians of the medieval period were convinced that God's righteousness was expressed in the manner in which he chose to redeem mankind in Christ. The difficulties associated with this understanding of the righteousness of God, particularly in connection with the correlative *iustitia Dei* and *iustitia hominis* were were never, however, fully resolved." See especially the author's discussion on the notion of the "righteousness of God" in medieval thought; *ibid.*, at 51–70. *Cf. also* G. Del Vecchio, *Justice—An Historical and Philosophical Essay* (A.H. Campbell, ed., Edinburgh 1952) p. 5, note 2 at 9, p. 24, note 6 at 30.

350. Thomas Aquinas, *Summa Theologiae*, Ia, *Quaestio* 21, Art. 1. After describing the two forms of justice, the author states that commutative justice does not relate to God: "Et haec non competit Deo, quia, ut dicit Apostolus, *Rom.* [11, 35], *Quis prior dedit illi, et retribuetur ei?*" He emphasizes that God is not anyone's debtor: "Et licet Deus hoc modo debitum alicui det, non tamen ipse est debitor, quia ipse ad alia non ordinatur, sed potius alia in ipsum." *See also id., Summa contra Gentiles*, Lib. 1, Cap. 93, §789: "Non igitur sibi competit commutativa iustitia, sed solum distributiva." In this sense already the teacher of Aquinas, Albertus Magnus (1206–1280), *Super Ethica Commentum et Quaestiones*, lib. V, in *Opera Omnia edenda curavit Institutum Alberti Magni Coloniense*, B. Geyer Praeside, Tomus XIV, Pars I (W. Kübel, ed., Münster, 1968–1972) 378, v. 15–27: "Dicendum, quod iustitia potest dupliciter considerari: vel quantum ad actus finales, sicut est in aequalitate esse et summae rectitudini adhaerere, et sic est in deo et angelis, et sic loquitur *hic* et *Plato*, si debeat sustineri, et *theologi*. Aut quantum ad actus proprios, quibus est usus iustitiae in communcationibus civilibus, et sic non est in eis iustitia. Tamen sciendum, quod *Aristoteles* vult, quod *Plato* male dixit, et loquitur contra eum, quia vult, quod deus non sit iustus civiliter, sed sit supra hoc bonum."

accept in principle the idea of divine distributive justice.[351] This was the basic approach of the Franciscan scholars Ricardo de Mediavilla (Richard of Middletown) (1249–1308)[352] and Johannes Duns Scotus (ca. 1265–1308).[353]

The important French Dominican scholar, Johannes Capreolus (ca. 1380–1444), the "Prince of the Thomists,"[354] defends—against the contrary scholastic view—the opinion of Thomas Aquinas that God is not subject to commutative justice.[355] The arguments in favor of divine commutative justice are that God's punishment is according to guilt, and His reward according to merit, and that even in cases where distributive justice criteria are applied, there is an element of commutative justice. Moreover, retribution implies commutative justice. Capreolus objects that the essence of commutative justice is the application of an arithmetic proportion, the mean between two amounts. This measure is not applied in relation to divine punishment. The punishment is not measured according to the amount that the sinner took away from God by his guilt. It is not according to a comparison between punishment and guilt, but according to the proportion between two sins and two punishments: who sins more is punished more. This is rather like distributive justice applying a geometric proportion between things and persons. In the same way, rewards for merits are according to a geometric proportion, since the person who has more merits gets a greater reward than the person with fewer merits.[356] Moreover, the merits of the just in this world are substantially far from being an equivalent to the divine reward of eternal life.[357]

In relation to Thomas Aquinas, the Dominican Cardinal Thomas de Vio Cajetanus (1469–1534) raises in his commentaries on Aquinas's *Summa*

---

351. *Cf.* Thomas Aquinas, *Summa contra Gentiles, ibid.*

352. Ricardo de Mediavilla (Richard of Middletown) (1249–1308), *Super Quatuor Libros Sententiarum Petri Lombardi* (Brescia 1591) Lib. 4, Disp. 46, Art. 2, Quaest. 1–3, at 619–622.

353. *See supra* 35; *cf.* G. Del Vecchio, *Justice—An Historical and Philosophical Essay* (A.H. Campbell, ed., Edinburgh 1952) 12.

354. On Capreolus's work in general, *see John Capreolus On The Virtues* (transl. K. White and R. Cessario, O.P., Washington 2001) XI–XXXV, Foreword and Translators' Introduction.

355. Johannes Capreolus, *Quaestiones in IV libros Sententiarum, seu libri IV defensionum theologiae Thomae Aquinatis* (Venezia 1483–1484), Lib. I, Distinctio 45, Quaest. 1, pp. 701–703.

356. *Ibid.*

357. *See* the author's lengthy discussion on the basis of the reward of the just, *ibid.*, Lib.II, Distinctio XXVII, pp. 560–567. On his attempt to reconcile the apparent contradictory statements of Aquinas, *see infra* note 361.

Theologiae[358] the problem of an apparent contradiction between that author's statement in one place that commutative justice does not belong to God,[359] and the statement elsewhere that divine punishment is based on commutative justice.[360]

Cajetanus argues that Aquinas excludes, in relation to God, commutative justice in its strict sense, namely that which relates to transactional equality between the giving and the acceptance. There can be no such equality between Divinity and man, since *a priori* everything belongs to the former. However, in God's acts of distribution there can be an element of commutative justice, as in punishing offenders according to their crime, or in rewarding the meritorious according to their merits. Hence, there is no contradiction in Aquinas's two statements. It appears that Cajetanus considers divine punishment to be an act of distributive justice with a mode of commutative justice mixed into it.[361]

But, again, the attribution of distributive justice to Divinity depends ultimately on the existence of a duty. Thus, it has been argued by the French Dominican theologian Durandus of Saint-Pourçain (ca. 1275–1334) that since in relation to distributive justice the duty to apply it arises out of commutative

---

358. *Summa Totius Theologiae S. Thomae De Aquino Cum Commentariis Et Opusculis Thomae de Vio Caietani Cardinalis S. Xisti* (Venezia 1588) I, q. 21, art. 1, at 89a; II–II, q. 61, art. 4, at 142b–143a.

359. *Summa Theologiae,* Ia, *Quaestio* 21, Art. 1, *supra* n.350.

360. *Summa Theologiae,* II–II, *Quaestio* 61, Art. 4: "Ad primum ergo dicendum quod illa forma divini iudicii attenditur secundum rationem commutativae iustitiae, prout scilicet recompensat praemia meritis et supplicia peccatis." *Cf. also ibid.*, II–II, Quaest. 80, Art. 1, 108, Art. 2; IIIa, Quaest. 85, Art. 3.

361. *Ibid.*, II–II, Quaest. 61, Art. 4, at 142b–143a. There have been a number of alternative explanations of the apparent contradiction in Aquinas's writings: Johannes Capreolus (ca. 1380–1444), *Quaestiones in IV libros Sententiarum, seu libri IV defensionum theologiae Thomae Aquinatis* (Venezia 1483–1484), Lib.II, Distinctio XXVII, pp. 560–567. This author distinguishes between two views of merits; one that measures merit substantially, the other does it under the aspect of grace. In the former sense, there is no equality whatsoever between the reward of eternal life and the merit; hence no commutative justice. In the latter sense, by the grace of God, there is not an actual but an essential equality between merit and reward; hence the grant of eternal life constitutes a divine act of commutative justice. The Spanish Augustinian Petrus de Aragon (1545–1592), *In Secundam Secundae Divi Thomae Doctoris Angelici Commentaria.De Iustitia Et Iure* (Lyon 1596) Quaest. LXI, Art. IV, pp. 90–91, strongly objects to the explanation of Johannes Capreolus; he disagrees also with that of Cajetanus. In his view, relying on De Soto, divine reward is based upon distributive justice, divine punishment upon commutative justice. *See also* on this problem relating to Aquinas, Franciscus Suárez (1548–1617), *De Justitia Dei, Varia Opuscola Theologica, Operum Tomus Decimus* (Venezia 1741) Sect. III, §§33–35, pp. 311–312; Hurtadus De Mendoza (1578–1651), *Disputationes de Homine sive de Incarnatione Filii Dei* (Antwerpen 1634) Disp. 12, Sect.16, §§273, p. 125.

justice, one cannot properly speak in relation to Divinity of distributive justice.[362]

Thus, the Spanish Dominican scholar Francisco de Vitoria (ca. 1483–1546) observes that it is particularly doubtful whether God, when rewarding the good and punishing the evil, exercises distributive or commutative justice.[363] Indeed, God rewards beyond merit and punishes below the due. He mentions the opinion of Thomas Aquinas that commutative justice does not belong to God. De Vitoria argues that God does not have any duties toward men. But one can say that God owes the duty to Himself to reward the good, and therefore He, so to speak, exercises justice. But in God there is rather distributive justice than commutative justice, since He concedes us much more than we merit, and punishes less than our sins demand. It is not commutative justice based on equality, but distributive justice, since there is more of grace than of merit.[364]

Following closely in the steps of Thomas Aquinas is equally the Spanish Dominican scholar Domingo Báñez (1528–1604), professor of theology at Salamanca. Accordingly, in relation to God there is no commutative justice, but only distributive justice. Since God remains the absolute master of all, He can do no wrong even if He would annihilate everything.[365]

A different approach was adopted by the Jesuit scholar Gregorius de Valentia (1550–1603). In his view, there are two dimensions to the awarding of eternal life to the just: one of distributive justice and one of commutative justice. The measuring of the award according to the merits of the just applies

---

362. Durandus de S. Porciano, *In Petri Lombardi Sententias Theologicas Commentariorum Libri 4* (Venezia 1571) Lib. 4, Disp. 46, Quaest. 1, at 407b–408: "Et confirmatur, quia iustitia distributiva saltem propriem dicta ortum habet ex commutativa, ut dictum fuit, sed talis iustitia distributiva non potest in Deo ortum habere ex commutativa, ergo etc."

363. Francisco de Vitoria, *De justitia*, vol. 1 (V. Beltrán de Heredia, O.P., ed. Madrid 1934) 2.2, q. LXI, art. 2.

364. *Ibid. See also* the careful discussion of that topic by the Jesuit Cardinal De Lugo (1583–1660), *De Iustitia et Iure* (Lyon 1652), Tom. 1, Disp. 1, Sect. 3, nn. 60–61 p. 17. In that author's view, God applies distributive justice, but without being bound by it. *See supra* 51.

365. Dominicus Bañes, *Scholastica Commentaria In Primam Partem Angelici Doctoris S. Thomae. Usque Ad LXIIII Quaestionem*, Tomus Primus (Douai 1614) 259. The author rejects the view of some scholatics that God, by refusing to accept the atonement of sins by Christ, would be unjust: "Primo quia D. Tho. expresse docet, quod in Deo non est iustitia commutativa, sed solum distributiva, ergo nulli potest facere iniuriam. Patet consequentia. Quia nulli potest obligari. Item quia quantumlibet Deus conferat gratiae, virtutum, & meritorum alicui, semper ipse Deus manet dominus absolutus omnium, ergo si cuncta annihilaverit, nulli facit iniuriam."

the proportional criterion characteristic of distributive justice. On the other hand, the award of eternal life is based upon a promise of God, and therefore—given the preconditions of the promise—it is His duty to confer it, and the right of the just to obtain it. This is an application of commutative justice. The author deals with the argument that the reward of eternal life exceeds the objective value of the good deeds' merits and is therefore an act of grace. His response is that God's promise includes this excess of reward and therefore it becomes binding upon Him and constitutes thus an integral part of commutative justice. He supports his conclusion by means of an example: Assuming that a prince determines by law the price of a good higher than its actual value, this price will avail in the transaction between the citizens.[366]

In the view of the Jesuit Cardinal Robertus Bellarminus (1542–1621), Divinity exercises—when granting eternal life to the just in recompense of their good deeds—both distributive and commutative justice. But there is a difference: The substance of God's judgment is distributive justice; the form of it commutative justice. The substance is distributive justice because the recompense is strictly according to merit; God does not unjustly prefer any person. On the other hand, the form of the judgment is commutative justice because God not only grants recompense proportionally to the measure of the individual merit (which constitutes distributive justice), but there is a strict equality between the measure of the merit and that of the recompense (which constitutes commutative justice).

The author claims that even in the framework of distributive justice, there must be a promise of God. Generally, distributive justice does not require a promise. But this is true only where common goods are distributed. In case of private property, there is a need of a promise or contract. Since God distributes not common goods, but what belongs to Him, the recompense is based upon a promise.[367]

The contemporary Jesuit scholar Francisco Suárez (1548–1617) dedicated a special work to the question of divine justice on the background of

---

366. Gregorius de Valentia, *Commentarii Theologici, Tomus Secundus, Primae Secundae Divi Thomae* (Ingolstadt 1593) Disp. 8, Quaest. 6, pp. 1381–1384.

367. Robertus Bellarminus (1542–1621), *De Controversiis Christianae Fidei, Adversus huius temporis Haereticos*, Tomus Quartus (Venezia 1599), col. 983, d-984, e. The views of Cardinal Bellarminus were severely attacked and criticized by the English Protestant (Puritan) scholar, William Ames (1576–1633), professor of theology at the Dutch University of Franeker in Friesland: *Bellarminus Enervatus, sive Disputationes Anti-Bellarminiae*, Tomus Quartus (Amsterdam 1628), Liber Septimus, *De Meritis*, 193–218. Ames relies extensively on scholastic literature and biblical sources.

the Aristotelian distinction.[368] He starts mentioning the dominant view that excludes in relation to God the strict notion of justice;[369] thus, all theologians deny especially the applicability of commutative justice to Divinity.[370]

In relation to distributive justice, Suárez mentions the view that this form of justice, too, is inapplicable to God, since He rewards the just for their own, specific merits, and not in a proportional way by comparison to the merits of others.[371] The same argument is voiced in relation to punishment, which again resembles more commutative justice.[372] Suárez contests the validity of these arguments. The Holy Scriptures have more weight than the reasons of human philosophy. God's justice, unlike human justice, is comprehensively perfect; it is higher and more eminent.[373] When God grants goods to creatures, the universal and superior ownership of them remains nevertheless with Him; the situation resembles, by way of example, the particular ownership of citizens to property, a right that may coexist with the superior, sublime ownership retained by the state.[374]

---

368. Franciscus Suarez, *De Justitia Dei, Varia Opuscola Theologica, Operum Tomus Decimus* (Venezia 1741) 285–323.

369. Among the authors he mentions Duns Scotus (4, Disp. 46, Quaest. 1), who bases God's action on his kindness (*bonitas*) and will.

370. Among these authors he counts: Thomas Aquinas, Cajetanus, Durandus, Richardus, Soto. Suárez repeats in this connection the known argument that denies the possibility of rendering unto God any benefit, since everything belongs to Him; *ibid.*, Sect. I, §3, pp. 285–286. Hence, like a father cannot oblige himself toward his unemancipated son, nor a master toward his slave, God cannot render anything to a creature under a duty of commutative justice; *ibid*, §4.

371. *Ibid.*, §5, p. 286: "Non enim promittit Deus unicuique dare secundum proportionem ad alios, vel secundum merita sua: ergo retributio illa fit secundum proportionem rei ad rem: id est meriti ad praemium: & non secundum proportionem ad alios: sed si haec resultet, est quasi per accidens ad talem distributionem: ergo ibi non intervenit vera iustitia distributiva, quae per se respicit talem proportionem."

372. *Ibid.*, §6, p. 286. Among the scholars who adopt this opinion, Suárez counts: Alensis, Bonaventura, Duns Scotus, Durandus, Paludanus.

373. *Ibid.*, §17, p. 288: "Quocirca, quamvis, discurrendo per species humanae justitiae nulla posset in Deo salvari secundum formalem rationem ejus, nihilominus negandum non esset rationem formalem justitiae, ut sic, formaliter in Deo reperiri: quae in eo non esset talis, qualis humana, sed altior, & eminentior; complectens quidquid perfectionis est in humana, & imperfectiones excludens." The author adds that divine justice differs from human justice, like divine knowledge, logic and mathematics differ from the imperfect human ones.

374. *Ibid.*, §12, p. 287.

The author claims—against other scholars—that divine justice constitutes a specific and proper attribute of Divinity, distinct from the attributes of fidelity, charity, and compassion.[375]

The author then proceeds to elaborate upon the particular features of distributive and commutative justice, rejecting from the start Buridan's opinion that denied the distinction between them *in specie*.[376] The definition of commutative justice is, as mentioned above, the following: The constant and perpetual will to give everybody his own full right, i.e., what is his specific property or what morally is its equivalent.[377] The traditional opinion, that denies the reality of commutative justice in respect of God, relies on the specific human relationship with all its imperfections. Between human beings, commutative justice arises from transactions, voluntary and involuntary. But, formally, it is enough for the existence of commutative justice that the criterion of equivalence between things is applied, without having regard to the material circumstances that gave rise to the duty. Moreover, there is no need that the transactions took place between human beings: They can be made also between angels. Thus Lucifer and Michael can be held to duties under commutative justice. True, human beings cannot cause injuries to angels, but conversely the angels are capable of damaging the former. They can, therefore, be held to abstain from it under strict commutative justice.[378] Concerning human beings, they can—contrary to the opinion of scholars—do wrong (*injuria*) to Divinity under commutative justice. Even if the wrong cannot injure Divinity or the proper use of things, it nevertheless can detract from external benefits that relate to honor, glory, or esteem.[379] The person who injured God in this way is duty-bound not only to give Him satisfaction, but equally to repair the damage; this is the sign of commutative justice.[380]

375. *Ibid.*, §§20–25, pp. 288–290.

376. *Supra* at note 89.

377. *Ibid.*, Sect. II, §2, p. 292: "Nam, sicut justitia definitur, quod sit constans & perpetua voluntas, jus suum unicuique tribuens, ita justitia commutativa definiri potest, quod sit constans & perpetua voluntas unicuique tribuens jus suum proprium, id est, tale, ut vel sit proprium dominium rei, vel illi moraliter aequivaleat." The author affirms that this definition, even if differently worded, corresponds in its substance to the traditionally accepted one; *ibid.*, §5, p. 293.

378. *Ibid.*, §8, pp. 293–294.

379. *Ibid.*, §11, p. 294.

380. *Ibid.*, §12, p. 295: "At vero, si quis cum effectu talem injuriam in Deum intulit, quae in re ipsa damnum reliquit in bonis externis Dei reparabile per actionem ejusdem hominis,

Correspondingly, where a person promises something to God by means of a vow, it creates a strict, commutative-justice-obligation. There is no need that the promise confers a real benefit upon God: it is enough that it relates to His service and honor.[381]

Basically, commutative justice does not require an equivalence of a mutual giving and accepting. Thus, a promise of giving a gift confers eventually a full commutative justice right upon the promisee, without the latter being bound to reciprocate.[382]

However, in relation to the reward of the just, God is exercising commutative justice based upon the equivalence of mutual giving and taking (*secundum aequalitatem dati & accepti*): The just person offers merit and receives reward, offers penitence and receives pardon. There is no need that what the human being gives God is something that is of any utility to God; it is enough that it is given in His glory and according to His will.[383]

But in order for God to have a duty under commutative justice, there must precede an explicit promise or agreement by Him. Without such promise or agreement, no duty in justice can arise.[384]

In respect of distributive justice, God exercises it in relation to the reward of the just. The fact that the reward is measured according to the individual merit, and that its resource with Divinity is unlimited—this fact does not detract from the reward being measured comparatively according to a geometric proportion.[385]

It appears, therefore, that Divinity, in rewarding the just, applies at the same time both commutative and distributive justice. The author then attempts to explain the background and possibility of that situation: The reward of the just belongs to commutative justice, to the extent that he confers, with the grace of God, something worthy of reward, based upon an agreement or contract. However, God as a debtor cannot be subject to a strict duty like human beings,

---

relinquitur obligatio non solum ad satisfaciendum Deo pro injuria allata, sed etiam ad reparandum damnum illud, quod est signum propriae justitiae commutativae."

381. *Ibid.*, §17, p. 296.

382. *Ibid.*, §§19–21, pp. 290–291.

383. *Ibid.*, §34, p. 300: "Neque enim ad rationem justae commutationis necesse est, ut quod datur, in utilitatem cedat alterius, sed satis est quod fiat secundum exigentia voluntatis eijus, si alias habet aequalitatem cum mercedem."

384. *Ibid.*, §§39–41, p. 301; for an additional analysis of the problem, *see also ibid.*, Sect. VI, §§7–10, pp. 321–322.

385. *Ibid.*, Sect. III, §§23–26, p. 310.

since a human being's right is subject to a higher right or to the highest property right that God has in every creature and in every right of creatures. As a result, God cannot be coerced from the outside to implement that right; He will be inclined to do it only out of His intrinsic rectitude. Since the right of the just lacks the rigor of a strict right, it falls under distributive justice. The conclusion is that this justice of God belongs, formally and eminently, to both commutative and distributive justice.[386] The author ends his analysis by affirming that the duty of God under distributive justice has equally to be based upon an explicit promise or agreement.[387]

The author then dedicates a special section to the issue of Divinity's vindictive (punitive) justice.[388] He repeats his view that punishing a delinquent person by human justice is an act of commutative justice, not intrinsically from the viewpoint of the defendant, but because of the official duty of the judge toward the state to exercise his judicial function.[389] His conclusion in relation to Divinity is that punishing the sinners does not involve any kind of commutative justice. One cannot say that the sinner has a right to the punishment; it is rather to be subjected to another's right of punishing. Since God is the supreme master over the person, He may punish him at His will. If God does not punish beyond the measure, it is not the result of commutative justice, but of His benignity, compassion, and love toward His creature. God is equally the supreme governor and, therefore, not obliged to punish under a notion of (external) commutative justice, especially so, because of His being also the supreme master of all. Finally, there is no binding promise of rendering evil for evil. Hence, no kind of commutative justice is involved in this divine vindication.[390]

The author then refers to the opinion of a number of scholars—among them: Capreolus, Cajetanus, and Richardus—that divine punishment is a matter of distributive justice. Suárez rejects this opinion on the mentioned ground that the delinquent has no right to the punishment, since its omission constitutes only an injury to the state. Hence, the punitive action as such does

386. *Ibid.*, §§31–32, p. 311: "Justitia autem divina respectu unius & eiusdem iuris secundum diversas considerationes eius habet rationem commutativae & distributivae."

387. *Ibid.*, §§35–37, pp. 312–313: "Et ratio est eadem, quam saepe tetigimus: quia Deus absque promissione non potest constitui debitor simpliciter, ita ut sit iniustus negando debitum: iustitia autem propria de qua locuti sumus talis est, ut hanc necessitatem debiti includat."

388. *Ibid.*, Sect. V, §§1–20, pp. 317–320.

389. *Ibid.*, §9, pp. 317–318.

390. *Ibid.*, §§10–11, p. 318.

not belong to distributive justice. God is not subject to a proper duty of justice, except if it is founded upon a promise or agreement. However, divine punishment is not based upon a promise, but rather upon a menace.[391]

Suárez concludes that divine punishment is based upon a special notion of divine justice, called by him "providential justice" (*justitia providentialis*).[392] This kind of justice corresponds to the Aristotelian "legal" or "universal" justice that is relevant in human affairs. This divine justice does not exclude the application of arithmetic and geometric proportions in meting out punishment or in rewarding the just. However, the form of distributive justice (geometric proportion in comparison to other persons) is more common in rewarding the just, than in punishing the sinners, where the ordinary form is that of commutative justice (arithmetic proportion between punishment and sin).[393] Yet, in determining the measure of punishment, a comparison between guilts is appropriate.[394]

The Dutch-born Jesuit theologian Martin Van der Beek (1563–1624), professor of divinity in Mainz and confessor of Emperor Ferdinand II in Vienna, mentions briefly, in relation to the divine reward of eternal life, the contrasting opinions of Durandus (commutative justice), De Soto (distributive justice), and Cajetan (a combination of both kinds of justice).[395] The author tends to accept the latter view. God not only grants each person as much reward as he merits—which is a form of commutative justice—but the person with greater merit receives a greater reward, which is a form of distributive justice. However, it is not a case of rigorous commutative justice, since the merit of the just is based upon grace and a free divine promise. Moreover, according to the common opinion of scholastics, God remunerates the merits of the just beyond worthiness (*supra condignum*).[396]

---

391. *Ibid.*, §15, p. 319: "Haec autem promissio, quae specialem obligationem justitiae inducat, non habet locum proprie in inflictione poenarum: & ideo potius comminatio, quam promissio dici solet. Nam si consideretur respectu illius, cui Deus poenam comminatur, non potest inducere obligationem, cum talis inflictio sit illi involuntaria, cui libenter cederet, si posset."

392. *Ibid.*, §16, p. 319. The author calls it alternatively "*justitia gubernativa*." On the foundation of this concept, *see ibid.*, Sect. IV, §§8–12, pp. 314–316.

393. *Ibid.*, §17, p. 319.

394. *Ibid.*, §18, pp. 319–320.

395. Martinus Becanus, *SummaeTheologiae Scholasticae, De Beatudine & actibus humanis, Peccatis, Legibus, Gratia, Iustificatione, & merito*, Pars Secunda (Paris 1620) 938, 940.

396. *Ibid.*

The Italian Jesuit theologian Francesco Pavone (1569–1637) deals in his treatise on ethics briefly with the problem of divine justice.[397] He affirms that in Divinity there is legal, distributive, and commutative justice. God distributes gifts to the creatures according to their dignity and merits applying a geometric proportion. Commutative justice is exercised on the basis of a contract that God sometimes enters into with His creatures promising rewards for actions. Divine commutative justice is equally applied in relation to punishments for misdeeds.[398]

The Flemish Jesuit and exegete, Cornelis Cornelissen van den Steen (1567–1637), professor of Holy Scripture at Louvain and later in Rome, deals with the problem of divine justice in his famous *Commentary on the Epistles of St. Paul.*[399] His starting point is that according to the Scriptures, there is in God vindictive, distributive, and commutative justice. God punishes the damned and the sinners; He distributes glory to the blessed and rewards a recompense for the good deeds. However, there exists no formal, perfect, and absolute duty in God, neither of vindictive nor of distributive justice, and even much less of commutative justice. These kinds of strict duties can exist only between equal human beings. God is the absolute owner of everything and cannot bind Himself by a strict duty of justice. God's duty is based upon His truth and faithfulness. But the duty is nevertheless a kind of commutative justice, like the duty between father and son, where the father promised a recompense for good actions. God promised reward not for free, but in exchange of good deeds and merits, and therefore it is a debt of justice. The duty in justice does not detract from God's supreme dominion, since He could always rescind His promise without doing wrong. But being faithful and steady in His promises, He will keep, because of His infinite benignity,

397. Franciscus Pavonius, *Summa Ethicae: Sive Introductio In Aristotelis, Et Theologorum Doctrinam Moralem* (Oxford 1633), Disp. 3, Quaest. 2, Prop. 10, col. 331–335.

398. *Ibid.*, col. 333–334: "Est ergo in Deo tum Justitia legalis, quatenus tribuit creaturis ob bonum universi ea, quae creaturarum naturae exigunt, quae exigentia est lex naturalis; tum Justitia distributiva, quatenus unicuique creaturae tribuit ex suis bonis dona secundum uniuscujusque dignitatem, & meritum, servando in distributione proportionem Geometricam: tum Justitia commutativa, quatenus ex pacto quod interdum ob suam bonitate Deus init cum suis creaturis, reddit ratione actionum sibi a suis creaturis exhibitarum iuxta pactum initum, praemium illis actionibus debitum, servando quandam proportionem arithmeticam; quatenus culpas vindicat, & poenas peccantibus iniungit secundum demerita; quatenus suis legibus, & praeceptis iubet, ac ipse curat ut fiat iustum commutativum inter homines."

399. Cornelius Cornelii A Lapide, *Commentaria In Omnes Divi Pauli Epistolas* (Antwerpen 1635), *Commentaria in II. Epist. ad Timotheum*, Cap. IV, 801–802.

this obligation and debt of justice out of His free will. Between us and God is a kind of agreement creating a kind of a commutative-justice-obligation that is less strict than that existing between men.[400]

The French scholar François Du Bois (1581–1648) equally argues that nothing prevents it to consider God as being bound by justice to reward the just with eternal life for their good deeds.[401] Moreover, the author claims that God may be subject to commutative justice as a result of a promise made by Him, though the basic relationship between Him and His creatures differs from that prevailing between men. Men are mutually independent and can act as exclusive owners of property. In contrast, men are dependent upon Divinity who is the real owner of all property. Hence, commutative justice in human transactions has some specific characteristics that are absent in relation to divine rewards. But the latter can nevertheless be conceived as falling under the real notion of commutative justice.[402]

The Irish Jesuit scholar Peter Wadding (1581–1644) also arrived at an identical conclusion, claiming that it results from the Scriptures and from the definitions of the Council of Trent (1545–1563).[403] He argues that upon those, who deny the application of commutative justice in relation to Divinity, lays the burden of proof of demonstrating that the relevant texts of the Scripture have to be given a different sense. In his view, they failed in this task.

A similar view was adopted by the Spanish Jesuit scholar Pedro Hurtado de Mendoza (1578–1651), professor of theology and philosophy at Valladolid and Salamanca.[404] In addition to the traditional argument that Divinity can create, by an explicit promise of His, a right-duty relationship falling under

---

400. *Ibid.*

401. Franciscus Sylvius, *Commentarii in Totam Primam Secundae S. Thomae Aquinatis*, Tomus Secundus (Venezia 1726), Quaest. 114, Art. 3, Quaeritur 5, Concl. 1, p. 632. This seems to be also the conclusion of the Flemish theologian Johannes Wiggers (1571–1639), *In Tertiam Partem Divi Thomae Aquinatis Commentaria* (Louvain 1631), Quaest. 19, Dubium Quintum, p. 158, n. 52. The author deals at length with the (intertrinitarian) relationship between Christ's merits and God's justice; *ibid.*, 152–164. In the course of his arguments in favor of a strict justice relationship, he observes that according to the Scripture, the reward of the Saints is based upon justice. He does, however, not mention in this context the two kinds of justice.

402. *Ibid.*, Concl. 2–3, pp. 632–633.

403. Petrus Wadingus, *Tractatus De Contractibus In Genere, Et In Specie* (Graz 1644) 212–220. The author was professor of theology teaching at Louvain, Antwerp, Prague, and Graz.

404. Petrus Hurtadus De Mendoza, *Disputationes de Homine sive de Incarnatione Filii Dei* (Antwerpen 1634) Disp. 12, Sect. 17, §§273–291. The author affirms that commutative justice relates also to God: "Dico igitur in Deo esse iustitiam commutativam

commutative justice,[405] the author claims that there are other possible divine acts that belong to this category. Thus, let us take as an example Anton being a debtor of Peter for a certain sum of money. Now assume that God, out of His free will, gives Peter this amount of money for Anton's sake. God did not owe this payment to Peter, hence there was no debt of His. Nevertheless, in the author's view, the payment of the debt was an act of commutative justice, since it freed Anton from his debt that he owed to Peter.[406]

The Italian Jesuit scholar Francesco Amico (1578–1651), in a lengthy discussion of the various contrasting scholastic views, arrives at a negative conclusion: Between man and Divinity there can be no perfect, formal justice relationship.[407] The reasons for the absence of commutative justice are that between man and God there is no perfect legal independence (*alteritas iurium*) nor equality, no perfect duty of God toward man to fulfill an obligation (*perfectum debitum retribuendi ex parte debitoris*), and no perfect right of man to demand that fulfillment (*perfectum ius exigendi ex parte creditoris*).[408] Since man is the creation of God, everything belongs to Him, and hence even by agreement no perfect legal right (of remuneration) can be created.[409] The author equally denies the existence

---

propriè & absque metaphora. Haec autem iustitia non est commercialis, quam solam negaverunt antiqui." (*Ibid.*, §274, p. 125).

405. *Ibid.*, §§281–291, pp. 127–128. On the other hand, the author insists that human ownership is effective only as against other human beings; in relation to Divinity, all human property is subject to the latter's dominium, since everything belongs to Him. Hence God is free to use anyone's property, but he cannot without injustice deny the property rights of an owner as against other human beings (*ibid.*, §§284–291, pp. 127–128.

406. *Ibid.*, 125–126, §§274–280.

407. Franciscus Amicus, *Cursus Theologici Tomus Quintus De Iure et Iustitia* (Antwerpen 1650), Disp. XI, *De iustitia*, Sect. 16–17, pp. 145–153. The author, however, admits an analogical, nonformal concept of justice between man and Divinity: "Concedenda est Deo propria iustitia: sistendo in communissimo & analogico conceptu propriae iustitiae, prout a metaphorica distinguitur: & sine temeritate negari non potest, propter Scripturas, qua passim Deo iustitiam tribuunt" (at 146). He affirms: "Probabo 1. in Deo ad creaturam perfectam iustitiam esse non posse. 2. nec in creatura ad Deum 3. consequenter inferam, nullam speciem perfectae iustitiae, commutativae, neque distributivae, neque legalis in Deo erga hominem, aut in homine erga Deum reperiri" (at 148). Interestingly, the author distinguishes sharply between analogical justice and metaphorical justice, denying the latter notion in regard of God. *See also ibid.*, 153–154. He uses the notion of "iustitia potestativa."

408. *Ibid*, 148–152.

409. "Deducitur 1. inter Deum & homines non esse iustitiam commutativam, quia haec requirit perfectam alteritatem iurium, & debitum in activo iure creditoris fundatum; sed neque in Deo tale debitum, neque in nobis talis alteritas iurium esse potest: ergo unde ubicunque de hac iustitia disputat S. Tho. 1. p. q. 21. art.1, 1. con. gen. cap. 43. in 4. dist. 46, art. 1, ad. 1. qu. illam Deo simpliciter negat, & solum eam concedit secundum

of formal distributive justice in Divinity.[410] He rejects the view of Suárez, according to which God exercises simultaneously formal commutative and distributive justice. Francesco Amico objects that it is impossible to assume simultaneously a perfect, commutative justice obligation and an imperfect distributive one.[411] One excludes the other. Concerning the view of Thomas Aquinas, who admits that God exercises distributive justice, the author suggests that Aquinas did not consider the distributive obligation, but rather the geometric proportion that underlies the recompense of merits.[412]

The French Jesuit scholar Louis de Mairat of Troyes discusses, too, at a considerable length the problem of divine justice.[413] He denies the possibility of a strict right relationship between God and the human beings. He relies on the traditional grounds of Divinity's absolute ownership over human beings and, as a result, the absence of a perfect "otherness" between God and His creatures. In his view, even an explicit promise of God does not create a strict duty of His, since He remains the absolute owner of everything.[414] For the same reason, commutative justice has no place between God and human beings, since God remains the absolute owner of everything, even after any transaction. Moreover, God cannot be awarded a benefit, nor can He suffer damage. Hence, the basic elements of commutative justice are lacking.[415] The author equally denies the existence of strict distributive justice between God and human beings.

---

aliquem modum similitudinis: qui in eo consistit, quod sicut unus homo compensat, quod ab alio accepit secundum aequalitatem mercedis ad laborem; ita Deus compensat opera nostra facta ad ipsius gloriam, secundum aequalitatem praemij ad meritum, sine debito tamen legali ex parte sua, & alteritate iuris ex parte nostra" (at 152).

410. *Ibid.*, 152–153: "In Deo non esse iustitiam distributivam, constat, quia haec supponit debitum ortum ex iure activo creditoris, sed in Deo tale debitum esse non potest, ergo nec talis iustitia, cum ergo Deus distribuit praemia meritis, aut supplicia peccatis, vel adaptat vitutes rebus iuxta earum exegentiam, non facit actum iustitiae distributivae, sed providentiae, aut specialis, ut in retributione donorum supernat. aut generalis; ut in collatione proprietatum naturalium, & punitione peccatorum; quia non facit ex debito orto ex iure activo creaturae, sed vel ex decentia suae bonitatis, vel ex liberali sua promissione."

411. *Ibid.*, 153.

412. *Ibid.*: "Dico: S. Tho. in iustitia distributiva, non tam considerasse debitum distribuentis, quam geometricam proportionem rerum distribuendarum . . . quia licet Deus sine vitio possit uni potius, quam alteri ultra merita retribuere, id tamen non facit, sed semper retribuit iuxta meritorum proportionem."

413. Ludovicus Maeratius, *Disputationes in Summam Theologicam S. Thomae*, Tomus Secundus, Tractatus de Iustitia et Iure (Paris 1633) Disp. XIV, pp. 517–531.

414. *Ibid.*, Sect. II–III, pp. 518–523.

415. *Ibid.*, Sect. IV, pp. 523–525.

The contrary conclusion is suggested by the Jesuit scholar of Spanish extraction, Juan de Dicastillo (1584–1653).[416] He explicitly follows the view of Suárez that subjects God to commutative justice on the basis of a promise of His.[417] He accepts in this respect the arguments of Suárez and uses them against those scholastics who deny the existence of commutative justice in relation to Divinity. Thus, commutative justice does not require an exact equivalence between the benefits exchanged.[418] Moreover, the fact that God is the absolute owner of all things does not detract from the possibility of a legal relationship with human beings. In relation to distributive justice, the author equally tends to recognize it in relation to Divinity on the basis of a promise or agreement.[419]

The contemporary Irish Franciscan scholar Anthony Hickey (Antonius Hiquaeus) (1586–1641), in his commentary on Duns Scotus,[420] follows in a lengthy discussion Thomas Aquinas's above-mentioned view that commutative justice cannot be, simply speaking, in Divinity.[421] The complete lack of equality between man and God prevents the existence of a strict duty.[422] The situation remains the same even in case of an explicit promise. Since all and everything belongs to God, nothing can be given to Him, and no duty can arise of His giving something back in exchange. Hence the right arising out of God's promise is merely based on His benevolence, faithfulness, and truthfulness; it cannot be in the nature of a strict right. Moreover, man as a creature of God lacks independence, "otherness" (*alteritas*), and is, therefore, incapable of acquiring property from Him. Similarly, a father or master, in order to validly transfer ownership in property to a son or to a slave, the latter must have the

---

416. Ioannes De Dicastillo, *De Iustitia Et Iure Ceterisque Virtutibus Cardinalibus Libri Duo* (Antwerpen 1641) Lib. II, Tract. I, Disput. II, Dub. II, pp. 162–166. The author, born in Naples, served as professor of theology in Toledo, Murcia, and Vienna.

417. *Ibid.*, 162, §47: "Porro retributionem meritorum in Deo proprie esse actum Iustitiae commutativae, multorum sententia est; & quamvis magna ex parte videatur quaestio vocum, mihi maxime placet haec sententia, quam late contra Vasquez probat Suarez."

418. *Ibid.*, 163, §51: "Quamvis enim opera nostra ipsi Deo nihil prosint; cedunt tamen in illius honorem, & obsequium, & in utilitatem boni communis, cuius curam habet Deus."

419. *Ibid.*, 166, §63: "Ulterius, quod attinet ad Iustitiam distributivam, probabilius existimo esse in Deo, supposita promissione, & pacto. Quo posito fit Deus debitor." The author is, however, of the opinion that the geometric proportion is not essential to distributive justice.

420. Johannes Duns Scotus, *Quaestiones in libro IV sententiarum*, in *Opera Omnia*, t. 10 (Lyon 1639) Lib. 4, Dist. 46, Quaest. 1, pp. 243–251.

421. *Supra* 81, at note 350.

422. *Ibid.*, 244: "Nulla potest esse aequalitas inter nos, & Deum, quam exigit iustitia commutativa stricte sumpta."

capacity of acquiring rights on their own. This capacity can be obtained by manumissio in case of a slave, or by emancipatio in case of a son. Thus, e.g., a Franciscan monk cannot acquire property on his own as long as his legal incapacity is valid.[423] In relation to Divinity, the capacity remains excluded.[424]

The author then deals with the problem of justification—the relationship between righteous deeds and eternal life—on the background of the doctrinal statements of the Council of Trent (1545–1563).[425] They affirm, in the author's opinion, the absence of a strict right toward God, as well as the absence of equality. Eternal life is a gift by God based upon His mercy and Christ's merits. It is not based upon a strict right of the just. Thus, e.g., if a person makes a promise to give a great amount of gold to another person, as a favor without any cause, it may happen that this promise is conditioned upon a service; nevertheless, no strict duty emerges for the promising person, since the promise remains based solely upon his generosity. The added condition does not detract from the gift's nature.[426] Hence, the merit of the just, which is a gift of God, cannot give rise to a right under commutative justice. As a result, in no way can God be held to be a debtor under strict law, nor can a creature acquire such a right.[427] However, since the reward is according to the merit, there is—as Duns Scotus affirms—substantially a commutative justice proportion without constituting a strict right.[428]

---

423. *Ibid.*, 245.

424. *Ibid.*, 246: "Sed neque promissio Dei, neque pactum potest reddere creaturam sic capacem iuris proprij, quod non sit Dei, neque etiam transferre ius Dei in bona creaturae; ergo ratione pacti, aut promissionis nullum acquiritur ius creaturae tanquam alteri, licet Deus sibi quasi alteri, debeat ex fidelitate& vericitate, seu sua bonitate."

425. *Ibid.*, 246–248.

426. *Ibid.*, 247: "Hic dicendum, si aliquis alicui promittat maximum pondus auri pro obsequio nullius momenti, licet promissio fiat cum conditione operis; tamen non redundat debitum obsequenti secundum iustitiam strictam dati, & accepti, sed ex mera liberalitate, & dono promittentis, cui nihil derogat conditio apposita: alias certe si ex motivo iustitiae stricte sumptae liceret talem conventionem interpretari, & non ex dono promittentis, conventio declararetur iure nulla propter fraudem, & gravamen notabile partis, licet merces idonea, & proportionata obsequio constitui posset."

427. *Ibid.*: "Ergo neque ex promissione Dei liberali cum conditione operis, neque ex acceptatione consequente, vel vi promissionis antecedentis, neque etiam ex conventione in sola promissione fundata, potest Deus constitui debitor ex stricto iure, neque creaturae ius simile accrescere per exhibitionem talis operis."

428. *Ibid.*: "Ex his primo sequitur quod conventio facta inter Deum, & creaturam, non possit esse iustitiae commutativae proprie, & stricte, sed, ut dicit Doctor, aliqualiter, quatenus scilicet medium dati, & accepti, servatur quoad quantitatem rei, nempe meriti, & praemij, servata proportione, ita ut quantum crescit meritum, tantum etiam crescit praemium intuitu meriti." *See also ibid.*, 248.

The author then rejects the idea of viewing the relationship between God's right to property and that of men like the relationship between the state's *dominium universale* and private property. God's property rights in relation to His creatures are absolute, unlimited, invariable, and inalienable.[429] The author criticizes the contrary view of Suárez—who imputes commutative justice—as being unconvincing and not sufficiently consistent with religious faith.[430]

The author then proceeds to discuss distributive justice. According to Duns Scotus, God applies distributive justice in its full sense.[431] According to the author, Duns Scotus limits the divine application of distributive justice—contrary to Richardus, Cajetanus, and Soto[432]—to (divine) government or natural providence, but not to retribution for deeds. The author goes on to say that one has to pay attention that distributive justice in relation to God is not to be understood in its strict sense implying a strict duty. It signifies merely the application of a proportion in the government of nature which does not give rise to a moral or legal duty.[433]

A thorough and rather fierce defence of the opinions of Duns Scotus was undertaken by the Italian Franciscan scholar Bartolomeo Mastri da Meldula (1602–1673).[434] The author, who is well versed in the whole scholastic literature, painstakingly analyzes the different opinions on the question whether the just are rewarded by Divinity on the basis of justice. He mentions three different

429. *Ibid.*, 249: "Sed dominium Dei si dicatur universale, est alterius rationis: quia respicit totum quod est, & habet creatura, in omni casu, & circumstantia ex ratione primae causae, & ultimi finis, a quo essentialiter est creatura, & omnia eius opera bona, ideoque illimitatum, & invariabile omnibus circunstantiis positis, & semper manens, cui neque Deus ipse renunciare potest, ideoque stante tali dominio, nequit aliquid creaturae respective ad Deum esse capax materiae iuris stricte sumpti."

430. *Ibid.*, 249, §41: "Reiicienda proinde eius [Suarez] censura praeceps *in 3. p. tom. 1 disp. 4 sect.3. conclus. 3.* qua notat oppositam improbabilitatis, nec piam, nec fidei satis consentaneam." The author refers to the writings of Vasquez and Theodorus Smising.

431. Duns Scotus, *supra* 22, at note 78; Antonius Hiquaeus, *ibid.*, 249, §42.

432. The author states that Richardus and Cajetanus extend distributive justice to rewards and punishments, but Sotus only to rewards, since in the latter's view punishments are applied in a way similar to commutative justice; *ibid.*

433. *Ibid.*, 250, §43: "Advertendum est praeterea, ut *infra* ipse docet, licet distinctionem iustitiae particularis distributivae in deo admittat hic cum aliis: tamen eum non asseri in rigore, & secundum debitum strictum sumptum, sed duntaxat quantum ad similitudinem quandam, quae est proportionis Arithmeticae servatam in rerum gubernatione, quoad suas perfectiones naturales, ex quibus nullum debitum morale, aut iuris redundat."

434. Bartholomaeus Mastrius de Meldula, *Disputationes Theologicae In Tertium Librum Sententiarum Quibus ab adversantibus, tum Veterum, tum Recentiorum iaculis, Scoti Theologia Vindicatur* (Venezia 1675), Disputatio Tertia, Quaestio V, Art. 1–6, §§ 149–231, pp. 162–180.

opinions, among them two extreme ones; one that completely denies the possible existence of commutative justice in relation to God. Accordingly, the basis of the reward of the just lies exclusively in the divine virtues of gratitude or fidelity[435]; the other extreme opinion assumes the application of a proper and veritable commutative justice by God.[436] The third opinion—a medium one—assumes that in relationship between God and His creatures justice can intervene; however, not in the general, simple sense of justice (*simpliciter*), but in certain respects only of the notion (*secundum quid*).[437]

The author supports this third opinion which, in his view, is held by Duns Scotus and his followers. It means that the reward of the just by Divinity is not merely an act out of fidelity or gratitude, but equally one out of justice. On the other hand, God is not subject to a rigorous and strict duty of commutative justice, but merely to one *secundum quid*, like the imperfect justice relationship that exists between father and son, master and servant.[438] However, whereas the father can create a strict justice relationship with his emancipated son, and the master with his freed servant, no such possibility exists between Divinity and human creatures: God's rights of paternity and dominion are inalienable.[439] The author—after a lengthy and detailed refutation of all the arguments voiced in favor of a strict commutative justice relationship between God and human beings[440]—then proceeds to analyze the existence of a distributive justice relationship.[441] Here, the author adopts again the opinion

---

435. *Ibid.*, §153, p. 163. The author names the following scholars: Vasquez, Turrian, Arrubal, Alarcon, Lorca, Coninch, Amicus, Oviedus, Hiquaeus, Gallus, Smising.

436. *Ibid.*, §154. The author names the following scholars, though there are some differences among them: Suárez, Zumel, Valentia, Bellarminas, Montesinos, Caspensis, Tannerus, Ioan. a S. Thomas, Lezana, Arriaga, Poncius, Bellutus.

437. *Ibid.*, §155. The terms of *dicto simpliciter* and *secundum quid* are familiar with the scholastics and are connected to syllogistic fallacies mentioned by Aristotle, *Sophistical Refutations*, 5. *Cf. Enciclopedia Filosofica*, Vol. 4 (Venezia-Roma 1957) 636.

438. The author repeats many times the idea that the position of God prevents the general conditions of commutative justice; thus, between God and men there can be no simple equality of giving and accepting. He concludes therefore (*ibid.*, §168, p. 167, and *passim*): "Ergo ex defectu harum conditionum inter Deum, & homines vera, & propria iustitia commutativa reperiri non potest, nec rigorosa commutatio quae est talis iustitiae materia; atque ideo Deus in retribuenda pro meritis mercede iustitiam commutativam proprie dictam exercere non potest, sed tantum secundum quid, quae proinde melius retributiva diceretur, vel praemiativa, quam commutativa."

439. *Ibid.*, §186, p. 171.

440. *Ibid.*, §§205–217, pp. 175–178.

441. *Ibid.*, §§218–232, pp. 178–180.

of Duns Scotus, according to which, distributive justice is exercised by God in the proper and full sense of the notion.[442] When rewarding the just, the proportion to other persons' merits is also taken into account.[443]

In a later part of his work, the author deals at length—again in the characteristic detailed scholastic way—with the juridical nature of atonement of sins.[444] He discusses the following questions: By sinning are we committing an injustice toward God? Are we held by justice to atone for our sins? Is the atonement by the sacrifice of Christ an act of justice? The author adopts basically a positive answer to all these questions in the spirit of Duns Scotus, but in relation to God and Christ the notion of justice is again used by him in a less rigorous way, namely *secundum quid.*[445] The author notes that in this context of atonement of sins, the appropriate notion is not commutative justice, but rather *iustitia remissiva & condonativa.*[446]

The German Benedictine scholar Paul Mezger (1637–1702), in his work on the scholastic theology according to Thomas Aquinas, follows also in relation to this topic rather closely the great predecessor.[447] However, he denies the very possibility of formal distributive and commutative justice between man and Divinity because of the total absence of any equality of status. Hence, there can be no formal justice relationship between man and Divinity, and that in either direction.[448] God's justice is of an eminent, perfect substance (*justitia eminentialis*).[449] A similar conclusion reaches the Belgian theologian scholar Laurent Neesen (1612–1679): Divinity is not subject to a strict commutative justice, neither to a distributive one. There can be no strict duty of God toward human beings.[450]

---

442. *Ibid.*, §§220–221, pp. 178–179.

443. *Ibid.*, §227, p. 179: "Iam enim demonstratum est in divino iudicio merita non tantum considerari secundum aequalitatem meriti, & retributionis, sed etiam secundum aequalitatem proportionum inter personas, & merita."

444. *Ibid.*, Disputatio Quarta, De Satisfactione Christi, Quaest. 2–4, §§80–199, pp. 249–271.

445. *Ibid.*, §137, p. 261.

446. *Ibid.*

447. Paulus Mezger, *Theologiae Scholasticae Secundum Viam D. Thomae Aquinatis, Doctoris Angelici*, Tomus III (Augsburg 1719) Tract. XI, Disp. XXV, Art.I–III, pp. 251–255.

448. *Ibid.*, 252: "Non datur formalis justitia commutativa in DEO versus hominem"; 253: "Negatur formalis justitia distributiva in DEO"; 254: "Negatur justitia commutativa hominis erga DEUM."

449. *Ibid.*, 251, 255.

450. Laurentius Neesen, *Universa Theologia In Tomos Duos Divisa Ad Mentem SS. Augustini Et Thomae Exposita*, Tomus Primus (Lille 1693) 63–64: "Resp. quando Scriptura Deo justitiam tribuit, tunc illam non procedere in rigore philosophico, nec illam stricte sumere,

The same conclusion is adopted by the French scholar of theology at the Sorbonne, Honoré Tournély (1658–1729).[451] In relation to commutative justice, he relies on Vasquez and Aquinas. The reference in the Scriptures to God's justice has to be taken metaphorically, since in its strict sense it contradicts His nature.[452] God's ownership in the property of human beings is much more extensive than that of the prince's in that of his subjects. For the same reason, there is strictly speaking no distributive justice in relation to God; nor is He bound to exercise vindictive justice. Aquinas's contrary statement has to be understood as relating to justice in the large sense, namely of applying a geometric proportion.[453] On the other hand, on the part of a human being, there can be a strict duty in relation to Divinity.[454]

A contrary approach was taken by the Spanish Jesuit Juan de Ulloa (1639–1723). In a lengthy and rather sinuous discussion, the author attempts to establish his thesis that God can oblige Himself to a strict, commutative justice duty.[455] The example used by the author is the divine promise to grant glory to the just. He undertakes a considerable intellectual effort to overcome the objections based upon God's omnipotence and absolute dominion over human beings and their property. A major part of the discussion is dedicated to the problem of God's lack of power to deny the promised glory to the just. The author tries to defend his thesis on the basis of medieval, scholastic

---

sed illam loqui juxta modum vulgo usitatum, secundum quem is, qui alteri satisfacit, dicitur justus, & dare id, quod debet, sive interim sit obstrictus obligatione justitiae proprie dictae, sive fidelitatis: et sic Deus dicitur reddere coronam justitiae, non quasi stricto jure debitam, sed ex fidelitate, ratione nimirum sue liberalis promissionis." *See also* the same idea in relation to penitence: *Id., Theologia Moralis Christiana de Sacramentis Ad Mentem SS. Augustini Et Thomae* (Lille 1693) 129. On the other hand, the author recognizes the existence of a strict duty of man toward God: *id., Tractatus Tres De Justitia et Jure Ad Supplementum Theologiae Moralis Christianae* (Antwerpen 1693) 11.

451. Honoratus Tournely, *Cursus Theologicus Scholastico-Dogmaticus* (Köln 1734), *Tractatus de Justitia Et Jure*, 535–536.

452. *Ibid.*, 535: "Scriptura sine metaphora explicari debere quoties id rerum natura patitur: atqui non patitur Dei natura ut justitia de qua loquitur, Deo adscribatur, cum ea imperfectionis aliquid includat, quatenus supponit Deum aliquid stricte debere creaturis: haec enim debendi ratio supremum Dei dominium omnino subvertit, ut probatum est."

453. *Ibid.*, 536.

454. *Ibid.*

455. Joannis De Ulloa, *Theologiae Scholasticae Tomus Tertius De Tribus Virtutibus Theologicis Atque De Justitia Prima Virtutum Pure Moralium* (Augsburg 1719) Disp. VIII, Caput IV, pp. 332–338.

distinctions developed by logicians and used in connection with the vexing problem of divine foresight, predestination, and free will.[456]

The topic of the relationship between Divinity and the forms of justice remained a central issue in Christian theology producing an extensive literature.[457] It served equally as a permanent topic in academic

---

456. *Ibid.*, §§47–48, pp. 435–436. The author relies on the scholastic concept of "*in sensu composito*."

457. For a discussion of the various approaches see especially the important work of the Spanish Jesuit scholar Gabriele Vasquez (1549–1604) *Commentariorum ac Disputationum in Primam Partem S. Thomae Tomus Primus* (Ingolstadt 1609) Quaest. 21, Disp. 85–86, pp. 530–551; this author argues that in relation to God there is neither commutative justice nor distributive justice. *Cf.* G. Del Vecchio, *Justice—An Historical and Philosophical Essay* (A.H. Campbell, ed., Edinburgh 1952) 5, note 2 at 11. The view of Vasquez is adopted by Luisius Torrianus (Luis de Torres) (1562–1655), *Disputationum in secundam secundae D. Thomae, De Iustitia*, Tomus alter (Lyon 1621) Disp. VI, Dubium II, col. 81–82. But *see* the detailed arguments against Gabriele Vasquez's view, by Petrus Hurtadus De Mendoza (1578–1651), *Disputationes de Homine sive de Incarnatione Filii Dei* (Antwerpen 1634) Disp. 12, Sect. 16, §§257–291, pp. 122–128. In relation to distributive justice this author affirms: "Est igitur in Deo iustitia distributiva propria & absque metaphora. Hanc multorum esse sententiam fatetur ipse P. Vasquez" (*ibid.*, 125, §271). For an additional discussion, *see also* Gabrielis a S. Vincentio (1601–1671), *De Iustitia et Iure* (Rome 1663) Disp. 1, Q. 20, nn. 287–321, at 98–111. The Italian Jesuit scholar Domenico Viva (1648–1726), *Cursus Theologicus Ad Usum Tyronum elucubratus, & in quotidianis Praelectionibus Suis Auditoribus traditus*, Pars Quinta, *De Justitia, & Jure* (Ignatius Viva, ed., Köln 1716) Disp. III, Quaest. VI–VIII, pp. 157–191, argues in a lengthy discussion that between Divinity and human beings there can exist legal relationships in the strict sense. Thus, assuming a divine promise of reward for human acts—such as fasting—God will be legally bound to fulfill that promise. The author concludes, after painstakingly refuting a long series of objections, that imputing Divinity a strict commutative-justice-duty toward human beings does not detract from His supreme dominion over His creatures. Such a duty is based upon a divine promise, given by His free will. The author relies specifically upon the writings of Suárez and the Scriptures in rejecting the contrary view of Vasquez. See in addition the work of the Dominican Cardinal Vincentius-Ludovicus Gotti (1664–1742), *Theologia Scholastico-Dogmatica Juxta Mentem Divi Thomae Aquinatis Ad Usum Discipulorum*, Tomus Secundus (Venezia 1750), Tractatus 13, *De Jure & Justitia*, Quaest. 3, Dubium 2, pp. 557–558. The author affirms that Divinity exercises real distributive justice. He argues that denying God the exercise of both commutative and distributive justice, would signify that He in fact does no justice whatsoever "quod falsum est, imo absurdum." Moreover, when exercising retribution—by punishing the offenders and rewarding the just—God applies distributive justice, but there is mixed in a kind of commutative justice (*ibid.*, 558): "Deum in retributione supplicorum pro demeritis, sicut in retributione Gloriae pro meritis, servare propriem justitiam distributivam; cui tamen aliqua species commutationis admiscetur." The author expounds the same topic at length in his discussion on the foundations of the merits of the just; *ibid.*, Tractatus 8, *De Merito Justi*, Quaest. 1, Dubium 3, pp. 395–397. Rejecting the views of Medina and Vasquez, who deny in this context the exercise by God of any kind of justice, the author—adopting the "common view of the disciples of Saint Thomas"—claims, as mentioned, that God, when rewarding the just, applies distributive justice with an element of commutative justice. For an extensive discussion, *see also* the Jesuit scholar Antonius Mayr (1673–1749), *Theologia Scholastica Tractatus Omnes In Universitatibus Provinciae Germaniae Superioris Societatis Jesu Tradi*

disputations.[458] But in post-scholastic times, the problem lost much of its intensity.[459]

Solitos Et Quaestiones In Iis Praescriptas Complexa, Tomus II (Ingolstadt 1732) Tractatus IX, Disputatio III, Quaestio III, pp. 107–121. The author assumes that in view of God's absolute ownership over all creatures, men are bound under commutative justice to abide by divine orders. However, the corresponding acts of human beings can never be adequate in the full and strict sense of justice. Adopting the prevailing Thomist view, the author affirms that God cannot be obliged under commutative justice toward His creatures; only a kind of distributive justice can be related to Divinity. God cannot abdicate His absolute dominion over the creatures. Hence, even in case of an explicit divine promise, the recompense of eternal life for good deeds remains based upon God's faithfulness and not upon justice. For a denial of the possibility of a strict duty of God toward man, *see* the Jesuit scholar Thomas Holzclau, *Theologia Dogmatico-Polemico-Scholastica*, Tractatus II, *De Jure Et Justitia*, Pars II, *De Justitia* (Würzburg 1768) 8–10.

458. There are scores of examples of disputations in the framework of public examinations in universities and theological seminaries that deal with that issue. The substantive conclusions vary. *See, e.g.*, in the Jesuit Academy of Dillingen: Stephanus Vitus, Andrea Wiser, Jacobus Merck, *Disputatio Theologica De Iustitia, Iure, Contractibus Legitimis, Et Oppositis Eorum Malis ipsorumque Medelis* (Dillingen 1613). In this case, the authors support the views of Aquinas and of the "older scholars against the younger"; at 4; Amandus Hegwein, *Disputatio Theologica De Justitia* (Praes. Matthias Ram, Dillingen 1664) Quaestio II, §II, pp. 42–46 (Justice, insofar as it is obliging, has no place in God); Joannes Holzman, *Tractatus Theologicus, In Secundam Secundae Summae Theologicae S. Thomae Aquinatis Angelici Ecclesiae Doctoris, De Jure Et Justitia* (Praes. Carolus Schrenckh, Salzburg 1701) 42–50 (Between God and human beings there can be no perfect justice relationship: "Justitia perfecta, nec est in Deo erga creaturas, nec in homine erga Deum"; the author relies on Paul Mezger, *supra* nn. 447–449; *cf.* Gregorius Lochner, *ExercitatioTertia Menstrua Theologico-Historica Sive Positiones Ex Tractatu de Jure & Justitia Quas Magni Frisigensium Patris & Pontificis Corbiani Virtutibus & meritis interpolatas* (Praes. Carolus Meichelbeckh, Regensburg 1707) 19: "In Deo non datur Justitia legalis. Nec commutativa ad creaturas. Nec distributiva proprie talis. Datur igitur in Deo solum Justitia quaedam eminentalis, praecisis omnibus imperfectionibus. Justitia hominis ad Deum non est commutativa." A similar thesis was put forward in another academic dissertation: Edmundus Arnold, *Tractatus Theologicus De Jure Et Justitia* (Praes. Coelestinus Mayr, Salzburg 1715) Quaestio IV, Art. I–III, pp. 102–131. The author's view is that between God and human beings there can be neither commutative justice nor distributive justice. He deals at length with all the possible objections against his thesis. But see the contrary view forcibly put forward in another academic dissertation: Stephanus Felix Vintschger, *Theoremata Theologica De Iure Et Iustitia* (Praes. Ludovicus Simonzin, Innsbruck 1705) Quaestio IV, pp. 98–179. According to this author, human beings can oblige themselves, under commutative justice, toward God, and, correspondingly, God, by means of an explicit promise of His, can oblige Himself under commutative justice toward Christ and human beings. The author, in a lengthy discussion of a multitude of objections, refers to the vast scholastic literature. He deals at length with the position of Christ in relation to God on the background of his salvatory function toward humanity.

459. *Cf., e.g.*, the approach of Cardinal R. Bellarmini (1542–1621), *Opera Omnia* (ed. J. Fèvre, Paris 1875), t. 8, p. 645 (God can oblige Himself to all forms of justice). *See also, e.g.*, the simple answer given in a Benedictine booklet summerizing Thomist views: P. Virgilio Sedlmayr, *Systema Theologiae Dogmatico-ScholasticaeJuxta Methodum S. Thomae Aquinatis*

Nevertheless, some mention should be made of the use by some theologians of the Aristotelian distinction in relation to the heated and prolonged controversy between Catholics and Protestants on the nature of justification, a controversy that arose in the wake of the Reformation.[460] Thus, the Polish Cardinal Stanislaus Hosius (1504–1579), a papal legate at the Council of Trent, relies upon the distinction between commutative and distributive justice in order to explain the award to the just of eternal life's glory. Since there can be no quantitative (arithmetic) equality between the earthly merits of the just and the heavenly reward, it must be a matter of proportional (geometric) equality, i.e., the application of distributive justice. The author explains the topic by means of an example: The semen of a tree, though being quantitatively much smaller than the tree itself, nevertheless contains all the latter's qualities. Likewise, the act of the just, though quantitatively far from being equal to the glory, nevertheless contains in its qualities, by the grace of the Holy Spirit, the eternal life.[461]

However, notwithstanding the objections to some fundamental tenets of Catholicism, some Reformed scholars continued to rely on scholastic literature. Thus, the English theologian Thomas Jackson (1579–1640), chaplain and president of Corpus Christi College in Oxford,[462] observes in relation to the covenant between God and Abraham:

> The word *Covenant* in our English, is sometimes equivalent to what the Latines call *pactum*, or *conventum*, to wit, any contract or bargain, wherein there is, *quid pro quo*, somewhat given, and somewhat taken. And in this sense every Covenant or bargain is an act of commutative justice, wherein there is, *ratio dati & accepti*, a mutual bond between parties contracting upon some valuable considerations. A Covenant of

---

(Augsburg 1754) 102: "Utrum in Deo versus creaturam sit justitia formalis et proprie dicta? R. Affirmativè."

460. *Cf. supra* at note 425.

461. Stanislaus Hosius, *Opera* (Lyon 1564), Cap. 73, at 264–265. The metaphor of the semen and the tree appears in this context already in the treatise of the French Dominican scholar Johannes Capreolus (ca. 1380–1444), *Quaestiones in IV libros Sententiarum, seu libri IV defensionum theologiae Thomae Aquinatis* (Venezia 1483–1484), Lib. II, Distinctio XXVII, Quaest. 1 (vdIb Köln, p. 560); it is repeated in connection with Aquinas by Petrus de Aragon (1545–1592), *In Secundam Secundae Divi Thomae Doctoris Angelici Commentaria.De Iustitia Et Iure* (Lyon 1596) Quaest. LXI, Artic. IV, p. 91.

462. On the life, religion and works of this author: S. Hutton, "Thomas Jackson, Oxford Platonist, and William Twisse, Aristotelian," 39 (1978) *Journal of the History of Ideas* 635.

> this rank there cannot be properly said or imagined betwixt God and mere man as *Abraham* was; for who can give any thing to God, which was not his own before, by a more sovereign right and more peculiar title than it is, or can be his that would take upon him to make God his Debtor by deed of gift. And for this reason the acutest Schoolmen resolve us, that commutative justice cannot be *formally* in God. But when we read that Justice is one of God's Essential Attributes, or when we say that God is truly and *formally* Just; this must be meant of distributive Justice, the ballance of whose scales are *poena* and *praemium*, matter of punishment, and matter of reward.[463]

In relation to the question of *antipeponthos*, Jackson has an interesting and quite original solution; he says:

> *Aristotle* did rightly deny Retaliation, or Counterpassion to be ἀυτοδικαίον, *exact justice*, and yet it may be, *Pythagoras* his thoughts did soar much higher than his, when he pitched upon the affirmative. In ordinary offences committed by unequal or extraordinary persons, *Pythagoras* his tenent, is not universally true. As if a great Person should beat his far Inferior, without just cause, it stands neither with the Law of God, or Rule of Equity, to beat him in the same fashion, or according to the same measure again. But when Kings and Monarchs do extraordinary wrongs unto their Subjects, or practice Prodigious Cruelties upon their Inferiors, they usually suffer the like harms or plagues themselves.[464]

The author then goes on to illustrate lengthily, by means of very detailed biblical and historical examples, the divine retaliatory punishments that befell upon great princes. Some are inflicted according to the geometrical proportion of distributive justice, others according to the arithmetic one of commutative justice.[465]

---

463. Thomas Jackson, *A Treatise Of The Consecration Of The Son Of God, To His Everlasting Priesthood. Being The Ninth Book Of Commentaries Upon The Apostles Creed* (London 1672), Chap. XVI, p. 985.

464. Thomas Jackson, *A Treatise Of The Divine Essence And Attributes*, Book VI, Part I (London 1672), Sec. IV, Chap. XXXI, p. 260.

465. *Ibid.*, Chapts. XXXII–XXXVII, pp. 262–286. The names of the chapters are indicative: "Of the geometrical proportion or form of distributive justice; which the Supreme Judge

Jackson's treatise provoked a sharp polemic attack by William Twisse (1578–1646), theologian and rector of Newbury.[466] Twisse, adhering to a supralapsarian Calvinism, blamed Jackson of Arminanism and even Pelagianism.[467] Being well versed in scholastic literature, Twisse made only a short comment in relation to our topic,[468] since his main interest lay in the more profound theological problems of divine attributes, such as predestination and election.

A more detailed discussion of the various forms of justice in relation to Divinity, one finds in the work of the German-Dutch theologian Conrad Vorstius (1569–1622), who extensively relies on biblical sources.[469] The author starts with a notion of judiciary justice which can be divided into cognitive and retributive justice.[470] The latter itself is divided into *iustitia remunerativa* and *iustitia vindicativa*.[471] In relation to the Aristotelian distinction, the author basically assumes that both forms of justice, in their strict sense, cannot be applied to Divinity.

---

sometimes observes in doing to Great Princes as they have done to others"; "How the former law of retaliation has been executed upon princes, according to arithmetical proportion, or according to commutative justice"; "The sins of parents visited upon their children according to the rule of retaliation"; "Grosser sins visited upon Gods Saints, according to the former rule of counterpassion"; "Of sins visited or punished according to the circumstances and places wherein they were committed"; "What manner of sins they be, which usually provoke Gods judgments, according to the rule of counterpassion. And of the frequency of this kind of punishment fore-signified by Gods Prophets."

466. William Twisse, *A Discovery of D. Iacksons Vanitie, Or A perspective Glasse, whereby the admirers of D. Iacksons profound discourses, may see the vanitie and weaknesse of them, in sundry passages, and especially so farre as they tende to the undermining of the doctrine hitherto received* (Amsterdam 1631).

467. On this polemic, *see* S. Hutton, "Thomas Jackson, Oxford Platonist, and William Twisse, Aristotelian," 39 (1978) *Journal of the History of Ideas* 635, 647–652.

468. Twisse, *ibid.*, ch. XXI, p. 697: "It is true some Schoolmen think that distributive justice may be properly enough attributed unto God but not commutative; not because this includes *rationem dati & accepti*, but rather because it includes, *aequalitatem dati & accepti*. Yet others are of opinion that justice distributive can be attributed unto God with no greater propriety, then justice commutative: as may be seen in Vasque 1. in 1. part. disput. 86."

469. Conradus Vorstius, *Tractatus Theologicus De Deo, Sive de Natura & Attributis Dei* (Steinfurt 1610). The work made the author suspect of Socianism. It caused eventually the condemnation of his theological views at the Dordrecht Synode in 1619 and his removal from the professorship at the Leiden University.

470. *Ibid.*, 100, thesis 34: "Haec judiciaria seu judicativa Justitia ut plenius intelligatur non inepte distribui potest in *Cognoscentem & Retribuentem*. Illa praesribit, ut omnium causae placide audiantur, & legitime cognoscantur." According to the author, retributive justice belongs to distributive justice; *ibid.*, 105, thesis 56.

471. *Ibid.*, 100, thesis 37.

They can be applied only "analogically."[472] However, especially inapplicable to Divinity is the concept of commutative justice, since there can be no equality of exchange. In lengthy notes to his basic theses, the author severely criticizes the "Papists" for interpreting biblical texts literally, instead of reading them metaphorically.[473]

A short reference to the scholastic approach relating to divine justice, one finds also in the work of the great Scottish Presbyterian theologian, Rev. Samuel Rutherford (ca. 1600–1661), professor of divinity at the University of St. Andrews.[474] He affirms that there is no equality between the promise of divine reward and human works. Hence, there is no place of commutative justice between God and human beings:

> The virtue of justice stands in the equality of that which is given and received. Now there is a two-fold equality, one *rei ad rem* between thing and thing, an Arithmetic justice, so many ounces of natural actings, and the same number of ounces of grace and glory: This commutative justice is not in God, as the soundest and learned'st School-men teach. There is another justice of proportion *duarum rerum ad duas alias res*, of two things proportionally answering to two things, distributive justice is this, and it keeps a Geometrical proportion.[475]

The promise of grace is a free promise:

> If a promise as a promise should make an equality between one thing and another, and so lay a band of strict commutative justice upon God, then should every promise do the like, *quod convenit* καθ' αὐτό *convenit*

472. *Ibid.*, 408–409: "Sed tamen haec divisio ad *divinam* justitiam non satis apte referri potest: tum, quia *commutatio* proprie dicta, inter Deum & nos, siquidem exacta rerum aequalitas spectetur, revera exerceri non potest: tum, quia *distributio* praemiorum, non tam dignitate, ac merito nostro, itidem proprie dicto, quam gratiosa *Dei* dignatione, ac liberali pactione, tanquam fundamento nititur. Interim si *metaphorae*, ac *catachreses*, hic quaedam recipiantur, & prudenter juxta mentem Spiritus S. rebus propositis accomodentur, non videtur odiose de *vocabulis* ipsis litigandum. Negari enim non potest, aliquid saltem *analogum* verae commutationi Arithmeticae, veraeque *distributioni* Geometricae, in ipsa justitiae divinae, praesertim judicariae, praxi atque exercitio reperiri."

473. *Ibid.*, 410–413.

474. Samuel Rutherford, *The Covenant Of Life Opened Or, A Treatise of the Covenant Of Grace* (Edinburgh 1655) 42–43. The author had an eventful life. Because of his political book *Lex Rex*, he was summoned, lying on his death bed, to answer a charge of high treason. The parliament in Edinburgh voted to let him die in the college.

475. *Ibid.*, 42.

> κατά παντός, but that cannot be said: For then if God should promise glory of ten thousand millions of degrees above the glory that Angels and men now enjoy, for speaking one good word, that should be a free promise, but that promise should not make an equality between so huge and rich a reward of glory, and so hungry and poor a work as the speaking of a good word, so as God should fail in Justice, if he should deny a reward so great, for so small a work: For the denying thereof should be against the veracity and faithfulness of God, if he should not fulfill his promise, but he should not fail against strict Justice either in not rewarding the work with a condigne reward, or not in giving to the man that spake the good word his own. For there is no just equality between work and wage here.[476]

However, the situation is different in relation to the intertrinitarian covenant, i.e., between God and Christ. The deliverance from satisfactory punishment is due to human beings under a commutative-justice-duty of God toward Christ.[477]

The idea that God cannot be subject to commutative justice was equally adopted in a short statement by the important German Lutheran theologian Johann Gerhard (1582–1637).[478] It was similarly affirmed by many other Protestant theologians, among them: Abraham van der Heyden (1597–1678), professor of theology in Leiden[479]; the English Puritan theologian Richard Baxter (1615–1691)[480]; the Orthodox Lutheran philosopher and theologian,

---

476. *Ibid.*, 43.

477. *Ibid.*, 249–250. The exact understanding of justification, salvation, and predestination is a most intricate topic that divided the different Protestant denominations. The author here argues against the theological views of Arminius and Socinus.

478. Iohannes Gerhardus, *Locorum Theologicorum Cum Pro Adstruenda Veritate, Tum Pro Destruenda Quorumvis Contradicentium Falsitate Per Theses Nervose, Solide & Copiose Explicatorum Tomus Primus* (Jena 1610) 319–320: "Justitia commutativa non competit Deo, quis enim prior ipsi tribuit? Sed distributiva." But in relation to the reward of eternal life to the just, see the comment of the German Calvinist Marcus Friedrich Wendelin (1584–1652), *Christianae Theologiae Libri II* (Editio Novissima, Amsterdam 1650) 887: "Ita ex justitia nobis dat Deus vitam aeternam: quia ex gratia eam promisit obedientibus. Idem, alii ita eloquuntur: Deus dat vitam aeternam ex *justitia constantia*, propter promissionem: non ex *justitia distributiva*, propter merita operum."

479. Abrahamus Heidanus, *Corpus Theologiae Christianae* (Leiden 1686) 165–166. In the author's view, distributive justice may be referred to Divinity; it includes remunerative and punitive (vindictive) justice.

480. Richard Baxter, *The Divine Life: In Three Treatises*, in *The Practical Works of the Late Reverend and Pious Mr. Richard Baxter, in Four Volumes* (London 1707), Chap. XIII, p. 695: "Hence we must conclude, and reverently and willingly confess, that further than he

Johannes Andreas Quenstedt (1617–1688), professor in Wittenberg[481]; the Dutch Calvinist theologian, Andreas Essenius (1618–1677)[482]; and the Dutch neo-Calvinist scholar and professor in Gronigen, Johannes Braun (1628–1708).[483] The same view was voiced by the Reverend Stephen Lobb (d. 1699), who denied the existence of commutative justice even in the relationship between God and Jesus Christ; the latter's merit is only according to the rule of distributive justice.[484] Moreover, the notion that according to the rule

---

voluntarily doth oblige himself to us, it is *impossible* that God should be *our Debtor*, and consequently that upon terms of *commutative justice* we should *Merit* anything of God. For what can we render to him but his *Own*? And how should he (properly and antecedently) be indebted to for his *Own*"? Baxter, who was involved in many theological controversies, encountered legal troubles and spent some time in prison for his views until his release by the Declaration of Indulgence in 1687.

481. Iohannes Andreas Quenstedt, *Theologia Didactico-Polemica, Sive Systema Theologicum In Duas Sectiones, Didacticam Et Polemicam, Divisum* (Wittenberg 1691) 292, Thesis XXXV.

482. Andreas Essenius, *Triumphus Crucis Sive Fides Catholica De Satisfactione Domini nostri Iesu Christi* (Amsterdam 1649) 336: "Neque unquam potest esse proportio inter opus qualecunque a mera creatura praestitum, & praemium vitae aeternae, neque justitia commutativa dari potest inter Creatorem & creaturam suam."

483. Johannes Braunius, *Doctrina Foederum, sive Systema Theologiae Didacticae & Elencticae;-Perspicua atque facili Methodo* (Editio altera, Amsterdam 1702) 90: "Hoc enim locum habere non potest, nisi inter homines, qui sunt pares & ejusdem conditionis. Nos autem, cum simus creati a Deo, ab eoque dependeamus, nostrique juris non simus, sed Deo adstricti, nullum nobis competit jus in Deum quo nobis adstringeretur."

484. Rev. Stephen Lobb, Sermon XVIII, in Samuel Annesley, *The Morning Exercises at Cripplegate*, Vol. III, *A Continuation of Morning-Exercise Questions and Cases of Conscience practically resolved By Sundry Ministers in October 1682*, in *The Morning Exercises at Cripplegate, St. Giles in the Fields, and in Southwark* (5th ed., London 1844) Vol. III, p. 419: "Merit as to *commutative* justice does necessarily include in it the passing of somewhat over unto God, unto which God had no right antecedent unto this transaction. But God is an absolute Lord and Sovereign, who has a right unto all things: Jesus Christ himself, as man, is God's propriety [property]; and all that Jesus Christ could give, must be considered as Christ's, either as he is God, or as he is man. Whatever belongs to him as God, is God's; and as he is man, whatever he has, it is God's: for which reason, Jesus Christ himself is not excepted, when it is said by the apostle, 'Who hath first given him, and it shall be recompensed unto him again?' (Rom. xi. 35.) 'Who?' As if it had been said,'There is none, no, not one, not Jesus Christ himself, [who] could give first unto God, could give that unto God unto which God had not, antecedently to that gift, a right;' that is, so to give unto God, as to pass-over a new right unto God, for which God should be under the obligation of recompensing it. Commutative righteousness is inconsistent with the absolute sovereignty and dominion of God: whence it must be acknowledged, that either God is not the absolute Sovereign and Lord of the universe,—which if not, he is not God,—or there is no such thing as commutative righteousness in God, and that Christ himself, much less man, could not merit of God any thing to the rule of commutative righteousness. That Christ merited according to *distributive* justice, is asserted by alll sound Protestants, and by Vasquez and other Papists." In this sense, *see* the Jesuit

of commutative justice man may merit of God is in the author's view absurd, since man cannot give God anything which is of a value proportional to eternal life, to infinite excellence. The author then adds in this connection:

> However, notwithstanding the ridiculousness, as well as falseness, of the notion, there are many among the Papists (if we may believe Arriaga) who assert it. It is true, Vasquez explodes it, with an essay to evince that the Papists generally reject it; but Arriaga, a later Jesuit, freely rebukes Vasquez, affirming that commutative righteousness is in God, and may be found to be between God and man, and that this is generally received in the church of Rome. "For," says he, "this is the opinion of Suarez, Valentia, Granadus (who introduces Medina and Alvarez, to agree with him in this point), Hurtado de Mendoza, Ragusa, Tannerus, and Albertinus, and Molina also; who, though he expresses himself with caution in one place, yet elsewhere doth freely enough own it. Besides, Capreolus and the Thomists generally," says Arriaga, "do agree with him in this"; and that therefore Vasquez is greatly to be blamed for affirming that so many were of the contrary opinion; whereas this about merit *quoad iustitiam commutativa*, ["as to commutative justice"] has many more authorities than Vasquez could produce for his sense of it. In fine, Arriaga corrects Vasquez' mistake, in saying that Hosius and Scotus were against commutative righteousness, and then proceeds to an attempt of demonstrating the truth of this doctrine.
>
> By this it is apparent that, if we may believe Arriaga, the Papists generally assert merit according to commutative justice; in which sense it is mostly oppugned by the Protestant writers, as a ridiculous doctrine: the which, from what has been already suggested, has been manifested. But seeing this doctrine contradicts our reason, our endeavours

---

scholar Antonius Mayr (1673–1749), *Theologia Scholastica Tractatus Omnes In Universitatibus Provinciae Germaniae Superioris Societatis Jesu Tradi Solitos Et Quaestiones In Iis Praescriptas Complexa*, Tomus II (Ingolstadt 1732) Tractatus IX, Disputatio III, Quaestio III, Art. VIII, §399, p. 117. But see the contrary view of the Scottish theologian Patrick Gillespie (1617–1675), *The Ark Of The Covenant Opened: Or, A Treatise Of The Covenant Of Redemption Between God And Christ, As The Foundation Of The Covenant Of Grace* (London 1677) 61: "Christ is a doer and obedient fulfiller of the Law, hath a reward in Justice by the promise of this Covenant: For (I humbly conceive) he had his reward of debt, and merit, having paid a condign price to the Justice of God; therefore his reward is due to him, by commutative Justice."

> must not be how to improve it; we must immediately reject it as false and unreasonable.[485]

This evident disrespect for the scholastic literature is not an isolated incidence. A further good example of this tendency—that appears to be growing in the wake of the reformation—constitute the writings of the English Puritan minister John Owen (1616–1683), Dean of the Christ Church College in Oxford. In his *Dissertation on Divine Justice*,[486] he undertakes the task to refute the extreme thesis, adopted by the "Socinian heresy," of the purely voluntary character of divine punishment. Referring to some of the scholastic discussions on the notion of justice, he refers to the authors (such as Duns Scotus, Durandus, Paludamus, Cajetanus, Gabriel, Pesantius, and Suárez) as "hair splitters," "triflers," and "bunglers."[487] Owen then adds:

> They resemble those advocates in Terence, whose opinion, after Demipho, embarrassed by the cheats of Phormio the sycophant, had asked, he exclaims, "Well done gentlemen; I am now in a greater uncertainty than before!" so intricate were their answers, and resembling the practices of the Andabatae.[488]

Suárez's view on the merits of Roman Catholics with God, Owen calls a "rotten fiction." He then suggests dismissing "these bunglers (who know not the righteousness of God)" from his dissertation, in order to attend to "the more sure words of prophecy."[489]

---

485. *Ibid.*, 420. The same approach is adopted by the English Puritan preacher, Rev. Peter Vinke (d. 1702), Sermon V, in Samuel Annesley, *The Morning Exercises at Cripplegate*, Vol. IV, *Casuistical Morning-Exercises*, in *The Morning Exercises at Cripplegate, St. Giles in the Fields, and in Southwark* (5th ed., London 1844) Vol. IV, p. 272. The author, after stating that there is no commutative justice between God and His creature, affirms: "We can give no equivalent for the least mercy, the least crumb, the least drop, to be sure, as coming from God"; he then adds: "God gets nothing by all our holiest performances, devoutest prayers, and most spiritual duties. Our righteousness cannot profit him."

486. First edition in Latin: *De Divina Justitia Diatriba* (1653); the English translation in 1794. The text has been retrieved by us from http://www.ccel.org/ccel/owen/justice.html.

487. *Ibid.*, Part 1, Chapter 2.

488. *Ibid.* The translator explains the *Andabatae*: "A kind of fencers who fought on horseback hood-winked."

489. *Ibid.*

FIVE

Jewish Commentators

IT IS A MOST NOTEWORTHY FACT that in the whole classical Jewish (rabbinic) literature one does not find an attempt of defining the notion of justice, neither that of law. Generally, it appears that the rabbis were considerably more interested in concrete solutions than in abstract legal concepts.[490] Moreover, the Jewish scholars first learned the ideas contained in Aristotle's *Ethics* through the intermediary of the Arab philosophers, probably only in the twelfth century.[491]

However, even after Aristotle's *Nicomachean Ethics* became known to Jewish scholars, there was—in great contrast to the Christian scholastics—no interest in Aristotle's specific analysis of the notion of justice. The interests lay elsewhere. Very few Jewish scholars mentioned at all the Aristotelian distinction; an analysis of Aristotle's distinctions relating to the forms justice was undertaken by even fewer ones, namely by those three to four scholars who composed an original commentary on Aristotle's *Ethics*. Nevertheless, there is considerable interest in these rare attempts of analyzing the Aristotelian distinction on the background of the Jewish legal tradition.

---

490. This is equally true in relation to divine justice. There was a felt tension between God's justice and God's mercy: B.D. Smith, *The Tension Between God as Rightous Judge and as Merciful in Early Judaism* (Lanham, Maryland 2005), especially at 292–296. However, the rabbis were not overly disturbed by the conceptual inconsistency between the two notions. *See also* the comprehensive work from a Christian perspective: M. Zehetbauer, *Die Polarität von Gerechtigkeit und Barmherzigkeit—Ihre Wurzeln im Alten Testament im Frühjudentum sowie in der Botschaft Jesu: Konsequenzen für die Ethik* (Regensburg 1999).

491. *See* S. Harvey, "The Sources of the Quotations from Aristotle's *Ethics* in the *Guide of the Perplexed* and the *Guide to the Guide*," *Joseph Baruch Sermoneta Memorial Volume, Jerusalem Studies in Jewish Thought*, Vol. XIV (A. Ravitzky, ed., Jerusalem 1998) 87 (in Hebrew). The author deals with the literary sources of Aristotle's Ethics that were at the disposal of Maimonides (1138–1204) and Shem-Tov Falaquera (1225–1295). No doubt, Aristotelian ideas in other fields were well known much earlier, *see, e.g.*, the philosophical work of Saadia Gaon (882–942); H.A. Wolfson, "The Double Faith Theory in Clement, Saadia, Averroes, and St. Thomas, and Its origin in Aristotle and the Stoics," 33 (1942) *The Jewish Quarterly Review* 213, 230–243.

An early Hebrew source dealing with Aristotle's *Ethics* was the translation of Averroes' *Middle Commentary on the Ethics* made from the Arabic by Samuel ben Judah of Marseilles in 1321/22.[492] It seems, however, that this translation had relatively little impact on Jewish philosophy.[493] A first (direct) Hebrew translation of Aristotle's *Nicomachean Ethics* was made from Robertus Grosseteste's Latin version by R. Meir (Harofe) Alguadez of Castile in 1405.[494]

As a matter of fact, Aristotle's *Ethics* became quite popular among Jewish scholars in Spain, especially among those who were committed to philosophy.[495] Moreover, one can discern the influence of scholasticism, and more

---

492. On this translation, *see* especially L.V. Berman, *Averroes' Middle Commentary on Aristotle's Nicomachean Ethics in the Hebrew Version of Samuel Ben Judah* (Jerusalem 1999) 23–53 (in Hebrew). *Id.*, "Greek into Hebrew: Samuel ben Judah of Marseilles, Fourteenth-Century Philosopher and Translator," *Jewish Medieval and Renaissance Studies* (A. Altmann, ed., Cambridge, Mass. 1967) 289, at 295.

493. H. Tirosh-Rothschild, "Jewish Philosophy on the Eve of Modernity," *History of Jewish Philosophy* (D.H. Frank and O. Leaman, eds., London and New York, 1997, 2003) 499, 559–560, note 154; for the reasons of that lack of impact, *see* especially, *Id., Happiness in Premodern Judaism: Virtue, Knowledge, and Well-Being* (Cincinnati 2003) 258–259.

494. The Jewish National and University Library, Ms. Heb. 28° 3524. *See* on this translation L.V. Berman, "The Latin-to-Hebrew Translation of the *Nicomachean Ethics*," *Shlomo Pines Jubilee Volume on the Occasion of his Eightieth Birthday* (M. Idel, W.Z. Harvey, E. Schweid, eds., Jerusalem 1988) 147 (in Hebrew); H. Tirosh-Samuelson, *Happiness in Premodern Judaism, op. cit*, 398–399; M. Zonta, *La filosofia antica nel Medievo ebraico: Le traduzioni ebraiche medievali dei testi filosofici antichi* (Brescia 1996) 83–85, 114–116, 258–260.

495. Among the important Jewish scholars who referred to a variety of Aristotle's writings, one has to mention Joseph Albo (fifteenth century), the author of *Sefer ha-Ikkarim, Book of Principles* (ed. I. Husik, Philadelphia 1946). However, the author does not refer to the here relevant Fifth Book of the *Nicomachean Ethics. See* generally H. Tirosh-Rothschild, "Jewish Philosophy on the Eve of Modernity," *History of Jewish Philosophy* (D.H. Frank and O. Leaman, eds., London and New York, 1997, 2003) 499, at 535–536; *see also* L.V. Berman, "Le Commentaire moyen d'Ibn Rushd sur l'Ethique à Nicomaque dans la littérature hébraïque du moyen âge," 13 (1977) *Archives Juives* 19. The author mentions specifically Joseph Ibn Caspi (1279–1347) who composed in 1329 an abridgment of the Hebrew translation of Ibn Rushd's commentary; *ibid.*, at 26–27; this work by Ibn Caspi, called *Terumat Hakesef*, remained in manuscript. For additional Jewish scholars who quoted Aristotle's *Ethics*, *see* B. Septimus, "Yitzhak Arama and Aristotle's *Ethics*," *Jews and Conversos at the Time of the Expulsion* (Y.T. Assis and Y. Kaplan, eds., Jerusalem 1999) 1, 12. *See also* S. Harvey, "The Sources of the Quotations from Aristotle's *Ethics* in the *Guide of the Perplexed* and the *Guide to the Guide*." *Joseph Baruch Sermoneta Memorial Volume, Jerusalem Studies in Jewish Thought*, Vol. XIV (A. Ravitzky, ed., Jerusalem 1998) 87 (in Hebrew). The author deals with the literary sources of Aristotle's *Ethics* that were at the disposal of Maimonides (1138–1204) and Shem-Tov Falaquera (1225–1295). Finally, another important Jewish scholar who was critically dealing with Aristotle's philosophy was the Italian Rabbi Ovadia Sforno (ca. 1470–1550); Chaim Shine, *Men, Society, and*

specifically that of a number of leading Christian theologians, such as Thomas Aquinas.[496]

A first commentary on the *Ethics* was written by Josef Ibn Shem Tov in Spain (1400–1460) in 1455, using the Hebrew translation of R. Meir (Harofe) Alguadez.[497] In relation to the Fifth Book, the author follows basically the analysis of Aristotle, but refers in many places to Jewish Talmudical sources that correspond, in his opinion, to Aristotle's views and can serve as their illustration. He explains at length the difference between the geometric proportion in the framework of distributive justice and the arithmetic proportion in commutative justice. He states that in the former one looks at the persons, in the latter at the acts. In relation to the known problem of *contrapassum*, namely, the above-mentioned apparent internal contradiction in Aristotle's approach, the author adopts a solution similar to that of the scholastics: hitting a prince means an increase in the actual damage.[498] It causes shame to the prince and to the entire people. He mentions that, in relation to retribution, the Jewish sages had laid down the corresponding principle: "Everything is in accordance with the person causing the indignity and the insulted party."[499] The author then critically mentions the commentary of Ibn Rushd, according to which in Aristotle's view a prince who hits an ordinary

---

Laws in R. Ovadia Sforno's Thought (Tel-Aviv 2001) (in Hebrew). But it seems that this author did not refer to the Aristotelian forms of justice.

496. On the influence of Christian scholasticism on Jewish philosophers in Italy, Spain, and Provence, *see* now especially M. Zonta, *The Hebrew Scholasticism in the Fifteenth Century: A History and Source Book* (Dordrecht 2006) 1–31, and *passim*; *see also* H. Tirosh-Rothschild, "Jewish Philosophy on the Eve of Modernity," *op. cit.*, at 503–505, 513; A terminological observation: The Hebrew terms for distributive justice that were used already in medieval times: צדק מחלק, צדק מתחלק; recently, some authors use: צדק חלוקתי. The terms for commutative justice were: צדק מאמת, צדק מיישר, צדק מתחלף, צדק מחליף; today the usual term is: צדק מתקן, that corresponds to the concept of "corrective justice." It has to be noted that in a number of early translations, the term for justice is not צדק but שווי, or יושר.

497. Oxford, Bodleian Library MS Mich. 404, Cat. Neubauer, OX 1431; Jewish National and University Library, Manuscript Reading Room, Microfilm F 22511. On the background and personality of Joseph ben Shem Tov ibn Shem Tov, as well as his theology and specific interest in Aristotle's *Ethics*, *see* the extensive discussion of his writings by H. Tirosh-Samuelson, *Happiness in Premodern Judaism: Virtue, Knowledge, and Well-Being* (Cincinnati 2003) 397–411.

498. Joseph Ibn Shem Tov, *ibid.*, 100b–101. On the possible influence of Thomas Aquinas upon Ibn Shem Tov, *see* B. Septimus, "Yitzhak Arama and Aristotle's *Ethics*," *Jews and Conversos at the Time of the Expulsion* (Y.T. Assis and Y. Kaplan, eds., Jerusalem 1999) 1, 14, note 56; H. Tirosh-Samuelson, *Happiness in Premodern Judaism*, *op. cit.*, 401.

499. Mishna, Baba Kama, 8:1: "הכל לפי המבייש והמתבייש".

person should be punished more severely than the contrary situation where an ordinary person hits a prince.[500]

In the author's view, even if there is some truth in the idea that a person's higher standing may increase the severity of his delict, this cannot be Aristotle's opinion in relation to retribution. He suggests the possibility that Ibn Rushd used a garbled text of Aristotle, since in the present correct version, the contrary solution is mentioned. The criterion under commutative justice is not the quality of the person as such, but the quantity of the actual damage.[501]

Rabbi Yizhaq Arama (1420–1494), a Spanish Talmudist and philosopher, is another most influential Jewish scholar who was familiar with Aristotle's *Ethics* and with the commentary of Josef Ibn Shem Tov.[502] In his major work, *Aqedat Yizhaq* (עקידת יצחק), Arama refers to the known problem of Aristotle's comments on retribution (*contrapassum*).[503] After stating the apparent contradiction between the elements of commutative justice, which disregard the status of the litigants, and the later comments of Aristotle on retribution, the author states:

> Indeed, commutative justice does not consider the value of the other people, but it retaliates according to the actual deed of a person, and if he caused a damage of ten dinars, it will command that he will be damaged for ten dinars; and if a person suffers damage for ten dinars, it is appropriate that he will gain in return ten dinars. Commutative justice requires to evaluate the quality and the quantity of damage. In the manner that law considers the difference in the quantity of damage, it should consider its quality, since quality is connected to quantity. As a result, the hitting of an ordinary person by a Prince is not of equal shame and injury as the hitting of the Prince by an ordinary person. And if the Prince, who hit an ordinary person, is punished by being hit himself, the shame and injury caused to him is of a much greater measure than that caused by him, thus constituting an eminent injustice. Equally, when an ordinary person, who had hit the Prince, is merely hit

500. *Supra* note 43.

501. Joseph Ibn Shem Tov, *ibid.*

502. *See* in this context the important work of B. Septimus, "Yitzhak Arama and Aristotle's *Ethics*," *Jews and Conversos at the Time of the Expulsion* (Y.T. Assis and Y. Kaplan, eds., Jerusalem 1999) 1.

503. J. Arama, *Sefer Akedath Jtzchak*, (Pollak, ed., Pressburg 1849), vol. II, pp. 126b–127 (in Hebrew).

> in return, that person has not suffered a punishment that is equal to what he did. Indeed, everything should be according to the position of the insulter and that of the person insulted. Thus, the law judges both on an equal basis, since, when it is lenient in this way towards the Prince, it does not remit, because of his princehood, anything of his appropriate punishment; it does so because the Prince did not cause the ordinary person a greater injury that the punishment meted out to him. Equally, when the ordinary person is punished with more than a blow, this is not because of his inferior status, but because the injury suffered by the Prince through him is greater than a mere blow in retaliation. As a result, all persons are equal under this justice, the insignificant as the mighty, the just as the wicked; as they did, so shall be done to them, equal to equal.[504]

In 1480 Baruch Ibn Yaish composed another Hebrew commentary on the *Nicomachean Ethics*. He based his commentary on two new fifteenth-century Latin translations.[505] This Hebrew commentary, too, remained in manuscript form.[506] The commentary on the Fifth Book of the *Ethics* is rather succinct, and it lacks originality.[507] Moreover, no Jewish sources are mentioned in the commentary.

The next comprehensive commentary on the *Nicomachean Ethics*, entitled *Penei Mosheh*, was written by Moses Almosnino (ca. 1518–1581) of Salonika.[508] The author used the mentioned Hebrew translation of Meir

---

504. *Ibid.*, 127 (author's translation).

505. The Latin translations used by Ibn Yaish were those of the humanists Leonardo Bruni (1416) and of Ioannes Argyropoulos (1457). *See* M. Zonta, *La filosofia antica nel Medievo ebraico: Le traduzioni ebraiche medievali dei testi filosofici antichi* (Brescia 1996) 167, 273–274; *see* now especially *id., The Hebrew Scholasticism in the Fifteenth Century:A History and Source Book* (Dordrecht 2006) 111, 115–155; H. Tirosh-Samuelson, *Happiness in Premodern Judaism: Virtue, Knowledge, and Well-Being* (Cincinnati 2003) 423, note 83, at 540–541.

506. Paris—Bibliothèque Nationale heb. 1001, 1002, 1003; Jewish National and University Library, Manuscript Reading Room, Microfilm, F 1486, F 1487, F 1488; on the origin of these manuscripts and the scholastic (Christian) sources of the commentaries, *see* M. Zonta, *The Hebrew Scholasticism, op. cit., ibid.*

507. I would like to thank Dr. Abraham David, Senior Researcher at The Jewish National and University Library, for his help in deciphering this manuscript.

508. On Almosnino in general, *see* M.Z. Bnaya, *Moshe Almosnino of Salonika: His Life and Work* (Tel Aviv 1996) (in Hebrew); Moše ben Baruk Almosnino, *Regimiento de la vida; Tratado de los suenyos* (Salonika 1564) (J.M. Zemke, ed., Tempe, Ariz., 2004) Introduction, 2–10. For an analysis of Almosnino's approach to ethics, happiness, and perfection, *see* especially H. Tirosh-Samuelson, *Happiness in Premodern Judaism, op. cit.*, at 423–438.

(Harofe) Alguadez. Unfortunately, this commentary, too, remained unpublished and has been preserved in an apparently only partial manuscript.[509]

However, Moses Almosnino published a book on Jewish ethics,[510] where he dedicates three chapters to the virtue of justice.[511] He expounds in a rather summary way the Aristotelian distinction between distributive and commutative justice.[512] The author basically follows Aristotle; he links the substance of justice to the rules of Jewish law.[513] He notes that in relation to Divinity, distribution of benefits is not a form of justice, but an act of pure mercy and compassion since God has no obligations.[514] The author mentions the fact that in the framework of commutative justice, one has to disregard the litigants' respective virtues; however, he refers this rule to the biblical commandment of the judges' duty to a strict impartiality.[515] He mentions the Talmudical saying that every judge who judges a true judgment according to the truth becomes a partner to the Holy One, blessed be He.[516] It is not enough

---

The authoress notes that Almosnino's moral philosophy fuses Aristotelian philosophy and Kabbalah, *ibid.*, 426.

509. Oxford, Bodleian Library MS Mich. 409, Cat. Neubauer, OX 1435; Jewish National and University Library, Manuscript Reading Room, Microfilm F 22515. The manuscript contains only 3 chapters (I, II, X), and lacks the here relevant chapter V of the Nicomachean Ethics. *Cf.* H. Tirosh-Samuelson, *Happiness in Premodern Judaism, op. cit.*, 540, note 81. The authoress describes the influence of Buridanus upon Almosnino, *ibid.*, 541–542, note 88.

510. The book was originally published in 1564 in Salonika, in Spanish with Hebrew letters (Ladino); *see* now Moše ben Baruk Almosnino, *Regimiento de la vida; Tratado de los suenyos* (Salonika 1564) (J.M. Zemke, ed., Tempe, Ariz., 2004); for an earlier edition in Spanish letters, *Id., Regimiento de la vida* (Amsterdam 1729). We shall refer to the Amsterdam edition, but indicate in brackets the corresponding pages in the new critical edition by Zemke.

511. Almosnino, *ibid.*, 203–219 [288–304]. *See also* Almosnino's (Hebrew) introduction to his book in the English translation of J.M. Zemke, *op. cit.*, at 65–66.

512. *Ibid.*, 206–215 [291–301].

513. *Ibid.*, 208 [293]: "Y por que todos estos generos de justicia están más espesificadamente declarados en Nuestro Talmud, y todo significado en Nuestra Santissima Ley no me alargo más en esta materia, más que darte a entendér, que todas quantas especies de Justicia puzieron los Sabios Antiguos, en todos reparticiones, estan incluidas en Nuestra Santissima Ley." On this method of Almosnino, in general, *see* H. Tirosh-Samuelson, *Happiness in Premodern Judaism, op. cit.*, 431.

514. *Ibid.*, 210 [295]. The author relies on Psalm 62:13.

515. *Ibid.*, 211 [295–296].

516. *Ibid.* [296]. The talmudical source is TB. Shabbat, 10a. The author adds: "Queriendo dezir que pues D.B. no cata respecto en la igualdad distribuitiva, más que la pura verdad, por la verdad en si."

to adjudicate according to truth, if it is done out of fear or out of other external reasons; justice must be done exclusively for the sake of truth.

The author then refers to the rejected view of the Pythagoreans. He explains that, in accordance with the rabbinical sources, the difference in retribution between persons of different social status is not based upon any inherent quality of these persons, but upon the difference of the injury.[517]

The philosophical approach among Jewish scholars, that was rather widespread in Spain (until the expulsion of the Jews in 1492), in Provence and equally in Italy, lost much ground in the sixteenth century until its near disappearance in rabbinical circles.[518] A major reason for that change was most probably the rapid and vast spread of Jewish mysticism, the Kabbala, throughout the whole Jewish world. This movement became intrinsically hostile to the rationalistic Greek philosophy as well as to the scholastic project of its adaptation to religion.[519] A relevant example of the shift from rationalism to mysticism presents Yohanan Alemanno (1433–1503), who in his *Song of Salomon's Virtues* deals specifically with the virtue of justice.[520] However, the author—very remote from the formal distinctions of Aristotle—includes in the notion of justice a "right will," harmony between faculties of the soul, and, principally, the mystical ascent toward God in the framework of Kabbalistic symbolism.[521]

---

517. *Ibid.*, 212–213 [298–299].

518. On the recurrent controversies about the study and use of philosophy in rabbinical Judaism, M. Halbertal, *People of the Book: Canon, Meaning, and Authority* (Cambridge, Mass. 1997) 109–119.

519. *Cf.* H. Tirosh-Rothschild, "Jewish Philosophy on the Eve of Modernity," *History of Jewish Philosophy* (D.H. Frank and O. Leaman, eds., London and New York, 1997, 2003) 499, 548–549. M. Zonta, *The Hebrew Scholasticism in the Fifteenth Century: A History and Source Book* (Dordrecht 2006) 30: "In Italy, there is evidence of the persistence of an interest in the works of some Jewish philosophers active in the sixteenth century, such as Ovadiah Sforno (ca. 1470–1550). However, sixteenth century Jewish philosophy in Greece and Italy seems substantially different from late medieval Jewish Aristotelianism, since it involved an eclectic fusion of various doctrinal trends: Aristotelianism, Renaissance Platonism and Humanism, and also kabbalah, which had begun to replace philosophy as the major expression of Jewish thought." On the cultural and spiritual reasons that induced the rabbinical circles in Italy to move away from scholastic philosophy, *see also* R. Bonfil, *The Rabbinate in Renaissance Italy* (Jerusalem 2005) 173–206 (in Hebrew).

520. H. Tirosh-Samuelson, *Happiness in Premodern Judaism: Virtue, Knowledge, and Well-Being* (Cincinnati 2003) 412–423.

521. A. Lesley, *The Song of Salomon's Ascents by Yohanan Alemanno: Love and Human Perfection According to a Jewish Colleague of Giovanni Pico della Mirandola*, Ph.D. Diss., University of California, Berkeley (1976) 518–553 (in Hebrew); 163–192 (English summary);

No wonder, that for the next Jewish scholar to publish a commentary on the *Nicomachean Ethics*, one had to wait until the eighteenth century for the Jewish enlightenment movement (*Haskala*). It was the Jewish scholar and philosopher, Isaac Satanow (1732–1804), who published an extensive commentary in Hebrew together with the mentioned medieval Hebrew translation of Meir (Harofe) Alguadez of Castile of 1405.[522] The author, who was a complex and controversial personality,[523] was familiar with the commentary of Josef Ibn Shem Tov,[524] to which he referred, in a number of instances, in a critical way.[525]

In relation to commutative justice, the author explains the difficult Aristotelian notion of equalizing gain and loss in delictual situations:

> The judge will try to assess in order to equalize the pleasure of the injurer with the pain of the injured. And this he will achieve by causing pain to the injurer according to the measure of the pleasure the latter had when

---

H. Tirosh-Samuelson, *Happiness in Premodern Judaism, op. cit.*, 418. It is, however, noteworthy that the author alludes to the different functions of justice, an allusion that may be a remote echo of Aristotle's distinction; A. Lesley, *op. cit.*, at 524–525: והיושר במדות הנפש ילך אחריו בלי ספק היושר בעסק ובממשלה ויהיו כענפים ממנו ובכלל היושר הוא הסדר הנאהב אם במדות ואם במשא ומתן לקחת הראוי ולתת הראוי ואם בתקון המדינה שתסודר בסדר הדומה לסדר חלקי הנפש עד שתהיה בסדורה ותכונת חלקיה.

522. **ספר המדות לאריסטוטליס מפורש ושום שכל על ידי איצק סטנאב**, חלק ראשון (ברלין 1790). The work has been reprinted in Lemberg in 1867. See the short comment by H. Tirosh-Samuelson, *Happiness in Premodern Judaism: Virtue, Knowledge, and Well-Being* (Cincinnati 2003) 445.

523. S. Werses, "Isaac Satanow and His Mishley Asaph," 32 (1963) *Tarbiz* 370–392 (in Hebrew); M. Pelli, "Isaac Satanow: Metamorphosis of Judaic Values—*Mishlei 'Asaf* As Reflecting the Haskala Ideology," *The Age of Haskalah: Studies in Hebrew Literature of the Enlightenment in Germany* (Leiden 1979) 151–170; *Id.*, *Isaac Satanow: A Heretic and a Believer in the Beginning of Hebrew Haskalah Literature in Germany* (Beer Sheva, 1973) (mimeographed; in Hebrew); N. Rezler-Bersohn, "Isaac Satanow: An Epitome of an Era," 25 (1980) *Leo Baeck Institue Yearbook* 81–100.

524. *Supra* 113–114.

525. In his Preface to the First Part, after stating the difficulties of the text, the author notes that the commentary of Ibn Shem Tov was the only one that was at his disposal, and that many times he deviated from it because it seemed to him to be incorrect: וגם פעמים רבות נטיתי מדרך ביאורו כי לא ישר בעיני ביאורו. In his Introduction, the author adds that the manuscript of Ibn Shem Tov was acquired after great troubles and by means of a great amount of money paid by a rich patron of his [probably Daniel Itzig]. He repeats: ובמקומות רבים נטיתי מביאור הר"שט יען ראיתי כי טוב לפרש בענין אחר המסכים יותר אל האמת. The author also mentions that he spoke with Moses Mendelssohn about the project of publishing the *Ethics*. Mendelssohn agreed to undertake the project, but his death prevented its execution.

> injuring his neighbor out of malice and wickedness and by causing pleasure to the injured from the assets of the injurer or by causing the injurer pain as revenge according to the measure of the injured's pain.[526]

The author then states that, since individuals differ in their affection when submitted to bodily assaults, a judge inflicting exactly measure for measure would do wrong justice. He continues:

> Hence the right justice is when the judge assesses and fills the pain with the pleasure of money, as the sages said "eye for eye means money for the eye" and they said "one assesses the corporal punishment." When compensating injuries that differ among persons, the judge will equalize the pain with the pleasure according to each individual's value: the great and important person will be given more, the lesser will get less. And in this sense, it was said [by Aristotle] "taking away the gain,"[527] meaning that he eliminates the pain of the injured person by means of the money of the injurer, that the latter gained, and not that it will be paid from the latter's body which is like a kind of capital that will not be called "gain." This seems to me to be the right interpretation of Aristotle's words. But, Rabbi Josef Ibn Shem Tov interpreted it differently, namely that the judge will try to equalize it by equalizing the pain with the pleasure according to the actual injury. He explained "gain" as referring to the pleasure, and "loss" to the pain. And I wrote what seemed to be right according to my humble opinion.

The author then deals with the Aristotelian text concerning retribution (*contrapassum*) and the criticized view of the Pythagoreans. The author first explains the difference in respect of the measure of punishment between the case of an ordinary person hitting a prince or governor, and the case of the latter hitting an ordinary person. He then illustrates this principle by means of Jewish sources. The first case corresponds to the biblical story of Shimei the son of Gera, who was eventually put to death because he had cursed and insulted King David.[528] The second case is illustrated by the Talmudic principle

---

526. *Ibid.*, at fol. 61b.

527. *Supra* 6 at note 18.

528. 2 Samuel 16:5–13; 1 Kings 2:8–9, 36–46.

that if a sage committed an offence that is punishable by excommunication, he will get a lighter punishment of shame and disgrace.[529]

The author then continues:

> Do not think that when Aristotle says that the punishment is according to the honor, he contradicts what he said in the preceding chapter, namely that commutative justice, of which he spoke, is not applied according to the honor of persons, but according to the measure of the injury: With the measure that a person measures, so it is measured out to him,[530] the honorable person like the ignoble one, as he [Aristotle] wrote: "For it makes no difference whether a good man has defrauded a bad man or a bad one a good one." Because there he spoke of pecuniary laws and of matters that do not relate to the body, [hence, of a matter] that is equal and equalizes the great and the small, because it is not concerned with honor or with shame. But here justice concerns duties of the body that have an influence upon honor. Hence, the punishment considers the value of each person's honor. Such was the question and such was the answer given by Rabbi Josef Ibn Shem Tov, and I had my say in the preceding chapter that the condition of Aristotle's view was that the judge should try to assess in what places the punishment should be ransomed by money and capital, taken away from the profit of the person, namely from his property. There is a great difference between voluntary and involuntary, since sales and other transactions are executed with the consent of the owners, whereas injuries and their compensation are made without the consent of the owners, both fall under commutative and corrective justice, as explained in the fourth chapter. In any event, their legal regime is not identical, since in case of voluntary transactions no attention is paid to the persons, but to the exchanged objects in order to be mutually equal. The owners, i.e., the buyer and the vendor, may be one a master and the other a slave, or both slaves, or both masters; however the nature of the sale remains identical in both cases, since everything follows the value of the exchanged things, not that of the owners; It is

529. According to Jewish law, a sage is, in principle, not subject to a public excommunication. *Cf.* TB Moed Qatan, 17a; Maimonides, Mishneh Torah, Hilkhot Talmud Torah, 7,1; Shulhan Arukh, Yoreh Deah, §334, 42.

530. Mishna Sota, 1:7: במדה שאדם מודד בה מודדין לו.

different in cases of involuntary [transactions], namely damaging acts, such as bodily injuries. Justice in relation to them is according to the value of the owners, as explained by [Aristotle] by the example of the Prince's blow. So the Sages said: "Everything is in accordance with the person causing the indignity and the insulted party."[531] If it would be otherwise, you would render impossible human life, since "the youth will be insolent to the elder and the base to the honorable,"[532] and they would pay him for his shame a fixed sum of money as if he were one of the ignobles. This seems to me to be the meaning of Aristotle's sayings.[533]

531. *Cf. supra* note 499.

532. This is a quotation from Isaiah 3: 5.

533. *Ibid.*, at fol. 63a. The author then criticizes the view of Josef Ibn Shem Tov, according to which "involuntary" means acts done be the injurer "inadvertently" (בשוגג), and not without consent from the injured person. The author insists that in the present context his interpretation is the correct one. He then expounds the difference between the proportional justice under commutative justice and that under distributive justice (EN 1132b 32). In the case of distributive justice, the proportion is between the owners themselves and between them and the distributed objects; in the case of voluntary transactions, the proportion is merely beteen the exchanged objects; *ibid.*, at fol. 63a. At the end of the chapter the author adds a lengthy comment on the history and economic function of money, *ibid.*, fols. 64b–66b.

SIX

Post-Scholastic Writers

THE TRANSITION FROM SCHOLASTICISM TO POST-SCHOLASTICISM was evidently a gradual matter. It signifies on the one hand, a critical approach toward medieval scholastic thought by a direct return to the classical thinkers of the antiquity. It is the period of the so-called Renaissance characterized by the activity of the humanists.[534] But, on the other hand, it could also mean a critical approach to Aristotle himself.[535] The critique of Aristotle was considerably enhanced during the succeeding era of the Enlightenment.[536] In the limited framework of our study, we will concentrate on the Aristotelian distinction of justice.[537] Naturally, not all humanist scholars added original

---

534. There is much scholarly discussion and controversy on the exact relationship between humanism and scholasticism, *see* D.A. Lines, *Aristotle's Ethics in the Italian Renaissance (ca. 1300–1650): The Universities and the Problem of Moral Education* (Leiden 2002) 1–23.

535. *See* in relation to the different aspects of the position of Aristotle's thought in this period: Ch. B. Schmitt, *Aristotle and the Renaissance* (Cambridge, Mass. 1983) *passim*; D.A. Lines, *Aristotle's Ethics in the Italian Renaissance (ca. 1300–1650), op. cit.*, 19–21; on the impact of humanism on translations of Aristotle's ethics and commentaries, *ibid.*, at 49–54. Many of the founders of the Reformation were equally critical of Aristotle and the scholastic literature: M. Deslandes, *Histoire Critique de la Philosophie*, vol. 4 (Amsterdam 1756) 124: "Je dois remarquer ici que Luther & les autres premiers réformateurs se déchaînèrent contre Aristote, & parlèrent de sa Logique avec beaucoup de mépris . . . Luther même fit soutenir à Heidelberg en 1518 une thèse célèbre, où il maltraita fort Aristote."

536. James Gordley, "Enforcing Promises," 83 (1995) *Calif. L. Rev.* 547, 556: "In the seventeenth and eighteenth century the authority of Aristotle was challenged and ultimately destroyed by the founders of modern critical philosophy. One of the casualties was his theory of distributive and commutative justice . . . When modern philosophers rejected Aristotle's conception of human nature, they pulled out the prop that supported the ideas about just distribution of wealth and equality in exchange." As our work will demonstrate, this statement is only very partially true: the formal aspects of the Aristotelian distinction continued to dominate the jurisprudential discourse.

537. *See* in this context U. Langer, "The Renaissance Novella as Justice," 52 *Renaissance Quarterly* (1999) 311–341. This essay examines short narrative as reflection of different models of justice within the Aristotelian-Ciceronian tradition. Thus, the author reveals the Aristotelian ideas of distributive justice, reciprocity and commutative justice in

ideas to the classical distinction; many limited themselves to a rather succinct description of Aristotle's writings.[538] This is especially true for the literary genre of compendiums for students of Aristotle's *Ethics*, works that concentrated on the original text.[539] Besides the reliance on Greek and Roman sources, one finds in the post-reformation theological-moral literature an enhanced reference to biblical quotations in support of the Aristotelian notions of justice.[540]

The Flemish Judocus Clichtoveus (1472–1543), a Catholic humanist, theologian, and influential teacher at the University of Paris, analyzes in his commentary on Aristotle's *Nicomachean Ethics*, the notion of justice on the background of the classical writings of the antiquity.[541] He affirms that in the framework of distributive justice, the distribution of benefits is better and more dignified than the distribution of evils and punishments. Distribution of benefits assimilates man to the intelligible and celestial world.[542]

---

three novellas of the *Decameron* (8,7; 8,8; 2,5). He assumes that the link between short narrative and justice illuminates the more general relationship between literature and moral language in the Renaissance.

538. *See, e.g.*, the Swiss scholar and Protestant Deacon Otto Werdmüller (1513–1552), *De Dignitate Usu Et Methodo Philosophiae Moralis Quam Aristoteles ad Nicomachum filium conscripsit, Libri duo* (Basel 1544) 265–274. The author explains the importance of Aristotle's ethics for jurisprudence, *ibid.*, 95–114.

539. *See, e.g.*, the summary, by way of questions and answers, published by Theophilus Golius (1528–1600), Professor of Greek and Ethics at Strasburg University, *Epitome Doctrinae Moralis Ex decem libris Ethicorum Aristotelis ad Nicomachum* (Cambridge 1634, London 1662) 128–141; for a more general summary on ethics, *see, e.g.*, Gerard Langbaine (1609–1658), *Philosophiae Moralis Compendium, Juventutis Academiae Studiis Accomodatum; Ex Veterum Scholarum placitis in hodiernarum usum concinnatum* (Cura Thomas Barlowe, London 1698) Cap. XXVI, col. 86–90. The latter author states that tyranny—like the regime of Dionysus—the acception of persons (προσωποληψία), the neglegt (*socordia*) of granting rewards to the worthy, and of punishing the delinquents, all these are contrary to distributive justice.

540. *See, e.g.*, Gulielmus Colvillus (William Colvill) (d. 1675), *Philosophia Moralis Christiana* (Edinburgh 1670) Cap. IX, pp. 191–194.

541. Jacobus Faber Stapulensis (Jaques Lefèvre d'Etaples) (ca. 1460–1536), *Artificialis Introductioin Decem Ethicorum libros Aristotelis, adiuncto Familiari Commentario Iudoci Clichtovei declarata* (Freiburg/Breisgau 1542) 82–94. *See* E. Kessler, "Introducing Aristotle to the sixteenth century: the Lefèvre enterprise," *Philosophy in the Sixteenth and Seventeenth Centuries: Conversations with Aristotle* (C. Blackwell and S. Kusukawa, eds., Aldershot 1999) 1–21.

542. *Ibid.*, 88: "Atqui distributio bonorum melior est & dignior, nam per eam assimilatur homo mundo intelligibili & coelesti, in quo aequissima est bonorum pro ratione meriti

Moreover, it is more enjoyable for the just man, since distribution of evils causes sadness and compassion.[543] Commutative justice in commerce exists only where there is human need (*indigentia*). It alleviates or removes that need. In heavens, since there is no need, there can be no commutative justice. Hence, there the more dignified distributive justice is practiced. In the world of darkness, where need is at its utmost, commutative justice is not conspicuous. Commutative justice of commerce is practiced in this world of senses, where there is partially sufficiency and partially need.[544]

The author affirms that distributive justice is of a geometric proportion: benefits according to merits (two different merits, two different benefits); punishment according to the measure of guilt (two different delicts, two different punishments).[545] Commutative justice observes an arithmetic proportion. The measure of commutative justice is determined by human need (demand); the greater the demand the greater the price. A thing is not valued according to its natural dignity, but according to the human need. If something is not needed, there is no exchange.[546]

---

distributio & non malorum. Distributio autem malorum minus est digna & perfecta, similisque quodam modo distributioni poenarum, quae fit in regione tenebrarum, ubi nulla est bonorum compensatio. In hoc autem mundo sensibili, ut utriusque mundi extremi, scilicet superioris & inferioris medio, fit distributio nunc bonorum, nunc malorum."

543. *Ibid.*, 88a–b.

544. *Ibid.*, 88b–89a: "Unde illic solum est iustitia commerciorum commutativa, ubi est indigentia quae per sufficientiam potest levari atque repelli. In coelo autem nulla est indigentia, sed summa sufficientia, quocirca non est ibidem iustitia commerciorum commutativa. Hinc deprehenditur iustitia communium distributiva esse dignior ea quae commercia commutat, ut cuius exemplar in coelo relucet . . . In regione autem tenebrarum summa est indigentia, & quae per sufficientiam minime depellitur, ideo neque in ea conspicitur iustitia commerciorum commutativa, sed duntaxat in hoc mundo sensibili, in quo partim est sufficientia, & partim indigentia. Et ergo recte medius dicitur, ut qui utriusque mundi extremi aliquid participet."

545. *Ibid.*, 89b–90a.

546. *Ibid.*, 91a–b: "Neque aestimatur res secundum naturalem earum dignitatem, sed secundum indigentiae humanae rationem. Alioquin mus pluris aestimandus esset quam massa auri: urtica omnibus esse divitijs praeferenda, cum sit natura dignior & in superiore entium gradu. Id tamen falsum est: quia murem & urticam non quaerunt homines: quod ijs ad usum non indigeant. Similiter existente humana indigentia, fit commutatio: & ipsa non existente, non fit commutatio. Si enim homines nullo egerent, neque inter eos ulla quidem rerum commutatio fieret. Est igitur indigentia humana, vera commutabilium mesura: & nummus solummodo commutationis instrumentum." The idea that the value of a thing is measured according to human need (demand) and not according

The Aristotelian distinction was equally analyzed by the great humanist jurist and theologian of the Reformation, Philipp Melanchton (1497–1560). He insists, on the basis of Aristotle's work, that there are only two forms of particular justice, commutative and distributive.[547] Commutative justice is based on an arithmetic proportion and includes punishment[548]; distributive justice applies a geometric proportion in bestowing upon persons private and public functions and offices.[549] The author then illustrates that division of justice by a series of examples.[550] Thus, he recounts Aesop's fable on the animals which, after hunting together, divide the quarry (three oxen) under the lion's governance: The luckless jackass and horse apply, respectively, commutative and distributive justice[551]; the clever fox safeguards the

to natural dignity, as well as the example of the natural dignity of a mouse versus the value of gold, can be found already in Thomas Aquinas's writings, *see supra* at note 72.

547. Philipp Melanchton, *Ethicae Doctrinae Elementa Et Enarratio Libri Quinti Ethicorum* (Wittenberg 1560) 99: "Sunt autem duae species iusticiae particularis distributiva & commutativa, nec sunt plures"; *ibid.*, 199; reprinted in *Philippi Melanthonis Opera Quae Supersunt Omnia*, Vol. XVI, (Bretschneider and Bindsell, eds., Halle 1850) col. 165–275, 363–416, at col. 224.

548. *Id., Ethicae, op. cit.*, 100–101, 187, 191; *Opera*, col. 224–225, 366, 369.

549. *Id., Ethicae, op. cit.*, 101–104, 187–190; *Opera*, col. 225–226. The author adds (at 102; col. 225): "Haec personarum ordinatio cum maxime necessaria sit, Plato dixit, Optimum Reipublicae statum esse, si sit constitutus Geometrica proportione." The same ideas are expressed by the author in his *Philosophiae Moralis Epitomes Libri Duo* in *Opera*, Vol. XVI, *op. cit.*, col. 65–69; reprinted in *Melanchtons Werke*, III. Band, *Humanistische Schriften* (R. Nürenberger, ed., Gütersloh 1961) 202–207; *cf.* H. Heineck, *Die Aelteste Fassung von Melanchtons Ethik* (Berlin 1893) 23–27, 46–49. Melanchton defines distributive justice as a combination of two commutative justices: "Iustitia distributiva est propriissime collatio duarum commutativarum in qua medium constituitur iuxta proportionem geometricam, et habet locum non solum in distribuendis poenis et praemiis sed etiam in contractibus ubicunque personae ac gradus plures occurrunt. Ut si amphora vini venit aureo in vindemia loclupletiore duobus aureis aestimanda erit cum dimidium crevit. Si opera unius diei denario aestimatur, bidui operae duobus denariis aestimandae erunt. Eadem plane ratio est in poenis ac praemiis . . . In his exemplis cerni potest quod distributiva vere ac simpliciter sit collatio duarum commutativarum (*ibid.*, 24)."

550. *Ethicae, op. cit.*, 196–214; *Opera*, cols. 372–383.

551. The ass divides the game into equal parts, the horse gives the lion a whole ox. In Melanchton's version the hunting group consists of lion, fox, wild boar, horse, and ass.

"lion's share."[552] In the author's view, the story demonstrates a tyrant's confounding of the two forms of justice.[553]

Another typical humanist work is the commentary on Aristotle's *Nicomachean Ethics* by the eminent Florentine philologist Pietro Vettori (1499–1585).[554] His commentary follows the Greek origin and its Latin translation. Totally unconcerned with the scholastic discussions, he concentrates more on the philological aspects and tends to rely on classical sources for the illustration of some ideas.

An additional trend in post-scholastic literature is the emphasis on Roman law. Thus, the French humanist jurist François Connan (1508–1551), after stating the Aristotelian distinction between the two forms of justice, adduces a number of examples from Roman succession law in order to illustrate the difference between arithmetic and geometric proportions.[555]

---

552. *Ethicae, op. cit.*, 201–202; *Opera*, col. 376: "In Apologo Aesopi exemplum illustre proponitur, quod monet confundi hanc proportionem a tyrannis: Leo, vulpes, aper, equus et asinus, simul venati, tres tauros ceperant, leo iubet asinum dividere praedam, is secat tauros omnes in quinque aequales partes, et tribuit singulis, qui una venati erant, unam. Hic leo iratus, dilaniat asinum, inquiens: sibi plus deberi, quam caeteris, quia antecellat aliis robore, et plus laborasset, quam caeteri, iubet igitue equum partiri, qui admonitus exitu asini, et cogitans aliquanto plus deberi leoni, attribuit ei integrum taurum, singulis caeteris dimidium. Leo et hunc concerpit, iam non allegans operas, sed ait plus honoris, tanquam regi, sibi tribuendum esse. Tandem iubet vulpem dividere praedam, haec cumulat omnes partes, et iubet leonem auferre universam praedam. Interrogata vulpes, unde didicisset hanc partitionem, respondit: ab his purpuratis doctoribus, id est, a laceratis divisoribus, significans tyrannos saevire in iudices, seu consiliarios, non servientes ipsorum cupiditatibus."

553. *Ibid.*: "Servaverat autem asinus proportionem Arithmeticam, equus Geometricam, tyrannus utranque conturbat." He adds ironically: "Sic in Synodo, qui singulis è vulgo iudicandi potestatem concedi volunt, asini divisionem imitantur. Qui deligunt idoneos, servant Geometricam proportionem, sed tyranni, more leonis, conturbant eam, & ad sese rapiunt omnia." The exact source of Melanchton's version of Aesop's fable is not quite clear to us. In the versions available to us (there exist an enormous number of editions), we found only the story of the lion, the donkey, and the fox without the participation of a horse that divided the quarry according to a geometric proportion. Compare, *e.g.*, Martin Luther, *Fabeln* (Bogeng, ed., Heidelberg 1924) 9, §VII; Aesopus, *Fabularum quae hoc libro continentur, interpretes atque autores sunt hi. Guilelmus Goudamus etc.* (Leipzig 1535?) 40–41; *Aesopi Phrygii Fabulatoris Celeberrimi Vita, Et Lepidissimae Fabulae Graecae, Et Latine* (Venezia 1747) 100; *Aesopi Phrygis Fabulae Graece Et Latine Cum Aliis Quibusdam Opusculis* (Basel 1616) 186–187; *Aesopi Phrygis Et Aliorum Fabulae* (Zürich ca. 1560) 189; *Fabularum Aesopicarum Collectio. Quotquot Graece Reperiuntur Accedit Interpretatio Latina* (Basel 1780).

554. Petrus Victorius, *Commentarii in X Libros Aristotelis De Moribus Ad Nicomachum* (Firenze 1684).

555. Franciscus Connanus, *Commentariorum juris civilis libri X* (Basel 1557), Lib. V, Cap. I, §§1–4, pp. 471–474.

A typical humanist approach one finds in the oration on justice of the German scholar Nicolaus Agricola (b. 1520), that he delivered as rector in Regensburg in 1555.[556] The classic sources are his starting point for sayings and examples on the notion of justice as well as for the Aristotelian distinction. The orator describes the political importance of distributive justice that, based on a geometric proportion, attributes offices, benefits, and punishments.[557] He emphasizes the fact that the arithmetic proportion[558] of commutative justice is equally applicable to involuntary contracts. Thus, Orestes who killed his mother was convicted under Greek law to the capital punishment.

However, the laws for punishing delicts differ in the various states. They are just if they conform to God's will and to human reason. The laws are enacted out of distributive justice considerations, taking into account the circumstances of the persons, the places, and the times. Once these laws have been so established, they are rightly considered to be orders of commutative justice that are applied by the judge in order to achieve equality between the delict and the injury.[559] In the whole nature a measure of equality between agent and patient is necessary, otherwise things perish. A lack of equality is like a too strong medicine that causes the destruction of the body, or a too strong light that blinds the eyes. Finally, need (*indigentia*) lies at the basis of the measure of equality in relation to commodities and services.[560]

556. Nicolaus Agricola, *Oratio De Iustitia Habita In Schola Ratisponensi* (Regensburg 1555).

557. *Ibid.*: "Porro distributiva respicit, ac discernit personas, & singulis suum locum & convenientia officia, poenas & praemia tribuit."

558. The author notes that the equality under commutative justice is called "*aequalitas numerorum*," as against the "*aequalitas proportionum*" of distributive justice.

559. *Ibid.*: "Orestes interficit matrem, caedes iniustissima est. Orestes igitur, ne plus habeat tollatque iustitiam, iudicium Graecorum iuxta legem decernit retributionem, videlicet poenam capitalem. Alibi quidem aliae leges latae sunt quibus puniuntur delicta, ut aliae fuere in republica iudaica, aliae vero nunc sunt passim in imperijs, & politijs, & quidem diversae, omnes tamen si cum voluntate Dei, & ratione humana consentiunt, iustae sunt. A iustitia enim distributiva, de qua dixi, promulgatae habentur consideratis circumstantijs personarum, locorum & temporum. Et postquam illae sic lata sunt, iustitiae commutativae recte putantur voces esse, quas in foro profert iudex in efficienda aequalitate delicti & damni. Et ideo probantur iura legislatorum quia ortum trahunt ex legibus naturalibus. Quare inter delicta & damna arithmetica aequalitas est, quam leges naturae & positivae decernunt per iudicem est vero eadem quae in contractibus voluntarijs."

560. *Ibid.*: "Caeterum causa, quae redigit merces, vel etiam operas, ad aequalitatem, est indigentia.Haec enim eius mercis, qua magis indigemus, maiorem gradum precij constituit, quam eius, cuius aliqua copia est, vel parum egemus."

Another important post-scholastic jurist is the Flemish Matthias Wesenbeck (1531–1586), who, after joining Protestantism, became Dean of the Law Faculty in Jena and later rector of the University of Wittenberg. He is one of the founders of the early *usus modernus pandectarum*. In his influential commentary on the Pandects, he discusses the Aristotelian notions of justice.[561] He identifies the virtue of particular justice with the famous Roman definition of Ulpianus: *Constans e perpetua voluntas ius suum cuique tribuens*.[562] The author then illustrates the geometric proportion applied in the distribution of public functions and rewards by means of a variety of positive Roman legal rules. He then states that nowhere is the application of a geometric proportion more conspicuous than in the distribution of punishments. Though the law in general and in the abstract establishes for punishment an arithmetic proportion—by measuring it according to the delict according to the *lex talionis*—it nevertheless adapts it in the concrete case to the person of the offender and to that of the victim according to a geometric proportion.[563] On the other hand, in transactions no attention is paid to the difference in the status of the contracting parties. The author refers the primary reasons (*causa efficiens*) of the two forms of justice to divine design and relates their functions (*finis & effectus*) to the service of Divinity and the welfare of society.[564]

In a book published in 1572,[565] the author Detlev Langenbeck describes the geometric proportion by the example of the human stomach that distributes the food to the various parts of the body according to their nature and dignity: the heart, the eyes, and the brain receive the best one, the hands and feet according to their quality. True, all are human beings, but there are differences in their quality and circumstances. Likewise, the earth gives each plant food according to its nature.[566] The arithmetic proportion is applied in

561. Matthaeus Wesenbecius, *In Pandectas Juris Civilis & Codicis Justinianei Libros Commentarii* (Basel 1629) Digest. Lib. I, Tit. 1, col. 7–14, §§10–13.

562. *Ibid.*, §10: "Est igitur justitia particularis (ut ex authoritate Simonidis definiunt nostri) constans & perpetua voluntas, jus suum cuique tribuens"; see on this identification, *infra* at note 690. The source of Ulpian's definition is Digest. 1.1.10. pr.

563. *Ibid.*, §11, col. 9–10. The author mentions the popular saying: "Duo, cum idem faciunt, non est idem," and adduces a series of illustrations to this effect from legal provisions.

564. *Ibid.*, §§12–13, col. 11–13.

565. Detlevus Langebekius, *Der andere Teil des Regentenbuchs; de justitia, jure et aequitate; Von der Rechtfertigkeit* (Wittenberg 1572).

566. *Ibid.*, p. 42b: "Denn in dieser *Proportion* wird allein de gleichheit der qualitet verstanden."

contracts, acts, obligations, and offenses. Here, the great and powerful is bound to keep his contract and punishable for offenses like the low one.[567] Since there is a great difference between these proportions, the prudent man must know, especially if he sits in government, which one to apply. The author then mentions the story of the young King Cyrus of Persia as recounted by Xenophon[568]:

> The young King Cyrus committed a grave mistake in relation to these proportions and as a result was severely punished by his teacher of justice. A big boy with a little tunic, finding a little boy with a big tunic on, took it from him by force, giving him his little tunic. The case came before the young King who decided that the little boy should keep the little tunic, the other boy the big one. However, it would have been

---

567. *Ibid.*: "Denn in alle denen dingen und dergleichen/ mus one alles ansehen und unterscheid der Personen/ gleichheit sein/ und Exempels weise/ so mus der Grosse und gewaltige/ seiner Contract halben/ so wol verpflichtet sein/ auch glauben halten/ zu dem seiner unthate und mishandlung halben gestraffet werden/ als der Nidrige/ Wiewol an form und masse der straffe/ unterscheid gehalten werden kan/ gilt auch gleich/ ob einem armen gewalt und unrecht geschehen sey/ oder einem Reichen. Item/ ein geringer mus so wol gehöret/ und zu rechte gefordert werden/ als ein fürnemer und gewaltiger etc. So wird in dem Contracten auch schier allein die gleicheit der dinge—so an beiden seiten verhandelt werden/ geachtet/ denn so bald in demselbigen grosse ungleicheit verhanden/ wird stets falscheit/ betrug/ und hinterlist vermutet."

568. For the original story, *see* Xenophon, *Cyropaedia* I (The Loeb Classical Library with an English translation by Walter Miller, Cambridge Mass. 1960) I. iii. 16–17, pp. 41–43. The story is already mentioned in this context by Philipp Melanchton (1497–1560), *Ethicae Doctrinae Elementa Et Enarratio Libri Quinti Ethicorum* (Wittenberg 1560) 192, who observes: "Erraverat autem Cyrus in discernenda aequalitate, iudicaverat secundum Geometricam proportionem, cum aequalitas non personarum, sed rerum tantum esset facienda Arithmetica proportionem, ne alter damno afficeretur." A reference to the story appears equally in Matthaeus Wesenbecius (Matthias Wesenbeck) (1531–1581), *In Pandectas Juris Civilis & Codicis Justinianei Libros Commentarii* (Basel 1629) Digest. Lib. I, Tit. 1, col. 13, when speaking of violations of commutative justice: "Item analogia Geometrica, hoc in contractuum argomento: ut cum Cyrus injustam vestium permutationem, juxta proportionem Geometricam facit." (The first edition of this book appeared in 1563.) The story is mentioned also by Hugo Grotius, *De iure belli ac pacis*, Lib. I, Cap. I, §8, 3, and in his wake by Leibniz, "Praefatio Codicis Juris Gentium Diplomatici," published in the edition of the Akademie der Wissenschaften, Vierte Reihe, Politische Schriften, Fünfter Band (1692–1694) (Akademie Verlag 2004), I. *Rechtswesen*, N.7, 48, p.62; in the English translation: Leibniz, "On the Notions of Right and Justice. 1693," *The Monadology* (R. Latta, transl., Oxford 1898) 281, 290. In another place Leibniz alludes to the story in relation to the right of property: "For it is not permitted to deprive the rich of their goods to accommodate the poor, nor to deprive a man of his coat which does not suit his size in order to give it to another whose size is better suited to it"; Leibniz, "Meditation on the Common Concept of Justice," in Leibniz, *Political Writings* (Patrick Riley, ed., Cambridge, 2nd ed., 1988) 45, 64. *See also infra*, note 576.

> much more equitable and just that each should have got back the ownership of his own tunic, without paying attention to any difference between the persons or to their standing. For in this case not the geometric proportion, but the arithmetic one should take place.[569]

The French jurist and political philosopher, Jean Bodin (1529–1596), also starts from the Aristotelian distinction between corrective and distributive justice, but he criticizes the assumption of their dichotomous, mutually exclusive character.[570] In his view, the two forms of justice have to be combined in a harmonious way. Thus, he claims that Aristotle was wrong in assuming that punishment, in distinction to rewards, should be imposed according to an equal, arithmetic justice. He states that, as a matter of fact, aristocratic people always received a milder punishment. Had Aristotle been a judge, or at least read and understood the laws of his country, he would never have written that punishment should be meted out according to arithmetic justice. The right measure is a combination of geometric and arithmetic, i.e., harmonic justice. Moreover, Aristotle errs when postulating that in sanctioning offences one had to ignore the good or evil character of the offender. On the contrary, that should be the foremost factor in the eyes of the judge. Equally, in relation to corrective justice, it is not enough that a thief always restores the mere loss of the victim.

In some ancient laws, he was obliged to pay the double, the triple or more of the stolen object's value. Even in cases of mere civil liability for damages, the concrete situation of the litigants was decisive for the existence of liability and the measure of interest. All this is the result of the application of harmonic justice, the combination of distributive and corrective justice.[571]

A typical representative of the humanist approach is the German Professor of Ethics at the University of Jena, Wolfgang Heider (1558–1626). He refers directly to Aristotle's text and to the classical literature, disregarding the

---

569. Langenbeck, *op. cit.*, 43a.

570. Jean Bodin, *Six Livres de la République*, Liv. VI, chap. 6.

571. On Bodin's notion of harmonic justice, *see* S. Goyard-Fabre, *Jean Bodin et le droit de la république* (Paris 1989) 255–269. On the question whether harmonic justice is a third form of justice in addition to that of corrective and distributive justice, *see* the discussion between between G. Del Vecchio, *Justice—An Historical and Philosophical Essay* (A.H. Campbell, ed., Edinburgh 1952) §6, note 5, pp. 58–59, and H. Nef, *Gleichheit und Gerechtigkeit* (Zurich 1941) 97–100. For a harsh critique of Bodin's treatment of Aristotle, *see* M. Villey, "La Justice Harmonique selon Bodin," *Jean Bodin: Proceedings of the International Conference on Bodin in Munich* (H. Denzer ed. Munich, 1973) 79–81.

scholastic endeavors.[572] His concrete examples, relating to the two kinds of justice, are taken from classic authors: Homer, *Iliad*,[573] Plutarch, *Apophthegmata Regum*,[574] Laertius, *Lives of Eminent Philosophers*,[575] Xenophon, *Cyropaedia*,[576] and Gellius, *Noctae Atticae*.[577]

The author notes that distributive and commutative justice differ in their action (division and exchange), in their object (things to be distributed and contracts), and in their proportion (geometric and arithmetic). In relation to punishment, the author suggests that it falls under both forms of justice. It conforms to corrective justice, since loss and profit are removed and brought to an equality that resembles an arithmetic proportion. Moreover, the punishment has to correspond exactly to the offense, as done in retaliation. However, it can also be classified under distributive justice, because it takes into account a person's merits.[578] In this context, the author defends the Pythagorean notion of *antipeponthos* against Aristotle's critique. In his view, the Pythagoreans did not conceive retaliation as a simple equal act, but rather something proportional, taking into account the specific merits of the case. Thus, if somebody imprudently causes death, reciprocity certainly does not mean to kill the offender, but to punish or exile him.[579]

---

572. Wolfgang Heider, *Libellus De Ira Cohibenda, Ex Aristotele, Seneca, Plutarco; et aliis auctoribus collectis. Ad quem accessere Disputationes; I. De Justicia. II. De Ratione Disputandi. III De Ratione Institutionis Scholasticae* (Jena 1608) 64–74.

573. *Ibid.*, §50, p. 66; comparisons between qualities of the heroes.

574. *Ibid.*, §58, p. 68; the story of King Antigonus and Thrasillus Cynicus, Archelaus, and Euripides: "Hanc ad Iusticiam refer Antigoni regis, qui Thrasillo Cynico petenti Drachmam, non est inquit munus regium & Cynico subjiciente: talentum itaque dato: non est inquit Cynicum tale munus accipere. Et Archelaus cum quidem ab ipso poculum aureum peteret: id Euripidi tacenti jussit dari, & tu quidem inquit dignus es, qui petas, sed hic qui accipiat."

575. *Ibid.*, §60; Diogenes Laertius, *Lives of Eminent Philosophers* (The Loeb Classical Library with an English translation by R.D. Hicks, London, New York 1931) vol. II, Book VI, *Crates*, p. 89:

"Set down for the chief ten minas, for the doctor
One drachma, for the flatterer talents five,
For counsel smoke, for mercenary beauty
A talent, for a philosopher three obols."

576. *Ibid.*, §82, p.72, the story of the big and little tunic, *supra* at note 568.

577. *Ibid.*, §83. Aulus Gellius, *Noctes Atticae*, Lib. 7, Cap. 14 (reasons for punishment); Lib. 14, cap. 4 (Chrysippus's description of the figure of justice); Lib. XX, Cap.1 (discussion of Sextus Caecilius and Favorinus about the lex talionis of the Twelve Tables).

578. *Ibid.*, §§83–85, pp. 72–73.

579. *Ibid.*, §§86–91, pp. 73–74.

The Oxford philosopher and physician John Case (ca. 1540–1599), characterized by Charles Schmitt as an "eclectic Aristotelian,"[580] actually closely followed in his work on ethics Aristotle's analysis of the two forms of justice.[581] The author, using in his work a Socratic method of oppositions and responses,[582] fully defends the Aristotelian approach. In relation to the example of the commoner who, after being hit by the ruler has no right to hit back, the author gives the classic explanation that retaliation is excluded not because of dignity, but in view of the greater damage caused to the community.[583] The author's original addition relates to the position of kings and rulers. They have to be honored even if they lack virtue. Kings are subject to nobody except to Divinity and nature. Hence, there is no right to rebel against rulers.[584] The author mentions in this context the biblical story of David restraining himself twice from killing King Saul, and his putting to death the young informant who (falsely) vaunted himself to have killed Saul.[585]

The German philosopher and Protestant theologian Bartholomäus Keckermann (ca. 1571–1608), follows basically the Aristotelian analysis.[586] Distributive justice is based upon a geometric proportion, taking into account the higher persons' status and dignity or their merits. He insists that punishment makes part of distributive justice.[587] The same is true for retribution (*ius talionis*).[588] According to Aristotle's criticism of the Pythagoreans'

---

580. C.B. Schmitt, *John Case and Aristotelianism in Renaissance England* (Kingston and Montreal 1983) 139–190.

581. Iohannes Casus, *Speculum Quaestionum Moralium, In Universam Aristotelis Philosophi Ethicen* (Oxford 1596) Question. Lib. V, pp. 264–290.

582. C.B. Schmitt, *op. cit.*, 87, observes that this structure was characteristic of Oxford philosophical education of the period.

583. *Ibid.*, 276: "Quod vero non liceat principi percutienti vim inferre, non dicitur respectu dignitatis, sed respectu laesae communitatis, quae vulnerato principe maximum damnum ac nocumentum patitur, Iustitia in hoc casu non dignitatem viri, sed inaequalitatem damni respicit."

584. *Ibid.*, 278–279.

585. 1 Samuel 24, 26; 2 Samuel 1.

586. Bartholomaeus Keckermannus, *Sistema Ethicae, Tribus Libris Adornatum & publicis praelectionibus traditum in Gymnasio Dantiscano* (London 1607) 169–185.

587. *Ibid.*, 173: "Obiectum iustitiae Distributivae sunt honores, dignitates, praemia, & contra poenae, supplicia, castigationes, simulque personae quibus ista tribuntur."

588. *Ibid.*, 176: "Ad iustitiam distributivam reducitur ius Talionis. Alii Ethici hoc ius referunt ad iustitiam commutativam, quae qualiter fiat, non video. Scriptura sane sacra illud ius ad poenas refert, poenae autem non ad commutativam iustitiam pertinent, sed ad distributivam."

notion of *antipeponthos*, it does not signify simple, identical reciprocity but an analogical, proportional one. Thus, if a person injures, by means of words or acts, a public orator while standing on the rostrum, he must be punished more severely, not only because of the person's circumstances, but also in view of the location.[589] The concept of judicial justice (*iustitia iudiciaria*), that prohibits to take into account personal qualities which are not relevant to the issue in litigation, makes also part of distributive justice.[590] Moreover, distributive justice includes equally defensive and preventive justice (*iustitia defensiva, iustitia propulsatrix*) that protect innocent, vulnerable persons from being injured.[591]

On the other hand, commutative justice applies an arithmetic proportion and does not pay attention to the personal qualities of the contracting parties, but only to the things exchanged.[592] However, the required equality between the things exchanged does not mean the exclusion of any profit-making in the commercial transaction.[593]

The German Calvinist scholar, Abraham Scultetus (1566–1625), preacher and iconoclast,[594] considered the notions of distributive and commutative justice to be too restricted.[595] In his view, they do not include the virtues of

---

589. *Ibid.*, 177. The author refers here to the argument against *ius talionis* as recounted by Gellius, *supra* note 184.

590. *Ibid.*, 178.

591. *Ibid.*, 179: "Pertinet etiam ad iustitiam distributivam iustitia defensiva & propulsatrix, quando nempe ab innocentibus propulsantur iniuriae, & defenduntur ii, qui seipsos tueri non possunt."

592. *Ibid.*, 179–185.

593. *Ibid.*, 182: "Nam sub fine cap. dicit [Aristoteles] signum commutationis esse, quando ij, qui commutarunt, post factam permutationem tantundem habent, quantum habebant ante permutationem, ita ut neutra pars possit vel de lucro gloriari, vel de damno coqueri: unde sequi videtur, quod omnis mercatura sit contra iustitiam commutativam, utpote cuius finis sit aliquid lucrari. Sed respondetur, Aristot. tantum hic respicere proportionem aequalitatis inter res de quibus contrahitur; non autem respicere medium & mensuram istitus permutationis, ex quo medio oriri possit lucrum secundum iustitiam commutativam." The author then analyses the economic factors that influence the measure and evaluation of commercial goods' prices.

594. Scultetus who served as counseler of the Elector of the Palatinate, Frederic, the short-lived King of Bohemia, was responsible for the iconoclastic destruction of Lucas Cranach's altar in the Cathedral of Prague.

595. Abrahamus Scultetus, *Ethicorum Libri Duo* (Oberursel 1603), Lib. I, Cap. XXVIII, p. 86: "Sed tamen sive ea sit rei difficultas, sive, quod potius reor, ea iudicii mei infirmitas: non semel mihi in mentem venit de distributionis huius veritate dubitare. Nam cum latissimum Iustitiae campum mentis oculis contemplor angusta vero, quibus distributiva, quibus item correctiva circumscribuntur, spatia considero: huc nonnunquam delabor: ut tam

veracity, gratitude, and *innocentia*[596] that are subjects of justice. On the other hand, he considers the essence of all justice to be the function of distribution, since between *suum cuique tribuere* and *suum cuique distribuere*, there seems to be no difference. Moreover, the arithmetic proportion is applicable not only in relation to contracts, but equally to delicts and punishment. Hence, some call punitive justice commutative justice, others distributive justice. As a result, he suggests that the whole Aristotelian distinction is unsatisfactory.[597]

These objections did not remain unanswered. Valentin Wudrian, the respondent in an academic disputation, argued that Scultetus himself confounded between immediate and mediate distinctions.[598] Thus, e.g., the virtue of gratitude will fall—if referred to particular justice—under distributive justice. Likewise, veracity does not in itself constitute a kind of particular justice, but relates to the matter of agreements. The same is true for honesty and abstention from wrongdoing (*innocentia*) that belong to commutative justice. Since these virtues constitute an indirect, mediate part of particular justice, they, by no means, exclude the immediate kinds of justice.[599]

The idea that all forms of justice are based upon the virtue of "giving everybody his due" ("*suum cuique tribuens*") is not to the point, since not all cases fall under distributive justice. Distributive justice is the standard for the distribution of things, commutative justice, on the contrary, for the exchange of things.[600]

---

exiguis Iustitiae distributivae & correctivae terminis totius amplitudinem Iustitiae minime posse includi existimem: praesertim cum non videam: quid Veracitati, Innocentiae, quae & ipsae Iustitiae subiectae, relictum sit loci. Rursum cum animum ab hac divisione ad iustitiae totius naturam perpendendam avoco: in eam devenio opinionem: ut totam Iustitiae vim in distributionis officio sitam esse credam: quandoquidem suum cuique tribuere, & suum cuique distribuere aut parum mihi tum aut nihil etiam differre videntur. Ut ita distributiva Iustitia non species Iustitiae, sed ipsa sit Iustitia."

596. The author defines that notion as abstention from causing injury: "Innocentia est Iustitia nemini nocens."

597. *Ibid.*, 86–87.

598. Valentinus Wudrianus, *De Justitia* (Disputatio XII, Praes. Joachimus Krakevitz, Greifswald 1637) §16: "[Scultetus] sed confundit eo ipso divisionem immediatam & mediatam, cum ea, siquidem sub particulari justitia locanda sint, non immediate sed mediantibus hisce specibus reponantur ibi, v.g. gratitudo si ad justitiam referenda est, ad distributivam referenda est, ut proinde eis recte hic nondum facta sit mentio, ubi distributivam speciatim non attingimus."

599. *Ibid.*: "Tanquam mediata justitiae particularis pars, immediatas nostras neutiquam excludit."

600. *Ibid.*

In relation to punishment, the author notes that the majority of scholars consider it to be part of distributive justice. However, he objects to that view for four reasons: 1) Punishment is not an object of distribution: It is not property of the state that can be distributed among the citizens. 2) Objects that are distributed on the basis of distributive justice are given according to the individual's position in the state, qua citizen and member of the community. Punishment is meted out not in the offender's capacity as a citizen, but because the delict he committed deserves punishment. 3) Objects that are distributed on the basis of distributive justice are to be distributed among all citizens. Punishments, to the contrary, are imposed solely upon criminals. 4) Aristotle agrees to that conclusion, since he refers the compensation of involuntary contracts—which are nothing else than the punishment of delicts—to contractual justice and not to distributive justice.[601]

In addition, the author states that he does not join the view of most scholars, according to which punishment is based upon a geometric proportion.[602] In his opinion, punishment is a matter of commutative justice for a number of reasons: It involves equality between the delict and the penalty; and insofar the condition of a person is taken into account, it is merely in order to assess the quantity of a thing and not the form of the equality.[603] The law prescribes the measure of punishment according to an arithmetic proportion and requires to impose it without paying attention to the person's status. Moreover, if the geometric proportion would be appropriate in imposing punishment, then, for an identical offense, the more dignified person should be punished more severely than the less worthy one. This, however, is absurd.[604] Finally, the author declares that commutative justice lies in the equality of exchange and not in its inherent physical quality or

---

601. *Ibid.*, §18. The author relies on Horneius (1590–1649), *Philosophiae Moralis Sive Civilis Doctrinae De Moribus Libri IV*, Lib. 3, Cap. 13.

602. *Ibid.*, §22.

603. *Ibid.*: "E, si quis obvertat; ita adaequationem delicti & ponae, hic respici, ut tamen conditio personae non excludatur, ei *Cajetani* verbis quantum veri illud involvat sic declaramus: *commutativa justitia non attendit conditionem personae, sed praesupposita rei quantitate tam ex personae, quam cujuscunque alterius circumstantiae conditione, adaequare uni rei rem alteram absolute quaerit: distributiva v. in constituendo aequalitatis formam conditiones personarum assumit, quasi mensuras aequalitatis rerum &c.consideratio prima est ad materiam, sc.ad quantitatem rei, ista v. ad aequationis formam.*"

604. *Ibid.* At the end of his argumentation, the author notes that—in respect of the classification of punishment —Aristotle, Thomas Aquinas, and Cajetanus, as well as among the more recent scholars, Henning Arnisaeus (1575–1636) and Conrad Horneius (1590–1649), agree with him as to his conclusion.

natural essence. Its measure is determined by its need and utility in the human life.[605]

Identical conclusions on similar grounds we find in another, later dissertation on commutative justice published in Leipzig in 1670.[606] The author insists—again against the opinion of a majority of scholars—that punishment for delicts constitutes commutative justice based upon an arithmetic proportion.[607] True, different persons may be punished differently for the same offence. Thus, e.g., a simple theft may be committed by a person in a public office or by an ordinary person. The punishment will be different: For the official it is enough to be removed from office, but the ordinary person may be punished by lashes. Still, it constitutes commutative justice on the basis of arithmetic equality, since the persons are not considered *per se*, as it is done in distributive justice.

Here, the position of the delinquent person is taken into account *per accidens*, in order to equalize the punishment. If both would get the same punishment, the more honorable person would suffer pain and in addition to it lose his dignity, whereas the private person would merely suffer pain. In order to achieve equality, the punishment is not based upon a simple comparison of the public and private person, but attention is foremost paid to the delict and the punishment.[608]

Distributive justice is different: It divides common things to the members of the community; benefits are distributed according to the citizens' position and dignity in the state. Punishments are meted out to persons not qua citizens, but qua delinquents.[609] The author, after discussing the measure of

605. *Ibid.*, §23: "*Aequalitas a. illa ex aestimatione rerum permutandarum petitur, quae 1. non dependet proprie ex perfectione naturali earum*, puta magnitudine, numero l. qualitate physica, l. in universum nobilitate essentiae. *nec 2. ex hujus vel illius judicio*, qui forte privato arbitrio ingeminat trita illa: Ich kans dafür bekommen / es ist Marckgänck und gebich, sed 3. *ex constitutione publica, fundata in rerum collatione rationabili ad se invicem, uitlitate item & indigentia earum in vita humana.*"

606. Johannes Michael Gutbier, *Discursus Ethicus De Justitia Commutativa* (Praes. Johann Caspar Pflaume, Leipzig 1670).

607. *Ibid.*, §§29–41.

608. *Ibid.*, §38: "Ut igitur adesset aequalitas, quae vult, ut poena tanta sit, quantam gravitas delicti requirit, non facta fuit simplex comparatio inter personam publicam & privatam, sed primario respectum fuit ad delictum & poenam, visumque a Judice, ut suum cuique tribueretur."

609. *Ibid.*, §40: "Praemia distribuenda dari qua civibus, ita ut cujusque locus ac dignitas in Republ. attendatur: (id enim ratio **Personarum** hic denotat) si vero poenae infligantur, hoc fit non qua Civibus sed qua delinquentibus." The author notes (*ibid.*), apparently in

equality in transactions and the function of money,[610] comments on Aristotle's critique of the Pythagorean notion of *antipeponthos*.[611] In his view, there is an affinity between the *jus talionis* and the notion of justice, even if not a full identity. Retaliation should be understood not as a simple equality, but as implying a proportion between delict and punishment.[612]

A different approach toward the distinction was voiced in an earlier dissertation, presented at the University of Wittenberg under the direction of the Lutheran theologian Nicolaus Hunnius (1585–1643) by the respondent G.-F. Rosa.[613] In relation to both commutative and distributive justice, the author starts with rejecting the view of the Anabaptists according to which the very exercise of these forms of justice runs counter the Christian faith.[614] In commutative justice, both the arithmetic and geometric proportions are applied.[615] The former applies in relation to persons: the differences in their respective merits have to be disregarded. Geometric proportion is used when comparing different things or comparing things to services. In these cases, equality is not measured according to quantity but according to value. Thus, in case of a sale of wood, the quantity of gold for its payment is not equal to that of the wood, but equality is measured according to their respective value.[616] The value of an object includes also labors or other services that

---

an ironical stance: "Quis vero asserat poenas inter Cives communes & ita dividendas est, ut illorum singuli partem habeat; ego, si res sic haberet, perpetuo partem meam cui arrideret relinquerem."

610. *Ibid.*, §§42–52.

611. *Ibid.*, §§54–59.

612. *Ibid.*, §58: "Quod si enim per hanc Talionem non nudam illam & simplicem aequalitatem, sed analogicam intelligas, quae fit secundum proportionem, qt. sc. poenae & delicta ad certam aequalitatem proportionabiliter sunt redigenda, non video quid hoc erroris habeat."

613. Georgius-Fridericus Rosa, *Disputationum Ethicarum IX, De Iustitia* (Praes. Nicolaus Hunnius, Wittenberg 1621).

614. *Ibid.*, III, §2, IV, §1. The presiding professor of theology, Nicolaus Hunnius, was famous for his fierce opposition to Protestant denominations that deviated from strict Lutheranism. The Anabaptists' negative view in relation to the exercise of particular justice by Christians was mentioned and rejected in an additional dissertation: Andreas Winzigerus, *Exercitationum Ethicarum Disputatio XX, De Justitia Distributiva* (Praeses Johannes Deutschman, Wittenberg 1653) §4.

615. *Ibid.*, III, §3: "Commutatio in contractibus versatur, qui commutant opes cum opibus; vel opes cum officio. Utraque ut justa sit, tamquam norma dirigit ἀναλογία seu proportio; tum γεομετρίκή, tum ἀριθμητική; utramque exacte observandam praecipit justitia."

616. *Ibid.*, III, §4: "Cum *res confertur cum re* 1. *Aequalitas utriusque rei non quantitatis, sed caritatis & dignitatis.* Ut ligna emturus non teneatis tantum auri quantitatem expendere,

have been performed in its connection. However, only those expenses are taken into account that were necessary for the thing to be sold.[617]

After a rather lengthy discussion about the legitimacy of taking interest (*usura*),[618] the author then classifies punishment as falling under the heading of distributive justice.[619] The punishment has to be measured according to the gravity of the criminal act, by taking into account the surrounding circumstances. Thus, taking away a penny from a poor man might be more serious than taking away a pound from a rich man.[620] Similarly, an offence committed by a public officer is graver than that of a private person. Moreover, the frequency of a crime requires harsher punishments, such as the death penalty for theft.[621]

The problem of classifying punishment occupied also the Dutch Calvinist scholar and theologian Antoine de Waele (1573–1639), professor of divinity at Leiden. In his summary of the Aristotelian ethics,[622] he suggests, in order to reconcile the different sayings of Aristotle, to distinguish between public and private delicts. The retribution of the former falls entirely under distributive justice. The author illustrates the application of distributive justice to a public offence by means of the reaction of King David to the shame caused to his envoys by the Ammonites: not an equal act of retaliation but public war.[623] However, in case of a private delict, both forms of justice may be applied. As far as the delict causes damage to the public, distributive justice and a geometric proportion are required; as far as the damage concerns private citizens, commutative justice and an arithmetic proportion have to be applied. In this way, both the state and the private person get simultaneously satisfaction.

---

quanta est lignorum, hic enim justitia aequalitatem faciat, lignum, quantum ab auro superatur aestimatione, seu dignitate, tantum vicissim superare debet aurum quantitate; ut defectum dignitatis expleat copia."

617. *Ibid.*, III, §6.

618. *Ibid.*, III, §§7–12.

619. *Ibid.*, IV, §5: "Poenarum distributionem similiter non aliunde, quam geometrica proportione aestimanda ducimus."

620. *Ibid.*: "Utpote, si diviti thalerum auferas, vix tantum abstulisti, ac si pauperi grossum: huic enim tantus est, (si non major) grossus, quantus ditiori thalerus."

621. *Ibid.*, IV, §6.

622. Antonius Walaeus, *Compendium Ethicae Aristotelicae Ad Normam Veritatis Christianae Revocatum* (Leiden 1647).

623. 2 Samuel 10.

Another Dutch scholar, Franco Burgersdijck (1590–1635), professor of logics and ethics at Leiden, gave an identical answer to that problem.[624] He assumes that punishment, as such, falls under distributive justice, but the satisfaction of delicts may involve both forms of justice, one (distributive) in relation to the damage caused to the state, the other (commutative) to that caused to the private citizen.[625] The *jus talionis* (*antipeponthos*), in its strict sense, does not conform to either of the two forms of justice.[626] It does not take into consideration the difference in status nor the specific circumstances of a delict, such as the mental state of the perpetrator. Moreover, in certain crimes, such as adultery, exact retaliation is impermissible. Even in voluntary contracts it is inapplicable, since the differences in regions and desires prevent that identical things are exchanged.[627] However, when the idea of equality is applied not in the strict sense of identity, but by way of analogy, then retribution (*jus talionis*) constitutes an integral part of commutative justice that is applicable to all transactions, voluntary and involuntary.[628] It signifies adequate compensation.

An interesting classification of the various terms relating to justice is suggested by the influential English Protestant (Puritan) scholar, William Ames (1576–1633), professor of theology at the Dutch University of Franeker in Friesland. The basic distinction is between distributive and emendative justice.[629] He states:

> Emendative justice is either Commutative, or Corrective. Commutative Justice, presupposeth some Injustice, and is either civill or criminall.

---

624. F. Burgersdicius, *Idea Philosophiae Tum Moralis Tum Naturalis Sive Epitome Compendiosa utriusque ex Aristotele excerpta, & methodice disposita* (Editio quarta, Oxford 1637).

625. *Ibid.*, Cap. XXII, §8, col. 292: "Quare non in muneribus tantum & praemiis conferendis, sed etiam in poenis & suppliciis pro merito infligendis consistit distributiva justitia"; *ibid.*, §17, col. 299: "Delicta partim ad justitiam distributivam, partim ad commutativam pertinent; quia non solum privatis sed etiam Reip. nocent, si non ipso facto, saltem exemplo. Quare & privatis satisfaciendum est, & Reip. illis secundum proportionem Arithmeticam: his, secundum Geometricam."

626. *Ibid.*, §§19–23, col. 300–307.

627. *Ibid.*, §19, col 301: "In contractibus voluntariis talioni non est locus; quia regionum & studiorum diversitas non permittit, ut eadem reddantur pro iisdem."

628. *Ibid.*, §20, col. 302–303: "Quod si jus talionis consideretur secundum equalitatem analogicam, hoc est, si non idem unicuique reddatur, sed aliquid quod ei proportione respondeat, erit ipsissima justitia commutativa, habebitque locum tum maleficiis ac contractibus invitis, tum in permutatione rerum, ac contractibus voluntariis."

629. William Ames, *The Marrow of Sacred Divinity, Drawne out of the holy Scriptures, and the Interpreters thereof, and brought into Method* (London 1642), Chapter XVI, §§65–77.

> Civill doth chiefly correct the injustice of the cause. Criminall doth chiefly correct the injustice of the person. To corrective Justice pertaineth revenge, and restitution. Revenge is an act of corrective Justice, whereby punishment is inflicted on him, who hath violated Justice... Restitution is an act of corrective Justice, whereby another is set againe into the possession of that thing of his own whereof he was unjustly deprived.

These distinctions were basically adopted later in the work of the German-Dutch, Reformed philosopher and theologian Peter van Mastricht (1630–1706), professor at the University of Utrecht.[630]

A typical humanist approach to the problem of justice, one finds in the work of the famous, controversial French Protestant theologian Moïse Amyraut (Moses Amyraldus) (1596–1664), professor at the University of Saumur.[631] Following rather closely the analysis of Aristotle, the author relies on illustrations from the Bible and classical literature; in relation to the latter, he uses especially examples taken from Cicero's *De officiis*.[632] Punishment makes part of distributive justice applying a geometric proportion by taking into account the disparity of persons. The author, however, states that not everybody agrees here with Aristotle: Some ancient and modern scholars prefer the practice of Rhadamantes, applying the rule of *lex talionis* (*antipeponthos*). The author believes that this problem belongs rather to the political legislator than to moral philosopher. It is important to abide by the law. But basically he believes that Aristotle is right in assuming that the gravity of a delict depends on the victim's disparity of dignity.[633] In a lengthy chapter on

630. Petrus van Mastricht, *Theoretico-Practica Theologia* (Editio Nova, Utrecht 1699), *Idea Theologiae Moralis*, Liber Tertius, Cap. I, *De justitia versus proximum in genere, & injuria*, 1144: "*Emendativa*, quae suum cuique *reddit*, estque rursus vel. 6. *Commutativa*, quae consistit in aequalitate redditi & accepti, de qua suo loco ex professo: Vel. 7. *Correctiva*, injustitiam aliquam praesupponens corrigendam: sive illa sit: 8.*Civilis*, corrigens injustitiam *rei*; sive 9. *Criminalis*, corrigens injustitiam *personae*. Ad hanc spectat: cum *vindictae*, quae poena infligitur ei, qui justitiam violavit; tum *restitutio*, qua alter istum statuitur, in possessione rei suae, qua fuit injuste privatus."

631. Moyse Amyraut, *La Morale Chrestienne A Monsieur De Villarnoul, Seconde Partie* (Saumur 1654) 423–544.

632. The examples are taken from Cicero, *De Officiis*, Book III, §§XII–XV.

633. *Ibid.*, 429–433: "Au fonds, j'estime qu'Aristote a raison de croire que les delicts sont plus ou moins grands selon la disparité de la dignité des personnes contre qui on les commet. & que qui se contenteroit d'arracher un oeil à une personne privée qui en auroit arraché un oeil à un Magistrat, luy appliqueroit une punition plus petite que son crime."

commutative justice, the author deals with the problems of just price, fraud, natural law, and usury.[634]

The Dutch scholar Adrianus Heereboord (1614–1661), professor of philosophy at the University of Leiden, equally follows in the steps of Aristotle.[635] Distributive justice relates to public benefits and charges applying a geometric proportion[636]; commutative justice is concerned with private transactions subject to an arithmetic proportion. In relation to the latter, the author distinguishes between voluntary and involuntary transactions: in the former, the compensation refers only to the object matter of the transaction; in the latter to both the damage and the offense.[637] Contrary to distributive justice, commutative justice does not take into account a person's status or merits. Thus, a prince and a plebeian will pay the same amount for a pair of shoes. Similarly, a colonel and a simple soldier will pay the promised rent for their home.[638] A public official has to pay for his private deals from his own money. In case of involuntary transactions, at least one party does not agree to the act, such as in case of theft, adultery, and poisoning. The author then refers to the question what are the gains and losses in these cases. His answer is that the gain of the person who kills another consists in the satisfaction of his vengeance or hatred.[639]

In relation to punishment, the author insists that, since its measure is according to the gravity of the offense, it applies an arithmetic proportion. In this respect it partakes of commutative justice. This, however, does not mean that for an equal delict all offenders must be punished by an identical penalty. Thus, the removal of a public officer from his office might constitute a heavier punishment than the whipping of a plebeian. On the other hand,

---

634. *Ibid.*, 434–544. The author equally deals with the function of money and commerce. Also here the influence of Cicero's writings is recognizable.

635. Adrianus Heereboord, *Collegium Ethicum, Seu Philosophia Moralis* (London 1658) 228–244.

636. In describing the geometric proportion, the author uses the illustration of the classical contest between Ulysses and Ajax about the arms of Achilles and Patroclus. Since Ulysses's contribution to the victory over the Trojans was considered greater than that of Ajax, the former was awarded the more precious arms, namely those of Achilles; *ibid.*, 243–244.

637. *Ibid.*, 235.

638. *Ibid.*

639. *Ibid.*, 239: "Sed roget quis, Quodnam hic est lucrum, quod damnum, quod tamen utramque in justitia commutante esse debet? Resp. Qui alium occidit, pro lucro habet vindictae aut odii expletionem: occisus pro damno habet omissionem vitae: sic in adulterio, aliisque, similiter se res habet."

the fact that punishment is imposed by a public officer constitutes an aspect of distributive justice. As a result, punishment belongs partially to the two kinds of justice.[640]

The English Puritan theologian Richard Baxter (1615–1691), distinguishes in relation to punishment between the commutative justice aspect of compensating the victim and the distributive justice aspect of satisfying the public interest; in his words:

> But here you must distinguish betwixt *satisfaction* in Commutative Justice, for a Debt, or *injury*, and *satisfaction* in *distributive Governing* Justice, for a *fault* or *crime*. The measure of the former satisfaction, is so much as may compensate the owners loss; not only so much as the thing was worth to another, but what it was worth to him: But the measure of the *later* satisfaction is, so much as the *ends of Government* instead of actual obedience; or so much as will suffice as to the *Ends of Government*, to repair the hurts which crime hath done, or avoid what it would do.
>
> And here you may see the answer to that question: *Why a Thief was commanded to restore fourfold by the Law of Moses?* For in that *restitution* there was a conjunction of both sorts of *satisfaction*, both in point of *Commutative* and *Distributive* Justice: So much as repaired the owners loss was *satisfaction* to the owner for the injury. The rest was all *satisfaction* to God and the Common-wealth for the public injury that came by the *crime* or violation of the Law. Other answers were given by some, but this is the plain and certain truth.[641]

A major and most influential figure of the enlightenment was Hugo Grotius (1583–1645). He accepted basically the Aristotelian dichotomy of distributive and corrective justice, translating them, as mentioned, with the

---

640. *Ibid.*, §§VIII, X, pp. 240–242, 244. In the author's view, punishment, since it is not fully one single kind of justice, belongs to the scholastic category of *potentiales*: "Et fortasse non errant, qui eam inter partes justitiae particularis propriae dictas non numerant, adeoque nec distribuentem, nec ad commutatentem, proprie eam referunt, sed ad partes justitiae particularis reducunt *potentiales*, quas sic vocant *Scholastici* ex *Aquin.* 2.2. *quest.* 101."

641. Richard Baxter, *A Christian Directory, The Practical Works of the Late Reverend and Pious Mr. Richard Baxter, in Four Volumes* (London 1707) 871.

Latin terms of *iustitia attributrix* and *iustitia expletrix*.[642] He introduced into the distinction two new terms: *aptitudo* and *facultas*. The latter term designates a legal right in the strict sense, like: personal freedom, paternal authority, ownership, and obligation. The former concept, aptitude, constitutes the potential of obtaining a right; in the framework of distributive justice it is the Aristotelian *axia*, the merit (called in Latin *dignitas*) serving as criterion for the proportional distribution. The *facultas* is the object of the corrective justice, since the latter is aimed at restoring rights to their owners. Distributive justice, by considering the *aptitudo* of a person, is the companion of those virtues that benefit the other members of society, such as generosity, compassion, and guiding care.[643]

However, Grotius is critical of Aristotle's mathematical analogies. He claims that, contrary to Aristotle's assumption, corrective justice is not always a two-term arithmetic proportion, and distributive justice is not exclusively a four-term geometric proportion. Thus, the social contract is implemented by a geometric proportion; on the other hand, where only one person is found to be apt for a public office, the distribution will be based merely on an arithmetic proportion.[644] Hence, the difference between the two forms of justice is not to be found in the use of different kinds of proportions but in the nature of the objects to which they respectively relate.[645]

---

642. Hugo Grotius, *De iure belli ac pacis*, Lib. I, Cap. I, §VIII. At another place, Grotius calls the distributive justice *iustitia assignatrix*; Lib. II, Cap. XVII, § II, 2.

643. As a matter of fact, in scholastic literature the question has been discussed whether acts of compassion and charity may be sold for a price. Some have argued that the duty of assisting a person in extreme need is based upon a notion of justice, *iustitia subsidiaria*. According to some authors, the duty under this form of justice is equal to that under commutative justice. *See* on this topic the Jesuit scholar Stephanus Fagundez (1577–1645), *De Iustitia, & contractibus, & de acqusitione, & translatione dominij, Libri Septem* (Lyon 1641) 396–398, §§22–31. On the Christian doctrine that almsgiving by the rich from their superfluity to relieve those in extreme need is an act of strict duty, *cf.* D.D. Raphael, *Concepts of Justice* (Oxford 2001) 59–60.

644. *Ibid.*, Lib. I, Cap. I, §VIII, 2.

645. Dutch jurists generally followed this opinion of Grotius: Arnoldus Vinnius (1588–1657), *In Quattuor Libros Institutionum Imperialium Commentarius Academicus & Forensis* (Leiden 1709), Lib. I, Tit. I, *De Justitia et Jure*, §2, p. 5: "Illud quoque perpetuum non est, quod plerique tradiderunt, a justitia commutativa respici proportionem simplicem, quam arithmeticam vocant, a distributiva comparatam, quam appellant geometricam. Quae mathematicis & revera sola proportio est, neque enim per se justitia commutativa a distributiva differt tali proportionum usu, sed objecto & materia, circa quam versatur." *See also* Charles Herbert, *The Introduction to Dutch Jurisprudence of Hugo Grotius, Now First Rendered Into English* (London 1845), Book I, Ch. I, Sect. XIII, p. 3, note*; the author mentions that the annotators of Paulus Merula (1558–1607) remark that the Aristotelian

Grotius then proceeds to refute the opinion of those who claim that distributive justice concerns the common goods of society and corrective justice those of the private individuals. Grotius argues that granting a legacy out of private property constitutes a matter of distributive justice. On the other hand, when a state restitutes to citizens, out of the common property, the expenses made by them in the public service, then it fulfills merely a duty of corrective justice.[646]

Grotius dedicates a special section to the classificatory problem of punishment.[647] Here are his comments:

> (1) But opinions differ as to whether punishment falls within the sphere of attributive or of expletive justice. For, on the ground that he who has committed the greater sin is punished more heavily, and he who has committed the lesser is punished more lightly and that the penalty is given as it were by the whole to the part, punishments are assigned by some to the sphere of attributive justice.
>
> However, this first principle which they lay down, that attributive justice comes into play whenever an equality is established between more than two terms, we have shown to be untrue at the beginning of this work; then, as regards the fact that those who have done greater injury are punished more severely, and those who have done less injury are punished more lightly, that happens only as a consequence, not because it is aimed at first and for its own sake. For first and its own sake a balance is aimed at between the guilt and the penalty . . .
>
> (2) Neither is the second principle which they lay down more true, that all punishments come from the whole to the part; this will appear from what we have to say. We have, in fact, shown above that the true nature of attributive justice properly consists neither in such balance nor in the transference from the whole to a part, but in taking account of the aptitude, which does not contain in itself right strictly so called, but furnishes an opportunity for it. Although, to be sure, he who is punished ought to be fit or worthy to be punished, this does not mean that something should befall him which attributive justice demands.

doctrine of Arithmetical and Geometrical Proportion "is exploded." Among these authors, who prefer the definition of Grotius, he counts Voet, Noodt, and Averanius.

646. *Ibid.*, Lib. I, Cap. I, §VIII, 3.

647. *Ibid.*, Lib. II, Cap. XX, §II, 1–4.

Nor yet do those give a better explanation who claim that expletive justice, which they commonly call commutative, is exercised in punishments. For in so doing they consider this a business transaction, as if something were paid to the wrongdoer, in accordance with the usage of contracts. They are deceived by current speech, whereby we say that punishment is due to him who sins. This is plainly "misleading." For he to whom something is properly owed has a right against another. But when we say that punishment is due to some person we mean nothing more than that is proper for him to be punished.

(3) Nevertheless, it is true that expletive justice is exercised in penalties primarily and for its own sake, because he who punishes, that he may punish rightly, must have the right to punish; and this right arises from the crime of the guilty. In this matter, therefore, there is something that approaches the nature of contracts. For just as he who sells, even if he says nothing specifically, is considered to have obligated himself to all the things which are naturally involved in a sale, so he who does wrong seems by his own will to have obligated himself to a penalty, because a serious crime cannot be unpunishable; hence whoever directly wills to sin, by consequence has willed to deserve a punishment. In this sense the Emperors say to a person, "You yourself have subjected yourself to this punishment," and those who take evil counsel are already punished at that time, that is they are said of their own will to have contracted for the recompense of punishment. In Tacitus a woman who had married a slave is said to have agreed to subject herself to slavery, because that penalty had been ordained for such persons.

(4) Michael of Ephesus, *On Aristotle's Nicomachean Ethics,* Book V, says: "There is here a kind of giving and receiving, which constitutes the essence of contracts; for whoever has taken property or stolen anything else pays the penalty for it." Later again "the ancient termed contracts not merely what men have willingly agreed to perform toward one another but also the things that are forbidden by the laws."[648]

Grotius's comments on Aristotle provoked a considerable controversy by later authors. But before examining the scholarly reactions to Grotius's approach to the Aristotelian distinction, a look at Thomas Hobbes's (1588–1679)

648. H. Grotius, *De iure belli ac pacis libri tres,* vol. 2, Book II (Transl. F.W. Kelsey, reprint New York, London 1964) 463–465. *Cf. also id.,* Lib. II, Cap. XX, §VI, 1; *ibid.,* §§XXXII, 1–2; XXXIII.

treatment of it is appropriate. Dealing with the secondary laws of nature, Hobbes first distinguishes between "justice of manners" (which is conceived by him as the expression of a man's general character: justice as virtue) and "justice of actions" which denominates men guiltless or guilty in relation to a concrete act.[649] Hobbes then goes on to say:

> Justice of actions is by writers divided into *commutative and distributive*; and the former they say consisteth in proportion arithmetical, the latter in proportion geometrical. Commutative, therefore, they place in the equality of value of the things contracted for, and distributive in the distribution of equal benefit, to men of equal merit. As if it were injustice to sell dearer than we buy, or to give more to a man than he merits. The value of all things contracted for is measured by the appetite of the contractors, and therefore the just value is that which they be contented to give. And merit (besides that which is by covenant, where the performance on one part meriteth the performance of the other part, and falls under justice commutative, not distributive) is not due by justice, but is rewarded of grace only. And therefore this distinction, in the sense wherein it useth to be expounded, is not right. To speak properly, commutative justice is the justice of a contractor; that is, a performance of covenant in buying and selling; hiring and letting to hire; lending and borrowing; exchanging, bartering, and other acts of contract.
>
> And distributive justice, the justice of an arbitrator—that is to say, the act of defining what is just. Wherein, being trusted by them that make him arbitrator, if he perform his trust, he is said to distribute to every man his own; and this is indeed just distribution, and may be called, though improperly, distributive justice; but more properly equity; which is also a law of nature, as shall be shown in due place.[650]

Hobbes then explains that latter comment under the heading of the eleventh law of nature:

> Also if a man be trusted to judge between man and man, it is a precept of the law of nature, that he deal equally between them. For without

649. Th. Hobbes, *Leviathan*, Part 1, Ch. 15 (Oxford 1957) 97.

650. *Ibid.*, 98; *see also* the similar development of that theme in Hobbes, *De Cive* III, 6 (*Man and Citizen*, ed. B.Gert, 1991) 139–140.

> that, the controversies of men cannot be determined but by war. He therefore that is partial in judgment doth what in him lies, do deter men from the use of judges, and arbitrators; and consequently, against the fundamental law of nature, is the cause of war. The observance of this law, from the equal distribution to each man, of that which in reason belongeth to him, is called EQUITY, and, as I have said before, distributive justice: the violation, acception of persons, προσωποληψία.[651]

The impression one gets from Hobbes's opposition to the Aristotelian distinction is that he is wary of giving substance to the notion of distributive justice on the basis of supposedly natural rights that would contradict his own assumptions on the nature of these rights.[652] In relation to commutative justice, Hobbes denies the existence of an *a priori* binding principle of just exchange: the only requirement of justice is the performance by the parties of their agreed undertakings.[653]

---

651. Leviathan, ibid., 101. The term "acception of persons" is the old English expression for the Hebrew משוא פנים.

652. *Cf.* M.M. Goldsmith, *Hobbes's Science of Politics* (New York and London, 1966) 102: "'Distributive Justice' requires that there be a natural and obligatory order of merit according to which benefits may be distributed. But there is no natural order. In the state of nature, all men are, or are presumed to be, equal. We are not obliged to give equally to all; we are only obliged to fulfill our covenants and beyond that we have liberty to do as we please."

653. *See* in this sense also the critique of Aristotle by K. Hildenbrand, *Geschichte und System der Rechts—und Staatsphilosophie: Das klassische Altertum* (Leipzig 1860) 297: "Was nämlich zunächst die Gleichheit der Leistung und Gegenleistung bei Tauschverträgen betrifft, so ist dieselbe ein *wirtschaftliches*, nicht aber ein rechtliches oder sittliches Postulat. Da die Tauschverträge wie die Verträge überhaupt auf freier Uebereinkunft der Partheien beruhen, so kann sittlich und rechtlich nur gefordert werden, dass die Leistungen beider Parteien ihrer Uebereinkunft entsprechen. Das wirthschaftliche Interesse wird die Partheien allerdings bestimmen, sich gegenseitig Gleichwerthe zu bedingen, wenn sie aber aus was immer für Motive dies nicht thun, so ist das ein ökonomischer Fehler aber nicht ein Verstoss gegen die Gerechtigkeit." On Hobbes's view, *see also* D.D. Raphael, *Concepts of Justice* (Oxford 2001) 76. For an attempt to analyze Hobbes's theory of justice in relation to contemporary debates, *see* A.L. Allen and M.H. Morales, "Hobbes, Formalism, and Corrective Justice," 77 *Iowa L. Rev.* (1992) 713. For a critique of Hobbes's approach to commutative justice, *see* Abrahamus Besselius, *Dissertatio Ethica De Justitia et Jure Quam Consensu Amplissimi Ordinis Philosophici* (Helmstedt 1667) §15. The author mentions the duty not to deceive the other party to a contract: "At vero iis, quae produxit, exemplis, res nondum conficitur. Etenim si res suas mercator vendere instituat, quanti velit, non habito mercis valore, is decipere praesumitur alium, adeoque vel hoc nomine in justitiam peccat commutativam." In relation to distributive justice, the author notes: "[N]eque sperari potest paritas ex aequalitate naturae, quam contra Aristotelem tantopere urget Hobbes."

As mentioned, some scholars were rather critical of Grotius's approach to the Aristotelian distinction. Thus, the German philosopher and jurist, Johannis a Felden (d. 1668), criticized Grotius for insisting on the dichotomy of two forms of justice (attributive and expletive justice), whereas Aristotle recognized in that author's opinion a third form, namely that of retributive justice (*antipeponthos*). In relation to punishment, the author blames Grotius for confusing two different meanings and functions of *poena*: deterrence and retribution.[654]

One of the more renowned critics of Grotius is Samuel Pufendorf (1632–1694), who in his work on the Natural Law and Law of Nations examines the Aristotelian notions of justice in the light of the conceptions of Hobbes and Grotius.[655]

Pufendorf equally uses the distinction of Grotius between perfect and imperfect rights, but in a completely different way. As mentioned above, according to Grotius the "attributive" (distributive) justice is concerned with imperfect rights, the "expletive" (corrective) justice enforces perfect rights. In Pufendorf's view, imperfect rights are the object of what Aristotle called "universal justice," conceived by the latter as the exercise of complete virtue in relation to others; on the other hand, perfect rights are the object of particular justice. As a result, Pufendorf observes in relation to Grotius's view:

> [H]is expletive justice does by no means exactly agree with commutative, nor his attributive with distributive; and that his division is not on the same basis as ours. For our division is taken primarily from the matter which is due, and from the origin of the obligation, but his from the manner and the degree to which something is owed. And so it is clear why the distribution of the profits in the contract of a society belongs, in his opinion, to expletive justice, in mine to distributive . . . As for the example of Grotius: "If only one person can be found who is fitted for a public position, the award will be made to him on the basis

---

654. Johannis a Felden, *Annotata in Hug. Grotium de Iure Belli et Pacis* (Amsterdam 1653) I p. 9–15 (on Lib. I, Cap. I, § VIII); II 91–94 (on Lib. II, Cap. XX, §II, 1–4); *cf.* G. Del Vecchio, *Justice—An Historical and Philosophical Essay* (A.H. Campbell, ed., Edinburgh 1952), §6, n.9, pp. 63–64.

655. S. Pufendorf, *De jure naturae et gentium libri octo*, II (transl. C.H. Oldfather and W.A. Oldfather, Oxford 1934). Some of his basic ideas on the forms of justice Pufendorf published already in one of his earlier works: *id.*, *Elementorum jurisprudentiae universalis libri duo*, II (transl. C.H. Oldfather, Oxford 1931) Book I, Definition XVII, §§1–4, p. 175–178.

of a simple proportion only," we must inquire further, whether he has a perfect or imperfect right to that position. If it is the latter, the case will be one for universal justice, if the former, we agree what he says about proportion, that usually, but not always, a geometrical proportion is employed in distributive justice. But we have not taken our distinction between the two kinds of justice from the use of a different proportion. And so also the assigning of legacies belongs not to distributive but to universal justice; and when a state pays from its treasury the amount that some citizens have expended for a public undertaking, this is an exercise of commutative and not distributive justice, because the reason for the obligation does not come from an agreement by which the state received the citizen into its fold, but from a special and very different contract.[656]

---

656. S. Pufendorf, *De jure naturae et gentium libri octo*, II (transl. C.H. Oldfather and W.A. Oldfather, Oxford 1934) Book I, Ch. VII, § 9, p. 120–121; *see also* his discussion of Grotius, *ibid.*, 121–123, §11. *Cf.* the critical commentary of Jean Barbeyrac, *ad locum*, who claims that Pufendorf's distinction is imperfect, since there are strict duties that are not based upon contract, but on the nature of things, like the duties to abstain from injuring and to compensate for damages; Pufendorf, *Le droit de la nature et des gens ou Système général des principes les plus importants de la morale, de la jurisprudence, et de la politique* (Jean Barbeyrac, trad., 2è édition, Amsterdam 1712) Liv. I, Chap. VII, §9, note 1: "Cette division est incomplette, puis qu'elle ne renferme que ce que l'on doit à autrui en vertu de quelque Engagement où l'on est entré, ou d'une Société particulière que l'on a contractée: or il y a bien des choses, que le Prochain peut exiger de nous à la rigueur, indépendamment de toute Société particulière, de toute Promesse & de toute Convention; comme, qu'on ne lui fasse point de mal, qu'on répare le dommage qu'il a reçû de notre part, qu'on le regarde comme un Etre qui nous est naturellement égal &c." *See* in this connection the academic thesis of Ludovicus Wentzius, *Dissertatio Philosophica De Justitia In Genere* (Praes. Lucas Burcardus, Basel 1742) §§11–16, pp. 6–8. The latter author supports Pufendorf's view that the difference in proportion (arithmetic versus geometric) is not the decisive criterion of the distinction. He adduces the following example in order to show that both forms of justice may be applied in one case: The merits of Titius are threefold of those of Cajus. Under distributive justice, the former receives a benefit that is three times greater than that of Cajus. However, the same result is achieved under commutative justice, when we replace Titius by three persons. The merit of each of the three is now equal to that of Cajus. Since according to simple equality, Titius should obtain the same amount as his three substitutes, it is evident that he receives under commutative justice three times the benefit of Cajus, exactly the same amount as he should receive under distributive justice. The author concludes that—given the fact that both kinds of justice tend to the same result—it is no wonder that Kemmerichius calls the distinction to be of "little usefulness" ("*parum utilem*"), and Budaeus as "useless" ("*ineptam*") (*ibid.*, §13). The author's intention is 1) to the German Professor and Privy Councillor Dieter Hermann Kemmerich (1677–1745), *Pufendorfius enucleatus sive elementa juris naturae et gentium* (Leipzig 1716), ad Lib. I, Cap. II, §14; and 2) to the German Philosopher and Theologian Johann Franz Budde (1667–1729), *Elementa Philosophiae Praticae* (Editio tertia, Halle 1707), reprinted in: Johann Franz Budde, *Gesammelte Schriften*, Band III (W. Sparn, ed., Hildesheim, Zürich, New York 2004) Pars Secunda, Cap. II, §46: "Iustitia expletrix inepte in commutativam

Discussing Aristotle's forms of particular justice, Pufendorf states that there are three different kinds: distributive (διανεμητική), corrective (διορθωτική), and retaliation (τὸ ἀντιπεπονθός).[657] Concerning the involuntary transactions, "they are seen in crimes, where what is properly an involuntary transaction takes place, because, for example, in a case of robbery my property has passed to a thief against my will, and so an inequality has arisen, in that he has more than he should, and I have less. This is corrected by taking from him what he has in excess of his due, and giving it to me."[658] In relation to the third kind of justice, retaliation, Pufendorf explains that it regulates the manner in which men exchange things among themselves, "whereby things which are different and unequal are compared and finally made equal, on laws of a geometrical proportion. For instance, when a horse and a pair of shoes are to be exchanged, it must first be decided how many pairs of shoes the horse is worth, and, if it is set at twelve, the "retaliation," τὸ ἀντιπεπονθός, would be observed if one took twelve pairs of shoes for one horse."[659]

In Pufendorf's view, retaliation is different from punishment, since it is exclusively concerned with restitution. Indeed, Pufendorf considers punishment, vindictive justice, as a different form of particular justice.[660]

Referring to Grotius's above-mentioned analysis of punishment, Pufendorf in a lengthy paragraph rejects the notion that punishment makes part of corrective justice.[661]

Rejecting also the idea that punishment makes part of distributive justice, he observes:

> Distributive justice takes place whenever an equality is established between more than two terms, that is, so often as something must be

et distributivam: rectius in *rectoriam* et *aequatoriam* dividitur: illa inter inaequales, haec inter aequales versatur. Rectoriae tot sunt species, quot sunt societatis, in quibus alii imperant, alii parent. Aequatoriae tot sunt species, quot sunt officiorum, quae homo erga hominem, civis erga civem, praestare tenetur, genera. Sic alia est, quae alterum non laedit, alia quae pacta servat, etc."

657. *Ibid.*, §12, p. 123–124.

658. *Ibid.*, 123.

659. *Ibid.*, 124.

660. *Ibid.*, §10, p. 121; an extensive discussion of the relation of punishment to the forms of justice is in Book VIII, Ch. III, §5; Pufendorf stated his basic view on punishment already in his earlier work, *id. Elementorum jurisprudentiae universalis libri duo*, II (transl. C.H. Oldfather, Oxford 1931) Book I, Definition XVII, §4, p. 176.

661. *De jure naturae et gentium libri octo*, II, Book VIII, Ch. III, §5, p. 1166–1170.

divided proportionally between more than one. For in the contract of a partnership the dividends are divided *pro rata* when there is more than one stockholder, and yet in this contract the dividends are owed in a very different way from that in the rewards or penalties are owed. For it is surely obvious that penalties are not owed because of a pact, nor does any man in subjecting himself to a state agree that punishment shall be laid upon him for crimes And so the imposition of penalties in no way squares with distributive justice as we described it above. In the next place, the fact that the more guilty are punished more severely, and the less guilty less severely, comes about only by consequence and by accident, not because that was intended primarily and for its own sake.[662]

In relation to corrective justice he remarks:

Grotius, Bk. II, ch. XX, § 2, writes that expletive justice, primarily and for its own sake, is observed in the infliction of punishments, and this for the reason, that, "in order for him who punishes to punish lawfully, he should have a right to punish, which right arises from another's crime." Yet here the ambiguity of the term "right" has led him astray, for to have a right to do something, and to have a right to receive something from another are two very different things. The former means that the power belongs to me to perform some act, in the exercise of which no one should hinder me; the latter means that I have such a right to have something from another that he is also under an obligation to give it to me. And yet when we speak of expletive justice, the word right is taken not in the former but in the latter sense, and this right lies in him who receives a thing, not in him who gives it.[663]

In relation to Grotius's assumption that the criminal, when committing a crime by his own will, has obligated himself to a penalty, the author comments:

Yet it is not proper to say on this account that any man has directly or immediately given his consent to his own punishment, or, better, has by his own agreement obligated himself to undergo that punishment.

662. *Ibid.*, 1167.

663. *Ibid.*, 1167–1168.

> For no man ever commits a crime without having the hope that by concealment or in some other way he will avoid the penalty.[664]

Pufendorf then goes on to explain that the obligation arising from a crime is that of repairing the damage, not to bear a penalty. He states:

> And this obligation is properly based not on the fact that a man has agreed to a penalty, but because natural law, after the introduction of dominium in things, produced the necessity of making that restitution ... But the reason why the obligation to repair a damage is classed by [Aristotle] under an involuntary contract, is because, for example, in the case of a loan it rests upon the will of the creditor as to whether the debtor shall receive the money, while, for example, the fact that a thief is obligated to restore to me either the article which he took from me or its value, is due to the deed having been done without my consent, and his having laid upon himself that obligation without my consent ... Therefore, upon the commission of a crime there lies in the injured person a right to demand reparation for the loss, and upon the injurer an obligation to repair it, and this is the concern of expletive justice. But in so far as a crime is a deviation from the law, there resides in the governors of states a power to require a fitting penalty, but no obligation in the offender to pay the penalty of his own accord; and on this score the exaction of penalties does not agree with expletive justice.[665]

Pufendorf therefore concludes that punishments belong to neither species of justice, but fall under a branch peculiar to itself.[666] He adds that although one might prefer to say that the imposition of penalties as well as the distribution of rewards, on which there has been no agreement in advance by a special pact, are parts of the prudence which is connected with the duty of ruling others, and so it is referred to universal justice.

A somewhat more positive echo to the distinction suggested by Grotius between attributive and expletive justice, one finds in the work of the Dutch

---

664. *Ibid.*, 1168.

665. *Ibid.*, 1169–1170.

666. See the critical comment on that conclusion by A. Trendelenburg, *Historische Beiträge zur Philosophie*, Vol. III (Berlin 1867) 406–407. But see the critique of Trendelenburg's approach by G. Del Vecchio, *Justice—An Historical and Philosophical Essay* (A. H. Campbell, ed., Edinburgh 1952), §6, note 9, pp. 64–65.

Remonstrant (Arminian) theologian Philippus van Limborch (1633–1712).[667] The author concentrates on the notion of commutative justice and his analysis is of considerable interest. He observes that the exchange in a commercial transaction has not always to be of an identical nature. Thus, a doctor who cures a mortally sick person will not receive an identical performance. In many cases the exchange of identical goods is even economically useless. The idea of reciprocity is realized by means of determining the price of the exchanged good and by its payment in terms of money.[668] In case of violation of contractual duty or the performance of delict, a quasi third kind of justice emerges, commonly called corrective justice. It concerns the restitution of the thing detracted from another person. However, sometimes attention is nevertheless paid to the status of a person, since that may influence the extent of the injury.

Thus, God recognized in His law that offences committed against parents, officials, widows, and orphans are more serious than against others. In these cases, the taking into account of a person's status is legitimate, since it is connected to the issue.[669] Retribution (*talio*) too does not always require a rigidly identical act. Sometimes exact reciprocity would induce an inequality to the highest degree. Thus, e.g., where a one-eyed person blinds the eye of another person, the reciprocal blinding of his eye would deprive him of his sight and so cause him a much heavier damage.[670] Moreover, persons differ in their health, as well as in relation to the economic utility of their respective limbs. Finally, an adulterer with another's wife cannot be punished by suffering an equal act to his own wife. The author then affirms that the *lex talionis* established in the Bible does not mean always a literal, rigorous reciprocity, but the injury's evaluation in money or an equivalent corporal punishment. This is, he remarks, also the view of the Jewish sages.[671]

At this point, the author refers to the alternative distinction between attributive and expletive justice, without, however, mentioning the name of

---

667. Philippus a Limborch, *Theologia Christiana Ad praxin pietatis ac promotionem pacis Christianae unice directa* (Amsterdam 1686), Cap. XXXVIII, *De Justitia*, §§XV–XX, pp. 540–541.

668. *Ibid.*, §XVI, p. 540.

669. *Ibid.*, §§XVII–XVIII, p. 540–541.

670. *Ibid.*, §XIX, p. 541. Similar arguments have been raised in the Talmud, TB Baba Kama, 84a; *cf.* for an identical argument, R. Yehudah Halevi (ca. 1075–1141), *The Kuzari: In Defense of the Despised Faith* (Northvale, N.J., Jerusalem, 1998), Book III, 47.

671. *Ibid.*

Grotius. In the author's view, this distinction coincides with the traditional Aristotelian notions.[672] The author then deals—relying on biblical sources—with the conditions for the legitimacy of prices and profits and with the problem of usury.[673]

A completely different critical voice one hears from a theologian and preacher, John Hartcliffe (1651–1712), Fellow of King's College at Cambridge, Canon of Windsor.[674] Evidently, not a friend of legal scholarship, he blames Grotius (without naming him) and others for inventing new terms:

> Now Justice taken in this Sense is twofold, either commutative or distributive or as some learned Men affect to call it, *Justitia expletrix* or *assignatrix*; here by the way, we may take notice of a vanity in many great Scholars, of innovating the ordinary and known names, under which things have passed; thus Mr. *Hobbes* hath been thought as the prodigy of the age, as very a *deviser*, as if he had found out Gunpowder, or Printing, only for dressing *common acknowledged things* in *new Phrases*, and then *trimming* them up for new *Discoveries*; so *Ramus* is notoriously Guilty of this fault ... for as my Lord *Bacon* wisely observes, nothing hath more hindred the Growth of learning, than Peoples studying of *new Words*, and spending their time in *Chaptring*, *Modelling*, and *Marshalling of Sciences*. The learned Author of this new language of *Expletrix* and *Assignatrix*, instead of the old Dialect of *Commutative* and *Distributive* Justice, may take his share patiently in this reproof.[675]

The author after praising the wisdom of Justinian, who prohibited scholarly legal expositions—as distinguished from short summaries (*paratitla*)—deplored the "torrent of writers" in legal science:

> It is not much more, than 400 years, since *Irnerius* and *Accursius* began to write; but there followed upon them such a Rabble of Scribblers, that our whole Libraries have been too little to hold them; so fertile

672. *Ibid.*, §XX, p. 541: "Quae distributio sensu cum nostra coincidit, ita ut Attributrix sit justitia nostra Distributiva: Expletrix vero utramque comprehendat, & Commutativam, & Correctivam."

673. *Ibid.*, §§XXIII–XXXIII, pp. 542–545.

674. John Hartcliffe, *A Treatise of Moral and Intellectual Virtues; Wherein Their Nature is fully explained, and their Usefulness proved, As Being The best Rules of Life* (London 1691).

675. *Ibid.*, 225–226.

> have their wits been, either by opening the paths of *Justice*, or in contriving *by ways* to *injustice*: if therefore you would hear more concerning *Justice*, I must recommend you to *Aristotle*, or to the Interpreters of the *Law*, if at least their multitude do not confound you.[676]

Among the critics of Grotius, one finds also the outstanding and influential Italian philosopher, historian and jurist, Giambattista Vico (1668–1744).[677] The latter suggests another Latin translation of Aristotle's two forms of justice: *iustitia rectrix* for distributive justice and *iustitia equatrix* for commutative (corrective) justice.[678] Vico defends the Aristotelian distinction between the geometric and arithmetic "measures" against Grotius's criticism.[679] The commutative justice considers exclusively the inequality of things and not the inequality of persons, who are viewed to be equal. It concerns therefore the transactions. Distributive justice concerns the community of unequal persons and takes into account the merit, the dignity of the individual for distribution. Commutative justice is at the basis of restitution and prevails in every community of equals.[680] Hence, two partners who invested different sums of money into the enterprise receive an arithmetic measure of the profit, and not, as Grotius thought,[681] a geometric measure, since the latter considers the

---

676. *Ibid.*, 244. *See also ibid.*, 225, where the author speaks of the "Lawyers, who call themselves *Sacerdotes Justitiae*, have done in those infinite and immense Volumes, which they have written *de justitia et jure* against the express charge and command of *Justinian* their Original and prime Author." The author extols the role of equity. He finishes his section on justice (at 244): "And that we may conclude this Head in the language of *Aristotle*, out of an *Arithmetical Government* (as we may call it) by rigour of Law, and that *Geometrical* Judgment at the pleasure of a *Chancellour*, well tempered together, the *sweetest harmony* of *Justice* must needs arise."

677. On Vico's general methodological objections against Grotius's approach toward law, *see* N.S. Struever, "Hobbes and Vico on Law," 19 (2001) *New Vico Studies* 63, 71.

678. G. Vico, *De universi juris uno principio et fine uno* (Napoli 1841, Italian translation by E. Amante) (Napoli 1858, Italian translation by F.S. Pomodoro) §LXII. Reprint of the original: Ioh. Baptistae Vici, *De Universi Iuris Uno Principio Et Fine Uno, Liber Unus* (Napoli 1720), in *Scrittori d'Italia*, G.B. Vico, *Il Diritto Universale* (F. Nicolini, ed., Bari 1936). A recent English translation has been made by J.D. Schaeffer: Giambattista Vico, *On the One Principle and One End of Universal Law*, in 21 (2003) *New Vico Studies* 33. The latter translates the two notions: "rectorial and aequatorial law"; *ibid.*, 73.

679. *Ibid.*, §LXI, and on the two measures, *see* especially §XLIV.

680. On this difference between community of equals and unequals, *see* G. Del Vecchio, *Justice—An Historical and Philosophical Essay* (A.H. Campbell, ed., Edinburgh 1952) 53–54, note 17, at 69–70.

681. I doubt very much that Grotius considered the example of investment by partners to be a case of geometric proportion. The example is used by Aristotle (EN 1131b29–31) and its

dignity of a person and not the money. Indeed, each partner takes an equal part of the profit according to simple arithmetic measure. The money is at the basis of the equality and not the personal dignity; each takes that measure of the profit that he would have received if he had been the only investor.[682]

On the other hand, contrary to Grotius's view, the father who, by dint of his prerogative, makes a legacy in his will by considering the merit (dignity) of a person makes use of distributive justice.[683] The family is like a little state, and the state like a big family.[684] Corrective justice is at the basis of all restitutionary claims; in these cases, we ask from the defendant nothing more than to restore the possession of our property.[685]

Vico pays special attention to the problem of categorizing punishment. He says:

> One should not think that considerations about punishments pertain to aequatorial [corrective] justice just because Aristotle in his *Ethics*, elegantly says punishment is justified by an "involuntary contract." The term is improper because it implies that some things deserve, require, or are owed punishment, as if on the one hand, where the punishment is not meted out, someone will be owed something else, or on the other hand, if someone does suffer punishment, the offended party somehow recovers something of which they have been deprived by the crime. But when we say something "deserves punishment" it is not simply on behalf of the injured party it is deserved, but more generally it is deserved for the sake of civil society. For civil power is able to impose such punishments justly, as the laws require, because the defendant had consented to the laws on which the civil society is founded and against which the supposed crime has been committed. Rectorial [distributive] justice obtains in public affairs; aequatorial [corrective] justice in private affairs.[686]

---

interpretation gives rise to some difficulties. It seems, however, that it is Aristotle, who considered it to be a case of geometric proportion in a transactional setting. *See* Gauthier and Jolif, *op. cit.*, II, 1, at 359–360; Vico's critique is relevant, therefore, to Aristotle's approach.

682. *Ibid.*, §LXI, 1.

683. *Ibid.*, §LXII, and in greater detail §LXIII, 6.

684. *Ibid.*, §LXIII, 6.

685. *Ibid.*, §LXIII, 3.

686. *Ibid.*, §LXIII, 6; J.D. Schaeffer, translation, *op. cit.* 21 (2003) *New Vico Studies*, chapter 63(6), 75.

In a final paragraph,[687] Vico notes that the distinction between distributive and corrective justice is valid in theory, but in the practice of life they are not separated. Thus, if the citizens deal among themselves on the basis of equal rights, this is so because the government obliges them to do it; and if the civil authority governs its subjects, this is so because the latter have consented to that power by a common promise. "Finally, all people are obligated by the principle of equity [*aequum bonum*] because reason dictates its truth [*verum*], and reason dictates it because a certain sociability and equality has been established. Humans cannot grasp this equality any other way. Other than by recognizing that they are created by God according to the one principle of nature."[688]

Vico then states that in distributive justice one finds corrective justice and vice versa. Where distributive justice reigns, there is frequently equality between the subjects; and where equality is lacking, distributive justice is equally wanting. Thus, where there are many equals, they regularly follow distributive justice, and where there are many superiors, they regularly apply corrective justice among themselves. For that reason the persons who were above the law understood that between all of them a certain affinity had been established; hence, a law of nature governed them according to equity; and, therefore, the monarchs, when waging war on one another, recognized each other as *hostes* (enemies), that means as *equals*.[689]

It seems, however, that those scholars, whose main interest lay in Roman law, were not overly concerned with the Aristotelian distinction. They presumed that Aristotle's notion of justice does not contradict the traditional Roman definition by Ulpian: *Justitia est constans ac perpetua voluntas jus suum cuique tribuendi*.[690] A good example is the commentary on the Pandects

---

687. *Ibid.*, §LXIV.

688. *Ibid.*, J.D. Schaeffer, translation, *op. cit.*, 77.

689. *Ibid.*, §LXIV, 2.

690. Digest. 1.1.10.pr. *See, e.g.*, Johannes Kahl, alias Calvinus Wetteranus, (1550–1614), *Magnum Lexicon Juridicum* (Geneva 1759) 832, "*Justitia* particularis, quam praecipue Jureconsulti considerant, est constans & perpetua voluntas, jus suum cuique tribuens . . . Et haec quidem species justitiae ab *Aristot.* rursus dividitur in distributivam . . . et commutativam . . . " In the same sense already Ioachimus Mynsingerus a Frundeck (Joachim Münsinger von Frundeck) (1514–1588), *Apotelesma, Sive Corpus Perfectum Scholiorum ad Quatuor Libros Institutionum Iuris Civilis* (Venezia 1569) 9. After quoting Aristotle's distinction, the author refers it to Ulpian's definition of justice (*ibid.*, §§9, 19): "Hinc igitur *particularem Iustitiam* definit hic Iustinianus ex Ulpiano, autque eam esse constantem & perpetuam voluntatem, Ius suum cuique tribuendi . . . Porro ut duplex est iustitia, ita hic duplex intelligitur ratio tribuendi ius suum cuique: nempe in distributionibus

by the jurist Johann Brunnemann (1608–1672), professor at the University of Frankfort on the Oder.[691] The author merely repeats the traditional criteria of the distinction, observing that distributive justice relates not only to rewards but also to punishment; then he adds that, nevertheless, sometimes the arithmetic proportion is applied in punishment—like in case of homicide—and sometimes the geometric proportion obtains in contracts, such as in case of corporation.[692] Similarly, the Dutch jurist Paulus Voet (1619–1667), after shortly mentioning the basic traditional criteria of the Aristotelian distinction, observes that under their own (Roman) law, even in some commutative justice situations, the condition, quality and dignity of persons are taken into account.[693] Thus, in specific cases, the opinion of the most dignified creditors is accepted by the Praetor.[694]

Johannes Voet (1647–1713), the son of the former, adds in his commentary on the Pandects[695] a number of additional cases where, under Roman law, the dignity or quality of persons, are taken into account in commutative justice

---

poenarum & praemiorum pro meritis, & in commutationibus rerum ne cui fiat iniuria, & servetur aequalitas." In this sense also the Italian Protestant theologian Hieronimus Zanchius (Girolamo Zanchi) (1516–1590), *De Natura Dei, Seu De Divinis Attributis, Libri V* (Neustadt an der Weinstrasse 1590) 354–355. For a critical comment on the view that the Roman *suum cuique tribuere* is identical to Aristotle's notion of distributive justice, D.D. Raphael, *Concepts of Justice* (Oxford 2001) 58–59.

691. Johannes Brunnemannus, *Commentarius in Quinquaginta Libros Pandectarum* (Freiburg 1714) Tit. I, p. 1.

692. *Ibid.*: "Particularis justitia vulgo in distributivam & Commutativam dividitur. Illa circa res communes tribuendo; Haec circa res singulares versatur: Illa res cum persona; Haec res inter se confert: Illam in praemiis non tantum, sed & poenis observandum puto; ita tamen ut in poenis interdum Arithmetica proportio, ut in homicidio & aliis; interdum in Contractibus, v. gr. Societate & simil. etiam Geometrica proportio obtineat." As a matter of fact, a great number of academic theses were dedicated to the topics of justice and law on the background of Roman law. Most of them started with the definition of Ulpian and added the Aristotelian distinction in a rather casual and simplistic way: *see, e.g.*, Jacob Sturtz, *Disputatio de Justitia et Jure* (Rostock 1627) Thes. III–IV, pp. A2–A3; *infra* at note 703.

693. Paulus Voet, *In Quattuor Libros Institutionum Imperialium Commentarius*, Pars Prior (Utrecht 1668) Lib. I, Tit. I, *De Justitia & Jure*, 32–33: "Non tamen id silentio possum praeterire, quod uno atque altero casu in jure nostro expresso, etiam in justitia commutativa habeatur ratio conditionis, qualitatis & dignitatis personarum."

694. *Ibid.* The author mentions the rule in Dig. 2.14.8.

695. Johannes Voit, *The Selective Voet being the Commentary on the Pandects [Paris edition 1829] and the Supplement to that Work by Johannes Van Der Linden [1756–1835]* (translated with explanatory notes by P. Gane), vol. 1 (Durban 1955) Sects. 9–10, pp. 13–15.

situations.[696] In relation to distributive justice—which has to do with rewards and penalties—the author notes that often, though not always, respect is paid to persons and that thus the geometrical proportion is preserved.

However, "penalties and rewards which looked at in themselves are unequal, will yet, because they are applied to persons differing in age, origin, dignity, sex, be equal, in so far as a penalty lighter in itself weighs no less heavily on a man of more honourable degree than one which, though appearing heavier when looked at in itself, weighs on a man of more humble degree."[697] The author then adds that it is generally known that fines of definite amount are fixed generally by law for all persons of whatever sex, dignity, or position. This was common with the Romans and is also not foreign to the usage of the present day. In a separate section,[698] the author refers to the mentioned Grotian distinction between expletive and attributive justice, noting that there is no great difference between that distinction and the Aristotelian one. In his view, Grotius's division is aimed at distinguishing between legally sanctioned rights and duties, and merely moral ones that are based on equity and natural reason.

The contemporary Dutch jurist, Gerard Noodt (1647–1725), after shortly describing the Aristotelian distinction, equally remarks that, under their law, the criteria of the distinction do not always prevail.[699] Thus, in commutative justice situation, the (Roman) law may grant privileges to orphans, minors, women, and soldiers, privileges that are denied from other people. Likewise, the action in fraud is not given to children or servants against their parents or masters.[700] Moreover, there are examples where under distributive justice an arithmetic proportion is observed and, conversely, a geometric proportion under commutative justice. Thus, in relation to delicts, that according to Aristotle are subject, like contracts, to an arithmetic proportion, the Roman jurists measure the punishment according to a geometric proportion: the more distinguished persons get a lighter punishment, the less worthy a heavier one. Finally, the delicts are measured according to the person of the

---

696. The author refers, *ibid.*, 13, note 1, to Dig. 2.7.19; 2.14.8; 42.5.16; and to Cod. 4. 66. 4; 3.37.1.

697. *Ibid.*, 14.

698. *Ibid.*, Sect. 10, pp. 14–15.

699. Gerardus Noodt, *Opera Omnia*, Tomus II (Editio Tertia, Leiden 1760), Commentarius ad Digesta seu Pandectas, Lib. I, Tit. I, De Justitia & Jure, p. 2.

700. Dig. 4.3.11.1.

wrongdoer and that of the victim. Sometimes, the more distinguished persons are punished more than the others, as in the case of an embezzlement committed by an official during his public office. He is punishable by death; others will get a lighter punishment.[701]

Finally, the German jurist, Johann Gottlieb Heineccius (1681–1741), who taught also in Holland, adopted fully the ideas of Grotius: The rights and duties under *iustitia expletrix* are fully binding and can be enforced; those under *iustitia attributrix* are rather based upon good will and, therefore, do not admit coercion. The Aristotelian distinction between commutative and distributive justice is in most cases based upon the arithmetic and geometric proportion, but not always.[702]

As a matter of fact, the topic of justice was treated during the sixteenth, seventeenth, and eighteenth centuries in numerous academic dissertations, often in a very cursory form, and generally the reference to Aristotle's distinction was rather succinct, lacking original ideas. It usually came after Ulpian's famous definition as mentioned in Justinan's *Digesta*.[703] Nevertheless,

---

701. Inst. 4.18.

702. Johannes Gottlieb Heineccius, *Elementa Iuris Civilis Secundum Ordinem Pandectarum Commoda Auditoribus Methodo Adornata* (Amsterdam 1731) Pars I, Lib. I, Tit. I, §§4–7, pp. 2–3.

703. The following, chronologically arranged list, is by no means exhaustive. It serves as a mere illustration of a general tendency existing at that time in a variety of academic institutions throughout Europe. We include the academic dissertations that continue the scholastic tradition, especially in Catholic institutions. The list represents the literature we personally encountered in a number of libraries: Ottho Eysenreich, *De Iustitia Iudiciis Servanda* (Praes. Gregorius de Valentia, Ingolstadt 1579) 12–13: "Nam si ob amicitiam, vel cupiditatem, vel odium sententiam ferunt, quam aut sciunt, aut arbitrantur iniustam aut etiam de qua dubitant, sit ne iniusta, bifariam peccant; primo contra Iustitiam commutativam, cuius rationem tunc Aequitatem (opinione saltem aut suspicione sua) violant. Secundo contra Iustitiam distributivam, hoc ipso videlicet, quod sententiam favorabilem in eius gratiam ferunt, quem illa indignum esse censent"; Joannes Wirth, *Theses Ethicae De Justitia* (Marburg 1592); Ioannes Lagonychus, alias Hasenklaw, *De Justitia theses, cum quibusdam aliis Philosophicis positionibus* (Marburg 1593). (The author considers punitive justice to be part of distributive justice: "Haec [justitia] est duplex: Distributiva, & commutativa. Nam punitivam, quem Franciscus Vallesius addit, nos subjicimus distributiva."); Leonhardus Koppelius, *Disputationis Iuridicae Primae, De Justitia & Iure*, Pars Tertia (Wittenberg 1593) VIII, p. A3; Zacharias Prantl, *Theses De Iustitia Et Iure, De Legibus Et Longa Consuetudine* (Rostock 1595) Thes. I, 8; J.C. Herdesianus, *De Fortitudine Et Justitia* (Herborn 1595) §§39–41; Iohannes Leonhardus Fleiner, *Disputatio Philosophica De Iustitia* (Praes. Michaelis Zieglerus, Tübingen 1596) (The author distinguishes between distributive and corrective justice. The latter is conceived in a remedial way. Its exclusive function is to correct injustices caused by inequality in distribution or in contractual transactions or by wrongful injuries.); Dominus Virgilius Maurer, *Disputatio Theologica De Iure Et Iustitia in Communi* (Praes. Iacobus Gretserus, Ingolstadt, 1601) §§63–69 (Vindictive justice makes part only of potential justice, since

some dissertations merit special mention, in view of their specific qualities.

---

it does not compensate the victim of the delict); Michael Zellerus, *Disputatio De Iustitia et Iure* (Strassburg 1602) Thes. I, 2; Johannes Lauterman, *Disputatio Ethica De Iusticia Et Jure* (Greifswald 1602); Georgius Beccerus, *Themata Ethica De Justitia. Ex libro V. Ethicorum Aristotelis ad Nicomachum methodice concinnata* (Marburg 1603) A2–A3 (In relation to punishment, the author observes that the geometric proportion of distributive justice is applied. He adds: "Tametsi enim in abstracto citra aliquem personarum respectum poenam constituit, Arithmetica proportione: tamen haec justitia cum legem exsequitur & in concreto; de poena personae applicanda disputat, rem ad proportionem Geometricam reducit. Nec tantum quid de facto debeatur: sed & quid de jure personae utrobique congruat expendit."); Adamus Willichius, *Disputationum Philosophiae Moralis, Duodecima De Justitia Et Iure* (Praes. Christophorus Butelius, Stettin 1603); Aegidius Held, *Disputatio Theologica De Iure Et Iustitia* (Ingolstadt 1603) §XIII; Albertus Alberti F. Clampius, *Disputatio Ethica De Iustitia Ad V. Lib. Nicomach. Summi Aristotelis* (Helmstedt 1609), §§11–62; Johannes Schraderus, *Disputatio Ethica De Iustitia Et Iure. Ex 5. Arist. Ethic. Libro deprompta* (Praes. Georgius Calixtus, Helmstedt 1609) §§13–26; Georgius Gollius, *Disputatio Ethica De Iustitia* (Praes. Laurentius Thomas Walliserus, Strassburg 1609) *passim*; Georgius Bruggmann, *Disputatio Theologica De Iustitia Et Iure, In Catholica Et Celebri Academia Ingolstadiensi* (Praes. Adamus Tannerus, Ingolstadt 1609) 12–14 (The author follows closely Thomas Aquinas; he rejects Buridan's view.); Andreas Poplizius, *Theses De Iustitia Et Iure* (Zerbst 1613), III, IV. (The author notes that when electing a worthy person, the worthier non-elected one does not have a claim for compensation; *cf. supra* at note 95; A. Wiser, I. Merck, *Disputatio Theologica De Iustitia, Iure, Contractibus Legitimis Et Oppositis Eorum Malis, ipsorumque Medelis* (Praes. Stephanus Vitus, Dillingen 1613) 1–4, 14–15 (A succinct summary of scholastic opinions.); Jeremias Reusnerus, *De Iustitia Et Iure* (Wittenberg 1617) Theorema II; Johannes Fritzsch, *De Iustitia et Iure*, in Jacobus Blümelius, *Partis Prioris Collegii Juridici* (Lipsia, Leipzig 1618) Disp. I, p. A3 (According to this author, the definition of justice should relate to the Aristotelian notion of universal justice, since the latter obliges obedience to all laws.); Johannis Trygophori Philosophiae Magistri atque In Academia Gryphiswaldensi P.P. Exercitationum Ethicarum ex Aristotelis Ad Nicomachum Ethicis Exercitat. IX, *De Justitia Universali Et Particulari, Talione, Jure & Aequitate*, Respondente Casparo Schwartzen (Greifswald 1619) 141 (The author refers to Jean Bodin's idea of harmony, (*ibid.*, §23, pp. 148–149; *cf. supra* 131)): "Inter utramque, hanc Bodinus lib. 6. de Republ. Harmonicam interijcit, a qua reliquas tantum differe dicit, quantum aqua tepida a frigidissima."); Iacobus-Ulricus Kern, *Disputatio Ethica De Justitia* (Praes. Iohannes Baptista Weiganmeierus, Tübingen 1621) (Distributive justice concerns public persons, commutative justice private ones.); Dionysius Mertens, *De Iustitia et Iure*, in Christianus Krembergk, *Collegii Institutionum D. Iustiniani Imperatoris Disputationes* (Wittenberg 1623), Disp. Prima, p. A2; Johannes Simon Weinmann, *Disputatio Ethica De Justitia & Jure* (Praes. Johannes Baptista Weiganmeierus, Tübingen 1624) 7–10; Johannes Jacobus Zobelius, *Disputatio Ethica De Justitia & Jure* (Praes. Iohannes Baptista Weiganmeierus, Tübingen 1625) 7–10 (Corrective justice is said of the judge's function to restore—without paying attention to the parties' dignity—the injustice caused by a voluntary or involuntary transaction.); David Cuselius, *Disputatio Philosophica De Justitia Et Jure Stylo Aristotelico* (Stettin 1644); Petrus Ernestus Goetefleisch, *Dissertatio Iuridica De Iustitia Et Iure* (Praes. Henricus Hahn, Helmstedt 1647) §§14–19 (In the author's view, relying on Grotius, Lib.II, Cap. XX, §II, *supra* at note 647, punishment makes part of commutative justice, since they can be assimilated to a kind of contractual duties.); Paulus Müller, *De Iustitia Exercitatio Moralis Quam Amplissimi Philosophorum Ordinis Auctoritate* (Helmstedt 1657) §§31–66;

Moreover, they represent the rather high standard of discussion prevailing at a number of academic institutions in that post-scholastic, humanistic period.

A good example constitutes the academic disputation on the subject of distributive justice held at the University of Wittenberg in 1653.[704] After relying on the analysis of Melanchton in relation to the Aristotelian distinction, the author rejects Buridan's view[705] by affirming that the distinction

---

Constantinus Caldonatius, *Disputatio Theologica Selectarum difficultatum De Iure Et Justitia* (Praes. Bernardus Waibel, Salzburg 1660) 31–42 (The object of distributive justice is a lesser strict right than that of commutative justice; vindictive justice is part of commutative justice based upon a contractual duty of the judge to adjudicate according to the laws of the state.); Amandus Hegwein, *Disputatio Theologica De Justitia* (Praes. Matthias Ram, Dillingen 1664) 2–31 (Distributive justice confers as strict a right as commutative justice; restitution is evidently based upon commutative justice, since in respect of the specific part to be restored, it applies an arithmetic proportion. Vindictive justice is neither commutative justice nor distributive justice, though the intended equality between guilt and punishment has some analogy to the former.); Joannes Laurentius Hoffmann, *Asserta Theologica Ex Tractatu Juridico-Theologico De Justitia Et Jure* (Praes. Ioannis Hermannus Maystetter & Laurentius Flucke, Bamberg 1676) §1 (Commutative justice is the only kind of rigorous justice; vindictive justice equalizes the punishment with the delict.); Zacharias Esbergius, *Disputatio Philosophica De Justitia* (Uppsala 1684) 77–123 (The author mentions in relation to the issue of punishment that it is controversial whether it falls under commutative or distributive justice. It is a fact that noble and virtuous people are punished more leniently. However, he agrees to those who classify it under commutative justice, since no common goods are distributed; *ibid.*, 118–120); Georgius Lohrer, *Statera Justitiae Quam Cuique Ad Jus Suum Expendendum, Appendit Publice In Alma, & Archiepiscopali Universitate Salisburgensi* (Praes. Honorius Aigner, Salzburg 1695) (Restitution exclusively based upon commutative justice); Balthasar Sardagna, *Tractatus De Justitia Et Jure* (Praes. Ludovicus Babenstuber, Salzburg 1699) 5–8; Marianus Wourstin, *Tractatus Theologico-Thomisticus Scholastico-Dogmaticus De Jure & Justitia* (Praes. Maurus Ott, Tegernsee 1751) 4 (Only commutative justice is endowed with the full rigor of justice.); Joannes Wilhelmus Emmericus Metzen, *Principia Juris De Justitia, Et Justis* (Praes. Georgius Christophorus Neller, Trier 1754) 7–8; Felix Sutor, Marcellinus Prunner, Udalricus Lederer, *Theses Theologicae Ex Tractatu De Jure, & Justitia ac Sacramentis In Genere* (Praes. Alipius Gottschneider, München 1760) §§2–3 (Vindictive justice makes part of commutative justice; the author states in relation to Divinity: "Repugnat in Deo erga hominem Justitia commutativa stricte & rigorose talis, Datur tamen Justitia distributiva in Deo erga hominem."); J.B. Camus, G. Siegnitz, I. Thill, *Theses Theologicae De Quatuor Virtutibus Cardinalibus, Prudentia, Justitia, Fortitudine & Temperantia Necnon Religione* (Praes. Damianus Burgers, Luxemburg 1766) 4; Bartholomaeus Billen et al., *Theses Theologicae Dogmaticae Morales De Actibus Humanis, Conscientia, Legibus, Praeceptis Ecclesiasticis, Peccatis, Fide, Spe, Caritate, Religione, Justitia* (Trier 1777) 33–34.

704. Andreas Winzigerus, *Exercitationum Ethicarum Disputatio XX, De Justitia Distributiva* (Praes. Johannes Deutschman, Wittenberg 1653).

705. *Supra* at note 89.

designates a real difference in kind. They differ in their form of proportion (arithmetic, geometric), in their object (private property, public honors), in relation to the persons (private, public).[706] The author then refers to the etymology of the word "*distribuere*" connecting it to "*tribus*" (tribe), "*tributum*," "*tribunus*," and "*tributio*."[707] The just distribution has to take into account the dignity of the individual. This is vital for the preservation of the state.[708]

There are a number of conditions for the proper application of the geometric proportion. First, the person administering it must be of reasonable age, of a public status and endowed with moral and intellectual virtue. Experience shows that those who lack virtue, hate virtuous persons out of jealousy, or malice, or any other reason. Second, the persons who are to benefit from the distribution have to be distinguished according to their merits. If all are treated alike, a great confusion will be created in the human life. Two examples from classical literature illustrate that point: first, Achilles' refusal to engage—in favor of the Greeks under Agamemnon's rule—into the dangers of war and battle, since with Agamemmnon the bravest and the most cowardly receive equal honor[709]; second, the complaint of the Theban Philosopher Crates about the disregard of the respective dignity and merit in the distribution of rewards and salaries to professionals (cook, physician, flatterer, philosopher).[710] Finally, the object of distribution influences the criterion of distribution. Thus, when public money is distributed, the poor should receive more. In case of honors and dignities, the erudites and virtuous should be preferred; in case of charges and contributions, the wealthy should bear more than the poor, since they have more property.[711]

---

706. *Ibid.*, §§11, 12.

707. *Ibid.*, §13.

708. *Ibid.*, §15; the author relies on a verse (in Latin translation) from Euripides' Hecuba: "*Nam id perire plurimas urbes facit, Si vir probus fortisque mactus pectore, Non aufera plus praemii, quam pessimus.*" (Hercuba, Lines 306–308; the answer of Odysseus to Hecuba's complaint).

709. *Ibid.*, §16. The author refers generally to Homer's Iliad.

710. *Ibid.* See the relevant quotation from Diogenes Laertius, *supra* note 575. The author adds here his actual, personal wish: "Utinam cum veteribus temporibus etiam veterum querelae essent sepultae, & nova justitia distributiva cum novit temporibus exsurgeret! Sed optandum illud, non sperandum."

711. *Ibid.*, §16.

Another typical example costitutes a dissertation of 1670 at the same University and on the same topic of distributive justice.[712] After analyzing the notion and application of distributive justice, the author deals at length with the classification of punishment.[713] After presenting the arguments for the various contrasting views, he enters into a detailed defense of the opinion that considers punishment to be part of commutative justice. The fact that a variety of positive laws take into account the status of offender and victim does not detract from the basic classification. One has to distinguish between the assessment of the offense's gravity and the very infliction of the punishment: in relation to the former a geometric proportion may be admitted, but in the latter a purely arithmetic proportion must be applied.[714] In his arguments, the author relies on scholastic and post-scholastic sources.

Another interesting example of an academic dissertation is the one publicly defended in 1667 at the Catholic University of Salzburg for the obtention of a degree in theology.[715] The author, after dealing at considerable length with the notion of "legal justice," enumerates five differences between distributive and commutative justice.[716] 1) In distributive justice, the community, or its representative, deals with a private person; in commutative justice, private persons, or those who conduct themselves like private persons, deal with another private person. 2) The former orders distributions, the latter transactions. 3) Contrary to distributive justice, the basis of commutative justice is a property right or a quasi property right. 4) Commutative justice, as such, regards an arithmetic proportion, which constitutes an exact equality between exchanged things; distributive justice considers a geometric proportion that constitutes a proportional equality between things to be distributed and the condition of the recipient persons. 5) A duty of restitution

---

712. Georgius Christianus Meusell, *E Philosophia Pratica De Distributiva Justitia Dissertatio* (Praes. Godofredus Wildvogel, Wittenberg 1670).

713. *Ibid.*, §§7–17.

714. *Ibid.*, §16: "Tandem ut omne tollatur dubium, discernenda caute est delictorum aestimatio ab ipsa poenarum inflictione. Ibi namque personarum circumstantiarumque habitudo et differentia, cum negligi non possit, Geometrica teneri facile concedimus: at hic dispar plane est ratio, & proportio non nisi arithmetica. Non tamen dignitas personae, quod adhuc monendum, unquam per se attenditur, sed prorsus per accidens, in quantum vel delicti vel poenae quantitas exinde aestimare potest."

715. Philippus Paumfelder, *Disputatio Theologica De Justitia Et Jure* (Praes. Maurus Oberascher, Salzburg 1667) 5–22; exactly the same dissertation was also published under the name of Gregorius Puecher (Bayerische Staatsbibliothek 4 Diss. 3713, 11; 4 Diss. 2094).

716. *Ibid.*, 16–18.

arises from the violation of commutative justice, but not from the violation of distributive justice as such. However, in some situations the distributive justice includes commutative justice; as a result, in case of an unjust distribution, a duty of restitution arises. This is the case where the distributor of public benefits is bound by a contract to act in accordance with a geometric proportion. He will be liable to pay compensation for the damage caused to the community by the bestowal of benefits or offices to the unworthy. The same is true where a person is charged to distribute money according to some proportional criteria.

A violation of the criteria constitutes a violation of both distributive and commutative justice. The recipients have acquired a strict right to the benefit and the distributor is, in addition, under a commutative-justice duty toward the donator. But, in some distributive-justice situations, there is no commutative-justice-right involved. This is the case where a public office has to be granted to the most worthy person. Here, distributive justice does not include commutative justice. Thus, the election to the office of a less worthy person does not give the worthier one a right of restitution.[717] Vindictive justice constitutes in respect of the judge's position and function an act of commutative justice. He is charged by contract to care for the common good, as well as to protect the citizens from crimes. A neglect of his task will oblige him to pay compensation for the damage. However, the very task of imposing punishment in proportion of the delict may be considered as an act of distributive justice, since it is executed in the name of the community.

Finally, it has to be admitted that the motive of imposing punishment in order to safeguard the common good according to the law makes part of legal justice (*justitia legalis*), but its actual execution belongs to distributive justice.[718]

---

717. *Ibid.*, 18: "Caeterum quando fit distributio rerum, quae non debentur stricto Jure secundum conditionem personarum (ut evenit in distributione beneficiorum & officiorum, quae debent quidem conferre dignioribus, non tamen ita, ut ipsi jus strictum ad illa habeant) tunc Justitia distributiva non includit commutativam saltem in comparatione ad personas; quibus eiusmodi res distribuendae sunt, adeoque cum distributor eiusmodi res confert minus digno relicto digniori, non infert digniori injuriam, quae distributorem obliget ad restitutionem faciendam digniori, quem praeterivit." Incidentally, we came across a later dissertation, submitted at the same university, that copied, partly literally, the arguments of the fifth difference: Joannes Holzman, *Tractatus Theologicus, In Secundam Secundae Summae Theologicae S.Thomae Aquinatis Angelici Ecclesiae Doctoris, De Jure Et Justitia* (Praes. Carolus Schrenckh, Salzburg 1701) 38–39.

718. *Ibid.*, 20–22.

An additional example of a high-standard academic dissertation is the one publicly defended in 1672 at the Catholic University of Ingolstadt.[719] Referring to a great number of scholastic sources, the author concludes that distributive justice is not based upon a strict right. He shows that in cases where a strict right is recognized, it is grounded upon a specific contractual commutative-justice-right.[720] He distinguishes between the distribution of common goods that is primarily in the interest of the recipients, and the conferral of public functions, that lies in the interest of the state. In the former case, the recipients have a right of restitution against the wrongful administrator; in the latter case, the right of compensation is primarily given to the state, except if the candidates have acquired a strict right under a contract.[721] In relation to vindictive justice, the author admits that the judge by ordering, according to his public duty and function, the punishment for the delict or its compensation, executes an act of commutative justice. However, vindictive justice, seen as such, does not belong to any kind of real justice, since it is not concerned with rendering somebody his right.[722]

A thesis, submitted to the Catholic University of Innsbruck in 1705, starts with the assumption of four different kinds of justice: distributive, legal, commutative, and vindictive justice.[723] Among these, commutative justice is the strictest and most properly called justice. The author identifies commutative justice with the classical definition of Ulpian[724] and maintains its specific

---

719. Josephus Angerer, *Disputatio Theologica De Iustitia Et Iure In Catholica Et Electorali Universitate Ingolstadiensi* (Praes. Jacobus Illsung, Ingolstadt 1672).

720. *Ibid.*, Quaestio I, Caput II, §I, pp.12–21. The author analyzes the different situations of distributive justice. He emphasizes that the community must act qua community. As a result, God, or the Pope, when distributing benefits and rewards according to a geometric proportion, is not—*proprie dictu*—executing a distributive justice act (*ibid.*, 21, §II).

721. *Ibid.*, §II, pp. 29–32.

722. *Ibid.*, Caput IV, pp. 36–45. "Motivum formale Iustitiae vindicativae est tantum aequalitas poenae cum culpa, non vero cum jure communitatis, vel personae laesae, quamvis finis extrinsecus, & ipsius inferentis, vel subventis poenam, possit esse aequalitas debita cum praedicto jure: ergo Iustitia vindicativa nec est, nec spectat ad speciem proprie dictae Iustitiae, cujus est, cuique tribuere jus suum" (45).

723. Stephanus Felix Vintschger, *Theoremata Theologica De Iure Et Iustitia* (Praes. Ludovicus Simonzin, Innsbruck 1705) Quaestio I, Art. I, pp. 1–3.

724. *Ibid.*, Art. II, pp. 3–4.

nature in relation to the other kinds of justice and virtues. He defends that thesis—in a typical scholastic way—against a long series of objections.[725]

Firmly in the Thomist tradition is an additional noteworthy dissertation of 1715 submitted in Augsburg.[726] The author concludes—on the basis of the traditional arguments—that the difference in the proportion is an insufficient criterion for the distinction between commutative and distributive justice.[727] There is a difference in the underlying legal duty: distributive justice is based not upon a strict right of property—like commutative justice—but upon a legal right grounded in the adequacy of merit (*condignitas*).[728] The duty of restitution derives from a contractual commutative justice obligation. Vindictive justice is not a different kind of justice. If exercised by a judge for the common good, it makes part of commutative justice, that on its part has been ordered by the higher legal justice. If vindictive justice's purpose is merely the good of the individual, then it is solely based upon a contractual commutative justice.[729]

In connection with the reliance on the Roman law tradition, mention must be made of Gottfried Wilhelm Leibniz (1646–1716), the great jurist, philosopher, mathematician, scientist, and diplomat. His general definition of justice is "*caritas sapientis*," the "charity of the wise man."[730] Nevertheless, he uses in his writings Aristotle's division between universal and particular justice. The resulting three notions of justice—namely, universal, distributive, and commutative justice—he identifies with the general precepts of the

---

725. *Ibid.*, Art. II–III, pp. 4–24.

726. Edmundus Arnold, *Tractatus Theologicus De Jure Et Justitia* (Praes. Coelestinus Mayr, Salzburg 1715).

727. *Ibid.*, Quaestio III, Art. II, §I, pp. 90–91.

728. *Ibid.*, 91–92.

729. *Ibid.*, §III, pp. 98–102.

730. Leibniz, "Meditation on the Common Concept of Justice," in Leibniz, *Political Writings* (Patrick Riley, transl.& ed., 2nd ed., Cambridge, 1988) 45, 54, and *passim*; the same idea appeared already in an earlier writing of Leibniz, "Praefatio Codicis Juris Gentium Diplomatici," published in the edition of the Akademie der Wissenschaften, Vierte Reihe, Politische Schriften, Fünfter Band (1692–1694) (Akademie Verlag 2004), I *Rechtswesen*, N.7, 48, at 61; the here relevant passages have been earlier published in English translation: Leibniz, "On the Notions of Right and Justice. 1693," *The Monadology* (R. Latta, transl., Oxford 1898) 281, 283–284. *Cf.* H. Cairns, "Leibniz's Theory of Law," 60 (1946) *Harv. L. Rev.* 200, 217–219; reprinted in *id.*, *Legal Philosophy from Plato to Hegel* (Baltimore 1949) 295, 316–318; D.D. Raphael, *Concepts of Justice* (Oxford 2001) 82–83. On the evolution of Leibniz's idea of justice, *see* Robert J. Mulvany, "The Early Development of Leibniz's Concept of Justice," 29 (1968) *Journal of the History of Ideas* 53.

Roman legal tradition[731]: *honeste vivere, suum cuique tribuere* and *neminem laedere.* In Leibniz's words:

> And while justice is only a particular virtue, when one leaves out of consideration God or a government which imitates that of God; and while this limited virtue comprises only what are called commutative and distributive justice; one can also say that as soon as it is founded on God or on the imitation of God, it becomes universal justice, and contains all the virtues... And universal justice is stamped with the supreme precept *honeste (hoc est probe, pie) vivere,* just as *suum cuique tribuere* was in conformity to particular justice, whether in general or (taking it more narrowly) as distributive justice (which distinguishes men); and as *neminem laedere* stood for commutative justice, or for the *ius strictum* as opposed to equity, according as one takes the terms [in different ways].[732]

It is likely that Leibniz's notion of strict right as commutative justice has been influenced by the scholastic literature.[733] In an earlier work, Leibniz referred—when dealing with the Aristotelian forms of justice—to the above-mentioned specific terminology of Hugo Grotius[734]:

> The precept of bare Right or Right *in the narrow sense* [jus strictum] is that *no one is to be injured,* lest if it be within the state, the person should have ground for an action in law, or if it be without the state, he should have the right to make war. From this there comes the justice which the philosophers call *commutative* and the right which Grotius calls *right proper* [facultas]. The higher degree I shall call

---

731. Dig. I, 1: "Iuris praecepta sunt haec: honeste vivere, alterum non laedere, suum cuique tribuere."

732. Leibniz, "Meditation," *op. cit.*, 60.

733. But see the comment of P. Riley in his introduction to Leibniz, *Political Writings* (Patrick Riley, transl. and ed., Cambridge, 2nd ed., 1988) 21: "One of the most important things about Leibniz's theory of practical justice, when joined with the gradations of the Roman law, is that he allowed no sharp breaks between duty and benevolence: in Leibniz there is none of Kant's differentiation between 'perfect' and 'imperfect' duties to others. Justice for Leibniz is a *continuum,* as everything in his philosophy tends to be: there is an unbroken continuity, with no 'gaps,' between the lowest substance and God, between life and death, between rest and motion, just as there is a *continuum* between abstaining from injury and doing good."

734. *Supra* at note 643.

> *equity*, or if you prefer it charity (that is, in the narrower sense), which I extend beyond the rigour of bare Right to those obligations also on account of which those to whom we are obliged have no ground to compel us to perform them, such as gratitude, pity, and the things which are said by Grotius to have *imperfect right* [or *fitness, aptitude*] not *right proper* [*facultas*]. And as to the precept of the lowest degree was to do injury to no one, so that of the middle degree is to do good to everybody; but that so far as befits each person or so far as each deserves, since we cannot befriend all men. Therefore to this place belong *distributive* justice and that precept of Right [*jus*] which bids us *give to each his own*. And to this political laws in the state are related, laws which have to do with the happiness of subjects and which usually bring it about that those who had only moral claim [*aptitudo*] acquire a jural claim [*facultas*], that is to say, that they are enabled to demand what is fair that others should give. But while in the lowest degree of Right no regard was paid to the differences among men (except to those which arise from the particular matter in hand), and all men were regarded as equal, now in his higher degree merits are weighed, and hence privileges, rewards, and punishment appear.[735]

It has been noted by a number of scholars that Leibniz's identification of commutative justice with the legal precept of *neminem laedere* deviates from

735. Leibniz, "On the Notions of Right and Justice. 1693," *The Monadology* (R. Latta, transl., Oxford 1898) 281, at 288–290; for the original Latin text, *see* Akademie der Wissenschaften, *supra* note 730, at 61–62; *see also id. Nova Methodus Discendae Docendaeque Jurisprudentiae (1667)*, Akademie der Wissenschaften, Sechste Reihe, Philosophische Schriften, Erster Band (1663–1672) (Darmstadt 1930) 261, §§ 73–74, at 343–344; *cf. id. Notae Ad Jac. Thomasium*, *ibid.*, at 50–51. In an additional writing, Leibniz expresses the idea of a different equality in the two forms of justice in the traditional Aristotelian terminology. Thus regarding the lowest degree of right (commutative justice), he states: "This is that equality which is commonly called *arithmetical*, that all are so far regarded as having the same merit, and no account of persons being taken, each receives just as much as he gave up"; and further he says: "The distribution of goods and evils is often made in proportion to people's virtues and merits, or vices and faults, and this is called *geometrical* equality, because in this very inequality an equality of ratios is observed, so that unequal things are given to unequal persons, the same proportion being kept between the things given as there is between the persons"; *id. De tribus juris naturae et gentium gradilus*, as quoted by R. Latta, in his notes to Leibniz, "On the Notions of Right and Justice, 1693," *op. cit.*, 290, note 34, from the publication of Georg Mollat, *Rechtsphilosophisches aus Leibnizens ungedruckten Schriften* (Leipzig 1885) 15, 16. In the same writing (at 14), Leibniz states that "Commutative justice has to do with private right, distributive with public right."

Aristotle's original conception of the forms of justice.[736] As one scholar puts it: "Leibniz's theory of justice, then is a complex amalgam of Christian charity, a metaphysic of Platonic perfection, Roman law, and transmogrified Aristotelian terminology; its relation to his pure philosophy is, to say the least, problematical, but taken in itself it has integrity and force."[737]

Among the legal scholars of the seventeenth and eighteenth centuries, we find a strong tendency to criticize Aristotle's distinctions, sometimes with ironical undertones directed against those jurists who spent time and intellectual efforts to elaborate these distinctions. An influential voice is Christian Thomasius (1655–1728), professor of law at the University of Halle. He argues in relation to Ulpian's definition of justice that the attempt to explain it on the basis of Aristotle's writings is even more awry than the attempt to explain the books of Protestant theologians on the basis of the writings of the Popes.[738]

The weekly dissertations held in the summer of 1750 at the University of Göttingen under the direction of Johannes Andreas Hannesen (d. 1751),[739] are another good example of this kind of criticism. The authors note that at a time when the Roman law penetrated Germany, the jurists' mind were

---

736. P. Riley in his introduction to Leibniz, *Political Writings* (Patrick Riley, transl. and ed., Cambridge, 2nd ed., 1988) 20; R. Latta, in his notes to Leibniz, "On the Notions of Right and Justice. 1693," *op. cit.*, 290, note 34; *see* especially D.D. Raphael, *Concepts of Justice* (Oxford 2001) 57–58, 85–86. The latter author remarks that it seems odd to identify the precept "to harm no one" with commutative justice: "To make sense of this strange conclusion we have to put aside the literal meaning of *justitia commutativa* ('the justice of exchanges') and recall that Aristotle's corrective justice, which had come to be known as commutative, deals with the rectifying of all wrongs to individuals, not solely in transactions of exchange."

737. P. Riley in his introduction to Leibniz, *Political Writings*, *cit.*, 21–22. On the possible sources of influence upon Leibniz in this direction, *see* Robert J. Mulvany, "The Early Development of Leibniz's Concept of Justice," 29 (1968) *Journal of the History of Ideas* 53. The author suggests influences by the Jesuit Friedrich Spee and by Johann Heinrich Alsted's *Encyclopedia*, *ibid.*, at 67–68. *Cf.* the general critique by D.D. Raphael, *op. cit.*, 86: "Leibniz's attempt to tie up his own thoughts with the tradition of jurists and earlier philosophers is no doubt commendable as an exercise in synthesis, but it does not really bring enlightenment to the subject." For a critique of Leibniz's fusion of ethics with law, *see* G. Del Vecchio, *Justice—An Historical and Philosophical Essay* (A.H. Campbell, ed., Edinburgh 1952) 25–27.

738. Christianus Thomasius, *Dissertationum Academicarum Varii Inprimis Iuridici Argumenti*, Tomus Primus (Halle 1773) 741: "Stoici fuerunt ICti ex quibus Pandectae sunt collectae. Horum tradita ex libris Aristotelis velle explicare magis absonum est, quam si quis libros theologorum Protestantium ex scriptis pontificiorum exponere vellet."

739. Ioannes Andreas Hannesen (Praes.), *Dissertationes Hebdomadales De Iustitia & Iure* (Göttingen 1750) §§25–27, pp. 61–67.

occupied with the philosophical question of justice under the influence of Aristotle: "Nobody would commit the fragile boat into the very vast sea of jurisprudence without Aristotle sitting as steersman at the rudder."[740] All, teachers and disciples, were infected by this philosophical disease. The distinction between universal and particular justice is inadequate.[741] After shortly describing the traditional criteria of the distinction between commutative and distributive justice, the authors state that these distinctions are useless and contribute little to clarity. The proposition that in distributive justice a geometric proportion is observed reveals itself, by a close inspection, to be completely false. Thus, where a war leader promises a certain reward to the soldier who will first climb up a valley or wall, no attention will, indeed, be paid to the status of the soldier; putting first his foot upon the bulwark, he may be a common soldier, a corporal, an ensign or a captain.[742]

The proposition that in commutative justice situations there is always an application of an arithmetic proportion is, in the authors' view, equally false. One example of the falsity constitutes the plurality of unsecured creditors who often are, in case of insolvency, paid according to a geometric proportion.[743] It appears that in the authors' view, any further analysis of the distinction is a waste of time and of intellectual energy.[744]

On the other hand, the authors agree with Grotius's distinction between *iustitia expletrix* and *iustitia attributrix*, as an expression of the difference between a perfect legal right and an imperfect one.[745] The former creates a legally enforceable obligation, the latter a merely moral duty.[746]

Finally, the authors refer to the problem of classifying punishment. Again, their discussion has a clear ironical dimension. After mentioning the differences

---

740. *Ibid.*, §25, p. 61: " . . .& nemo, nisi Aristotele gubernatore, vastissimo iurisprudentiae pelago fragilem committebat navem."

741. *Ibid.*, 62.

742. *Ibid.*, 62–64.

743. *Ibid.*, 64. The authors refer to a judicial decision called "Classifications-Urthel."

744. *Ibid.*: "Sed diutius hisce quisquilliis non immoramur, quum iudice Thomasio (In iurisp. divin.lib. 1, c.1, n. 106), hac divisione Aristotelica, ad id magis ut ingenia torqueantur, quam ut excolantur, apta, merito careamus, & nulla in iure sit controversia, quae sine his tricis commode dirimi nequeat."

745. *Ibid.*, §26, pp. 64–65. On this distinction, *see supra* at notes 642, 643.

746. The authors use also the expressions: *iustitia externa* (*iuridica*) and *iustitia interna* (*moralis*).

of opinion between scholars—one part defining it as distributive justice,[747] another as commutative justice[748]—they claim that neither of the two forms is appropriate. Commutative justice is inapplicable, since in a series of legal provisions in Roman law, the social status of the offender is taken into account.[749] Moreover, one can ask what is exchanged in meting out punishment. "Perhaps, you would say, the wicked life before the deeds, the mutilation of limbs, the bad reputation, the diminished property is exchanged against the punishment; but, in the same line, I would affirm that when a good life before the acts, a undiminished property, a good reputation and the limbs' integrity are exchanged against rewards and honors, then they pertain to distributive justice."[750]

Distributive justice is inadequate for punishment, since it presupposes a community. However, punishments are not held in common: the criminal alone is fully liable. Some are of the opinion that punishment constitutes a third kind of justice, *iustitia vindicativa* or *vindicatrix*. There is no need for that additional distinction; it suffices that punishments should conform to the delicts and be established for the welfare of the state. Since the awkward Aristotelian distinctions are of no use, the controversies among the scholars relating to the classification of punishment are idle.[751]

The German Pandectists of the nineteenth century, too, were not specifically interested in the scholastic discussions of the Aristotelian notions of justice. Thus, e.g., Anton Friedrich Justus Thibaut (1772–1840), in his famous *System des Pandekten-Rechts*—after mentioning Grotius's distinction between *iustitia attributrix* and *iustitia expletrix*[752]—simply adds that, for the history of science, the scholastic division between commutative and distributive is noteworthy.[753] Some Pandectist scholars used even a most disparaging language

747. *Ibid.*, §27, p. 66. The scholars mentioned are: Vinnius, Wesenbecius, Brunnemanus, and Heineccius.

748. The scholars mentioned here are: Struvius, Eckoldus, and Hahnius.

749. The Roman sources quoted are: Codex Justinianus, 9.44.2; Digesta 48.19.9.11, 48.19.16.3, 48.19.28.16, 48.19.38.2+3.

750. *Ibid.*

751. *Ibid.*, 67: "Tandem quum distinctiones **Aristottelis** salebrosae nullius sint usus (§. 25) recte inde colligimus, Doctorum varias disceptationes, ad quam iustitiae speciem in divisione Aristotelica sint referendae, plane otiosas esse."

752. *Supra* at notes 642, 643.

753. A.F.J. Thibaut, *System des Pandekten-Rechts*, Band I (7. Aufl., Jena 1828) §5, pp. 5–6. This author too conceives Grotius's two notions of justice as expressing the distinction

in relation to these classical notions of justice, claiming that their analysis was a waste of time, misleading, and a contraband of prohibited goods.[754]

In relation to punishment, the question remains what was Aristotle's exact understanding of its function, and why has he not more exhaustively expounded its nature in relation to the forms of justice. An interesting suggestion has been made by the nineteenth-century German scholar Karl Hildenbrand.[755] According to his opinion, Aristotle views punishment basically as a means of education. When stating that virtue has to do with pleasure and pain, Aristotle adds:

> This is further indicated by the fact that that punishment is inflicted by means of pain. For punishment is a kind of medical treatment to take effect through the introduction of the opposite of the disease.[756]

Aristotle returns to the idea of punishment as an educational means to achieve and maintain virtue at the end of the *Ethics*:

> But it is perhaps not enough that they receive the right upbringing and attention only in their youth. Since they must carry on these pursuits and cultivate them by habit when they have grown up, we probably need laws for this, too, and for the whole of life in general. For most people are swayed rather by compulsion than argument, and by

---

between performance of moral duties (*iustitia interna, attributrix*) and performance of legally sanctioned duties (*iustitia externa, expletrix*). In the author's view, this distinction—contrary to a common mistake—is not identical with the scholastic categories of commutative and distributive justice. Commutative justice is a strict, absolute one (*durchgreifende, absolute Gerechtigkeit*); distributive justice is a proportionate one, modified according to the circumstances (*verhältnissmässige, nach Umständen modificirte Gerechtigkeit*). *Cf. also* L.A. Warnkönig, *Rechtsphilosophie als Naturlehre des Rechts* (Freiburg im Breisgau 1839, repr. Aalen 1969) 206. The author briefly notes that Aristotle emhasized only one aspect of justice. He adds generally: "Einzelne scharfsinnige Bemerkungen finden sich bei den scholastischen Philosophen des Mittelalters."

754. Christian Gotthelf Hübner, *Berichtigungen und Zusätze zu den Institutionen des Römischen Rechts* (Leipzig 1801) 45: "Die *iustitia* in *expletrix, commut.* und *distrib.* u.s.w. eintheilen, und sich mit der Erklärung dieser begriflosen Begriffe im schriftlichen und mündlichen Unterrichte beschäftigen, das heisst, die Zeit tödten, Leser und Hörer irre führen, und verbotene Waaren einführen oder Schleichhandel treiben."

755. K. Hildenbrand, *Geschichte und System der Rechts—und Staatsphilosophie: Das klassische Altertum* (Leipzig 1860) 299–303.

756. EN, Book II, 1104 b 16–18.[M. Ostwald, transl., Indianapolis 1962]. See generally I. Englard, "The Example of Medicine in Law and Equity—On a Methodological Analogy in Classical and Jewish Thought," 5 (1985) *Oxford Journal of Legal Studies* 238–247.

> punishment rather by (a sense of) what is noble. This is why some believe that lawgivers ought to exhort and try to influence people toward (a life of) virtue because of its inherent nobility, in the hope that those who have made good progress through their habits will listen to them. Chastisements and penalties, they think, should be imposed upon those who do not obey and are of inferior nature, while the incorrigible ought to be banished abroad.[757]

It follows that Aristotle conceives punishment, apparently in the wake of Plato, as a means to education, having thus rather the utilitarian function of deterrence and rehabilitation (healing).[758] This rationale seems to distance punishment from the idea of justice as interpersonal equality.[759]

The idea of geometric proportion has been criticized by modern authors on the ground that even if in the abstract it sounds good, in practice it is in many cases impossible to quantify by numbers the difference of persons' merits. Thus, even if one knows that one person is more virtuous than another, how can this difference be expressed in exact numbers?[760]

A general observation on the development of the distinction between distributive and corrective justice: Aristotle's emphasis was on the virtue of justice, which means the doing of justice. Hence, his major interest concentrated on the nature of the just act and correspondingly that of the unjust one. He found it in the notions of equivalence and proportion in their arithmetic and geometric sense. Aristotle was not concerned with the legal dimension of justice, namely, justice as an institution conferring legal rights and imposing correlative legal duties. It is true that he mentions the judicial function of restoring the equivalence in relation to the arithmetic proportion. But he did

---

757. EN, Book X, 1180 a 1–10.[M. Ostwald, transl., Indianapolis 1962].

758. Hildenbrand, *op. cit.*, 302–303. But see the radical view, according to which Aristotle's notions of corrective and distributive justice can be used, in relation to punishment, in support of the thesis that an adequate education by the state (among other state duties furthering "initiation into compliance with law") is a precondition for the legitimacy of punishment: Randall R. Curren, "Punishment and Inclusion: The Presuppositions of Corrective Justice in Aristotle and What they Imply," 8 (1995) *Canadian Journal of Law and Jurisprudence* 259. In our view, there is very little basis for this thesis, if at all, in Aristotle's writings.

759. For this reason Paul Lapie, *De Justitia Apud Aristotelem* (Paris 1902) 64, note 1, rejects the view of Hildenbrand. *Cf.* generally L. Günther, *Die Idee der Wiedervergeltung in der Geschichte und Philosophie des Strafrechts*, Abteilung 1 (Erlangen 1889, repr. Aalen 1966) 103–107.

760. J.H. von Kirchmann, *Erläuterungen zur Nikomachischen Ethik des Aristoteles* (Leipzig 1876) 93–94.

it in order to illustrate the functioning of corrective justice in restoring the arithmetic equivalence.

However, in the scholastic literature, the issue of the nature of the legal right under the different forms of justice became predominant. The traditional approach tended to define distributive justice—the function of which was to distribute goods belonging to the collectivity—as a nonperfect right of the recipient and a nonperfect duty of the distributor. Distribution of common goods was conceived to be the privilege of the prince, the ruler, who was not subject to any legal enforcement. This approach was criticized by some authors as going beyond the Aristotelian distinction.[761] Later it was argued that the traditional approach was based upon the idea of sovereign immunity, an idea that was no more valid.[762]

761. *See* Gabriele da San Vincenzo (1601–1671), *supra* at notes 274, 275.

762. A.-J. Faidherbe, *La justice distributive* (Paris 1934) 59–60.

SEVEN

The Modern Use of Aristotle's Forms of Justice

THE TRANSITION TO MODERNITY is again evidently a very gradual process that cannot be reduced to a specific moment in history. Being aware of its inevitable arbitrary character, we assume that for our specific purposes, the modern trends start with the eighteenth century. However, the criterion for modernity is not to been seen exclusively in the specific period of time, but rather in the change of certain ideas. Thus we can still see, in this assumedly modern period, (late) scholastic works—especially by Catholic authors—that do not substantially differ from those of their predecessors in earlier times.[762a]

Generally, the modern tendency appears to distance itself from the notion of justice as a moral virtue in the Aristotelian sense; it inclines to relate justice to law as a public institution.

Another phenomenon that can be conceived as a sign of modernity is the linkage of the Aristotelian forms of justice to the distinction between public and private law. The idea itself that commutative justice relates to private acts, distributive justice to public ones, was already explicitly expressed by Aristotle. It was later applied in practice by scholastic authors, who used the Aristotelian distinction as a means for the basic classification of legal fields that ran somewhat parallel to that of public and private law. Thus, e.g., the Jesuit Thomas Sanchez of Cordoba (1550–1610), in his book on Justice and Law, groups under commutative justice the matters of property rights, damage and injuries, promises and gifts, sales and leases, games and bets; under distributive justice: acception of persons,[763]

762a. For a modern author who builds his legal theory upon the scholasticism of Thomas Aquinas, *see* Jean Dabin, "General Theory of Law," in *The Legal Philosophies of Lask, Radbruch, and Dabin* (K. Wilk transl., Cambridge, Mass. 1950) XXXV–XXXVI; on the three kinds of justice (commutative, distributive, legal), *ibid.*, 443–452.

763. On this notion *see supra* note 651.

bestowal of benefices (*de beneficiis*), simonia, taxes, and fees (*de tributis et vectigalibus*).[764]

However, a close analysis of the exact relationship between the two sets of concepts was apparently made first by Donatus Hoffman (1703–1783), rector at Kempten, professor of philosophy and theology.[765] He states that distributive and commutative justice can be relevant in both public and private law. Thus, the state may engage into buying and selling like private persons; correspondingly, the head of a family may distribute among its members rewards and charges. Hence, it is appropriate to distinguish between *public* distributive and commutative justice, and *private* distributive and commutative justice.[766] Thus, the prince—when decreeing war or peace by treaties, enacting laws, assessing prices of things, requiring taxes, establishing punishments for crimes, etc.—exercises *public commutative* justice; he exercises *private commutative* justice in contracts made for the sake of his own benefit. *Public distributive* justice relates to the institution of officials, the establishment of their prerogatives functions and charges, etc.; *private distributive* justice consists in the distribution of honors and duties to the servants of his court.

Conversely, any private citizen exercises *public commutative* justice when abiding by the just laws, by the treaties of commerce, of war and of peace,

---

764. Thomas Sanchez, *Consilia Moralia, De Iustitia et Iure*, Tomus primus (Cologne 1653), Lib. I, II. Mention should also be made of the work of the Portuguese Carmelite scholar Johannes Consobrinus (João Sobrinho) (d. 1475) *De iustitia commutativa* (Paris 1514). The author, who had studied theology at Oxford, conceived commutative justice basically as an economic, transactional notion between private persons. His work deals with property (*dominium*), contractual fraud, usury, and aleatory contracts. His work is important for the study of medieval economic doctrines: M.B. Amzalak, *Frei João Sobrinho e as doutrinas económicas da Idade Média* (Lisboa 1945). *See also* Andreas Sallius (Andrew Sall) (1612–1682), *Ethica Sive Moralis Philosophia Ex Veterum, & Recentiorum sententiis concinnata* (Oxford 1680) Disp. Septima, *De Justitia*, 158–161. The Irish author, a former Jesuit who joined the Church of England, enumerates under commutative justice twelve nominate contracts and includes in the notion any other consensual agreement.

765. The author used in his publication the following name: Donatus A Transfiguratione Domini, *Introductio In universam Philosophiam, Veterem, Et Novam, Exegeticam, Et Dialecticam; Usui, & commodo studiosae Iuventutis* (2a ed., Kempten 1754), Tomus IV, pp. 135–140.

766. The core of this idea can already be found in the very popular law dictionary of the Heidelberg Law Professor Johann Kahl, alias Calvinus Wetteranus, (1550–1614), *Lexicon Iuridicum Caesarei* (Geneva 1612) 1482, "Iustitia": "Utramque autem & magistratus, & privatus colere debet; Nam & commutativa utitur magistratus, cum ius dicit de sarciendo damno dato. Et distributiva utitur privatus, cum gradus officiorum observat erga parentes, liberos, amicos, hospites." The idea is literally repeated in the later edition of *id., Magnum Lexicon Juridicum* (Geneva 1759) 832, "Justitia particularis."

and when paying the taxes, etc. He exercises *private commutative* justice when contracting freely with citizens or equitably with the very community itself. He exercises *public distributive* justice when showing more reverence, compliance, and obedience to higher officials than to lower ones; *private distributive* justice is exercised when caring more for the spouse than for the children, more for the children than for the servants, and so forth.

In view of his new classification, the author denies the necessity of the separate category of "legal" or "general" justice. Moreover, the *iustitia vindicativa* can be classified partly as public commutative justice and partly as public distributive justice.

The author then states that in many cases it may happen, especially in the public context, that both commutative and distributive justice are violated. Whereas the violation of distributive justice may not require the reparation of the injury—because the violation did not affect a vested right (*ius quaesitum*), but merely one to be acquired (*ius querendum*)—reparation may nevertheless be required, because the same act may have violated commutative justice, by affecting adversely the vested right of another person. Thus, e.g., the prince, while distributing honors, prefers unworthy persons over worthy ones. He sins against distributive justice by violating the nonvested rights of the worthy persons, but he, nevertheless, is not held to repair the inflicted injury. However, the unworthy administrators may cause various damages to the state that has a vested right to its integrity. Hence, *public commutative justice* has been violated, and the prince is, without doubt, liable to repair the damages.

The same is true when the prince, without any reason, grants remission to one among a plurality of death convicts. He sins against distributive justice in relation to those who do not get pardon, but toward them he cannot be obliged to anything. However, with respect to the state, whose interest it is that offences should be punished, he doubtlessly sinned against *public commutative justice*, and he will be held to repair the damages caused by that pardon.[767]

767. *Ibid.*, 138–140. The author notes at the end of his analysis that the observations are of his creation and invites the criticism and corrections of scholars, that are reasonable and without prejudice: "Atque hae observationes, domi quidem meae subnatae, innumeris paene casibus lucem afferre posse videntur; at videntur fortasse mihi dumtaxat; quare doctiorum censurae, atque correctioni (rationabili tamen, & a praeiudiciis liberae) libens eas subiicio."

In more recent times, some authors simply identify commutative justice with private law, distributive justice with public law.[768]

A completely different meaning and use of Aristotle's notions of justice is suggested by Immanuel Kant (1724–1804) in his *Rechtslehre.*[769] His starting point is a sharp distinction between moral duties (*officia virtutis s. ethica*) and legal duties (*officia iuris*).[770] Justice is, therefore, not a personal virtue but a public institution. Kant's analysis of the forms of justice is very complex, since he connects them to his general philosophical premises relating to cognition.[771] Besides the concepts of commutative and distributive justice, he introduces a third form: the protective justice (*iustitia tutatrix*).[772] These three forms correspond to the three Kantian categories of modality: possibility (*Möglichkeit*), reality (*Wirklichkeit*), and necessity (*Notwendigkeit*).[773] Whereas the notion of commutative justice is still, to some extent, based upon the Aristotelian meaning of transactional justice between private persons, Kant's notion of distributive justice is very remote, if not completely divorced, from the original meaning of distributing public honors and benefits. In Kant's understanding, distributive justice is the decision handed down by a state court in the private law conflict. Kant affirms that what might *a priori* appear to be right under private law (commutative justice), could be viewed differently

768. Gustav Radbruch, "Legal Philosophy," in *The Legal Philosophies of Lask, Radbruch, and Dabin* (K. Wilk transl., Cambridge, Mass. 1950) 74: "Commutative justice is the justice of private law; distributive justice is the justice of public law." For an interesting discussion of the relationship between the three pair of concepts: formal and substantive justice, corrective and distributive justice, private law and public law, *see* R. Briner, *Zur Funktion der Gleichheit in der menschlichen Gerechtigkeit,* Zürcher Beiträge zur Rechtswissenschaft, N.F., Heft 158 (Aarau 1949) 109–124.

769. I. Kant, *Metaphysik der Sitten, Metaphysische Anfangsgründe der Rechtslehre,* Akademie-Ausgabe, Band VI (Berlin 1914) (cited AA); for a translation into English we refer to the Cambridge Text in the History of Philosophy, I., *The Metaphysics of Morals* (M. Gregor, transl. and ed., Cambridge 1996) (cited MM). However, the translation in the text are of the present author.

770. AA 6, Einleitung in die Rechtslehre, p. 239; MM. p. 31.

771. For a most interesting attempt to clarify Kant's *Doctrine of Law* (*Rechtslehre*) by means of seven parallel sets of three concepts, *see* "Introduction," *Kant and Law* (B.S. Byrd and J. Hruschka, eds., Aldershot 2006) xiii–xxix; *see also* especially E.J. Weinrib, "Law as a Kantian Idea of Reason," 87 *Columbia L. Rev.* (1987) 472, reprinted in *Kant and Law, cit.*, 3–39; B.S. Byrd and J. Hruschka, "Lex iusti, lex iuridica und lex iustitiae in Kants *Rechtslehre*," 91 (2005) *Archiv für Rechts und Sozialphilosophie* 484.

772. AA. VI, Rechtslehre I, Privatrecht, §41, pp. 305–307; MM. pp. 84–85.

773. *Ibid.*

under distributive justice, as applied by the court, since the latter has to take into account the idea of public law.[774]

Kant illustrates this contrast between commutative and distributive justice by means of four examples: the binding force of a contract of donation; the allocation of risk in a contract of bailment (*commodatum*); the principle of market overt; the application of a decisive oath in judicial litigation.[775] It is remarkable that in Kant's view, considerations of public law, such as the efficiency of the administration of justice, may change the substance of private law.[776]

An echo of the old scholastic discussion about divine justice, we find in Kant's Concluding Remark to his *Metaphysics of Morals*: Divinity has no duties, but only rights toward human creatures; correspondingly the latter have only duties and no rights toward God.[777] Kant's conclusion is that ethics is limited to the moral relations between human beings. The idea that under divine justice human beings have a right to reward or to remuneration is a contradiction; they can only be based upon love and charity (*benignitas*). The idea of a divine punitive justice is equally problematic, since it must be based upon the unconceivable concept of an injury (*Läsion*) to Divinity. Moreover, divine punitive justice runs counter the intended end of the Creator in creating the human race, namely the happiness of mankind.

Kant's moral and legal philosophy exercised an enormous influence upon modern thinkers—including his specific notions of justice—creating a vast literature. An analysis in depth of the Kantian notions exceeds by far the limits of this study, as well as the capacities of the present author.[778]

---

774. *Ibid.*, §36, p. 297.

775. *Ibid.*, §§37–40, pp. 297–305; MM. pp. 78–84.

776. Thus, Kant bases the principle, that a promise to give a donation can be enforced against the promisor, upon the ground that otherwise judicial adjudication would be rendered infinitely difficult, or even impossible; *ibid.*, §37, p. 298; MM. p. 79. Similarly, the allocation of risk in bailment (*commodatum*) is justified by the practical reason that a public judge cannot get involved in presumptions as to what each of the parties had in mind; *ibid.*, §38, p. 300; MM. 80. Finally, the principle of market overt is grounded in the distributive justice principle (*in favorem iustitiae distributivae*) that enables the court to adjudicate a right in relation to thing as a proprietary right (*als Sachenrecht*) in the easiest and most secure way; *ibid.*, §39, p. 303; MM. p. 82. *See* J.D. Harke, "Kants Beispiele für die *iustitia distributiva* im Privatrecht," 91 (2005) *Archiv für Rechts—und Sozialphilosophie* 459.

777. *Ibid.*, 488–491, *see also ibid.*, 241; MM. pp. 230–232, 33.

778. In addition to the mentioned literature dealing more specifically with Kant's particular use of the Aristotelian notions of justice, *see* D. Klesczewski, "Kants Ausdifferenzierung

Aristotle's ethical works remained an object of great scholarly interest in the nineteenth and twentieth centuries. But in the spirit of the time, great intellectual efforts were invested into the philological, textual, and editorial problems of these philosophical writings according to the so-called methods of "higher" and "lower" criticism. A major objective was the correct understanding of Aristotle's original intentions. A good example of this tendency one finds in a dissertation on Aristotle's notion of justice published in Paris in 1902, rather surprisingly in Latin.[779] The author, adhering strictly to the Greek text, critically analyses the various contemporary scholarly views. Thus, he sharply criticizes the widespread view classifying punishment under corrective justice.[780] In the author's opinion, a correct analysis of the Aristotelian texts implies that punishment makes part of distributive justice. It explicitly takes into account the mental state of the perpetrator and thus the latter's ethical dignity.[781]

In relation to Aristotle's discussion of *antipeponthos*, the author rejects the view of some scholars who consider it to be a third kind of justice. In his view, Aristotle opines that the *lex talionis*, in order to be just, has to be a combination of corrective and distributive justice.[782] That is the way one has to understand also Aristotle's example of the transactional exchange, between an architect and a shoemaker, of a house and shoes.[783] As a matter of fact, both forms of justice may be combined. The author then emphasizes the formal nature of these notions of justice.[784]

However, another most remarkable phenomenon of contemporary legal scholarship, especially in tort law, is the renewed interest in the ancient

des Gerechtigkeitsbegriffs als Leitfaden der Unterscheidung von Unrechtsformen," *ARSP Beiheft* 66 (1997) 77–103. *See* generally also A. De Luca, *Giustizia e legalità nella filosofia giuridica di Kant* (Napoli 1984).

779. Paul Lapie, *De Justitia Apud Aristotelem* (Paris 1902).

780. *Ibid.*, 27–35.

781. The author argues that Thomas Aquinas's explanation, that the difference in punishment is the result of the difference in the gravity of the injury, is insufficient, since it does not explain why the mental state of the offender (voluntary or involuntary act) equally influences the measure of punishment. As a matter of fact, the state of mind does not affect the quantum of injury; *ibid.*, 33, note 1.

782. *Ibid.*, 35–40. See the interesting analysis of Gustav Radbruch, "Legal Philosophy," in *The Legal Philosophies of Lask, Radbruch, and Dabin* (K. Wilk transl., Cambridge, Mass. 1950) 186–187.

783. EN 1133a et seq.

784. Lapie, *ibid.*, 45.

distinction between distributive and corrective justice. One pronounced tendency is to found tort liability on the premises of corrective justice. As it has been noted by one scholar:

> There is no indication that an organized body of tort law existed in ancient Athens. Nevertheless, Aristotle's notion of corrective justice appears well suited to the law of torts, and many modern legal scholars, with scant knowledge of Aristotle, have casually borrowed the term and used it to talk about corrective justice of tort law. In fact, corrective justice has become a cottage industry for tort law theorists.[785]

It seems that the first important (modern) scholar to relate the substantive rules of delictual liability to the classical Aristotelian distinction between distributive and commutative justice has been the German Josef Esser. The latter published in 1941 a seminal and most influential work on strict liability (*Gefährdungshaftung*).[786] The author deplores the exclusive application of the traditional fault principle in relation to the liability for damages. In his view, it was a mistake of the liberal ideology to base liability exclusively upon the (Kantian) ideas of freedom of will and equality. Since many damages were caused by nonfaulty activities, i.e., as a result of causes that could not be viewed as an abuse of freedom, the problem became one of allocation of accidental losses between innocent parties. The traditional fault approach could not offer a satisfactory solution to this problem. The idea that the victim had to bear himself all accidental losses, did not constitute a reasonable legal ordering, but was merely a manifestation of the impotency to chose between two "equally innocent people" according to justice.[787] Here, the author states:

> Out of this apparently insoluble situation conducts us the recognition that the distribution of accidental losses, as well as that of goods, is *not* the task of "*commutative,*" i.e., of retributive or reciprocal justice, but that of "*distributive,*" i.e., of apportioning and allocating *justice.*

---

785. R.O. Brooks, "The Many Busts of Aristotle on Display: A Review of Calnan's *Justice and Tort Law*," 36 (2001) *Tort & Insurance L.J.* 1105, 1106–1107. (Footnotes omitted.)

786. J. Esser, *Grundlagen und Entwicklung der Gefährdungshaftung* (München-Berlin 1941), *passim.*

787. *Ibid.*, 73.

In a footnote to this text, Esser explains:

> We are following here the fundamental insight of *Aristotle* into the existence of two independent functions (and criteria) of justice, of which the first is directed at the ordering of legal relations (of both the voluntary as well as the involuntary, delictual ones); the second being directed at the ordering of the allocation of goods (*Nicomachean Ethics*, Book 5, Chapter 5)[788]

It is noteworthy that Esser, in justifying the imposition of strict liability, relied on Otto Gierke's idea of the social function of private law.[789] However, the latter considered the imposition of strict liability, on the basis of causation, to be a postulate of *corrective justice*: "Corrective justice requires, as far as expediency and equity allow, a shifting of the damaging consequences."[790] Moreover, Gierke viewed the allocation of loss on the basis of causation to be founded—like fault—on a "moral principle," namely: that where a special risk for others was created through something which brought a special advantage to somebody, the latter should equally support the loss.[791]

We find here the first signs of the widespread and heated modern controversy about the correct understanding of the Aristotelian distinction in relation to the substantive rules of liability.

Esser himself emphasizes correctly the "empty" idea of distributive justice, because of its merely formal character.[792] In its framework, all possible substantive solutions are conceivable, as far as they are conform to the historical social situation. The substantive solutions may lie between the poles of a collective assumption of damages and the individual bearing of success and misfortune. He considers the finding of the just solution to constitute a historical task.[793] It may depend on society's measure of organization and the connected mental attitude toward the contrasting notions of "fate" and "rational planning."[794]

---

788. *Ibid.*, 73, note 2 (Author's translation). For a general description of this shift in the view about the function of tort law from commutative to distributive justice, *see* J. Finnis, *Natural Law and Natural Rights* (Oxford 1980) 180–181.

789. O. Gierke, *Die soziale Funktion des Privatrechts* (Berlin 1889).

790. *Ibid.*, 33.

791. O. Gierke, in *Verhandlungen des Deutschen Juristentags*, vol. 28(II) (1907) 115.

792. J. Esser, *Grundlagen und Entwicklung der Gefährdungshaftung*, *op. cit.*, 80.

793. *Ibid.*, note 1.

794. *Ibid.*, 81.

It has been widely recognized that in view of the formal and, therefore, "empty" character of the Aristotelian notions of justice, the latter cannot yield by themselves substantively "just" solutions.[795] In order to reach these solutions, one has to refer to independent moral values that are capable to supplement the formal notions of "merit" and "equality." In the words of the German scholar Helmut Coing, who undertook one of the many enterprises to elaborate these additional moral values: "The value 'justice' is in itself not completely unequivocal; it requires supplementation by means of other moral values that will grant the criterion of the just allocation. It points from itself to other criteria."[796]

The Aristotelian distinction between the two forms of justice lay dormant for many decades in the legal discourse. This does not mean that jurists were not aware of the difference in their respective aims. Distributive considerations played an important role in the analysis of legal liability, as well as in other fields, but very rarely reference was made to the conceptual framework of the classical distinction.

An important exception in the U.S. legal literature constitutes the most famous article, published in 1936, of L.L. Fuller and W.R. Perdue, Jr. on the "Reliance Interest in Contract Damages."[797] The authors make the following remark: "In passing from compensation for change of position to compensation for loss of expectancy we pass, to use Aristotle's terms again,

---

795. R. Stammler, "Privilegien und Vorrechte," *Rechtsphilosophische Abhandlungen und Vorträge*, Vol. I (Charlottenburg 1925) 205, 224. The author, referring to Aristotle's different systems of "merit," makes the following critical comment: "Hierin liegt jedoch der Mangel, dass die Feststellung der *Gleichheit*, und damit der sachlichen Gerechtigkeit in besonderem Rechtsinhalte, auf den *Wert* verwiesen wird, der dem Einzelnen gerade *nach einer konkreten Rechtsordnung* erst zukommt. Diese besonderen Satzungen und Einrichtungen sind aber bedingt und wechselnd und selbst schon Gegenstand der kritischen Prüfung; sie können daher das *allgemeingültige* Richtmass *nicht* liefern, das in dem Grundsatze der *Gleichheit aller* gedacht ist." *See also* N. Bobbio, *Introduzione alla filosofia del diritto* (Torino 1948) 187–190.

796. H. Coing, *Die obersten Grundsätze des Rechts—Ein Versuch zur Neugründung des Naturrechts* (Heidelberg 1947) 35. The author himself adds to distributive and commutative justice a third form of justice: "protective justice." In his view, it is close to commutative justice, and includes the "*iustitia vindictiva*," the punishment as imposed by the state; *ibid.*, 48, note 2. For a completely different view of the relationship between a "protective" and a "vindictive" justice, *see* Friedrich Julius Stahl (1802–1861), *Die Philosophie des Rechts*, 2. Band, *Rechts und Staatslehre auf der Grundlage christlicher Weltanschauung* (3. Aufl., Heidelberg 1854) 160–175; the author criticizes the traditional Aristotelian distinction as an inadequate combination of legality (*Rechtlichkeit*) and justice. In his view vindictive justice is part of distributive justice; commutative justice ("erfüllende Rechtlichkeit") makes part of protective justice (*ibid.*, 170–171).

797. L.L. Fuller and W.R. Perdue, Jr., "The Reliance Interest in Contract Damages," 46 (1936) *Yale L. J.* 52.

from the realm of corrective justice to that of distributive justice. The law no longer seeks merely to to heal a disturbed status quo, but to bring into being a new situation. It ceases to act defensively or restoratively, and assumes a more active role."[798] However, this particular reference to the Aristotelian distinction seems to have escaped scholarly interest for a very long period of time.[799] In U.S. case law, one finds one lonely reference to that passage.[800]

The whole situation changed dramatically in the early eighties of last century: A growing flow of scholarly papers started to appear U.S. law reviews—especially, but not exclusively,[801] in relation to tort law—all referring to the

798. *Ibid.*, 56. In our view, the authors' concept of corrective justice is much too narrow. Aristotle uses the concept of commutative justice in voluntary transactions where it possesses a pronounced active dimension. The duty to perform a promise in an exchange transaction has been understood throughout the ages to be an important part of this kind of justice. *See* James Gordley, "Enforcing Promises," 83(1995) *Calif. L. Rev.* 547, 551–556; *id.* "A Perennial Misstep: From Cajetan to Fuller and Perdue to 'Efficient Breach,'" *Issues in Legal Scholarship* (online edition): (2001) Article 4; *see also* the criticism of E.J. Weinrib, "Legal Formalism: On the Immanent Rationality of Law," 97 (1988) *Yale L. J.* 949, 983, note 74.

799. It seems that one had to wait until the 1980s for scholars paying attention to the authors' specific reference to the Aristotlian distinction: R. Birmingham, "Notes on the Reliance Interest," 60 (1985) *Wash. L. Rev.* 217, 242; A. Katz, "Reflections on Fuller and Perdue's The Reliance Interest in Contract Damages: A Positive Economic Framework," 21 (1988) *Univ. of Michigan J. of Law Reform* 541, 545, note 11; P. Benson, "The Basis of Corrective Justice and Its Relation to Distributive Justice," 77 (1992) *Iowa L. Rev.* 515, 517 note 3; R. Craswell, "Against Fuller and Perdue," 67 (2000) *U. Chi. L. Rev.* 99, 103, 121–128; D. Slawson, "Why Damages for Breach of Contract Must Be the Norm: A Refutation of the Fuller and Perdue 'Three Interests' Thesis," 81 (2003) *Nebraska L. Rev.* 839, 841, 859; E. Zamir, "The Missing Interest: Restoration of the Contractual Equivalence," 93 (2007) *Va. L. Rev.* 59, 108–110; J.M. Fischer, "The 'Right' to Injunctive Relief for Patent Infringment," 24 (2007) *Santa Clara Computer and High Tech. L. J.* 1, 24, note 103.

800. *Perma Research and Development v. Singer*, 542 F.2d 111, 127 (2nd Cir. 1976), in the dissenting opinion of Van Graafeiland, Circuit Judge. The judge omitted from the quotation the reference to Aristotle.

801. Reliance on corrective or distributive justice appears in relation to contracts, unjust enrichment, criminal liability, environmental regulations, constitutional issues, and a variety of additional topics. For contract law, *see, e.g.*, A.T. Kronman, "Contract Law and Distributive Justice," 89 (1980) *Yale L. J.* 472; James Gordley, "Equality in Exchange," 69 (1981) *Calif. L. Rev.* 1587. *Cf.* P. Benson, "The Basis of Corrective Justice and Its Relation to Distributive Justice," 77 (1992) *Iowa L. Rev.* 515. In relation to unjust enrichment, *see, e.g.*, the conceptual analysis of D. Klimchuk, "Unjust Enrichment and Corrective Justice," *Understanding Unjust Enrichment* (J. Nyers, M. McInnes, and S.G.A. Pitel, eds., London 2004) 111; *id.* "The Structure and Content of the Right to Restitution for Unjust Enrichment," 57 (2007) *Univ. of Toronto L. J.* 661, 674–680.

Aristotelian distinction of corrective and distributive justice.[802] At the origin of this still continuing controversy are the papers of two scholars dealing with tort liability: George Fletcher[803] and Richard Epstein.[804] Both used the notion of corrective justice in order to act counter the instrumentalist, economic approach that had won important scholarly support in the recent preceding years.[805]

The start was made by Fletcher, who first observed that the journals cultivated the idiom of cost-spreading, risk-distribution, and cost-avoidance; hence, "discussed less and less are precisely those questions that make tort law a unique repository of intuitions of corrective justice," such as the rationale

---

802. A glimpse into Lexis reveals that in the last ten years only, close to 300 papers are listed to refer to corrective justice and Aristotle.

803. G.P. Fletcher, "Fairness and Utility," 85 (1972) *Harv. L. R.* 537, 538.

804. R.A. Epstein, "A Theory of Strict Liability," 2 (1973) *J. Legal Stud.* 151, 165 note 42, where he shortly refers to Fletcher's article mentioning the latter's notion of corrective justice. In the next paper, *id.* "Defenses and Subsequent Pleas in a System of Strict Liability," 3 (1974) *J. Legal Stud.* 165, Epstein remarks that his intention is to show how tort law can be viewed as a system of corrective justice appropriate for the redress of private harms. At the end of his article (at 215), he notes that the common law of negligence and the system of strict liability "treat the tort law as a system not of resource allocation but of corrective justice." The concept of corrective justice became more prominent in Epstein's later articles, ever since it appeared in the title: *id.* "Nuisance Law: Corrective Justice and Its Utility Constraints," 8 (1979) *J.Legal Stud.* 49; *id.* "Causation and Corrective Justice: A Reply," 8 (1979) *J. Legal Stud.* 477. It has, however, to be noted that the author does not refer to Aristotle, nor does he specifically mention the Aristotelian distinction, and, consequently, his articles don't contribute much to the understanding of the historical notions.

805. It has, however, to be noted that in the Anglo-American legal literature the Aristotelian distinction had been mentioned before in connection with compensation and tort liability. Thus, in an article of W.J. Blum and H. Kalven, Jr., "The Empty Cabinet of Dr. Calabresi: Auto Accidents and General Deterrence," 34 (1966–67) *U. Chic. L. Rev.* 239, 268, the authors, referring to Aristotle, observe: "In large part corrective justice is concerned not with deterring the wrongdoer, but with satisfying the victim's feeling of indignation. If the victim recovers only from the fund, he will not gain the satisfaction of seeing his wrong righted. Nor will it be much different if, after paying the victim, the fund later recovers from the tortfeasor." The authors refer also (*ibid.*, note 65) to H.L.A. Hart, *The Concept of Law* (Oxford, 1961) 160. Hart, indeed, mentions there the Aristotelian distinction in relation to compensation. Hart was familiar with Del Vecchio's book, *Justice—An Historical and Philosophical Essay* (A.H. Campbell, ed., Edinburgh 1952), and as a result was aware of the scholastic discussions (*Concept of Law, cit.*, 251, note to page 153). Hart wrote a critical review of Del Vecchio's book in 28 (1953) *Philosophy* 348–352. Hart's personal copy of Del Vecchio's book has been donated to the Hebrew University, Faculty of Law library in Jerusalem; it contains handwritten marks and notes of Hart. It appears that the mentioned reference to Aristotle by Blum and Kalven induced Samuel Stoljar, "Accidents, Costs, and Legal Responsibility," 36 (1973) *Modern L. Rev.* 233, 234, to deal shortly with the relationship between the two forms of justice; *infra* note 871.

for an individual's "right" to recover for his losses.[806] And more explicitly, Fletcher remarked in relation to the economic argument of shifting losses to the individual who was in better position to distribute losses:

> This is an argument of distributive rather than corrective justice, for it turns on the defendant's wealth and status, rather than his conduct. Using the tort system to redistribute negative wealth (accident losses) violates the premise of corrective justice, namely that liability should turn on what the defendant has done, rather than who he is. See the *Nicomachean Ethics of Aristotle*, Book V, ch. 4, etc. What is at stake is keeping the institution of taxation distinct from the institution of tort litigation."[807]

This specific use of the Aristotelian distinction marks an important and decisive change seen from a historical point of view. Contrary to the medieval and late scholastic endeavors, aimed at the correct understanding of the Aristotelian notions of justice and of their application in practice, we encounter here their employment for a critical analysis of substantive solutions. The argument voiced here is that the distributive aims of tort liability are inherently inconsistent with corrective justice and therefore illegitimate in relation to the parties involved. The truth is that objections against the economic-utilitarian approach in tort law—based upon the Aristotelian distinction—had been raised already in the late nineteenth century in

---

806. G.P. Fletcher, "Fairness and Utility," 85 (1972) *Harv. L. R.* 537, 538. It is possible that the author subsequently somewhat changed his attitude toward the foundation of negligence: *Id.* "Corrective Justice for Moderns," 106 (1993) *Harv. L. Rev.* 1658, 1677–1678; *cf.* R.W. Wright, "The Standards of Care in Negligence Law," *Philosophical Foundations of Tort Law* (D.G. Owen, ed., Oxford 1995) 249, 254.

807. *Ibid.*, 547, note 40; *cf. also* 560, note 81. In a recent private conversation with Professor Fletcher, the latter told me that at the time he was familiar with the above-mentioned book of the German scholar Josef Esser on strict liability, and that it was quite probable that he had been influenced by it in referring to the Aristotelian distinction. It is noteworthy that in an (unpublished) paper of Ernest Weinrib, delivered at the University of Tel Aviv Law Faculty in 1999, he critizised "Fletcher's Footnote" for being only "a suggestive and unspecific reflection of Aristotle." He adds: "Fletcher was not concerned to align the particulars of Aristotle's account with the considerations deployed in his article. Perhaps even then he was of the view, expressed decades later, that Aristotle's conception was incapable of dealing with the problem of risk-taking that are central to modern tort-law." On Fletcher's subsequent view on the notions of justice, G.P. Fletcher, *Basic Concepts of Legal Thought* (New York, Oxford 1996) 79–94; the author distinguishes between four kinds of justice: distributive, corrective, retributive, and commutative. On the problem of risk-taking, *ibid.*, 90.

continental Europe.[808] However, these were less founded on arguments of an impermissible violation of the structural-conceptual coherence, than on the more functional reason that the two kind of justices could not be integrated (theoretically or practically) in one uniform principle of liability. In this context, it is noteworthy that Josef Esser did not see any inherent inconsistency in introducing distributive considerations into the domain of delictual liability.[809]

Be that as it may, the substantive argument, based on the notion of corrective justice, which was raised against the instrumental-economic approach in tort law, gained prominence and provoked a protracted scholarly controversy. The result was a direct return to Aristotle's original text and its renewed analysis on the background of the actual debate. Apart from very few limited exceptions,[810] the millennial treatment of the Aristotelian distinction was completely disregarded.

The intellectual effort was directed to different aspects of the two forms of justice, depending upon the respective scholar's basic conception concerning tort liability's foundation.[811]

---

808. *See* I. Englard, "Victor Mataja's *Liability for Damages from an Economic Viewpoint:* A Centennial to an Ignored Economic Analysis of Tort," 10 (1990) *Int'l Rev. Law and Econ* 173, 184–185.

809. *Supra* 183–184.

810. James Gordley, "Tort Law in the Aristotelian Tradition," *Philosophical Foundations of Tort Law* (D.G. Owen, ed., Oxford 1995) 131; the author refers very briefly to a number of scholastics in relation to private ownership, to the forms of justice and to delictual liability; namely, to Thomas Aquinas, Buridanus, Cajetan, Domenicus de Soto, Ludovicus Molina, and Leonardus Lessius; moreover he refers to these and to some other scholastic authors in a considerable number of additional publications dealing with a variety of topics in contract law and unjust enrichment: *id.* "Equality in Exchange," 69 (1981) *Calif. L. Rev.* 1587, 1603 and *passim*; *id. The Philosophical Origins of Modern Contract Doctrine* (Oxford 1991) 69–111; *id.* "Enforcing Promises," 83 (1995) *Calif. L. Rev.* 547, 551–556; *id.* "The Purpose of Awarding Restitutionary Damages: A Reply to Professor Weinrib," 1 (2000) *Theoretical Inquiries in Law* 39, 40–41, 43, 53; *id.* "Contract Law in the Aristotelian Tradition," *The Theory of Contract Law* (P. Benson, ed., Cambridge 2001) 265–334; *id. Foundations of Private Law: Property, Tort, Contract, Unjust Enrichment* (Oxford 2006) *passim*; *id.* "Morality and Contract: The Question of Paternalism," 48 (2007) *Wm. and Mary L. Rev.* 1733; *see* generally, *id.* "Why Look Backward," 50 (2002) *Calif. L. Rev.* 657. *See also* J. Finnis, *Natural Law and Natural Rights* (Oxford 1980) 161–197, esp. 184–185, where, in the context of justice, mention is made of Aquinas, of Cardinal Cajetan's work and that of Domenicus de Soto. The same author refers in other places to a number of additional scholastics. His treatment of the relationship between distributive and corrective justice shows clearly the influence of scholastic literature; *infra* at notes 868, 869. For a substantial reference to Thomas Aquinas, *see also* P. Benson, "The Basis of Corrective Justice and Its Relation to Distributive Justice," 77 (1992) *Iowa L. Rev.* 515, 529–547.

811. *See* Benjamin C. Zipursky, "Civil Recourse, Not Corrective Justice," 91 (2003) *Geo. L. J.* 695, 696. The author mentions four reasons for corrective justice theory's vitality as a focus

Those scholars who opposed the instrumental approach, being oriented toward economic efficiency, emphasized the postulate of corrective justice that required an exclusive concentration upon the concrete litigants on a basis of strict equality. This necessarily implied the disregard of the prior status of the parties, as well as of all possible objectives going beyond their personal interests. Seen from the perspective of the Aristotelian distinction, the critique assumed the dichotomous, i.e., the mutually exclusive, character of the two forms of justice. It meant that the very introduction of distributive considerations into the notion of liability constituted a violation of corrective justice and was, therefore, illegitimate.

Viewed from a historical perspective, the use of the distinction as a normative tool for examining the legitimacy of substantive solutions seems to be quite a novelty. As we have seen, the high scholastics, the late scholastics and the post-scholastics, all used the positive law as a criterion for the correctness of the distinction and not the other way around. It is interesting to note, that the challenge of tort liability's conformity to corrective justice was taken most seriously by many U.S. tort scholars. Hence, the great intellectual effort applied by many scholars to reconcile their suggested substantive solutions with the assumed requirements of corrective justice. Other scholars used the Aristotelian notions of justice in order to criticize legislative schemes of compensation.[812] Finally, some scholars—relying on the formal character of the distinction—used it in an expository way, aimed at explaining in a coherent way the normative structure of a legal regime in a certain field.[813]

of sustained legal theory: its aspiration to surpass law and economics by adequately interpreting the actual structure of tort law; its claim to articulate a commendable aspect of political order distinct from distributive justice and compatible with liberal individualism; its challenge to public law and public policy justifications in favor of a conception of private law; its place for a conceptualistic, rather than an instrumentalist, form of legal analysis.

812. *See, e.g.*, John G. Culhane, "Tort, Compensation, and Two Kinds of Justice," 55 *Rutgers L. Rev.* (2003) 1027, criticizing the September 11th Victim Compensation Fund of 2001; *see also id.* "What Does Justice Require for the Victims of Katrina and September 11?" 10 (2007) *De Paul J. Health Care L.* 177; *cf.* K.M. Wyman, "Is there a Moral Justification For Redressing Historical Injustices," 61 (2008) *Vand. L. Rev.* 127; A. Calnan, "Litigation and Compensation: Distributive and Corrective Justice Issues in Contemporary Tobacco Litigation," 27 (1998) *Sw. U. L. Rev.* 577. *Cf.* the critical assessment of the U.S. First Restatement of Torts, P.J. Kelley, "The First Restatement of Torts: Reform by Descriptive Theory," 32 (2007) *S. Ill.U. L. J.* 93, 124–131.

813. *See, e.g.*, A.J. Morris, "On The Normative Foundations of Indirect Discrimination Law: Understanding the Competing Models of Discrimination Law as Aristotelian Forms of

A precondition to this discourse was naturally the right understanding of the very notion of corrective justice and its relationship to the substance of law. Since we are not directly concerned here with the substantive legal solutions in tort (or in other fields of law), we will limit our discussion, as far as possible, to the specific use of the Aristotelian distinction. This is by no means an easy task in view of the fact that our conclusion about the formal character of the distinction has been contested by a number of modern scholars. The latter assume that the very notion of corrective justice implies substantive principles that determine the legal solution of the question of liability. This approach is in our view erroneous.

Corrective justice is formally concerned with restoring the antecedent equality between specific parties. But in order to establish the relevant notion of equality and the relevant initial position of the parties, extrinsic values will have to be invoked. More specifically, in tort cases, corrective justice relates to an involuntary transaction. The functional notion of corrective justice—undoing, by means of an award of damages, the wrong suffered by the plaintiff at the hands of the defendant—does not yield the criterion for the notion of wrong.[814] As it has rightly been stated, the notion of wrong embodying the principle of justice, as distinguished from the form of justice, has to be derived from a specific moral philosophy.[815]

A significant, influential, profound, and comprehensive analysis of the Aristotelian forms of justice in the modern context has been made by

---

Justice," 15 (1995) *Oxford J. Leg. Studies* 199. The author's conclusion (at 228): "Indirect discrimination law is better interpreted as an effort to compensate individuals for wrongs than to award them distributive benefits. Although distributive traces may be visible in the corrective scheme, its corrective character remains distinct . . . On the whole it consistently is apparent that the features of indirect discrimination law as conceived lack coherence and consequence if viewed according to the redistributive thesis but align neatly, coherently and effectively according to the corrective thesis." But see the critique of this conclusion: J. Gardner, "Discrimination as Injustice," 16 (1996) *Oxford J. Leg. Studies* 353.

814. *See* the critical comments on this incompleteness of corrective justice: L. Kaplow and S. Shavell, "Fairness Versus Welfare," 114 (2000–01) *Harv. L. Rev.* 966, 1046–1050. The authors argue (at 1048) that "practically any substantive principle, including the one we advocate, could be embedded in corrective justice." *Cf.* in this context *supra* at note 796.

815. E.J.Weinrib, "Toward a Moral Theory of Negligence," 2 (1983) *Law and Philosophy*, 37, 39–40. *Cf.* J. Finnis, *Natural Law and Natural Rights* (Oxford 1980) 178–179: "'Correction' and 'restitution' are notions parasitic on some prior determination of what is to count as a crime, a tort, a binding promise."

Ernest J. Weinrib.[816] This scholar's starting point remains the formal character of the Aristotelian notions of justice. However, the author affirms that despite its abstraction from particular prescriptions Aristotle's formalism is by no means empty: "Aristotle's attention to structure enables to appreciate both the internal coherence of the private law relationship and the categorical difference between private law and other legal orderings."[817] The author adds: "Despite his achievement, however, Aristotle's exposition, like all pioneer efforts, is seriously incomplete. Aristotle presents corrective justice as a transactional equality, but he does not tell us what the equality is an equality of."[818]

Weinrib's declared enterprise is to fill in this lacuna in Aristotle's account by connecting corrective justice to Kant's legal philosophy. As a result, the equality of corrective justice is the abstract equality of free purposive beings under the Kantian concept of right.[819] The connection between corrective justice and Kantian right implies a number of important substantive consequences, such as the exclusion of strict liability based on risk or causation without fault.[820] Weinrib's legal formalism, its concern with intelligibility of juridical relationships and with coherence, as well as his approach to tort liability and Kantianism, have provoked a considerable number of critical studies.[821] However, we limit ourselves to his specific understanding of the Aristotelian forms of justice.

A major critique of the formalist conception of corrective justice has been undertaken by Richard W. Wright.[822] The author attempts to derive substantive conclusions directly from the two forms of justice, in order to rescue the Aristotelian concepts of justice from their "formalistic evisceration."[823]

---

816. E.J. Weinrib, *The Idea of Private Law* (Cambridge, Massachusetts 1995) *passim.*

817. *Ibid.*, 57.

818. *Ibid.*

819. *Ibid.*, 58.

820. *Ibid.*, 171–203. *Cf.* P.M. Gerhart, "The Death of Strict Liability," 56 (2008) *Buffalo L. Rev.* 245, 272.

821. *See* the comprehensive critique of Weinrib's Kantian approach, R.W. Wright, "Substantive Corrective Justice," 77 (1992) *Iowa L. Rev.* 625, 631–664; *see also* D. Patterson, "The Metaphysics of Legal Formalism," 77 (1992) *Iowa L. Rev.* 741; J. Stick, "Formalism as the Method of Maximally Coherent Classification," 77 (1992) *Iowa L. Rev.* 773; R. Hyland, "The Spinozist," 77 (1992) *Iowa L. Rev.* 805, 815–819 for a discussion of Weinrib's moral notion of tortious liability, *see also* I. Englard, *The Philosophy of Tort Law* (Aldershot 1993) 44–57.

822. R.W. Wright, "Substantive Corrective Justice," 77 (1992) *Iowa L. Rev.* 625; *Id.* "Right, Justice, and Tort Law," *Philosophical Foundations of Tort Law* (D.G. Owen, ed., Oxford 1995), 159, 166–171.

823. "Substantive Corrective Justice," *op. cit.*, 629.

The author is well aware of the fact that the notion of distributive justice requires a determination of the relevant criterion of "merit," and, correspondingly, corrective justice a determination of the "unjust" loss or gain. However, in his view it is possible to derive substantive conclusions from Aristotle's general discussion of the relationship between justice and the good. As a result, "the Aristotelian concepts of corrective justice and distributive justice are not empty formalist shells. They have a powerful nonaggregative and egalitarian substantive ethical content."[824]

In our view, the author's reasoning is not convincing. No doubt Aristotle himself had very defined and clear notions about the contents of vice and virtue, of justice and injustice, of right and wrong. However, these (personal) ethical judgments have to be sharply distinguished from his conceptual insight into the structure of justice. Thus, when discussing distributive justice, Aristotle mentions the contrasting possibilities of defining the content of "merit," such as wealth in the political system of an oligarchy.[825] Now, it is well known that in Aristotle's view, wealth was not a component of the "good," and oligarchy certainly not the ideal political system.[826] One is, of course, free to accept Aristotle's ethical notions, but this can in no way detract from the purely formal character of the distinction between corrective and distributive justice.[827]

Let us continue with one of the great protagonists of the economic approach to tort law, Richard Posner. The latter seems to agree that the Aristotelian distinction is of a purely formal character.[828] His major argument

---

824. *Ibid.*, 702.

825. *Supra* 4, 6.

826. *See* generally on Aristotle's constitutional preferences, F.D. Miller, Jr., *Nature, Justice, and Rights in Aristotle's* Politics (Oxford 1995) *passim.*

827. In our view a similar criticism can be raised against the view expressed by S.J. Heyman, "Aristotle on Political Justice," 77 (1992) *Iowa L. Rev.* 851, according to which Aristotle's conception of justice was political because directed to the common good. Thus, according to this author, Aristotle's view of corrective justice and private law is not autonomous and separate from politics, but rather constituted in large part by politics. Here again, the author disregards the distinction between Aristotle's own political and ethical preferences and the structural essence of the two forms of justice. Similarly, the fact that the judge, by enforcing corrective justice between the parties, fulfills a political function, does not affect the formal features of corrective justice.

828. *See* especially Posner's critique of the various tort theories using the notion of corrective justice in order to derive substantive rules: R.A. Posner, "The Concept of Corrective Justice in Recent Theories of Tort Law," 10 (1981) *J. Legal Stud.* 187, 191–201. The author affirms that corrective justice is a procedural principle, the meaning of wrongful conduct must be sought elsewhere; *ibid.*, 203.

is that the Aristotelian concept of corrective justice is compatible with, and indeed required by, the economic theory of tort and, incidentally, contract and criminal law.[829] He states:

> To be sure, the Aristotelian judge is not to look "beyond the case at hand," but only in the sense that he is not to consider whether the defendant is a better man than the plaintiff, evaluated apart from the character of the injury; it does not follow that the social utility of the defendant's conduct is irrelevant to whether the injury was wrongful.[830]

Posner's conclusion is that corrective justice is an instrument for maximizing wealth, and that the concept of corrective justice in the *Nicomachean Ethics* is, and must be, a component of the economic theory of law.[831]

A final comment: No doubt, the formalist approach clashes with a substantive understanding of both distributive and corrective justice. However, it has to be remembered that even from a strictly formalist conception, the difference in the formal structures implies some important consequences for the substance. Form and substance become linked through the idea of coherence.[832]

In view of the widespread controversy and fundamental dissent among contemporary scholars about the nature of the two notions of justice, it is by no means easy to sum up the modern use of the Aristotelian distinction. The rather surprising fact is that the notion of corrective justice has exercised upon scholars, especially in tort law,[833] a most suggestive power. As a result, a huge intellectual effort has been applied by a great number of scholars to reconcile their substantive views on tort liability with the notion of

829. *Ibid.*, 188.

830. *Ibid.*, 192.

831. *Ibid.*, 206. *See also* R. Posner, "Wealth Maximization and Tort Law: A Philosophical Inquiry," *Philosophical Foundations of Tort Law* (D.G. Owen, ed., Oxford 1995) 99, 108–109.

832. *Cf.* in this context the discussion of Kelsen's and Posner's critique of Aristotle's formal notions of justice by M. Stone, "The Significance of Doing and Suffering," *Philosophy and the Law of Torts* (G.J. Postema, ed., Cambridge 2001) 131, 165–172.

833. As mentioned above (note 801), the concepts of corrective and distributive justice have been applied in other legal fields too; for a more recent use in contractual relations, *see, e.g.*, Marc Ramsay, "The Buyer/Seller Asymmetry: Corrective Justice and Material Non-Disclosure," 56 (2006) *Univ. of Toronto L. J.* 115.

corrective justice.[834] One could ask: What is fundamentally wrong with a liability based upon distributive considerations? Why the attempt to squeeze all suggested concrete solutions into the notion of corrective justice? In this context, Richard Posner somewhat caustically observed: "No doubt they like the favorable connotations of the term 'corrective justice'—why else use it?"[835]

The consequence of these efforts was a great diversity in the understanding of the notions of distributive and corrective justice. In view of the extremely vast literature on the topic in relation to tort law, as well as in relation to other fields, a detailed analysis of all the different views would become cumbersome and not very productive.[836] We will, therefore, limit ourselves to the more fundamental aspects of the discussion.

A special and quite vexing problem of Aristotle's analysis of corrective justice was raised by the relation between gain and loss. Aristotle himself noted that these terms are not always appropriate:

> For the term "gain" is used in a general way to apply to such cases, even though it is not strictly appropriate to some of them, for example to a person who strikes another, nor is "loss" appropriate to the victim in this case; but at all events the results are called "loss" and "gain" respectively when the amount of the damage sustained comes to be estimated.[837]

It follows that Aristotle was of the opinion that the terms of loss (ζημία) and gain (κέρδος) are not quite appropriate in delictual situations. But he still considered the result of the injurious act as a form of gain and loss. However, from an economic, material point of view, it often happens that the

---

834. As a result of the sharp disagreement among scholars, the meaning of the Aristotelian notion of corrective justice has become most controversial. For an illustration of the problems created by the uncertain meaning of corrective justice in relation to tort theory, *see* K.W. Simons, "Corrective Justice and Liability for Risk-Creation: A Comment," 38 (1990) *UCLA L. Rev.* 113, 126.

835. R.A. Posner, "The Concept of Corrective Justice in Recent Theories of Tort Law," 10 (1981) *J. Legal Stud.* 187, 194; *cf.* E.J. Weinrib, "Aristotle's Forms of Justice," *Justice, Law, and Method in Plato and Aristotle* (S. Panagiotou, ed., Edmonton, 1987) 133–134; reprinted in 2 (1989) *Ratio Juris* 211: "Corrective justice has frequently been invoked in recent tort theory, though more as a slogan or an independent ideal than as part of the rich mode of understanding in which it originally appeared."

836. For a description of some of the manifold attempts to reconcile positive legal rules with the two categories of justice, *see* John Keeler, "Thinking through the Unthinkable: Collective Responsibilities in Personal Injury Law," 30 (2001) *Common Law World Review* 349.

837. EN 1132a10–14 (Loeb-Rackham 275).

loss caused to the victim is disproportionate to the gain of the actor, even if the notion of gain is conceived in its broadest sense. Aristotle did not explain how the principle of arithmetic proportion (in the sense of symmetry) of corrective justice can be maintained in the case where the injured person's loss exceeds the wrongdoer's gain.[838]

The difficulty did not escape the pre-modern scholars, and, as we have seen, some of the post-scholastic commentators on Aristotle have applied great intellectual efforts in order to give sense to the notions of equalizing loss and gain in delictual situations, or, in Aristotle's term, in involuntary transactions. The problem received a renewed actuality in the writings of the modern tort scholars dealing with the foundations of corrective justice. Some authors, being critical of Aristotle's comprehensive conception of the necessary correlation between gains and losses in corrective justice situations, suggest to abandon this notion in delictual,[839] as well as in restitutionary contexts.[840]

Here again, Ernest Weinrib suggests to reinterpret Aristotle's original notions in the Kantian spirit.[841] In his view, the correlativity of gain and loss in

---

838. K. Hildenbrand, *Geschichte und System der Recht—und Staatsphilosophie: Das klassische Altertum* (Leipzig 1860) 297. The author mentions an additional difficulty, namely the case where restitution is impossible, such as in case of causing the death of a person. The author points to the possibility that Aristotle believed to leave the task of implementing corrective justice to the judge, the incarnation of the just. *Cf.* the comment by the Benedictine Cardinal Josephus Saenz de Aguirre (1630–1699), *Philosophia Moralis Ab Aristotele Tradita Decem Libris Ethicorum ad Nicomachum: A Joanne Argyropilo Byzantino latine reddita; Nunc perpetuo Commentario literali & Scholastico, plenissime illustrata*, Pars Prima (Rome 1698), Lib. Quintus, Cap. IV, p. 212: "Itaque acceptio propria non est, sed metaphorica, damni pro perpessione iniuriae; & lucri pro actione iniuriam inferente." *See also* in this context J. Gordley, *Foundations of Private Law—Property, Tort, Contract, Unjust Enrichment* (Oxford 2006) 182–183, who explains, according to the opinion of Thomas Aquinas, that "to gain" means to fulfill one's will: "One who took or used or harmed another's resources for his own ends had 'gained,' and therefore must pay compensation, whether or not his ends were achieved, and whether or not he had made a financial gain by pursuing them." The author relies on St. Thomas Aquinas, *Commentary on Aristotle's Nicomachean Ethics* (C.I. Litzinger, transl., Notre Dame, Indiana 1993) Book V, Lect. VI, §952, p. 302.

839. George P. Fletcher, "Corrective Justice for Moderns," 106 (1993) *Harv. L. Rev.* 1658, 1668; *id. Basic Concepts of Legal Thought* (New York, Oxford 1996) 88–90; Stephen R. Perry, "The Moral Foundations of Tort Law," 77 (1992) *Iowa L. Rev.* 449, 457.

840. Lionel D. Smith, "The Province of the Law of Restitution," 71 (1992) *Canadian B. Rev.* 672, 694–699. The author, who does not refer to the Aristotelian distinction, suggests to distinguish between compensation, restitution, and disgorgement. Compensation for wrongs and disgorgement of gains, as in cases of breach of fiduciary duties, don't require a correlation between defendant's gain and plaintiff's loss.

841. Ernest J. Weinrib, "The Gains and Losses of Corrective Justice," 44 (1994) *Duke L. J.* 277.

corrective justice has to be understood normatively rather than materially. At the heart of corrective justice, linking the two parties lies the correlativity of the normative categories of right and duty, as established in the Kantian legal theory.[842] Another author suggests reinterpreting the notions of loss and gain in a material way: The wrongful gain lies in the tortfeasor's acquisition and exertion of utter dominance over certain portions of the material world, namely, over the body or property of the victim. This gain corresponds to the loss of control by the victim. The amount of damage to the victim indicates the degree of the involuntary transfer of control between the parties.[843]

Another issue that got prominence in the modern discourse concerns the exact relationship between corrective justice and distributive justice.[844] Thus, it has been suggested that, since the function of corrective justice is merely to restore the original position of the parties, this form of justice is secondary in importance to distributive justice that determines the original position.[845]

---

842. Weinrib remarks (*ibid.*, 279): "Despite my focus on Aristotle's text, I conceive this task as philosophical rather than exegetical. My aim is not to draw conclusions from Aristotle's words, let alone to reconstruct his mental processes, but to follow through on the conceptual implications of his account." *See also* in this sense the approach of M. Stone, "The Significance of Doing and Suffering," *Philosophy and the Law of Torts* (G.J. Postema, ed., Cambridge 2001) 131, 154–155.

843. M.H. Kramer, "Of Aristotle and Ice Cream Cones: Reflections on Jules Coleman's Theory of Corrective Justice," 16 (1996) *Quinnipiac L. Rev.* 279. For a somewhat similar idea in the theory of punishment, *see* W. Sadurski, "Distributive Justice and the Theory of Punishment," 5 (1985) *Oxford Journal of Legal Studies* 47, 54–59. The author suggests that the fundamental benefit that a criminal acquires from violating the rules of criminal law is a benefit of non-self-restraint, that is to say, a benefit of freedom from burdens imposed by the criminal law. He notes (at 56): "The fundamental benefit, that is, the benefit of non-self-restraint, is a function of the violation of the protected sphere of liberty." However, in this author's view, the aim of punishment is to restore the equilibrium of benefits and burdens and not to restore the previous *status quo*. Hence, its function is one of redistribution.

844. Peter Cane, "The Anatomy of Private Law Theory: A 25th Anniversary Essay," 25 (2005) *Oxford Journal of Legal Studies* 203, 205: "The hottest current debate amongst justice theorists is the best way to understand the relationship between 'corrective' and 'distributive' justice in the explanation and justification of private law." For a general analysis of the relationship on the background of formal and substantive criteria, *cf.* M. Rosenfeld, *Affirmative Action and Justice: A Philosophical and Constitutional Inquiry* (New Haven 1991) 30–42.

845. A. Trendelenburg, *Historische Beiträge zur Philosophie*, Vol III (Berlin 1867) 399, at 412: "Die Gerechtigkeit hat im proportionalen Zutheilen (διανέμειν κατά τήν άζίαν) ihr ursprüngliches Wesen (πρώτως), sei es im Austausch des Verkehrs (δικαιοσύνη άλλακτική), sei es im Staat in der Vertheilung gemeinsamer Güter (διανεμητική τών κοινών), und erst wo Rechtsbeziehungen verletzt sind (δευτέρως), tritt die zweite Art der Gerechtigkeit ein, welche das Ungleiche ausgleicht (die διορθωτική, κατά τὸ ποσὸν)." In the same spirit: H.A. Fechner, *Über den Gerechtigkeitsbegriff des Aristoteles—Ein Beitrag zur Geschichte der alten Philosophie*

This specific topic received renewed interest in more recent times. According to what appears to be the dominant view among contemporary scholars, corrective justice presupposes the existence of entitlements which, presumably, are the creation not of corrective justice itself but of distributive justice. Hence, the function of corrective justice is to preserve a given distribution of wealth.[846] In this sense James Gordley declares that "according to Aristotle, distributive justice secures a fair share of resources for each citizen. Commutative or corrective justice preserves that share."[847]

(Leipzig 1855) 31 (" . . . zu der vertheilenden Gerechtigkeit nur eine consekutive Stellung einnimmt"); *id.* at 41; G. Del Vecchio, *Justice—An Historical and Philosophical Essay* (A.H. Campbell, ed., Edinburgh 1952) 53; the author, after affirming that the validity of contracts is based upon the idea of equal dignity of persons, then states (note 13, at 67): "This shows that commutative justice in reality presupposes distributive justice, which (understood in the wider sense as recognition of the value of persons) is therefore the primary and basic form of justice"; *see also ibid.*, §VIII, note 6, at 89–90. In this sense also Gustav Radbruch, "Legal Philosophy," in *The Legal Philosophies of Lask, Radbruch, and Dabin* (K. Wilk transl., Cambridge, Mass. 1950) 74: "Commutative justice is justice between persons co-equal as to their rights. Therefore, it presupposes an act of distributive justice which has granted to those concerned equality of rights, equal capacity to act, equal status. Distributive justice, then, is the prototype of justice (footnotes omitted)." Radbruch refers to the idea of Carl August Emge, *Geschichte der Rechtsphilosophie* (Berlin 1931) 34–35: "Das Schema zeigt, dass die 'ausgleichende' die 'austeilende' voraussetzt . . . Die Distributiva enthüllt sich somit als 'erstmalige Ordnung—Hypothesis—, die alles weitere bestimmt. Die Commutativa zeigt sich als Regulativ *auf Grund* eines positiven Anderen, so dass ihre Gerechtigkeit bloss gerecht im Sinne des Bestimmungsgemässen ist." The latter author, indeed, develops the same idea in *id. Einführung in die Rechtsphilosophie* (Frankfurt/M-Wien, 1955) 170; M. Kriele, *Kriterien der Gerechtigkeit* (Berlin 1963) 59: "Die iustitia commutativa meint nichts anderes als: Verhältnismässige Aufrechterhaltung des durch gerechte Distribution herbeigeführten status quo." In the same sense H. Coing, *Grundzüge der Rechtsphilosophie* (3. Aufl., Berlin 1976) 209. See equally Elise Charpentier, "Les fondements théoriques de la transformation du rôle de l'équilibre des prestations contractuelles," 45 (2004) *Les Cahiers de Droit* 69, 72–73: "La justice commutative suppose en effet la justice distributive. Elle ne peut donc pas être comprise indépendamment de la justice distributive, 'dont elle n'était à l'origine qu'un pronlongement.'" The authoress relies on M. Villey, *Leçons d'histoire de la philosophie du droit* (Paris 1962) 120, note 1. Villey notes that corrective justice's function is subsidiary to distributive justice. On the interplay between distributive and commutative justice seen from a religious outlook, Walther Schönfeld, *Über die Gerechtigkeit—Ein Triptychon* (Göttingen 1952) 7–8, 100–105.

846. For a description of this "current understanding of corrective justice," *see* P. Benson, "The Basis of Corrective Justice and Its Relation to Distributive Justice," 77 (1992) *Iowa L. Rev.* 515, 529–532. The author, who criticizes this conception, observes that "it is unusual to find this view explicitly articulated and defended" (*ibid.*, 529, note 25).

847. James Gordley, "Enforcing Promises," 83 (1995) *Calif. L. Rev.* 547, 549; in the same sense *id.* "Equality in Exchange," 69 (1981) *Calif. L. Rev.* 1587, 1589; *id.* "When Is the Use of Foreign Law Possible? A Hard Case: The Protection of Privacy in Europe and the United States," 67 (2007) *La. L. Rev.* 1073, 1086; *cf. id. Foundations of Private Law—Property, Tort, Contract, Unjust Enrichment* (Oxford 2006) 12–14. In this sense also: B.A. Wortley, *Jurisprudence* (Manchester 1967) 352, 353.

The autonomous character of corrective justice in the tort context has been denied by Joseph M. Steiner, on the basis of an additional, related argument, namely, that the definition of "improper" conduct is necessarily in distributive terms: what do I have a right to do; what do I have a right to be free of.[848] The author affirms:

> The right to act in certain ways and the right to be saved harmless from the consequences of certain conduct are as much forms of wealth as a piece of land or a sum of money. Thus the notions of corrective and distributive justice merge. The object of this branch of the law is to define that what is the victim's and to restore it to him if it has been taken away without his consent.[849]

This basic view has been forcefully contested by Peter Benson, who claims that corrective justice must consist in a specific mode of correcting violations of entitlements that is wholly rooted in a distinctive yet self-sufficient nondistributive justificatory structure. Distributive justice could also be said to postulate a mode of correction of its own: persons should receive what is their due according to the distributive criterion. "Correction takes its 'corrective' or 'distributive' character from the specific nature of the notions of entitlement and equality."[850] The author then proceeds to develop a "reasonably systematic justification of the nondistributive conception of entitlement"[851] that is consistent with the Aristotelian notion of corrective justice. Assuming that neither Aristotle nor Aquinas have addressed this problem, the author uses philosophical premises of Kant, Hegel, and Rawls ("abstract right," "personality," "constructivism"), in order to establish the moral justification of the nondistributive entitlement that is at the basis of corrective justice equality.[852] The author then deals, in relation to first principles of justice for transactions, with bodily

---

848. J.M. Steiner, "Economics, Morality, and the Law of Torts," 26 (1976) *University of Toronto L. J.* 227, 248. In a similar sense also A. Calnan, *Justice and Tort Law* (Durham, N.C. 1997) 297; *Id.* "Litigation and Compensation: Distributive and Corrective Justice Issues in Contemporary Tobacco Litigation," 27 (1998) *Sw. U. L. Rev.* 577, *passim.*

849. Steiner, *ibid.*; *cf.* A. Calnan, "The Fault(s) in Negligence Law," 25 (2007) *Quinnipiac L. Rev.* 695, 715, note 110.

850. P. Benson, "The Basis of Corrective Justice and Its Relation to Distributive Justice," 77 (1992) *Iowa L. Rev.* 515, 532.

851. *Ibid.*, 549.

852. *Ibid.*, 549–578.

integrity, first and derivative acquisitions.[853] In the final part of his essay, the author suggests that his constructivist theory of corrective justice does not rule out Rawls's substantively egalitarian conception of distributive justice.[854]

The idea of the autonomous character of corrective justice has been maintained by additional contemporary scholars—such as Ernest Weinrib, Stephen Perry, and Martin Stone—though with partly different argumentations. Thus, Weinrib claims that even if holdings were intelligible solely as distributive justice, the dependence of corrective justice on a previous distribution does not diminish the autonomy of the two forms of justice. The fact that corrective justice must accept the distribution as given does not mean that the justification of the distribution is an aspect of justification in corrective justice. What matters for corrective justice is that the distribution exists, not that the distribution is justified. Corrective justice's mode of justification can operate against the background of a distribution without incorporating into its justificatory structure the justification of the distribution.[855] Otherwise, corrective justice becomes a species of distributive justice, which runs counter the Aristotle's postulate of their being two separate forms of justice.[856]

Stephen Perry, dealing with corrective justice in relation to tort law, equally maintains its autonomous character by relying on the notion of harm.[857] In Martin Stone's view, the equality of corrective justice in the tort context signifies "to treat

853. *Ibid.*, 578–601.

854. *Ibid.*, 601–624. The relationship between John Rawls's principles of justice and corrective and distributive justice became a matter of academic dispute: A. Ripstein, "The Division of Responsibility and the Law of Torts," 72 (2004) *Fordham L. Rev.* 1811; S. Perry, "Ripstein, Rawls, and Responsibility," 72 (2004) *Fordham L. Rev.* 1845; K.A. Kordana and D.H. Tabachnik, "Rawls and Contract Law," 73 (2005) *Geo. Wash. L. Rev.* 598; *id.*, "On Belling the Cat: Rawls and Tort as Corrective Justice," 92 (2006) *Va. L. Rev.* 1279; S. Walt, "Eliminating Corrective Justice," 92 (2006) *Va. L. Rev.* 1311; *cf. also* A. Ripstein, "Private Order and Public Justice: Kant and Rawls," 92 (2006) *Va. L. Rev.* 1391.

855. E.J. Weinrib, "Legal Formalism: On the Immanent Rationality of Law," 97 (1988) *Yale L. J.* 949, 984, note 75, criticizing Radbruch's contrary view, *supra* note 845.

856. *Id. The Idea of Private Law* (Cambridge, Massachusetts 1995) 78–80. The author reacts here against the view of James Gourdley, *supra* at note 847. See the latter's response, James Gordley, "Tort Law in the Aristotelian Tradition," *Philosophical Foundations of Tort Law* (D.G. Owen, ed., Oxford 1995) 131, 132–137.

857. S. Perry, "On the Relationship between Corrective and Distributive Justice," *Oxford Essays in Jurisprudence* (Jeremy Horder, ed., 4th Series, Oxford 2000) 237. For a comparison between Benson's approach and that of Perry, *see* Dennis Klimchuk, "On the Autonomy of Corrective Justice," 23 (2003) *Oxford Journal of Legal Studies* 49. For a short description of some major contrasting views: Peter Cane, "The Anatomy of Private Law Theory: A 25th Anniversary Essay," 25 (2005) *Oxford Journal of Legal Studies* 203, 214–217.

the parties as equals by according equal status to their interests in acting (which includes their interest in being free from injurious interferences)."[858]

One author adopts a completely different approach: He claims that in view of the protective function of tort law achieved by means of establishing primary (tort) duties, the corrective justice interpretation of tort law—at least in the common law context—has to be completely rejected.[859] The author does not refer directly to the Aristotelian distinction, and, as a matter of fact, his conception of corrective justice, based exclusively upon the views of some modern tort theorists, is rather remote from the traditional understanding.

Since we do not intend to take position in this protracted controversy, we will limit ourselves to a general remark in relation to the view that commutative justice is secondary in importance vis-à-vis distributive justice. In our opinion, there are two relevant considerations in respect to that issue. First, why should an original distribution of goods be more important in terms of justice than the restoration of deprived goods? From a general, political point of view, it may be different, but justice is in my eyes much more important in its remedial function than in its distributive one. Second, the distinction between the two functions is from a positive-normative view far from being clear-cut. Seen from a purely formal point of view, legal norms are defined by their sanction. As a result, the original distribution of entitlements can only be determined by the remedial potential of the legal system. In other words, legal rights are co-extensive to their remedy: *Ubi remedium ibi ius*. This is most obvious in those cases where the object of the right is from the beginning in a person's possession, such as the body itself. The right to bodily integrity may be conceived as being part of an original division, but its actual extent is generally determined by corrective justice.[860]

---

858. M. Stone, "The Significance of Doing and Suffering," *Philosophy and the Law of Torts* (G.J. Postema, ed., Cambridge 2001) 131, 159. The author adds, *ibid.*: "The departure from equality in this situation consits, then, in doings which are wrongful, not because they upset a previously just distribution, or because they threaten a communal goal, but because they are inconsistent with the equal status of other affected agents."

859. H. Sheinman, "Tort Law and Corrective Justice," 22 *Law and Philosophy* (2003) 21–73.

860. *Cf.* in this context Julie Chi-hye Suk, "Antidiscrimination Law in the Administrative State," 2006 *U. Ill. L. Rev.* 405, 419–420: "The pursuit of corrective justice may also help shape and change prevailing notions of distributive justice. Often, a sense of wrong or injustice precedes the articulation of a conception of distributive justice. The attempt to remedy the wrong makes possible the articulation of the right that the offending act violates . . . Therefore, while principles of distributive justice do not depend on principles of corrective justice, the articulation of distributive justice has often been made possible by the operation of corrective justice regimes" (footnotes omitted).

This brings us to an issue that is related to the foregoing one: the classification of restitutionary duties in relation to the two forms of justice. As we have seen, in Aquinas's view, restitution is necessarily always an act of commutative justice.[861] Many scholastic theologians have defended this conclusion of Aquinas.[862] More recently, it has been argued that the identification of every restitutionary duty with commutative justice is a misfortune of history. In truth, so the argument goes, where a person received more than his due according to the criterion of distributive justice, his duty of restitution is still substantially founded in distributive justice.[863] It is merely the exterior, formal process that corresponds to corrective justice; the moral dimension, the "soul" of the ought remains to be distributive justice.[864]

A number of modern authors go much beyond this argument: they maintain that restitutionary claims, even if based on corrective justice, cannot be isolated from distributive considerations. According to their more comprehensive theory, corrective justice, as such, is subject to social policies.[865] This approach raises the fundamental question of the relationship between the two forms of justice, being mutually exclusive or complementary. To this problem we will now proceed.

The actual question is whether two forms of justice can be applied simultaneously in a given situation. As we have seen in the scholastic literature, many authors have assumed the possibility of their active coexistence in a number of specific circumstances. In this sense, John Finnis affirms that "the distinction between distributive and commutative justice is no more than an analytical convenience, an aid to orderly consideration of

861. *Supra* at note 70.

862. Molina, *supra* at note 138; Mastrius, *supra* 56; *cf. also* Vico, *supra* 158.

863. In this sense apparently already Petrus de Aragon (1545–1592), *In Secundam Secundae D. Thomae Commentaria. De Justitia et Jure* (Salamanca 1590), Q. 62, Art. 2, fol. 201b, 203a–b; José Barrientos Garcia, *El Tratado "De Justitia et Jure" (1590) de Pedro de Aragón* (Salamanca 1978) 207–208. For a different view, Th. Tack, *Fr. Pedro de Aragon* (Chicago 1957) 136: "[It] must be concluded that, regardless of his unqualified assertions, he is considering only those cases in which a violation of distributive justice contains in itself a violation of commutative justice."

864. A.F. Utz OP, in his (German) commentary on Thomas Aquinas, Summa Theologica II–II, 57–79, *Die deutsche Thomas—Ausgabe*, 18. Band, Recht und Gerechtigkeit (1953) 469–470. *See also* in this sense A.-J. Faidherbe, *La justice distributive* (Paris 1934) 129–137.

865. Hanoch Dagan, "The Distributive Foundation of Corrective Justice," 98 (1999) *Mich. L. Rev.* 138; *id.* "Encroachments: between private and public," *Unjustified Enrichment: Key Issues in Comparative Perspective* (D. Johnston and R. Zimmermann, eds., Cambridge 2002) 348; in relation to tort law, *see* P. Cane, "Distributive Justice and Tort Law," 4 (2001) *NZ L. Rev.* 401. *Cf.* generally M. Rosenfeld, *Affirmative Action and Justice: A Philosophical and Constitutional Inquiry* (New Haven 1991) 30–42.

problems.[866] Many actions are both distributively and commutatively just (or unjust)."[867] Speaking of the act of the judge in giving a judgment, the author states:

> The biased or careless judge violates distributive justice by using an irrelevant criterion (or by inappropriately using a relevant criterion) in apportioning the merits and awarding judgment and/or costs. But, finally, we can also consider the judge's duty to apply the relevant legal rules; in this respect his duty is one of commutative justice: faithful application of the law is simply what is fitting and required of him in his official dealings with others.[868]

This approach clearly resounds the voices of those scholastics who have defined the function of officials as based on a commutative duty toward the state.[869]

However, the possibility of combining in one substantive legal solution the two forms of justice has been strongly denied by some modern authors, principally amongst them Ernest Weinrib:

> Because corrective and distributive justice are categorically different and mutually irreducible patterns of justificatory coherence, it follows that a single external relationship cannot coherently partake of both. Aristotle's contrast of corrective and distributive justice does not determine whether the law should treat an incident correctively or distributively. But if the law is to be coherent, any given relationship cannot rest on a *combination* of corrective and distributive justifications. When a corrective justification is mixed with a distributive one, each necessarily undermines the justificatory force of the other, and the relationship cannot manifest either unifying structure.[870]

---

866. This statement of Finnis has been criticized by Richard Wright, who considers the two notions of being of substantive importance: R. Wright, "The Principles of Justice," 75 (2000) *Notre Dame L. Rev.* 1859, 1884–1892.

867. J. Finnis, *Natural Law and Natural Rights* (Oxford 1980) 179. The author dedicates a special section to the English law of bankruptcy as illustration: it gives effect to the commutatively just claims of the insolvent's creditors and at the same time subjects all those claims to a principle of distributive justice (*ibid.*, 188–193); *cf.* V.V. Miles, "Assessing Modern Bankruptcy Law: An Example of Justice," 36 (1996) *Santa Clara L. Rev.* 1025.

868. *Ibid.*, at 179–180.

869. *See, e.g.*, the view of Suárez, *supra* at note 121.

870. E. Weinrib, *The Idea of Private Law* (Cambridge, Massachusetts 1995) 73.

Many scholars adopt an opposite view, maintaining that the two forms of justice can be legitimately combined, or even necessarily interact.[871] Thus, Richard Wright asserts that "contrary to Weinrib's assertion, distributive justice claims and corrective justice claims may not only coexist in the same body of law, but also may apply simultaneously in the same situation."[872] Interestingly, a similar idea has been adopted by Lord Steyn in one of his speeches in the House of Lords:

> The truth is that tort law is a mosaic in which the principles of corrective justice and distributive justice are interwoven. And in situations of uncertainty and difficulty a choice sometimes has to be made between the two approaches. In my view it is legitimate in the present case to take into account considerations of distributive justice.[873]

---

871. In this sense, generally, G. Husserl, "Justice," 47 (1937) *International Journal of Ethics* 271, 307: "Corrective and distributive justice supplement each other; the materialization of the two together in historic reality produces an equilibrium of the legal status." The author refers to the role of equity. In relation to accident compensation, *see* S. Stoljar, "Accidents, Costs, and Legal Responsibility," 36 (1973) *Modern L. Rev.* 233, 234–235: "Still, the corrective and distributive principles, precisely because of their different aims, can easily co-exist in the same area. In particular, the distributive principle does not require us to say that tort-law should abdicate the field, or that the tortfeasor should be ignored." *See also* A. Ripstein, *Equality, Responsibility, and the Law* (Cambridge 1999) 270–271. The author notes the difference between his conception of the two forms of justice and that of Aristotle.

872. R.W. Wright, "Substantive Corrective Justice," 77 (1992) *Iowa L. Rev.* 625, 708; the same idea is repeated in *id.* "Right, Justice, and Tort Law," *Philosophical Foundations of Tort Law* (D.G. Owen, ed., Oxford 1995), 159, 173. The author adduces two examples illustrating his point: public takings of private property under the exercise of public domain, and private takings of private servitudes for public benefit as permitted by nuisance law. *See* our comments on these examples: I. Englard, "The Idea of Complementarity as a Philosophical Basis for Pluralism in Tort Law," *Philosophical Foundations of Tort Law* (D.G. Owen, ed., Oxford 1995), 183, 186. See in relation to constitutional torts, Berard D. Dauenhauer and Michael L. Wells, "Corrective Justice and Constitutional Torts," 35 (2001) *Ga. L. Rev.* 903, 907: "Within the realm of costitutional rights and duties, there is no conflict between corrective justice and distributive justice. On the contrary, corrective justice and distributive justice complement one another. A violation of distributive justice has already occurred and corrective justice now requires a remedy." The authors criticize the claim of Daryl J. Levinson, "Making Government Pay: Markets, Politics, and the Allocation of Constitutional Costs," 67 (2000) *U. Chi. L. Rev.* 345, 412, according to which "achieving corrective justice, therefore, will always entail some sacrifice of distributive justice. The only way to make the conflict between distributive and corrective justice disappear is to reduce the latter to the former."

873. *McFarlane v. Tayside Health Board* [2000] 2 AC 59, 83 (H.L. (Sc.)); *cf. ibid.*, 96, *per* Lord Hope of Craighead. The idea that tortious liability may be denied on grounds of distributive justice has been first mentioned in *White v. Chief Constable of South Yorkshire Police* [1999] 2 AC 455 (H.L. (E.)), at 503–504, *per* Lord Hoffmann. In the wake of these judicial sayings, the Aristotelian distinction was mentioned in a number of judgments: *Lee v. Taunton and Somerset NHS Trust* [2001] QB Fam Law 103, [2001] 1 FLR 419; *Parkinson v. St James and Seacroft University Hospital NHS Trust* [2002] QB 266 (CA), at 274–280, *per*

Referring to Lord Steyn's statement, Justice Crennan of the High Court of Australia remarked:

> The Aristotelian backdrop to the notions of "corrective justice" and "distributive justice" was a community whose common good included laws, both reflecting the community's common values and enabling individual members to achieve reasonable objectives. However, there remains a problem in Aristotle's analysis, relevant to this submission. In emphasising "corrective justice," even as added to by his consideration of "distributive justice," Aristotle left unexplored the dependence of "correction" on the prior establishment of principles (footnotes omitted).[874]

It is noteworthy, that the Aristotelian distinction—notwithstanding the vast scholarly literature—has been mentioned in relatively very few judicial decisions.[875]

Beneath the scholarly controversy, whether the Aristotelian forms of justice are mutually exclusive or may be legitimately combined, lie a number of different important theoretical and ideological premises and objectives. On the more theoretical level: Purism, formalism, postulates of intelligibility, and

---

Brooke, LJ, at 298–290, *per* Hale, LJ; *McLoughlin v. Jones* [2002] QB 1312 (CA), at 1323–1324; *Gwilliam v. West Herts Hospitals NHS Trust* [2003] QB 443 (CA), at 458–459, *per* Sedley, LJ; *Rees v. Darlington Memorial Hospital NHS Trust* [2003] All E. R. 987 (H.L.(E)), at 999, 1020, 1024; *Tameside and Glossop Acute Services NHS Trust v. Thompstone and other appeals* [2008] All E.R. 553 (CA). See the criticism on Lord Steyn's approach: Michael A. Jones, *Textbook on Torts* (Oxford 2002) 17–18; *see also* the critical comments by P. Cane, "Distributive Justice and Tort Law," 4 (2001) *NZ L. Rev.* 401, *passim.*

874. *Harriton v. Stephens* (2006) 80 ALJR 791, 843, at 844. *See also Cattanach v. Melchior* (2003) 77 ALJR 1312, at 1354, *per* Hayne J, dissenting).

875. Besides the mentioned decisions in Great Britain and Australia, judicial references to the Aristotelian distinction can be found in Israel case law: C.A. 10064/02 *Migdal Insurance Company, Ltd v. Abu Hana* (not yet published); H.C.J. 244/00 P.D. 56(6) 26, 66 (in distributive justice cases, considerations of corrective justice are taken into account); C.A. 5604/94 P.D. 58(2) 498, 519–521, *per* Justice E. Rivlin (relation between Learned Hand formula in tort law and corrective justice). For short references in Ireland and New Zealand: *Byrne v. Ryan* [2007] IEHC 207 (H.C.); *Accident Compensation Corporation v. Ambros* [2008] 1 NZLR 340 (CA). In Germany, there seems to be only one single explicit reference to Aristotle by the Federal Constitutional Court, in a dissenting opinion of the judgment of 8.5.1973: BVerfGE, 35, 41, at 56, *per* Dr. v. Schlabrendorff (distributive justice). *See* G. Robbers, *Gerechtigkeit als Rechtsprinzip: Über den Begriff der Gerechtigkeit in der Rechtssprechung des Bundesverfassungsgerichts* (Baden-Baden 1980) 77, note 343; *cf.* M.S. Jungbauer, *Die Verwendung des Begriffs "Gerechtigkeit" in der Rechtsprechung des Bundesverfassungsgerichts* (Hamburg 2002).

coherence clash with pragmatism and pluralism; on the more ideological, political level: Individualism, right-oriented personal autonomy contrast with instrumentalism, utilitarianism, economic efficiency, and social justice. Some authors rely directly on the Aristotelian distinction in order to buttress their premises and objectives,[876] others take it as a mere starting point, and others again contest its very correctness or relevance.[877] Our own view is that, whatever may be the exact relationship between the two forms of justice, the reality of law is a pluralistic normative system of contrasting values, combining specifically in tort law distributive and corrective justice considerations.[878] However, a critical analysis of all these different theoretical, philosophical, and ideological approaches lies far beyond the scope of this work.[879] The amazing fact is the centrality of the Aristotelian forms of justice in this modern controversy. No wonder that it succeeded in provoking a harsh negative reaction by some contemporary scholars.[880]

---

876. *See, e.g.*, James Gordley, "Tort Law in the Aristotelian Tradition," *Philosophical Foundations of Tort Law* (D.G. Owen, ed., Oxford 1995) 131, 132–133, who argues that Weinrib's interpretation of corrective justice "breaks with the broader Aristotelian tradition"; *id.* "The Purpose of Awarding Restitutionary Damages: A Reply to Professor Weinrib," 1 (2000) *Theoretical Inquiries in Law* 39, 42.

877. Thus, *e.g.*, in relation to constitutional torts it has been argued by Ken Cooper-Stephenson, "Theoretical Underpinnings for Reparations: A Constitutional Tort Perspective," 22 (2003) *Windsor Yearbook of Access to Justice* 3, 11, that "Once state actors are involved, Aristotle's distinction between the two types of justice is compromised: that tort law when it functions in the public domain fuses the two types of justice, and that a wrongful failure to respect the requirements of overall justice by government cannot easily be compartmentalized into the two suggested forms."

878. I. Englard, "The Idea of Complementarity as a Philosophical Basis for Pluralism in Tort Law," *Philosophical Foundations of Tort Law* (D.G. Owen, ed., Oxford 1995), 183. *Cf.* Michael D. Green, "Negligence = Economic Efficiency: Doubts >," 75 (1997) *Tex. L. Rev.* 1605, 1643: "Rather, tort law may be an amalgam of eficiency, corrective justice, and pragmatism, all leavened with whatever the contemporary cultural, political, and social attitudes happen to be"; *cf. ibid.*, note 180. For the view that the English law on contractual damages and on frustration of contracts carry a perspective of distributive justice J. Finnis, *Natural Law and Natural Rights* (Oxford 1980) 182–183.

879. For a criticism of various theories in relation to tort law, *see* I. Englard, *The Philosophy of Tort Law* (Aldershot 1993), *passim*; among the vast, more recent literature: Gary T. Schwartz, "Mixed Theories of Tort Law: Affirming Both Deterrence and Corrective Justice," 75 (1997) *Tex. L. Rev.* 1801; for a brief survey of the different theories, George P. Fletcher, "Remembering Gary—and Tort Theory," 50 (2002) *UCLA L. Rev.* 279; G.J. Postema, "Introduction: Search for an Explanatory Theory of Torts," *Philosophy and the Law of Torts* (G.J. Postema, ed., Cambridge 2001) 1.

880. Virginia E. Nolan and Edmund Ursin, "The Deacademification of Tort Theory," 48 (1999) *Kan. L. Rev.* 59, 90.

> As we reach the twenty-first century, however, it seems appropriate we acknowledge that modern corrective justice scholarship with its nineteenth-century conceptual apparatus is . . . an anachronism and should be treated as such. It should be relegated to a historical footnote in casebooks and anthologies of tort scholarship. Like a Model T Ford, the corrective justice approach may be interesting for some to look at—or even to tinker with—but few will view it as a way to get anywhere important.[881]

Finally, it is noteworthy that Aristotle's notion of *antipeponthos* (reciprocity) has equally been revived in the modern context, and rather surprisingly in relation to globalization.[882] Based on a short observation of Aristotle, the scholar Giampaolo Azzoni relates that kind of justice, called by him "catallactic justice,"[883] to the three Graces. Indeed, Aristotle writes in connection with *antipeponthos* the following:

> This is why we set up a shrine of the Graces in a public place, to remind men to return a kindness; for that is a special characteristic of grace, since it is a duty not only to repay a service done one, but another time to take the initiative in doing a service oneself.[884]

Azzoni then goes on to analyze the historical interpretations and iconography of the three Graces. He starts with classic authors of the antiquity, such as Chrysippus and Seneca,[885] continues with Shakespeare[886] and Goethe,[887] and ends with modern scholars. His conclusion is that reciprocity is under

---

881. The authors then suggest to inform the law students in casebooks with the following introductory paragraph (*ibid.*): "Warning! The material you are about to read presents what many torts scholars believe is an anachronistic approach, out of touch with reality and distinguished by obscurity. The (few) proponents of the corrective justice perspective do not even agree on a common frame of reference, and their work, which was dismissed at the outset by economists, has largely been ignored over the years by other torts scholars (let alone attorneys and judges). You should also be aware that this scholarship has no authentic claim to an Aristotelian pedigree; indeed, Aristotle's concept of corrective justice is in no way antithetical to the utilitarian goals excluded by these authors in the name of corrective justice."

882. G. Azzoni, "L'ídea di giustizia tra universale e particulare," http://www.unipv.it/deontica/opere/azzoni/giusti.pdf.

883. *Supra* note 29.

884. EN, 1133a 3–5. (Loeb-Rackham translation 281).

885. Seneca, *De Beneficiis*, I, iii, 2–10, iv, 1–6.

886. Azzoni, *ibid.*, 25, citing John M. Wallace, "Timon of Athens and the Three Graces: Shakespeare's Senecan Study," 83 *Modern Philology* (1986) 349–363.

887. Faust II, First Act, vv. 5299–5304.

the protection of the Graces and is implemented through the spontaneous initiative of men. It can be applied to persons who are citizens of different states. The normative relationship of justice as reciprocity is a threefold one (like the Graces and according to Aristotle's statement that "proportional requital is effected by diagonal conjunction"[888]): Person A, who satisfied a need of a second person B, acquires a "claim" that a third person X will satisfy a need of his in the measure of the benefit given by him to B. On his part B, whose need has been satisfied by A, acquires a "duty" to satisfy a need of a third person X, in the measure of the benefit received by him from A. Hence, in case of justice as reciprocity, the relationship is not exhausted bilaterally, but opens itself to third party. In this sense, justice as reciprocity is different from both contract and donation. The image of the Graces seems to be consistent with some of the new requirements of the era of globalization, by being apt to produce some indications for interventions in the world that go beyond the bipolar relationship of the universal-particular.[889]

---

888. EN, 1133a 5–7. (Loeb-Rackham, *ibid.*).

889. Azzoni, *ibid.*, 27.

Conclusion

OUR JOURNEY THROUGH THE WRITINGS of many generations of scholars on the Aristotelian distinction of distributive and corrective justice has reached its final destination. We have seen the enormous and fascinating intellectual efforts to understand, analyze, and apply the classical text. What is the conclusion? We certainly have no intention to determine the "correct" view about the Aristotelian notions of justice. This we leave to the individual reader if such an aspiration lies in his or her mind. The specific interpretations, evaluations, and applications of the two notions of justice are deeply imbedded in the culture and intellectual atmosphere of a given period of time as well as in the personal conviction and ideology of the individual scholar. On the other hand, concepts may shape the intellectual atmosphere and personal convictions. In other words, form and substance interact and intermingle. This insight lies at the basis of the method of *Begriffsgeschichte*, the history of concepts. We, therefore, will make an attempt to summarize in short the conclusions that derive in this sense from our description of the scholarly views throughout the ages.

Let us start with the revival of the Aristotelian Ethics in the period of Christian High Scholasticism (thirteenth to fourteenth centuries). The central figure is the Dominican Thomas Aquinas, the disciple of Albertus Magnus. Aristotle is viewed as an important authority in philosophy in general, and in ethics in particular. Aquinas analyzed the major problems created by the Aristotelian distinction and his answers defended the classical text. He concluded that retribution is at the basis of corrective justice. However, Aquinas introduced a substantive notion of justice that was oriented toward the common good, conceived ultimately in a religious sense. His theological outlook is also responsible for his view that Divinity cannot be subject to corrective justice. The interesting phenomenon is the subjection of the conceptual notions of justice under the theological premises concerning the absolute nature of Divinity. Another influence of the religious background consisted in the clear separation between the legal and a merely moral dimension of justice. The latter concerns exclusively the actor's conscience.

The Franciscan John Duns Scotus tended to view punishment as part of distributive justice and affirmed that distributive justice can be in God in an unqualified sense. Finally, the French scholar Jean Buridan denied the difference in kind between the two forms of justice.

The subsequent vast scholastic literature was clearly dominated by the work of Thomas Aquinas. He was considered to be an authoritative source for the right understanding of the Aristotelian distinction. The best legal minds of Dominicans, Franciscans, and, prominently, of Jesuits, as well as of members of some other religious orders, were discussing the right understanding of the Aristotelian distinctions. Since the different views on the formal notions of (human) justice didn't imply any basic theological differences, the ensuing controversy didn't provoke the tensions between Dominicans, Franciscans, and Jesuits that we encounter in some theological disputes.

A major topic of the discussion was the essential elements of the distinction between corrective (commutative) justice and distributive justice. The traditional assumption was that the principal distinctive element was to be found in the difference of proportions, arithmetic versus geometric equality. This assumption was weakened by a number of contrary practical examples: corrective-justice-situations where a geometric proportion is applied, such as contractual distribution of profits among partners according to the proportion of the respective investment; distributive-justice-situation where an arithmetic proportion is applied, such as in relation to a single candidate or benefit.

Though many scholars maintained that in these situations one has to distinguish between an essential and a merely accidental feature, one can discern a shift to an alternative distinctive element: the intensity of the right and the duty under the respective kinds of justice. Accordingly, only under commutative justice there was a perfect duty-right relationship; distributive justice created a much weaker claim against the distributor. This idea originated in the recognition that the prince or ruler, when distributing public honors, functions or benefits, enjoys a great measure of discretion that is beyond legal control.

Moreover, some scholars started from the political thesis that the (absolute) ruler is above the law. Consequently, it was assumed that the violation of distributive justice, as such, does not entail a legal sanction of compensation. The logical result of that view was that in any case where a duty of compensation was to be recognized, its foundation had to be in commutative justice. Another consequence of this approach was that the very dichotomous character of the distinction was considerably weakened: many scholars saw no problem in defining certain legal situations as a combination of the two forms of justice. Nevertheless, the great majority of scholastic scholars explicitly rejected Jean Buridan's view that denied the difference in kind between the two forms of justice. A few scholars even suggested that the great difference in the intensity and the nature of the respective rights turns the application of the notion of justice to both of them into a mere analogy, since they are not of one identical kind (*species*) of justice.

The classification of punishment was the object of a permanent controversy. The loyal Thomists defended Aquinas's view that it was part of commutative justice; the Scotists tended to view punishment as belonging to distributive justice. Many scholars suggested that the imposition of judicial punishment was a combination of different kinds of justice, some of them maintaining that vindictive (punitive) justice constitutes a separate kind of justice. All these discussions have continued to occupy also neo-scholastic Catholic moralists. It is noteworthy that some modern authors claim—especially when dealing with the notion of social justice—that rights under distributive justice are no less stringent than those under commutative justice. These authors conceive social justice to constitute part of distributive justice.

The Aristotelian distinction played a major role in the theological controversy about the nature of divine justice to which we dedicated a special chapter. The fundamental question was whether between God and the human creatures there could be a justice relationship, and if yes, what was the exact nature of this relationship.

The opinions among the theologians were deeply divided. Most of them assumed—following Aquinas—that God was not subject to commutative justice, since that would imply a strict right-duty relationship. Such a relationship was excluded in the light of God's omnipotence and sovereign dominion over His creatures. In view of the fact that distributive justice did not entail an obligation toward the recipient, it could, according to this view, be applied in relation to Divinity. However, some theologians even denied the possibility of a distributive-justice-relationship between God and human beings. On the other hand, a few theologians took the opposite view: Assuming a specific promise of God—such as eternal life to the just—it could be binding upon Him. Hence, God could be fully subject to both forms of justice. Some theologians adopted a medium way: The justice relationship between God and man was essentially different from that existing between human beings, but it nevertheless had some aspects of distributive and commutative justice.

The theological premise that the absolute perfection of divine justice made it essentially different from human justice accorded the theologians a great measure of flexibility in applying the Aristotelian distinction. It enabled them—each according to his specific theological tenets—to integrate divine justice with the divine attributes of omnipotence, grace, and mercy. It is noteworthy that Reformed scholars continued to rely on these Catholic scholastic discussions—even if in a more critical way—in order to resolve the theological problems connected to the notion of justification. A special theological problem constituted the intertrinitarian relationship between God and Christ; also here the existence of a commutative-justice-right was a matter of controversy.

The chapter on Jewish commentators illustrates the tendency to link the elements of the Aristotelian distinction to the substantive principles of Talmudic sources. However, in view of the enormous quantity of rabbinical legal literature, the barely handful of relevant commentators demonstrates the scanty interest of Jewish scholars in the formal definition of justice. This general tendency against categorial legal thinking was later enhanced by the anti-philosophical attitude of the dominant movement of Jewish mysticism, the Kabbala.

The chapter of post-scholastic writers concentrates on the works of humanists and of some outstanding representatives of the Enlightenment. The Aristotelian distinction constituted still an important topic but less in its theological context. The authors' eyes are turned directly toward the Aristotelian text and the classical sources. Their look became more critical and to some extent more pragmatic. Justice was brought into connection with economic and utilitarian considerations. A major topic was the classification of punishment. The solutions continued to differ: some viewed it as commutative justice, some as distributive justice, and some as a third, separate kind of justice.

An additional trend was the emphasis on Roman law in general, and Ulpian's definition of justice in particular. Among the great names treated in this chapter are: Philipp Melanchton, Jean Bodin, Hugo Grotius, Thomas Hobbes, Samuel Pufendorf, Giambatista Vico, and Gottfried Wilhelm Leibniz. The common denominator of these outstanding scholars was not only a most extraordinary, creative intellectual capacity, but equally an independent, critical mind toward the hitherto considered authoritative classic philosophers, such as Aristotle.

We open the modern age with the middle of the eighteenth century. The modern tendency distanced itself from the notion of justice as a moral virtue in the Aristotelian sense; it inclined to relate justice to law as a public institution. This is most prominent in Kant's philosophical analysis of the classic distinction. An additional consequence was the linkage of the Aristotelian forms of justice to the Roman distinction between public and private law. As a matter of fact, the formal categories lost much of interest in the eyes of the nineteenth-century German Pandectists who concentrated their attention on the Roman law heritage. True, Aristotle's ethical works remained an object of great scholarly interest in the nineteenth and twentieth centuries; but in the spirit of the time, the great intellectual efforts were invested into the philological, textual, and editorial problems of these philosophical writings according to the so-called methods of "higher" and "lower" criticism. A major objective was the correct understanding of Aristotle's original intentions.

In any event, the Aristotelian formal notions of justice lost most of their actual relevance. An amazing change occurred in the early 1980s in U.S. legal scholarship. The immediate trigger was the challenge of the economic approach to tort law that had won important scholarly support in the recent preceding years. It constituted a major attempt to ground tortious liability on instrumentalist foundations that were said to further social utility.

Consequently, it clashed with the traditional view that considered the foundation of tortious liability to be based upon moral blameworthiness. The opponents of the economic approach relied upon the Aristotelian distinction between corrective and distributive justice, arguing that the instrumentalist foundation of liability, by introducing distributive aims, violated its corrective justice foundation. The connotation was that public law penetrated illegitimately into a private law conflict.

Viewed from a historical perspective, the use of the distinction as a normative tool for examining the legitimacy of substantive solutions seems to be quite a novelty. The high scholastics, the late scholastics, and the post-scholastics, all used the positive law as a criterion for the correctness of the distinction, and not the other way around. Their endeavors were aimed at the correct understanding of the Aristotelian notions of justice and of their application in practice. The substantive argument, based on the notion of corrective justice, which was now raised against the instrumental-economic approach in tort law, gained prominence, and provoked a protracted scholarly controversy.

The result was a direct return to Aristotle's original text and its renewed analysis on the background of the actual debate. Apart from very few limited exceptions, the millennial treatment of the Aristotelian distinction was completely disregarded. The intellectual effort was directed to different aspects of the two forms of justice, depending upon the respective scholar's basic conception concerning tort liability's foundation. The challenge of tort liability's conformity to corrective justice was taken most seriously by many U.S. tort scholars. Hence, the great intellectual effort applied by them to reconcile their suggested substantive solutions with the assumed requirements of corrective justice.

A precondition to this discourse was naturally the right understanding of the two notions of justice and their relationship to the substance of law. The result of these inquiries was a vast literature and a great diversity of views. The age-old questions reappeared and exerted the minds of jurists and philosophers. Among these questions we find the following ones: The correlation between gain and loss in corrective justice; the problem of the autonomous character of corrective justice in relation to distributive justice; the classification of restitutionary duties in relation to the two forms of justice; the question whether the two forms of justice can be applied simultaneously in a given situation.

It is evident that the contrasting answers given to these questions are influenced by the individual scholar's theoretical and ideological premises and objectives. One could define the opposite values involved on the more theoretical level in the following summary way: Purism, formalism, postulates of intelligibility, and coherence clash with pragmatism and pluralism; on the more ideological, political level: Individualism, right-oriented personal autonomy contrast with instrumentalism, utilitarianism, economic efficiency, and social justice. The overriding issue seems to be the relationship between form and substance.

Finally, echoes of the scholarly, modern discussions on the Aristotelian distinction have recently been sounded in the courts in Great Britain, Ireland, Australia, New Zealand, and Israel. In all probability, once the classic distinction has recaptured the minds of legal scholars, it will remain with us for quite a time.

APPENDIX

The Iconography of the Aristotelian Distinction

THROUGHOUT THE AGES, the image of justice pervades art in all its variegated manifestations. Its worldwide spread is a sign of justice's centrality in human society. However, the artistic representation of the two Aristotelian forms of justice is relatively rare. We will concentrate on two major examples: 1) The very famous fresco cycle, painted by Ambrogio Lorenzetti in the years 1338–1340, decorating the Sala dei Nove in the Palazzo Pubblico of Siena, the council-room of the Sienese government; and 2) Two illustrated manuscripts, dating from the 1370s, of Aristotle's *Ethics* in French from the library of King Charles V of France. The king commissioned the translations of Aristotle's Latin texts into French from the important scholar Nicole Oresme (ca. 1323–1382).

Lorenzetti's Frescoes in Siena

Three walls of the council-room in Siena are covered with the fascinating frescoes of Ambrogio Lorenzetti (1295–1348). They represent the allegories of the Good Government (Buon Governo) and the Bad Government (Mal Governo).[890] Under the Bad Government, the bound female figure of Justice

890. Lorenzetti's source of inspiration for his portrayal of the good and bad government is a matter of an extensive scholarly controversy. According to the "orthodox" view, the painter was influenced both by Aristotelian and Thomistic ideas, the work having its roots in scholasticism. Quentin Skinner disagrees with that view arguing that Lorenzetti's cycle is best interpreted as an expression of the pre-humanist rhetorical culture of the Italian city-republics in the early years of the thirteenth century; in his view, a major source was Brunetto Latini's encyclopaedic *Li Livres dou tresor* compiled in the early 1260s: *Id.* "Ambrogio Lorenzetti: The Artist as Political Philosopher," 72 (1986) *Proceedings of the British Academy* 1–56; a revised version of this paper appeared in Q. Skinner, *Visions of Politics*, Vol. 2, *Renaissance Virtues* (Cambridge, New York 2002) 39–92. Some scholars emphasize, against the secular interpretation, the religious-biblical background of some elements in the painting; Ch. Frugoni, *A Distant City: Images of Urban Experience in the Medieval World* (W. McCuaig, transl., Princeton 1991) 118–188. In a more recent doctoral

writhes at the feet of the demonic Tyrant, her scales lying on the ground. In the depiction of the Good Government on the northern wall of the room, the figure of Justice appears twice.

To the extreme lefthand side of the enthroned ruler, symbolizing the City of Siena,[891] sits as a crowned counselor, the cardinal virtue *Iustitia*. Dressed in a red robe, she holds upright in her right hand the sword; below the sword's handle lies on her knee the severed head of a bearded man. In her left hand she holds a crown. As a virtue, Justice appears to relate to the governance of the depicted ruler.

It seems, therefore, that the ruler exercises justice by punishing the delinquents and rewarding the just.[892] The severed head and the crown symbolize these two functions. As we will see, these functions are actually carried out in the other, more central figure of justice, by an angel who represents the distributive justice.

The question is, of course, why the double representation of justice in the painting? One author, indeed, notes that he cannot think of any other medieval

---

dissertation, it has been suggested that the key for the correct interpretation of the frescoes lies in Dante's *Commedia*: Dagmar Schmidt, *Der Freskenzyklus von Ambrogio Lorenzetti über die gute und schlechte Regierung—Eine danteske Vision im Palazzo Pubblico von Siena* (Dissertation Nr. 2656, Universität St. Gallen, 2003) (retrievable under www.biblio.unisg.ch). On the problems of Lorenzetti's frescoes, *see also* P. Boucheron, "'Tournez les yeux pour admirer, vous qui exercez le pouvoir, celle qui est peinte ici.' La fresque du Bon Gouvernement d'Ambrogio Lorenzetti, 60 (2005) *Annales. Histoire, Sciences Sociales* 1135; *see* especially U. Meier, "Die linke und die rechte Waagschale der Justiz. Die Rezeption der aristotelischen Lehre der Teilgerechtigkeiten bei Albertus Magnus und Ambrogio Lorenzetti," *Gerechtigkeiten im gesellschaftlichen Diskurs des späteren Mittelalters, Festschrift zum 60. Geburtstag von Eberhard Isenmann* (G. Annas and P. Schulte, eds., Berlin 2008) (forthcoming).

891. N. Rubinstein, "Political Ideas in Sienese Art: The Frescoes by Ambrogio Lorenzetti and Taddeo di Bartolo in the Palazzo Pubblico," 21 (1958) *Journal of the Warburg and Courtauld Institutes* 179, 181: "The figure has been explained as 'an aged king,' the Good Ruler, Good Government,' or Justice; others believe that it is meant to personify the Commune of Siena. This is the most satisfactory explanation so far; in fact, the ruler is dressed in the colours of Siena, black and white; at his feet lies the Sienese Wolf with the Twins, and above his head we find the initials C.S.C.C.V. [*Commune Senarum Civitas Virginis*]" (footnotes omitted); in the same sense, U. Feldges-Henning, "The Pictorial programme of the Sala della Pace: A New Interpretation," 35 (1972) *Journal of the Warburg and Courtauld Institutes* 145, 146, 156. On the initials, *see* G. Rowley, *Ambrogio Lorenzetti*, Volume I Princeton 1958) 99, note 2; but in our view the better reading is "*Civitas*" and not "*Civitatis*."

892. *See* Q. Skinner, "Ambrogio Lorenzetti's *Buon Governo* Frescoes: Two Old Questions, Two new Answers," 62 (1999) *Journal of the Warburg and Courtauld Institutes* 1, 11–14; a revised version of this paper appeared in Q. Skinner, *Visions of Politics*, Vol. 2, *Renaissance Virtues* (Cambridge, New York 2002) 93–117, at 99–103. In the author's view, the ruler represents a supreme judge, a secularised image of the last Judgment, probably inspired by Giotto's painting in the Cappella degli Scrovegni in Padua.

work of art or text which contains two Justices, excluding instances involving separation into subcategories, such as commutative and distributive justice.[893] Moreover, to his knowledge, Justice's attributes of the severed head and proffered crown are not found beyond Ambrogio's mural and its close sphere of influence in Siena.[894] In that author's view, the central figure of Justice, at the right hand of the ruler, is of a higher, celestial order; she is the "*santa virtù*."[895] The other figure is a lesser, strictly secular Justice.

The intention of introducing two Justices was to separate Heaven's role in civic good government, which was still clearly acknowledged, from that belonging to man.[896] According to another view, the central figure illustrates the idea of justice or fairness as the essence of law; the other figure depicts justice as a personal attribute, hence as a separate concept.[897] In the same line of ideas, it has been suggested that the great figure of justice symbolizes a value that relates to the whole community, whereas the smaller one concerns the just conduct of the individual citizen or of the magistrate.[898]

In our view, the interpretation is somewhat different. Since decapitation and crowning in the central figure of justice are specifically designed as acts of distributive justice, the crown in the hand of the smaller figure and the severed head below her sword appear to be equally the elements of distributive justice.[899] According to Aristotle and Aquinas, distributive justice is basically a function of the ruling authority. Since in Lorenzetti's view, punishment makes part of distributive justice, the virtue of distributive justice—like the other seated virtues in the painting—belongs to the function of the ruler, here symbolizing the community of Siena. This explains, in our opinion, the absence of commutative justice in this figure of justice.

---

893. J. Polzer, "Ambrogio Lorenzetti's 'War and Peace' Murals Revisited: Contributions to the Meaning of the 'Good Government Allegorym,'" 23 (2002) *Artibus et Historiae* 63, 91–92.

894. *Ibid.*, 93.

895. *Ibid.*, 81.

896. *Ibid.*, 97–98.

897. Q. Skinner, *Visions of Politics*, Vol. 2, *Renaissance Virtues, op. cit.*, 72; the author observes that to claim that justice appears twice is misleading, *ibid.*, note 229. *Cf.* C.R. Sherman, *Imaging Aristotle: Verbal and Visual Representation in Fourteenth-Century France* (Berkeley 1995) 114 (the large figure corresponds to Legal or Universal Justice; the other to justice as a cardinal virtue).

898. Dagmar Schmidt, *Der Freskenzyklus von Ambrogio Lorenzetti über die gute und schlechte Regierung—Eine danteske Vision im Palazzo Pubblico von Siena, op. cit.*, 231–232.

899. But *see* G. Rowley, *Ambrogio Lorenzetti, op. cit.*, 101, who suggests that this figure represents vindictive justice as the third kind of justice.

Let us now turn to the central female figure of Justice in Lorenzetti's painting. She sits enthroned at the right hand of the ruler in a way that underlines her independent nature. She is the second largest figure, her open eyes turned upward to the crowned, celestial, winged figure of *Sapientia*, Wisdom. In a half-circle around Justice's blond head appears a text in golden letters: "*Diligite iustitiam qui iudicatis terram*"; it reproduces the Latin translation of the opening verse in Greek of the apocryphal Book of Wisdom of Solomon: "Love justice, you who judge the earth."[900] A large balance encompasses the figure of Justice. The figure of Heavenly Wisdom holds in her right hand the top of the balance's stem, its bottom is placed on the crowned head of Justice. The thumbs of Justice rest slightly on the sides of two scales keeping them in equilibrium. Each of the scales contains a winged, angel-like figure, both kneeling toward two larger men who are situated on the ground directly before them. Over these figures appear identifying texts; the one on Justice's right side reads "Distributiva," the other on her left side "Commutativa." Below Justice, in a less imposing chair sits the figure of Concordia. On her lap she holds with one hand a large carpenter's plane, signifying the smoothing of differences. Through her other hand runs a cord combining two strings, one coming down from the pan of commutative justice, the other from that of distributive justice.[901] The cord is transmitted to the 24 representatives of the Siena community and is ultimately knotted to the wrist of the ruler who holds upright his sceptre. This connection seems to demonstrate the governing authority's binding commitment to justice.[902]

Let us now have a closer look at the figures representing the two Aristotelian forms of justice. Their understanding has perplexed many scholars and a variety of contrasting interpretations have been suggested. On Justice's right side—under the title "*distributiva*"—the angel-like figure in red, kneeling in the pan, deals with two men: the one on her right, turning his back and neck toward her in a bowing position, arms bound behind him, is

900. For an interesting parallel in Dante's *Paradiso*, xviii, 91–93, Ch. Frugoni, "The Book of Wisdom and Lorenzetti's Fresco in the Palazzo Pubblico at Siena," 43 (1980) *Journal of the Warburg and Courtauld Institutes* 239; Dagmar Schmidt, *Der Freskenzyklus von Ambrogio Lorenzetti über die gute und schlechte Regierung, op. cit.*, 136, 209. It is noteworhty that the same sentence appears in Simone Martini's "Maestà," a fresco painted in 1315 in the Great Hall of the Palazzo Pubblico in Siena.

901. On the image of the rope of concord (*vinculum concordiae*), Q. Skinner, *Visions of Politics*, Vol. 2, *Renaissance Virtues, op. cit.*, 48–49, 96; Ch. Frugoni, *A Distant City: Images of Urban Experience in the Medieval World, op. cit.*, 132–134.

902. Q. Skinner, *Visions of Politics*, Vol. 2, *Renaissance Virtues, op. cit.*, 79.

about to be decapitated by the sword she holds in her right hand. Blood starts flowing from his neck where touched by the sword. Besides the man lie his weapons. The other man, kneeling and bowing in the direction of the angel, holds in his right hand a palm frond. He is in the course of being crowned by the angel.

On Justice's left side—under the title "*commutativa*"—the angel-like figure in white, kneeling in the pan, equally deals with two men. They confront the angel in a half-kneeling position, the conventional posture of donors, looking straight into her face. The one man is extending a cylindrical object to the angel, into which the latter puts her right hand. The other man holds two lengthy, stick-like objects, the angel grasping them with her left hand. This basic description of the depicted scenes is practically accepted by all,[903] as well as the portrayal's affinity to Giotto's figure of Justice in the Arena Chapel in Padua, the Cappella degli Scrovegni (1303–1309).[904]

However, two major problems have occupied the scholars, provoking a protracted controversy. The one relates to the scene of distributive justice: the inclusion of punishment under this heading has puzzled the scholars, since, as Quentin Skinner observes, "neither in the *Nicomachean Ethics*, nor in Aristotle's later analysis in the *Politics*, nor in any of Aquinas's comments on these texts is it ever suggested that Aristotle's concept of *iustum distributivum* is connected with the infliction of punishment."[905] The second problem concerns the simple understanding of the commutative justice scene, namely, what is the exact nature of the objects in the hands of the figures, and what is the significance of their acts? Briefly, what is going on in that scene?

In relation to the first problem, a radical solution has been suggested by Chiara Frugoni: During a restoration process of the painting, the titles of the scenes have

903. An exception makes S.Y. Edgerton, "The Aesthetic Image of Public Execution and Its Impact on Criminal Justice," 15 (2003) *Cardozo Studies in Law and Literature* 235, 242–243. In that author's interpretation, the distributive-justice angel rips with her left hand the crown from the head of an offender in a judicial divestiture ceremony. In this sense already E.C. Southard, *The Frescoes in Siena's Palazzo Pubblico, 1289–1539: Studies in Imagery and Relations to Other Communal Palaces in Tuscany* (New York/London 1979) 280. *Cf. also* W. Schild, *Bilder von Recht und Gerechtigkeit* (Köln 1995) 106, who mentions it as an alternative explanation. With all due respect, this interpretation is in our view unfounded.

904. E. Froimovič, "Giotto's Allegories of Justice and the Commune in the Palazzo della Ragione in Padua: A Reconstruction," 59 (1996) *Journal of the Warburg and Courtauld Institutes* 24, 45; A. Timmermann, "The Avenging Crucifix: Some Observations in the Iconography of the Living Cross," 40 (2001) *Gesta* 141, 148–149; Q. Skinner, *Visions of Politics*, Vol. 2, *Renaissance Virtues*, *op. cit.*, 100–101, 113.

905. Q. Skinner, *Visions of Politics*, Vol. 2, *Renaissance Virtues*, *cit.*, 74.

been mistakenly exchanged.[906] As a result, the original commutative justice scene has subsequently been wrongly entitled "*Distributiva*." This solution is not only historically doubtful, but creates no less serious problems for the understanding of the now exchanged scences of distributive and commutative justice.[907]

Other scholars have looked for early sources that may have induced Lorenzetti to depict punishment as being part of distributive justice. Thus, Quentin Skinner considers, as already mentioned, the pre-humanist encyclopaedic *Li Livres dou tresor*, compiled by Brunetto Latini in the early 1260s, as a major source of inspiration to the painting.[908] The German historian Ulrich Meier is of the opinion that Lorenzetti's motives of distributive and commutative justice are more in accordance with the explications of Albertus Magnus in his vernacular *Augsburger Predigtzyklus* (1257–1263).[909] In our view, the answer to the problem is not too difficult. As our study has shown, there was a broad scholastic trend that classified punishment under the heading of distributive justice, a major source being Duns Scotus (ca. 1265–1321).[910] It is highly probable that this quite common scholastic conception reached Lorenzetti.[911]

The interpretation of the commutative justice scene has equally been controversial. However, most scholars agree that it represents a peaceful

906. Ch. Frugoni, *A Distant City: Images of Urban Experience in the Medieval World, op. cit.*, 121–123, 191.

907. Q. Skinner, *Visions of Politics*, Vol. 2, *Renaissance Virtues, cit.*, 74–75; *cf.* J. Polzer, "Ambrogio Lorenzetti's 'War and Peace' Murals Revisited," *cit.*, 80, note 68 at 102.

908. *Ibid.*, 39–40. The author relies on Latini's notion of rectifying inequalities by means of an "*ygailleur*," who can do it by punishing the wicked and by rewarding the good. In this sense also R. Starn, "The Republican Regime of the 'Room of Peace' in Siena, 1338–1340," 18 (1987) *Representations* 1, 29, note 27; H. Hofmann, *Bilder des Friedens oder Die vergessene Gerechtigkeit* (München 1997)24. N. Rubinstein, "Political Ideas in Sienese Art," *cit.*, 183, connects the illustration of distributive justice to the Italian version of Giles of Rome's *De regimine principium* of 1288.

909. U. Meier, "Die linke und die rechte Waagschale der Justiz. Die Rezeption der aristotelischen Lehre der Teilgerechtigkeiten bei Albertus Magnus und Ambrogio Lorenzetti," *Gerechtigkeiten im gesellschaftlichen Diskurs des späteren Mittelalters, Festschrift zum 60. Geburtstag von Eberhard Isenmann* (G. Annas and P. Schulte, eds., Berlin 2008) (forthcoming). The sermons were published in Latin: "Alberts des Grossen Augsburger Prediktzyklus über den hl. Augustinus," 36 (1969) *Recherches de théologie ancienne et médiévale*, 105–147.

910. *Supra* at notes 76, 85.

911. In view of the real problem of classifying punishment according to Aristotle's notions of justice, Hofmann's critical and rather caustic comment toward Gustav Radbruch's conception of distributive justice (*Bilder des Friedens, cit.*, 25) seems hardly justified.

transaction between citizens under the guidance of the angel-like figure. Some assume that the objects, exchanged between a metal worker and a draper, are spears or lances and a bale of cloth.[912] Others identify the cylindrical object as a strongbox filled with money (*forziere*).[913] According to another view, the objects present two official measures of weight and length, namely the cylindrical object a *staio* (bushel)[914] and the two staffs a *canna* and a *passetto*.[915] Though the exact identification of the objects continues to constitute a problem,[916] the scene most certainly presents a commercial exchange.[917]

The Miniatures in Nicole Oresme's French Translation of Aristotle's Nicomachean Ethics

As mentioned, the King of France Charles V ordered from Nicole Oresme (ca. 1323–1382) a vernacular translation of Aristotle's Ethics. In the manuscript (1370–1375), kept at the Royal Library in Brussels, a miniature illustrates the Aristotelian notions of justice.[918] The miniature is divided into two registers; the upper zone depicts Legal or Universal Justice; the lower register illustrates Particular Justice, divided into Distributive and Commutative Justice. The illustrations follow rather closely Aristotle's definitions and are, therefore, not as enigmatic as Lorenzetti's frescoes. Moreover, its context is secular and earthbound. The preponderant, crowned, and upright female figure of Justice

912. Q. Skinner, *Visions of Politics*, Vol. 2, *Renaissance Virtues*, *op. cit.*, 76; the author adds in a note to this revised version of his original paper: "But in the light of the latest restoration of the frescoes I now feel less sure about this detail."

913. Ch. Frugoni, *A Distant City*, *op. cit.*, 122. *Cf.* M.L. Cohen, *Law: the art of justice* (New York 1992) 40: "[C]ommutative Justice seems to give money to one and arms to another."

914. M.M. Donato, "La'bellissima inventiva": immagini e idee nella sala della Pace," *Ambrogio Lorenzetti, Il Buon Governo* (Milano 1995) 23, 35.

915. *Cf.* J. Polzer, "Ambrogio Lorenzetti's 'War and Peace' Murals Revisited," *cit.*, 77.

916. *See* the reservations of Polzer, *ibid.*, 77–79, about the cylindrical object's identification as a "bushel"; the author now thinks that it may present a sieve; *ibid.*, 80.

917. In this sense Polzer, *ibid.*, 81.

918. *Les éthiques d'Aristote*, Brussels, Bibliothèque Royale Albert 1er, MS 9505–06 (formerly MS 2902), folio 89r. Unidentified scribe, close to Raoulet d'Orléans; illumination with the participation of Jean de Sy Master. The following description in the text is based upon C.R. Sherman, *Imaging Aristotle: Verbal and Visual Representation in Fourteenth-Century France* (Berkeley 1995) 94–108. On the historical context of Oresme's translation, *see ibid.*, 3–33; *see also* Maistre Nicole Oresme, *Le Livre De Ethiques D'Aristote* (A.D. Menut, ed., New York 1940) 3–91.

Légale shelters under her spread mantle six daughter-like smaller figures; four are named: Fortitude, Justice Particulière, Mansuétude (Gentleness), and Entrepesie (Conciliation). The kneeling figure of Particular Justice holds upright in her hand a sword.

The representation in the lower half of the miniature of the two forms of particular justice emphasizes their concrete function. On the left side, situated in a tricolor quadrilobe, the female figure of Distributive Justice stands behind a table that is covered with stacks of gold coins, vessels, and documents. These items symbolize the common goods to be distributed according to merit. Identified by the inscription unfurling above her head, she bears a widow-like headdress. Her right hand is upraised in a reflective gesture, her left one placed on the pile of coins in front of her on the table. Her head is turned toward four rectangular measuring rods representing the proportional equality of 6:3 = 4:2. These proportions are marked in (Roman) numbers on the short projecting sides of the proportionate rods. To her right stand four male figures, two of them depicted full length. The one closer to the figure of Distributive Justice holds a pile of coins and a document bearing a red seal. The other man holds a gold chalice.

We have, therefore, here a visual demonstration of the proportions indicated on the measuring rods: two awards (coins and document) as against one object (chalice). The act of distribution does not seem to have been terminated, given the actual attitude of Distributive Justice and the expecting glances of the recipients.

On the lower right quadrilobe, the miniature presents a scene of commutative justice. The female figure at the center appears to be a twin sister of Distributive Justice: She is equally dressed bearing an identical widow-like headdress. But her function is different. She acts as a judge between two litigants. The one to her left appears to be a tonsured cleric, the one to her right a fashionably dressed secular figure. Behind the litigants are bystanders or witnesses. Commutative Justice has her hands crossed in an act of taking something away from the one litigant and giving it to the other. Her position is one of evenhandedness and impartiality. From the expression of the litigants' respective faces, it seems that the secular person is on the receiving, winning side. Justice looks at the cleric with what could be viewed as an expression of compassion.[919] Justice touches the hands of the litigants, but

919. Sherman, *ibid.*, 106–107.

there is no material object of exchange. Visual instruments of commutative justice are suspended above the figures of the litigants. Over the head of the secular litigant is a balance; on the side of the cleric hang a scourge and a stock, and on the floor between him and Justice rests an axe. These instruments symbolize the function of commutative justice: equality and impartiality in commercial transactions and especially in punishment. By classifying punishment under the heading of commutative justice, the manuscript follows the approach of Thomas Aquinas.

Finally a few remarks on the second manuscript of Oresme's translation, kept at the Rijksmuseum in The Hague, containing a parallel miniature executed by a different illuminator in 1376.[920] In the top zone, a non-crowned Justice légale, shelters with her mantle the virtues. This time they are seven, not identified, standing female figures.[921] Another, more substantial change concerns the scene of distributive justice. Here, Justice apparently adjudicates claims of two parties, one, on the left side, represented by two clerics, the other one on the right side represented by a pair of secular people. Contrary to the first manuscript, on the table there are no gold coins, vessels, and documents to be distributed. On the table before the clerics lies a gold miter and before the secular people a sword. Justice holds a balance in her hand and the inscription at the bottom reads: "*departir a chascun selon les merites*" ("distribute to each one according to his merits"). Our impression is that there are no directly conflicting claims between the opposite parties, but each asks for a distinct public function; the clerics for the authority of bishopric, symbolized by the miter, and the other people for a secular authority, symbolized by the sword. Justice weighs each side's merits independently.[922]

In the scene of commutative justice, the figure of Justice sits upright looking straight forward, holding in her left hand a balance and in her right hand a sword. Below her the inscription reads: "*rendre a chascun le sien*" ("to render

920. *Les éthiques d'Aristote*, The Hague, Rijksmuseum Meermanno-Westreenianum, MS 10 D 1; scribe: Raoulet d'Orléans; illuminator: Master of the Coronation of Charles VI and workshop. For the description we are again relying on Sherman, *cit.*, 109–112.

921. Sherman, *ibid.*, suggests that the addition of a seventh virtue, permits the division into the traditional four cardinal and three theological virtues.

922. Sherman (*ibid.*, 109) has a different interpretation. In her view, the larger pan of Justice's scale comes down on the secular side, the struggle being between two competing sources of authority, the secular and ecclesiatic courts.

each one his due"). On both sides of her are figures who are described as "*advocas et tesmoins*" ("lawyers and witnesses"). Above their heads on the left side the inscription reads: "*discussion*," on the right side: "*execucion urgens*." The scene depicts, therefore, an actual trial, the lawyers submitting their arguments and awaiting the just and impartial judicial decision of Commutative Justice that will be executed without delay.

Table of Cases

United States, United Kingdom and Commonwealth

Germany

Israel

Index

Printed and bound by CPI Group (UK) Ltd, Croydon, CR0 4YY

The manufacturer's authorised representative in the EU for product safety is Oxford University Press España S.A. of El Parque Empresarial San Fernando de Henares, Avenida de Castilla, 2 - 28830 Madrid (www.oup.es/en or product.safety@oup.com). OUP España S.A. also acts as importer into Spain of products made by the manufacturer.
Printed and bound by CPI Group (UK) Ltd, Croydon, CR0 4YY
14/09/2026
02216304-0003